Critical Essays on

JAMES JOYCE'S
FINNEGANS WAKE

CRITICAL ESSAYS
ON
BRITISH LITERATURE

Zack Bowen, General Editor
University of Miami

Critical Essays on

JAMES JOYCE'S
FINNEGANS WAKE

edited by

PATRICK A. MCCARTHY

G. K. Hall & Co. / New York
Maxwell Macmillan Canada / Toronto
Maxwell Macmillan International / New York Oxford Singapore Sydney

G. K. Hall & Co.
Macmillan Publishing Company
866 Third Avenue
New York, New York 10022

Maxwell Macmillan Canada, Inc.
1200 Eglinton Avenue East
Suite 200
Don Mills, Ontario M3C 3N1

Macmillan Publishing Company is part of the Maxwell Communication Group of Companies.

Library of Congress Cataloging-in-Publication Data

Critical essays on James Joyce's *Finnegans wake*/edited by Patrick A. McCarthy.
    p. cm. — (Critical essays on British literature)
    Includes bibliographical references and index.
    ISBN 0-8161-8870-X (alk. paper)
    1. Joyce, James, 1882–1941. Finnegans wake. I. McCarthy,
Patrick A., 1945– . II. Series.
PR6019.O9F5757   1992
821'.912—dc20
                                     92–4217
                                         CIP

---

10 9 8 7 6 5 4 3 2 1

Printed in the United States of America

To Robert Boyle, S.J.:
for the greeter glossary of code

Contents

♦

General Editor's Note

◆

The Critical Essays on British Literature series provides a variety of approaches to both classical and contemporary writers of Britain and Ireland. The formats of the volumes in the series vary with the thematic designs of individual editors and with the number and nature of existing reviews and criticism, augmented, where appropriate, by original essays by recognized authorities. It is hoped that each volume will be unique in developing a new overall perspective on its particular subject.

Patrick McCarthy's volume on *Finnegans Wake* concentrates for the most part on the seminal essays of the last twenty years. He has selected those that deal with the broad issues of "structure, voice, narration, language, and interpretation, analyses of important recurrent themes, and readings of passages in ways that pose crucial questions about the *Wake* as a whole." His introduction is a thoughtful and judicious summary of the major *Wake* scholarship.

ZACK BOWEN
University of Miami

Publisher's Note

◆

Producing a volume that contains both newly commissioned and reprinted material presents the publisher with the challenge of balancing the desire to achieve stylistic consistency with the need to preserve the integrity of works first published elsewhere. In the Critical Essays series, essays commissioned especially for a particular volume are edited to be consistent with G. K. Hall's house style; reprinted essays appear in the style in which they were first published, with only typographical errors corrected. Consequently, shifts in style from one essay to another are the result of our efforts to be faithful to each text as it was originally published.

Introduction

PATRICK A. MCCARTHY

Writing in 1929 about *Anna Livia Plurabelle*, a separately published episode from James Joyce's *Work in Progress*, Arnold Bennett cited examples of the work's curious language, admitted his own inability to understand a single page of it, and concluded that *"Anna Livia Plurabelle* will never be anything but the wild caprice of a wonderful creative artist who has lost his way."[1] In the same year, however, there appeared *Our Exagmination round His Factifica- tion for Incamination of Work in Progress*, a collection of a dozen articles whose authors (including Samuel Beckett, Stuart Gilbert, and Eugene Jolas) certainly seemed more at ease with *Work in Progress* than Bennett did. Yet even these positive responses to Joyce's project, along with a few more discerning essays and the numerous fragments of *Work in Progress* itself that Joyce had published from 1924 on,[2] proved insufficiently comforting for many reviewers in 1939, a decade after the *Exagmination*, when the completed text of *Work in Progress* was finally unveiled as *Finnegans Wake*. Faced with over 600 pages of dense prose on which Joyce had labored since the 1922 publication of *Ulysses*, several reviewers complained that it was impossible to understand such a book on short notice; others seemed of the opinion that even a lifetime would not suffice for them to comprehend what Oliver Gogarty termed "the most colossal leg pull in literature since Macpherson's *Ossian*."[3] While paying tribute to Joyce's "genius" or the inventiveness of his language, more than a few commentators pronounced *Finnegans Wake* an artistic failure. Of course, there were some remarkably sensitive and well- conceived assessments of the book (by Harry Levin, William Troy, and Edmund Wilson, among others[4]), but these were relatively rare. With prepa- rations for World War II diverting his readers' attention from the book in which Joyce believed he had demonstrated the absurdity of war (Ellmann, 728), it is hardly surprising that *Finnegans Wake* was greeted with far less enthusiasm and comprehension than its author had hoped for. When Joyce died in January 1941, those readers who had depended on him to unlock the

1

book's mysteries could be forgiven for assuming that he had taken with him "the keys to dreamland" (615.28).[5]

The situation changed in 1944 with the publication of *A Skeleton Key to "Finnegans Wake"* by Joseph Campbell and Henry Morton Robinson.[6] Arguably the most important book in the history of *Finnegans Wake* criticism, the *Skeleton Key* had several advantages over *Our Exagmination*. With the full text of *Finnegans Wake* (and a small but respectable body of criticism) in front of them, Campbell and Robinson could see larger patterns of narrative development that eluded readers of the *Work in Progress* fragments; moreover, their collaboration on the study must have enriched their understanding of the book. (In a sense, Campbell and Robinson provided a small-scale model for the *Finnegans Wake* reading groups that have proved invaluable for many readers.) A further advantage was that instead of acting as Joyce's advocates in a dispute over a radical literary experiment or merely investigating a limited, and often arcane, aspect of the *Wake*, as the "exagminers" did, Campbell and Robinson were concerned with clarifying the general contours of *Finnegans Wake* for as wide an audience as possible. For that reason, they sought to present the *Wake* as a coherent (if complex) narrative combining a story about a rather commonplace Dublin family with a wide range of historical and mythic references—in short, an allegorical account of the human condition.

It is easy, in retrospect, to see the faults and limitations of the *Skeleton Key*. Campbell, who later wrote such important works on mythology as *The Hero with a Thousand Faces*, *The Mythic Image*, and the four volumes of *The Masks of God*, followed the Wakean injunction to "wipe your glosses with what you know" (304.F3) and emphasized the *Wake*'s mythic element so much as to exaggerate its relative importance within the book's fabric. In addition, there were numerous local judgments that later commentators, with the advantage of hindsight, can safely discard. A more serious problem is the reliance on paraphrase and synopsis throughout most of the study: after some important general commentary and a detailed explanation of the *Wake*'s opening paragraphs, the *Skeleton Key* alternates between simplified or abbreviated renditions of passages and bracketed summaries of the book's themes and actions. The problem is not so much that this method produces a reductive version of the text, since—as I have argued elsewhere[7]—every attempt to interpret *Finnegans Wake* results in a simplification of Joyce's work. Rather, the real problem is that the authoritative tone of the *Skeleton Key*, the book's format, and the lucidity of the presentation have led many readers to assume that its reading is definitive rather than just an exploration of *Finnegans Wake* from the perspective of myth criticism. (In the early 1960s, when other studies finally began to challenge the hegemony of the *Skeleton Key*, Viking Press took care to reinforce the appearance of authority by publishing a paperback edition with a cover design resembling that of the paperback version of the *Wake*.)

Despite these problems, it must be emphasized that Campbell and Robinson produced a remarkable book under difficult circumstances. Finding themselves lost in Joyce's "puling sample jungle of woods" (112.4), most readers of *Finnegans Wake* need a summary of the book's plot, themes, and characters in order to get their bearings, and the *Skeleton Key* was only the first of several attempts to make Joyce's formidable dream vision more accessible to beginning readers. For the most part, Campbell and Robinson's account of *Finnegans Wake* remained unchallenged until 1959, when William York Tindall devoted sixty pages of *A Reader's Guide to James Joyce* to the *Wake*. A decade later, Tindall expanded his analysis to a book-length study, *A Reader's Guide to "Finnegans Wake"* (1969), an occasionally useful book that contains a good deal of speculation and intelligent free association but does not really anchor its readings of individual passages in a clearly conceived view of the work as a whole. A more coherent (if simplistic) outline from the same era may be found in Anthony Burgess's *Re Joyce* (1965; British title: *Here Comes Everybody*), a rather derivative book that is mainly useful as a popularization of Joyce. Burgess was also responsible for *A Shorter Finnegans Wake* (1967), an unfortunate abbreviation of the Joycean text that connects chunks of *Finnegans Wake* with frequently dubious summaries of the intervening passages.[8] More recent overviews may be found in *Understanding "Finnegans Wake"* by Danis Rose and John O'Hanlon (1982); in my essay, "The Structures and Meanings of *Finnegans Wake*" (in *A Companion to Joyce Studies*, 1984, edited by Zack Bowen and James F. Carens); in John Gordon's *"Finnegans Wake": A Plot Summary* (1986); and in Margot Norris's succinct contribution to *The Cambridge Companion to James Joyce* (1990, edited by Derek Attridge). Rose and O'Hanlon rely heavily on the *Finnegans Wake* manuscripts (on which the authors are acknowledged experts) and on Joyce's use of his sources, while Gordon attempts to read backward from the text in order to lay bare the real-life story that he believes is transformed in the dream narrative of *Finnegans Wake*.

The best general study of Joyce published during the 1950s, Hugh Kenner's *Dublin's Joyce* (1956), contained a significant discussion of the dream situation and narrative structure of *Finnegans Wake*, but Kenner was primarily intent on examining selected aspects of the *Wake* rather than on providing a comprehensive account of the book's themes and structure. A more serious challenge to the *Skeleton Key* as a guide to the *Wake*'s narrative line might be located in another 1956 volume, Adaline Glasheen's *A Census of "Finnegans Wake."* Expanded in subsequent editions—*A Second Census of "Finnegans Wake"* (1963) and *Third Census of "Finnegans Wake"* (1977)—Glasheen's highly individualistic reading of the narrative line opens up important areas of the work without precluding others. All three editions of the *Census* contain useful, if occasionally eccentric, listings and discussions of what Joyce calls "the charictures in the drame" (302.31–32), the multitude of personages who appear or are mentioned in *Finnegans Wake*. In attempting to list all of the characters and discuss their functions within the book, Glasheen's first *Census* issued in the era of what is usually called "hard facts" scholarship. Other notable studies of this type are James S. Atherton's *The Books at the Wake* (1959), an examination of Joyce's literary sources that is still an essential volume of *Wake* scholarship; *Song in the Works of James Joyce* (1959) by Matthew J. C. Hodgart and Mabel P. Worthington, most of which was devoted to the *Wake*; several lexicons covering Joyce's use of foreign languages;[9] and Louis O. Mink's *A "Finnegans Wake" Gazetteer* (1978), a truly important work that provides reliable information and commentary on Joyce's references to places. A general volume of *Annotations to "Finnegans Wake"* (1980), compiled by Roland McHugh from more specialized studies, is an attempt at providing line-by-line glosses on all aspects of *Finnegans Wake*, but it is far from the comprehensive set of annotations for which it is often taken.

A second type of "hard facts" scholarship involves research into Joyce's notes and manuscript drafts for the *Wake*. An early, and important, example of criticism based on a study of archival materials is David Hayman's 1958 *PMLA* article, "From *Finnegans Wake*: A Sentence in Progress," which illustrated Joyce's techniques by following a single sentence through successive drafts. Hayman's work on the manuscripts subsequently led to his transcription of *A First-Draft Version of "Finnegans Wake"* (1963); to his collaboration with Danis Rose on the *Finnegans Wake* volumes (28–63) of *The James Joyce Archive*, which, under the general editorship of Michael Groden, makes available facsimiles of virtually all prepublication materials for all of Joyce's works; and to a recent book, *The "Wake" in Transit* (1990), which includes revisions of some of Hayman's more significant articles on Joyce's composition process. Other important work in the area of manuscript study includes A. Walton Litz's *The Art of James Joyce* (1961); Fred Higginson's *"Anna Livia Plurabelle": The Making of a Chapter* (1960), with its transcription of several drafts for that episode; Thomas Connolly's transcription of Joyce's *Scribbledehobble* notebook (1961); and Danis Rose's deciphering of *The Index Manuscript: "Finnegans Wake" Holograph Workbook VI.B.46* (1978). Here it might also be appropriate to mention the importance of *A Concordance to "Finnegans Wake"* by Clive Hart (1963), which includes not only an alphabetical listing of all the words in the *Wake* but also sections on "syllabifications" and "overtones." The frequency with which I have consulted the *Concordance* over the years has deepened my admiration for the pioneering Wakeans whose studies were produced without the assistance of such a word list.

As the author of a highly respected and influential critical study, *Structure and Motif in "Finnegans Wake"* (1962), and coeditor (with Fritz Senn) of *A Wake Newslitter*, Hart played a major role in shaping the debate over *Finnegans Wake* in the 1960s and 1970s. *Structure and Motif* set new standards for *Finnegans Wake* scholarship through its careful examination of archival materials as well as the published text and through its use of close reading to support Hart's analysis of the *Wake*'s dream structure and its narrative and thematic patterns. Even those aspects of Hart's study that have not been widely accepted by later critics—for example, his argument that there are several distinct dream levels in the *Wake*—have had a salutary effect on *Finnegans Wake* criticism by demonstrating the need to ground general interpretations in a specific knowledge of the text and by challenging standard views of the book's structure.

The combination of solid scholarship and iconoclasm that is evident in *Structure and Motif* may also be found in the pages of *A Wake Newslitter*, which began in 1962 as a set of stenciled notes and went into letterpress in 1964. In that journal, Hart and Senn emphasized factual scholarship (identifications, word lists, studies of the notebooks, and the like) and brief exegetical articles and encouraged debate over the principles of reading the *Wake*. *A Wake Newslitter* ceased regular publication at the end of 1980 (although it enjoyed a brief afterlife in the form of "occasional papers" and monographs that appeared through 1984); it has been succeeded by a similar publication, *A "Finnegans Wake" Circular* (edited by Vincent Deane), which continues the important work of encouraging close readings and collecting information based on Joyce's notebooks and other sources.

Stimulated in part by the presence of *A Wake Newslitter* and, beginning in 1963, the *James Joyce Quarterly*, *Finnegans Wake* scholarship enjoyed a boom throughout the 1960s. Aside from the books by Litz, Hart, Burgess, and Tindall already mentioned, as well as volumes on Scandinavian, German, and Gaelic languages in the *Wake*, the decade was notable for the publication of *Joyce's Benefictions* by Helmut Bonheim (1964); *Joyce-again's Wake: An Analysis of "Finnegans Wake"* by Bernard Benstock (1965); *Twelve and a Tilly*, a collection of essays edited by Jack P. Dalton and Clive Hart (1965); *A Wake Digest* (1968), in which Hart and Senn reprinted some of the best articles from the old, stenciled series of *A Wake Newslitter*; and Margaret Solomon's *Eternal Geomater: The Sexual Universe of "Finnegans Wake"* (1969). Bonheim's book, which investigates Joyce's anti-authoritarianism in *Ulysses* and *Finnegans Wake*, and Solomon's study of sex at the *Wake* have been faulted for their lack of rigor, but both opened up important areas of *Finnegans Wake* study. *Twelve and a Tilly* illustrates the range of studies published during the 1960s, including close readings, analyses of themes or subjects (especially James S. Atherton's "Sport and Games in *Finnegans Wake*"), and textual studies. *A Wake Digest* contains, among other things, Clive Hart's "The Elephant in the Belly: Exegesis of *Finnegans Wake*," an influential study of the principles underlying explication of the *Wake*.

Benstock's book, *Joyce-again's Wake*, was—after Hart's *Structure and Motif*—the most significant critical work on *Finnegans Wake* published during the decade. Although his announced intention was to write for the "middle-range" reader who would be intimidated by more specialized investigations, Benstock addresses such crucial areas as Joyce's characterization, his political and religious attitudes, and his use of autobiographical materials in *Finnegans Wake*; Benstock also discusses the *Wake*'s status as a "comic epic" and provides a close reading of "The Tale of Jarl van Hoother and the Prankquean" (21.5–23.15) as a paradigm for many of the book's themes and narrative patterns.

The pace of *Finnegans Wake* scholarship increased again in the 1970s, a decade that saw developments in several distinct areas. I have already discussed or alluded to important works of scholarship, published during this period, that focus on "hard facts" or archival sources: O Hehir and Dillon's *Classical Lexicon*, Glasheen's *Third Census*, Mink's *"Finnegans Wake" Gazetteer*, Rose and O'Hanlon's edition of *The Index Manuscript*, and the *Finnegans Wake* volumes of the *James Joyce Archive*. A more specialized volume dependent on manuscript and source study is Claude Jacquet's *Joyce et Rabelais: Aspects de la création verbale dans "Finnegans Wake"* (1972), which shows that Joyce drew on L. Sainéan's *La Langue de Rabelais* (1922) while writing *Finnegans Wake*. Mark Troy's *Mummeries of Resurrection: The Cycle of Osiris in "Finnegans Wake"* (1976) includes valuable material on Joyce's Egyptian sources and relates the Osiris myth to larger patterns in the book. John Garvin's book, *James Joyce's Disunited Kingdom and the Irish Dimension* (1976), contains enthusiastic, if not particularly rigorous, discussions of some of the Irish backgrounds for *Ulysses* and *Finnegans Wake*.

Two books that emerged from efforts to reconceive *Finnegans Wake* in broad terms and to trace its narrative and thematic patterns are *A Conceptual Guide to "Finnegans Wake"* (1974), edited by Michael H. Begnal and Fritz Senn, and *Narrator and Character in "Finnegans Wake"* (1975), by Michael H. Begnal and Grace Eckley. The *Conceptual Guide* contains thirteen essays by notable *Wake* scholars, each dealing with one or more of *Finnegans Wake*'s seventeen chapters. Few of the contributions include readings of individual chapters that open up the book as a whole, as the editors had planned, but most of the essays are successful in providing new and stimulating insights into areas of more specialized concern. The *Narrator and Character* volume is not a coauthored study but a pair of monographs that were not quite long enough to be published separately. Begnal's half of the book, "The Dreamers at the Wake: A View of Narration and Point of View," argues that *Finnegans Wake* actually has several dreamers (rather than the single dreamer usually posited); Begnal also discusses the book's various characters and their roles in the narrative. Eckley's half, "Queer Mrs Quickenough and Odd Miss Doddpebble: The Tree and the Stone in *Finnegans Wake*," traces a complex of images throughout the book and relates them to Joyce's characterization and his concept of the artist.

A shift in the direction of *Finnegans Wake* criticism during the 1970s may be seen through a comparison of the *Conceptual Guide* and *Narrator and Character* with two books published in 1976: Roland McHugh's *The Sigla of "Finnegans Wake"* and *The Decentered Universe of "Finnegans Wake"* by Margot

Norris. McHugh focuses on a group of signs, or "sigla," that Joyce used during the composition of *Finnegans Wake* and incorporated at various places in the text. Arguing that these sigla are not merely interchangeable with the book's characters but reveal its fundamental principles, McHugh uses the sigla as a key to the book's structure and to the relationship of its dominant themes. McHugh's work is important for its use of the *Finnegans Wake* notebooks and its development of a critical approach that is independent of traditional assumptions about novelistic design.

Norris is even more opposed to what she calls "the novelistic fallacy," the idea that there is a core of real, verifiable, conscious experience underlying the book's dream transformations. Instead, Norris locates the meaning of *Finnegans Wake* in the linguistic complexity which she reads as the dreamer's confused, but ultimately liberating, assault on the structures of authority. Drawing heavily on Freud, Heidegger, and their structuralist and poststructuralist successors, Norris develops a persuasive rationale for her interpretation of *Finnegans Wake* as both a reflexive examination of the dreaming state and a veiled critique of familial and social structures.

A highly original and stimulating perspective on *Finnegans Wake* is included in *James Joyce's Pauline Vision: A Catholic Exposition* by Robert Boyle, S. J. (1978). By playing *Ulysses* and *Finnegans Wake* against various other texts, particularly the epistles of St. Paul, *The Book of Kells, A Midsummer Night's Dream*, and Gerard Manley Hopkins's poetry, Father Boyle produces an engaging, and radically subjective, essay on Joyce's imagination. More dogmatic in its approach is Colin MacCabe's *James Joyce and the Revolution of the Word* (1978), which draws upon poststructuralist and Marxist theory to develop a political reading of Joyce's work. Another book of general interest that contains useful material on *Finnegans Wake* is Anthony Burgess's *Joysprick: An Introduction to the Language of James Joyce* (1973), while *The Wink of the Word: A Study of James Joyce's Phatic Communication* by A. M. Leo Knuth (1976) is informative in its treatment of Shem's riddle and other specialized subjects.

The momentum that built up during the 1970s continued into the next decade. 1980 saw the publication of three books on the *Wake*: Roland McHugh's *Annotations to "Finnegans Wake,"* which I have already mentioned; Barbara DiBernard's *Alchemy and "Finnegans Wake"*; and my own *The Riddles of "Finnegans Wake."* DiBernard analyzes Joyce's use of alchemical terminology and shows that one of the central metaphors of *Finnegans Wake* involves the comparison of artistic creation to alchemical transmutation. My book on riddles in *Finnegans Wake* also draws upon a traditional body of knowledge to illuminate an aspect of Joyce's work—in this case, the relationship between riddling and central thematic and structural concerns of *Finnegans Wake*. A similar strategy may be found in a later book, *James Joyce and Heraldry* by Michael J. O'Shea (1986), which includes an important commentary on the use of heraldic language in the *Wake*.

Two books of a less specialized nature, each by an already-established authority on *Finnegans Wake*, are Roland McHugh's *The "Finnegans Wake" Experience* (1981) and Michael H. Begnal's *Dreamscheme: Narrative and Voice in "Finnegans Wake"* (1988). McHugh's book discusses how to go about reading *Finnegans Wake*, offering his own experience as a model for others. Begnal returns to some of the fundamental questions of narration that he addressed in his earlier work and, in so doing, demonstrates that a common-sense approach to narrative in *Finnegans Wake* may still prove illuminating.[10] More narrowly focused in their approach, yet accessible to general readers, are *Children's Lore in "Finnegans Wake"* by Grace Eckley (1985), which is valuable for its research into Joyce's use of children's games, nursery rhymes, and the like, and Vincent John Cheng's *Shakespeare and Joyce: A Study of "Finnegans Wake"* (1984), which doubles as a reference book on Shakespearean allusions in *Finnegans Wake* and a critical study of those references.

Of the many books on *Finnegans Wake* published during the 1980s, the one that received the most attention, and stirred the greatest debate over its methods and conclusions, was *Joyce's Book of the Dark: "Finnegans Wake"* by John Bishop (1986). An erudite and witty study based on years of immersion in Joyce and an impressive array of sources, *Joyce's Book of the Dark* is devoted to the proposition that *Finnegans Wake* is literally a description of a dreaming state. Bishop imagines a dreamer who is both an individual person (with a body whose sensations impinge upon the dream) and a universal or collective protagonist; his sleep is at once a real night's sleep, the state of death or suspended animation between reincarnations, and the nightmare of Viconian (cyclic) history from which we cannot awake. The primary criticism of the book has focused on Bishop's appropriation of language from Joyce's text, which he integrates into his own sentences without regard for traditional concerns about context (although in response he disarmingly observes that if the book is about a dream, then the sleeping state provides its only significant context). Whatever the merits or defects of its methodology, *Joyce's Book of the Dark* has done more than any other recent volume to open up the rich imaginative possibilities of *Finnegans Wake*.

In addition to the books cited already, there are important discussions of the *Wake* in some recent general studies of Joyce, many of which show the influence of feminist theory, deconstruction, new historicism, or other aspects of current literary theory. Among the noteworthy general volumes published in the 1980s, the following deserve mention here: *Post-Structuralist Joyce: Essays from the French* (1984), edited by Derek Attridge and Daniel Ferrer, which includes Jacques Derrida's "Two Words for Joyce"; Bonnie Kime Scott's *Joyce and Feminism* (1984) and her *James Joyce* (1987); *A Companion to Joyce Studies*, edited by Zack Bowen and James F. Carens (1984); *Joyce the Creator* by Sheldon Brivic and *Joyce's Catholic Comedy of Language* by Beryl Schlossman (both 1985); *Joyce's Anatomy of Culture* by Cheryl Herr (1986); *Vico and Joyce*, edited by Donald Phillip Verene, and *Joyce's Uncertainty Principle* by

Phillip F. Herring (both 1987); Derek Attridge's *Peculiar Language: Literature as Difference from the Renaissance to James Joyce* (1988); and two 1989 volumes: *Crimes Against Fecundity: Joyce and Population Control* by Mary Lowe-Evans and *Reading the Book of Himself: Narrative Strategies in the Works of James Joyce* by Michael Patrick Gillespie. A worthy addition to this list is *James Joyce and the Politics of Desire* by Suzette A. Henke (1990), whose attempt to reclaim Joyce for feminism reaches its logical conclusion in a reading of the female voice in *Finnegans Wake* as an example of *écriture féminine*.

As we enter the 1990s, criticism of *Finnegans Wake* continues to be one of the most dynamic areas of Joyce scholarship. The Summer 1990 issue of the *James Joyce Quarterly* was the fifth in that journal's quarter-century history to be devoted to *Finnegans Wake*, and two important books on the *Wake* have recently been published: *The "Wake" in Transit* by David Hayman (1990) and *Wandering and Return in "Finnegans Wake"* by Kimberly J. Devlin (1991).[11] Hayman's study of Joyce's composition process focuses on the early development of the *Wake*'s framework (another volume, on "verbal substance and details," is promised); its combination of extensive work on the manuscripts and genuine critical acuity is a rarity in *Finnegans Wake* scholarship. Devlin's book is equally distinguished, but quite different in its approach. Applying to *Finnegans Wake* Freud's concept of the uncanny as the unconscious mind's disguised transformation of the familiar, Devlin traces ways in which the *Wake* explores questions of identity, subjectivity, and gender through innumerable turns and returns that include uncanny versions of scenes from Joyce's earlier work.

In this review of *Finnegans Wake* criticism, I have emphasized studies that have appeared in books, but it should be noted that some of the best criticism, including work that has had a major impact on subsequent scholarship, has been published in journals. An obvious example (reprinted in this volume) is Adaline Glasheen's 1954 essay, *"Finnegans Wake* and the Girls from Boston, Mass.,"* which demonstrates the importance of Morton Prince's *The Dissociation of a Personality* as a source for *Finnegans Wake*. The selections that follow include journal articles, essays that originally appeared in collections of Joyce criticism, and book chapters; in addition, Clive Hart's *"Finnegans Wake* in Adjusted Perspective,"* which first appeared a quarter century ago, has been substantially revised for this volume, while Vincent J. Cheng's "The General and the Sepoy: Imperialism and Power in the Museyroom," part of his work in progress on Joyce and imperialism, is published here for the first time.

As a whole, *Critical Essays on James Joyce's "Finnegans Wake"* is an attempt to bring together important and representative critical work on *Finnegans Wake*. No early reviews are included, since they are readily available in Robert H. Deming's *James Joyce: The Critical Heritage*, nor have I reprinted much other criticism that was first published more than two decades ago, since for the most part those works either have been reprinted elsewhere or have been superseded by later studies. I have also avoided the following kinds of criticism, regardless of their intrinsic value: studies of the *Finnegans Wake* text, the manuscripts, or the notebooks; word lists or other sets of annotations; highly theoretical articles concerned more with demonstrating a theoretical position than with interpreting the *Wake*; and essays on the influence of *Finnegans Wake* on later works. Instead, I have chosen criticism that deals with issues of broad concern: studies of structure, voice, narration, language, and interpretation, analyses of important recurrent themes, and readings of passages in ways that pose crucial questions about *Finnegans Wake* as a whole.

Finally, the essays in this book should illustrate how enjoyable an experience reading *Finnegans Wake* can be. Joyce frequently caricatures his critics, including the twelve authors of *Our Exagmination*—"Your exagmination round his factification for incamination of a warping process" (497.2–3)—and he is particularly severe on critics who take themselves too seriously and fail to catch the fun: "we grisly old Sykos who have done our unsmiling bit on 'alices, when they were yung and easily freudened" (115.21–23). In addition to their value as scholarly investigations of Joyce's themes and techniques, the studies that follow should also demonstrate what every Wakean knows, that there's "lovesoftfun at Finnegan's Wake" (607.16).

Notes

1. Arnold Bennett, "Books and Persons," *London Evening Standard*, 19 September 1929, 7; excerpted in *James Joyce: The Critical Heritage*, vol. 2, ed. Robert H. Deming (New York: Barnes & Noble, 1970), 404. Deming also includes numerous other early responses to *Work in Progress*, as well as reviews of the completed *Finnegans Wake*.

2. For a chronology of the composition and publication of *Finnegans Wake*, including excerpts published as *Work in Progress*, see A. Walton Litz, *The Art of James Joyce: Method and Design in "Ulysses" and "Finnegans Wake,"* corrected edition (New York: Oxford University Press, 1964), 145–48, and the "Draft Catalogue" appended to *A First-Draft Version of "Finnegans Wake,"* ed. David Hayman (London: Faber & Faber, 1963), 286–330.

3. Cited by Richard Ellmann in *James Joyce*, rev. ed. (New York: Oxford University Press, 1982), 722; hereafter cited in text as Ellmann.

4. For reprinted (and, in the case of Levin and Wilson, expanded) versions of these reviews, see Harry Levin, *James Joyce: A Critical Introduction* (Norfolk, Conn.: New Directions, 1941; rev. ed., 1960); William Troy, "Notes on *Finnegans Wake*," in *James Joyce: Two Decades of Criticism*, ed. Seon Givens (New York: Vanguard Press, 1948), 302–18; and Edmund Wilson, "The Dream of H. C. Earwicker," in Givens, 319–42, and in Wilson's *The Wound and the Bow* (New York: Oxford University Press, 1947), 243–71.

5. In this introduction and the essays that follow, *Finnegans Wake* citations include both page and line numbers (thus 615.28 is page 615, line 28); the letters R, L, and F in page references designate right-margin notes, left-margin notes, and footnotes in book 2, chapter 2. Citations refer to all editions of the *Wake*, both British (Faber & Faber) and American (Viking Press).

6. For a balanced assessment of the *Skeleton Key* and its contribution to Joyce scholarship, see Michael H. Begnal, "A Skeleton Key to Campbell and Robinson," in *Re-Viewing*

Classics of Joyce Criticism, ed. Janet Egleson Dunleavy (Urbana: University of Illinois Press, 1991), 36–45. The same volume includes significant essays on *Our Exagmination* (by Suzette A. Henke), Adaline Glasheen's *A Census of "Finnegans Wake"* (by Bonnie Kime Scott), James S. Atherton's *The Books at the Wake* (by Fritz Senn), and other seminal works of Joyce criticism.

    7.   See my "Reading the Letter: Interpreting the *Wake*," in *New Alliances in Joyce Studies*, ed. Bonnie Kime Scott (Newark: University of Delaware Press, 1988), 238–42, and " 'A Warping Process': Reading *Finnegans Wake*," in *Work in Progress: Joyce Centenary Essays*, ed. Richard F. Peterson, Alan M. Cohn, and Edmund L. Epstein (Carbondale: Southern Illinois University Press, 1983), 47–57.

    8.   For a more detailed look at Burgess's method in *A Shorter Finnegans Wake*, see Derek Attridge, *Peculiar Language: Literature as Difference from the Renaissance to James Joyce* (Ithaca, N.Y.: Cornell University Press, 1988), 210–18, 229–30.

    9.   Dounia Bunis Christiani, *Scandinavian Elements of "Finnegans Wake"* (Evanston, Ill.: Northwestern University Press, 1965); Helmut Bonheim, *A Lexicon of the German in "Finnegans Wake"* (Berkeley and Los Angeles: University of California Press, 1967); Brendan O Hehir, *A Gaelic Lexicon for "Finnegans Wake"* (Berkeley and Los Angeles: University of California Press, 1967); and Brendan O Hehir and John M. Dillon, *A Classical Lexicon for "Finnegans Wake"* (Berkeley and Los Angeles: University of California Press, 1977). Numerous articles have been published on the use of other languages in the *Wake*, many of them appearing in *A Wake Newslitter*. A "polyglossary" that will include all recognizable foreign language references in *Finnegans Wake* is forthcoming from the University of California Press.

    10.   Begnal has produced some particularly useful studies of narrative structure in the *Wake*: see his half of *Narrator and Character in "Finnegans Wake"* (Lewisburg, Pa.: Bucknell University Press, 1975), *Dreamscheme: Narrative and Voice in "Finnegans Wake"* (Syracuse, N.Y.: Syracuse University Press, 1988), and the essay reprinted in the present book. Other important work includes Bernard Benstock's "Every Telling Has a Taling: A Reading of the Narrative of *Finnegans Wake*," *Modern Fiction Studies* 15 (Spring 1969): 3–25, and Benstock's "Beyond Explication: The Twice-Told Tales in *Finnegans Wake*," in *James Joyce: The Centennial Symposium*, ed. Morris Beja et al. (Urbana: University of Illinois Press, 1986), 95–108. Benstock is now preparing a book on "Narrative Con/texts in 'Finnegans Wake.' "

    11.   A recent book whose publication was announced as I completed this introduction is *James Joyce's "Finnegans Wake" A Casebook*, ed. John Harty, III (New York: Garland, 1991).

HARDEST CRUX EVER: INTERPRETING *FINNEGANS WAKE*

◆

Finnegans Wake in Adjusted Perspective[1]

Clive Hart

I

In order to make some analytical progress with *Finnegans Wake* it may be profitable, as with scrutiny of the physical world, to set up hypotheses about its nature and purpose. It is nevertheless all too noticeable that hypotheses have been maintained in the face of plain evidence as to their fallaciousness or futility. Critics of *Finnegans Wake* have too often used the book to pursue their own obsessions.[2] That is not, of course, a phenomenon peculiar to Joyce studies. Critics of Shakespeare, among others, have been quite as aberrant in their pronouncements. The difference, in the case of Shakespeare studies, is that there the plain sense of the text keeps pulling the reader back to the common center, whereas we have no common center to which to relate ideas generated by *Finnegans Wake*.

What, first, might be assumed about the genesis and purpose of the book and about Joyce's attitude to it?

(1) Perhaps the earliest assumption—one that was made at least implicitly by Harriet Weaver when Joyce sent her his early sketches—was that Joyce was mad:[3] the book was the product of a mind totally alienated from the world of ordinary readers, from ordinary users of language. It might, like the literary products of certain schizophrenic patients, contain amusing, even interesting and enlightening passages, but as a whole it might be ignored as an unfortunate aberration of a once-great writer who had lost the power to make effective verbal contact with his audience.

This charge is easy to dismiss—too easy. There may be some truth in it. Joyce was indeed somewhat alienated from ordinary readers and ordinary users of language. Having little idea of the inevitable responses of his audience, he lived in a critical fantasy world, unable to comprehend why his book should not be widely read and accepted. He showed himself during most of his life to be a poor critic, both of his own work and of that of others. His literary training was scanty and his sense of artistic values odd.

An earlier version of this essay was published as *"Finnegans Wake* in Perspective," in *James Joyce Today: Essays on the Major Works*, ed. Thomas F. Staley (Bloomington: Indiana University Press, 1966), 135–65. The revised version was prepared for this volume and is published here for the first time by permission of the author.

Joyce's powers were confined to only one or two creative contexts, outside which he was worse than mediocre.

That is not, of course, the whole truth about Joyce's attitude to *Finnegans Wake*. He did at times accept the realities and protected himself with such statements as that the book would be understood after the passage of three centuries. But his distress at the poor reception accorded it in 1939 was genuine. He had made his book harder than he realized; he had partially failed in his aim because he did not altogether know what he was doing. Later I shall discuss the extent to which authorial intentions and aberrations should influence our own reading of *Finnegans Wake*.

Joyce not only made *Finnegans Wake* difficult, but also based some of it on irrational linguistic principles. Like other partially alienated writers—Lawrence, for instance—Joyce would accept reason only when it suited him. He protected himself from criticism for his use of Vico by saying that he would not pay much attention to Vico's theories of history and the origins of language but merely use them for all they were worth.[4] In respect of his own use of language, however, he was less clear-sighted. The truths of philology did not interest him. He used only those theories that suited his purpose and cohered with his own irrationally conceived picture of how the world was constructed. He used theories that bolstered an all-consuming superstition.

The adoption of such theories is of course unexceptionable as far as the internal coherence of a work of art is concerned. There is clearly no reason why a book should be philologically accurate in order that it be a fine work of art. But Joyce went further. He not only used language in internally coherent ways, but also relied on some of those theories to establish the external relevance of his book—in order, in fact, to communicate with his audience. Joyce used language in ways which would work fully for the reader only if certain irrational concepts about the function of words were true. His belief in the magical function of language is thoroughly well attested. He told Heinrich Straumann[5] that the reader should "let the linguistic phenomenon affect one as such," by which he seems to have implied that communication of some sort will take place even when the meanings of words, in the normal sense of "meaning," are not consciously apprehended. There is some truth in Beckett's assertion[6] that Joyce used words as things, that he subscribed to ideas of a racial linguistic unconscious. If the reader is to follow the lead that he often finds in the biographies, he will allow the phenomenon of *Finnegans Wake* to work on him without rational intervention. He will expect unknown words to stir him, just as he may be stirred by the sight of unknown objects of mysterious nature and of archetypal form. This attitude to the text has been adopted by a small number of critics, among whom perhaps the most serious was Sven Fagerberg, who in 1950 published a lengthy article entitled "Finnegan och det öde landet"[7] ("Finnegan and the

Waste Land"), in which *Finnegans Wake* is related to the unconscious needs and drives of modern man.

Joyce was, however, a schizophrenic type. His attitude to his book was by no means invariably as I have described it. At times he was capable of claiming that readers (such as Edmund Wilson) had failed to "understand" certain passages. He would even, on occasion, provide a glossary, as he did when writing to Miss Weaver about the opening passage (*Letters*, 247–48), or encourage others to provide glossaries, as in Stuart Gilbert's contribution to *Our Exagmination*.[8]

This all indicates, I think, some small degree of alienation, which may influence the reader's approach to *Finnegans Wake*. It is not so much the mystical beliefs about language that seem out of touch, as the frequent vacillations between the total commitment to the unconscious response and the rational semirepudiations of that commitment—the claim that explication and hard work are necessary.

(2) An even simpler assumption, made by countless hostile critics during the publication of "Work in Progress," is that Joyce was a charlatan. He threw language together into any old outrageous shapes and laughed behind the reader's back. This assumption is even easier to dismiss than is the first, but once again it includes, I believe, an element of truth which I shall discuss below. There was some irresponsibility in the composition of *Finnegans Wake*.

(3) A further widespread assumption, attributing conscious purpose but little order, is exemplified in the *Times Literary Supplement* review and developed in D. S. Savage's *The Withered Branch*.[9] Joyce is looked upon as the exponent of destruction, the prophet of the modern social crack-up. *Finnegans Wake* reflects the crack-up directly: Joyce wrote the book to express the dissolution of the universe, and hence the association of materials in the portmanteau words is, by intention, self-contradictory, self-destructive, fortuitous, based on unreason. A grandiose agglomeration of disparate materials has been produced by free-associative methods. Thus, although the reader may here and there glean some local sense by a similar process of associative reading, it is futile to try to derive any coherent statement from the book as a whole.

(4) An assumption contrary to number (2), and perhaps equally self-protective on the part of the critic, is that Joyce was a mastermind, incapable of error (as Stephen says of his ideal artist in "Scylla and Charybdis"). Many adulators during the twenties and thirties acted on this idea, and some criticism still appears under its influence. The mastermind assumption usually leads to the belief that in *Finnegans Wake* Joyce wrote about the whole of human life and history and that in doing so he created a work of art perfectly unified, brilliantly coherent, endlessly intricate in its internal relationships and in its external relevance to the world in which we live.

This sort of gushing "appreciation" would hardly warrant separate attention as an assumption bearing on the nature of the book if it were not that it has led, in practical criticism, to a special working hypothesis: the belief, held in some quarters, that Joyce (in reality, I believe, quite ill-read and limited in intellectual scope, at least by the best academic standards) knew more than any other reader can ever hope to know and that in *Finnegans Wake* everything interrelates meaningfully with everything else. I discuss, below, some of the results of the assumption of endless interrelationship, while elsewhere[10] I have tried to analyze the sentimentality inherent in such a critical approach.

The positive value of this sort of attitude lies in the fact that it assumes Joyce to have composed rationally, with conscious control over his materials. It is therefore a useful corrective to the attitude which would rank him with those who play on the reader's unconscious or semiconscious responses. While I believe that there is evidence to show that Joyce often flirted with the attractive idea of magical verbal communication, it seems to me that the emphasis should be placed squarely on the lucid, rational aspects of *Finnegans Wake*. The best representative of the opposite extreme is no doubt Gertrude Stein, whose relationship to Joyce might be likened to that between Jung and Freud: the one basically mystical, the other, in his best moments, rational; the one receptive, almost gullible, the other restrictive, empirical; both aspiring to cover the whole range of human experience.

It is possible, of course, to assume rationality, great architectural skill, and brilliantly conceived internal coherence without finding that *Finnegans Wake* has sufficient immediacy to move or delight. Some critics otherwise favorably disposed toward Joyce appear to feel that it is a work of brilliant but futile Alexandrian complexity. Samuel Goldberg and Joseph Prescott are in this category, while the attitude is seen in extreme form in a long attack by Francis Russell.[11]

II

How do these assumptions manifest themselves in practical criticism of *Finnegans Wake*? One can find meaning in *Finnegans Wake* very easily—far too easily. Depending on one's notions about its communicative techniques, it can mean whatever one wants it to mean. Before we can arrive at any useful conclusions about either the total meaning or the meaning of individual passages, it will therefore be helpful to try to determine the nature and limitations of those techniques.

In trying to discover how to read *Finnegans Wake* we are necessarily concerned with the bases of any form of verbal communication. The assumptions underlying normal discourse are brought to the surface for reexamination. It may be that *Finnegans Wake* should finally be thought of as communicating in more or less the same way as do other literary works,[12] but that does not at first seem to be the case, and careful thought is needed before the reader can feel confident.

Two distinct stages are involved in what has become the most common method of explication. The first concerns the reader's assumptions about the reference of the words in the text. To what system or systems of reference should the black marks on the page be referred?

We are used to literature which displays a multiplicity of meanings, but we are used also to a publicly apprehendable surface. "Mary Had a Little Lamb" may be a political allegory, but it is also, for the uninitiated, a simple, comprehensible narrative. *Finnegans Wake* often contains such a surface meaning, but equally often it does not. The following makes as much surface sense as does "Mary": "A baser meaning has been read into these characters the literal sense of which decency can safely scarcely hint. It has been blurtingly bruited by certain wisecrackers . . . that he suffered from a vile disease" (33.14). This second passage, on the other hand, is likely to mean nothing at all to many casual readers: "Ichts nichts on nichts! Greates Schtschuptar! Me fol the rawlawdy in the schpirrt of a schkrepz" (343.20).

"Mary Had a Little Lamb" calls upon an agreed system of signs and symbols. By common consent we do not go beyond these as we read. (As I try to show below, it is nevertheless possible to withdraw one's consent.) For much of its length *Finnegans Wake* does not seem to use an agreed-upon system such as that of "Mary." If we look with an open mind at the possible alternatives, we find that at least four different working assumptions may be made.

(1) We may retain the agreement where the black marks on the page are, as in the first example above, identical with the conventional signs for English words and phrases. Approximations to such signs may be interpreted in the same way as one interprets, for example, the everyday pun.

(2) We may assume that *Finnegans Wake* is an amalgam of typographical bits and pieces drawn from various accepted systems, each bit to be interpreted in terms of the system from which it appears to have been drawn. The contexts in question include, of course, not only natural languages, but also such things as proper names and the specialist vocabulary of any intellectual discipline.

(3) We may expand number (2) and assume that any sign or symbol in *Finnegans Wake* may be interpreted according to any agreed-upon linguistic or other system with one of whose signs or symbols it is identical, or to which it approximates. For example, the form "See" might be interpreted at all times as English "see" and/or German *See*— sea, lake.

(4) It may be assumed that *Finnegans Wake* is based on no agreed-upon system or systems, but that, in keeping with some of Joyce's apparent beliefs about the function of language, its words should be thought of

as having an irrational, mysterious, incantatory, or magical effect on the psyche. Receptivity, rather than analysis, would then be the basis of reading.

Justification for any or all of these assumptions may be sought either within the text or from external evidence. I shall discuss below the criteria of consistency. For the present, here is an example to clarify some of the consequences of the various assumptions. Consider the words "aqualavant to . . . kaksitoista" (285.16, 17). These might be taken to mean:

(1) "Equivalent to . . . cack (feces) and oyster(s)." Cats eat oysters? The idea of "sit" is somehow involved (shit?).
(2) "Equivalent to, and washing (*laver*) with water (*aqua*) . . . twelve (Finnish, *kaksitoista*)."
(3) All the above, plus such words and concepts as qual(ity), *avant*, ant, accidia, toy, etc.
(4) "Kaksitoista" as onomatopoeia, totem word, etc.

Provided that it is possible to distinguish the languages or contexts from which parts of words are derived, the second assumption may at first seem to be the most rational, but one is faced with the question of why Joyce chose to use foreign languages instead of plain English. "Aqualavant" is simple enough: it makes possible a multiple pun. But what is the point of using Finnish *kaksitoista* instead of English "twelve"? No pun is immediately suggested. The word is undistorted Finnish. It is not sufficient to say that Finnish is used because of its relevance to Finn the giant. We need to have some understanding of why that language is used here and not elsewhere. The passage begins a calculation of factorial twelve, with the numbers in Finnish, the identification of the language being embedded in the final phrase: "to the finish of helve's fractures" (285.22). The same result could have been achieved with any other of the several foreign languages relevant to the Finn story. It may seem rational to explain the choice of Finnish by giving tentative acceptance to the first assumption as well as to the second: *kaksitoista* is used because Joyce wants the various overtones of meaning which arise when we relate the word form to the English language. That is to say, we are asked to supply pun materials which seem relevant when a foreign word is used in an English context. But if the English overtones are relevant, why not accept those from any other language or context of discourse? Why not, in fact, make the third assumption?

At this point the second stage of the inquiry may begin. The questions are these: What kinds of thing are being said if those various assumptions are correct? Can the assumptions be justified or invalidated by the nature and quality of the ideas that emerge? To what system or systems of ideas should the meanings of the words be referred?

It might seem at first that the problem can be solved with relative ease by examining the coherence or otherwise of such meanings as arise and relating them to what we know of the meaning of the text where its sense is plain—that is, as a modern theorist might wish to put it, by breaking into the hermeneutic circle. That a solution is not so readily available may be seen from the following two examples of explication:

(a) Book II, chapter I, line 1, words 1 and 2:

Every evening at lighting up o'clock sharp and until further notice in Feenichts Playhouse.

(219.01)

It is clear that the opening phrase means "Every evening at precisely lamp-lighting time, and until further notice, in the Phoenix Playhouse" (assumption 1). But Joyce has distorted some words to add further meanings and, by implication, has invited the reader to add distortions of his own to the words which appear in plain English. Thus it is apparent that the play is to be about man's whole existence, starting from the Garden of Eden—else why speak twice about Eve? ("*Every evening* . . ."). Since there are two Eves in the phrase, it is to be presumed that Adam's first wife, Lilith, is implied in one of them, together with the Second Eve, Mary, while the expression "Every eve-" relates the idea of Eve to all women, daughters of Eve. But there is a further implication in the opening words: Every Eve may suggest the dramatic title *Everyman*. Therefore we have here to deal with a female counterpart of Everyman, which suggests in its turn the idea of change of sex, or even of transvestism, to tie in with changes of role elsewhere, especially with the pantomime sex changes on which James Atherton has commented.[13] If we look at the first two words in combination, we see that they contain the word "rye" (-ry e-). This recalls the rye-field which plays an important part in the discussion about Shakespeare in "Scylla and Charybdis." Anne Hathaway tumbled Shakespeare in a rye-field. The tumbling is, of course, a function of the Eternal Eve. The allusion to sexual activity strengthens the suggestion that the play performed in book 2, chapter 1 is to be about Eve as temptress. Because of the presence of the word "-very," which may be interpreted in its primary sense of truthful, we know also that it is to be a play about eternal verities. Joyce is not, however, wholly unsympathetic to Eve. He clearly sees women as creatures of some value; it is a representative of Eve who clears away the debris after the battles between the men. Thus we may read the second word as the present participle of the verb "to even": Eve is the soother, the ironer-out.

(b) The word "hatache" in the clause "has a block at Morgen's and a hatache all the afternunch" (127.30). The simple reader may see here the primary statement "has a block (constipation?) in the morning and a headache all the afternoon." But let us consider "hatache." This contains the letters

HCE in a common variant order: CHE. We all know that these letters stand for Humphrey Chimpden Earwicker, who is the subject of the clause in question. What, however, is the meaning of the residue of the word: "hata-"? *Hata* is, among other things, a Japanese word meaning "flag." What is the significance of that? The significance is hidden in one of Joyce's usual pieces of devious presentation. *Hata* is a name used in Nagasaki for the famous Nagasaki fighting-kite. It is so used because the kite carries the colors of the Dutch flag—those having been adopted during the period of the Dutch presence in Nagasaki in the seventeenth century. The point about this is, of course, that HCE is often seen as a Dutchman—a Flying Dutchman (just as the Nagasaki-Dutch were sailors, and as the hata-kite flies). HCE has eastern connections, as we see particularly in Book 4. If we move a little farther east we are in the Pacific, from which kites may originally have been imported into Japan. It is well known that the Polynesians thought of certain gods, such as Tane, in personified form as bird-kites.[14] Thus, if Earwicker has a "hatache" it is only because he is a hata-CHE, or kite-god struggling with the elements, just as the Flying Dutchman had to struggle.

These are, I believe, not unfair pastiches of many explications offered during the sixties and early seventies and occasionally still published today. What is happening in those examples?

First, in order to define possible limits of relevancy in the references of individual words, assumption number 3 has been made. Potentially, any meaning drawn from any linguistic system may be accepted. In practice, of course, the limits are more restricted, since only those meanings are accepted which provide a coherent set of conceptual interrelationships. The coherence is, however, potentially limitless. Joyce, the master craftsman, made *Finnegans Wake* so brilliantly and so inclusively that it is about anything that ever happened anywhere. Thus any reading is true, provided it has some meaningful link with some other idea in the context. The network of relationships may lead in any direction, though some relationships will be more immediate than others and may have more appeal to the individual explicator.

Such exegetical procedures amount, therefore, to a series of recognitions linked by association. Individual units of potential meaning, established by relating the word forms to parts of agreed-upon systems of signs and symbols, are automatically accepted as "readings" if they can be shown to form part of a coherent pattern. Coherence is the criterion. Typically, we are shown a series of associations which returns to itself:

$$a = b = c = d = e = a'$$

Term *d*, say, may be relevant only because it is a link in the chain. In the case of "hatache" we begin with HCE and we end with him (the Flying Dutchman–god—one of his best known manifestations). In the middle we have the fighting-kite whose value, in such an exercise, lies only in its linking function. The kite is, nevertheless, an essential part of the coherent pattern.

My two examples differ in at least one important respect. The first never moves outside the field of reference established by the "plain sense" of those parts of *Finnegans Wake* which can be read as we normally read "Mary Had a Little Lamb," while the second gets as far away from that field as possible, but uses the chain of associations to return, at the end, to the context of the plain sense. The comparative restraint of the first explication does not, however, make it necessarily more valid. How far may one go in weaving coherent patterns of meaning? Later I want to make a plea for weaving as few patterns as possible.

We need to remind ourselves that such explicative procedures are peculiar to *Finnegans Wake* studies only because we choose so to limit them. If we want to withdraw our consent to the linguistic and referential conventions in other cases, we can apply the same methods wherever we wish. Let us consider, for example, the first line of "Mary":

Mary had a little lamb . . .

If we assume that the words in this passage contain, let us say, anagrams of words in foreign languages, we may find that "had," read backwards, gives Sanskrit *dah*, which means "burn." The word is reversed. The reverse of burning is coldness. Mary is therefore to be thought of as frigid. (Thus far the outward excursion; now follows the return to the plain sense, only a little heightened.) That Mary is frigid explains her association with the little lamb and defines her identity more closely: a Little Lamb, the Lamb of God. Mary had—gave birth to—Christ. Both the Blessed Virgin Mary and Christ are, however, virginal, cold. This explication is, I suggest, entirely coherent. It is also very selective. Nothing indicates why we should read "had" in Sanskrit rather than in, say, one of the Papuan languages. As before, the potential meanings are selected on the basis of their coherence with the plain English sense.

Before we dismiss this as useless fantasy, we might examine a further example from *Finnegans Wake*: the clause "may the mouther of guard have mastic on him" (55.18). Reading the suggested English sense we find "may the Mother of God have mastic on him." What can be meant by "mastic on him"? The suggestion of mastication, to cohere with "mouther," may be relevant, evoking, perhaps, something to do with the Eucharist. There is, however, a more directly relevant concealed meaning. Although it is more common in French than in English, "mastic" is a synonym for putty. The clause therefore reads "may the Mother of God have putty on him." A pun is now evident: "may the Mother of God have pity on him."

Two issues arise here. First, what do we do with the putty? It seems to be only a link in the chain from mastication to pity. That is to say, it does not seem, in itself, to be more useful than was the hata-kite. The second issue arises from the first: if putty and the kite are equally irrelevant, what makes the "mastic" explication more cogent than the "hatache" one? The answer seems to lie in Joyce's introduction into his text of further controls. Long before we reach the end of the clause, we expect "pity" instead of "mastic." The question is how to get there, how to turn "mastic" into "pity."[15] In the case of "hatache" we do not expect from the context anything to do with the Flying Dutchman, or flying gods, however relevant these may be, in general terms, to HCE. The same applies to the general relevancy of Eve, etc., in "every evening." Eve is relevant to *Finnegans Wake*, and she is especially relevant at that point, but nothing indicates that she is indeed included in the words "Every evening" except by orthographical accident. In other words, we have still to consider the question of internal consistency—of the extent to which the book is self-determining. It is possible to prove, as I think the above example demonstrates, that *Finnegans Wake*, or any part of it, is about anything at all. Such a conclusion is plainly useless. We can lead the text wherever we like. To what conclusions, however, can the text, in its turn, lead us?

III

The controlling consistency of the text is not always as apparent as it is in the "mastic" example. Internal consistency is, indeed, a dangerous criterion because of the vagueness of the word "internal." What is internally consistent? What is internal in a work of literature? William York Tindall says: "A danger to be guarded against is free-wheeling interpretation. Your guesses about the meaning of any word or phrase must be justified by both immediate and general contexts. The text limits its interpretation. Not only ideas but tone and movement . . . can serve as limiting context."[16] This warning sounds sane enough at first, but it is difficult to put into practice when one comes to consider it in detail.

The text itself sometimes indicates which of the potential meanings may be accepted, at least in so far as some readings make effective literary sense while others produce only nonsense. This is not, however, always so. We must, I think, accept the fact that, provided it is handled with sufficient ingenuity, good sense—even profound sense—can be derived from any reading taken at random from among the limitless semantic possibilities. Since, therefore, the possibilities are endless, it may seem more useful to work at the other end of the scale: to accept only so much meaning as is necessary to make some sense of every semantic unit and, where there are several possibilities, to accept only so much as establishes the most persuasive sense.

It is common experience of readers of *Finnegans Wake* to find that a tentative reading of a passage will later yield priority to another which is obviously the central intention once one has certain specific information at one's disposal. Such cases occur so frequently that one is tempted to generalize and suggest that if a reading seems doubtful it is probably wrong, or at least omits the most vital points. Nathan Halper's hypothesis that we should accept not possible readings but only mandatory readings[17] reveals a healthy conservatism. It nevertheless seems to me unhelpful to be so rigidly prescriptive about the limits of relevancy. The following example may illustrate the difficulty of finding an adequate criterion for the priority of readings:

> It came straight from the noble white fat, jo, openwide sat, jo, jo, her why hide that, jo jo jo, the winevat, of the most serene magyansty az archdiochesse, if she is a duck, she's a douches, and when she has a feherbour snot her fault, now is it?
>
> (171.23 ff.)

What is "jo"? Is someone called Joe involved here? A case may be made for the relevance of several Joes, including the Fat Boy from *Pickwick Papers*.[18] Although "Jo" might mean something in a foreign language, the reader is led to believe that an English reading of the word has at least some bearing on the passage. *Jo* is a Scandinavian word for "yes," said in answer to a negative, like German *doch* and French *si*. It is often repeated in speech, as in the present context. This, I suggest, is a "possible" reading, but it is by no means mandatory. The context does not suggest Scandinavian elements, and we are not helped by the consistency of the text. Nor are we led, as with "mastic," to expect a meaning to which the form "jo" might be referred.

But let us reconsider the context. It contains at least two quasi-Hungarian words, "magyansty" and "feherbour," the latter representing fever-inducing *fehérbor*—white wine. Might "jo" therefore be Hungarian? Yes, *jó* is Hungarian for "good." Now it has come to be assumed by many Joyceans that in the light of such evidence "good" is in some sense a more "correct" and more valuable reading than "yes." We are not, however, led to expect the idea of "good" any more than we expect "yes." The assumption, an arbitrary one, requires examination.

There are some simple cases where the device is obviously justified by results. One such is the following passage, which was explicated by Nathan Halper:[19]

> Any vet or inhanger in ous sot's social can see the seen for seemself, a wee ftofty od room, the cheery spluttered on the one karrig, a darka disheen of voos from Dalbania, any gotsquantity of racky.
>
> (114.22 ff.)

Recourse to an Albanian dictionary, following the hint in "Dalbania," elucidates most of the obscure words in the passage. No one, I think, will quarrel with the statement that the two most obviously useful senses are those derived from our reading the words as (1) English and (2) Albanian. But when we start applying the technique to a passage like that on page 171, which I have been discussing, it becomes less obvious that one should apply the arbitrary rule "read odd-looking forms in the language alluded to by the context or especially relevant to it." The principle is excellent when, as in the Albanian passage, we immediately see a whole pattern of meaning emerge. But in the case of "jo" it is by no means clear that "good" is intrinsically more meaningful, more valuable, more illuminating, than "yes." The fact that Scandinavian elements do not occur elsewhere in the passage seems to be no more than an arbitrary and mechanical criterion. I believe that this rule of explication, like all others associated with exegesis of *Finnegans Wake*, should be applied only when and if it provides the kind of answers that engender sudden insight: the "uh-huh!" reaction. Pragmatism is the basis of the world of the book just as it is basis of Joyce's compositional techniques—indeed, of his whole practical philosophy of living. Too often one hears statements like "the word 'jo' is not 'yes'; it is Hungarian for 'good.' " Such statements seem to me to be as constrictive, and to show as little understanding of the function of literature, as those which tell us once and for all what the honey "means" in Yeats.

Furthermore, we need to come to terms with some of Joyce's expressed views concerning at least one point of explication—views that are far from limiting. In his letter to Miss Weaver dated 15 November 1926 (*Letters*, 247) he says, of the word "violer" (3.04): "viola in all moods and senses." It would seem that, in this case, all of the possible meanings, from among which Nathan Halper would have chosen only the essential, are relevant and "correct," at least in the opinion of the author. If this is true of "violer," what is to be our attitude to the rest of the text? It seems that, if we are to give any weight at all to Joyce's opinion about his work, the only satisfactory solution to the problem is to accept, in theory, all the potential meanings with which we have been dealing, but if possible to arrange them in a hierarchy. Some are plainly more helpful than others, and in some cases one reading is by so much the most illuminating that the others need hardly be considered. Let us retain "all moods and senses" as an aura of connotation, but in the present state of our understanding of *Finnegans Wake* we would do well to confine most of our attention to what we tentatively identify as the kernel of meaning.[20]

It is interesting that, in the passage quoted above, William Tindall used the words "your guesses." One wonders how far *Finnegans Wake* may profitably be read by the guesser, how much research and specialist knowledge are necessary. I have dealt with this subject elsewhere,[21] but some of the issues need further attention. If internal consistency is to be a criterion, what are we to do when the consistency of the text is interrupted? *Finnegans Wake* has, like *Ulysses*,[22] a fractured surface. Intentionalism may be dangerous when we are discussing meaning, but when we are concerned with the accuracy of the text it is of some importance. We are—or should be—wholly dependent on the author's arbitration as to what black marks are to be read on the page before us, yet in the case of *Finnegans Wake* there is often more than a little doubt as to what those marks should be, and, more important, Joyce seems at times to have renounced his control over them.

It appears almost certain that Joyce intended some flaws to appear in the texture. The book itself deals with man's place in a fallen and broken universe. Although, unlike Humpty Dumpty's shell, the cracked world can be put back together again, man experiences it only in its broken form—except, perhaps, for a few brief moments of blissful insight. The process whereby *Finnegans Wake* reached its final form was not unlike Gulley Jimson's painting of the "Creation": it crumbled during the very moments of composition. While Joyce was elaborating successive drafts, his typists and printers were simultaneously corrupting and simplifying them.[23] Joyce seems to have taken very little account of many of these corruptions—partly, no doubt, due to poor eyesight; partly, perhaps, due to a genuine artistic principle leading him to incorporate fortuitous materials and thus release the book to some extent from the artist's control;[24] partly, it may be, due to artistic irresponsibility or even charlatanry. During some periods of the book's composition Joyce was not very energetic. Although he took *Finnegans Wake* very seriously, he was by no means the devoted artist, the slave to his calling that some adulators have supposed him to have been. I make these points to emphasize the difficulty of knowing, in many places, what black marks should appear on the page. In the simplest sense of the term, some, at least, of *Finnegans Wake* may lack control; Joyce may have abandoned it to chance.

Quite apart from the critical questions raised by such a possibility, uncertainty as to the exact nature of the text often defeats any attempt to use consistency as the criterion of reading. As with some questions of modern physical theory, it is not that we could know but don't; it is rather that the information, the certainty, that we are seeking does not exist. Jack Dalton documented an interesting example of textual doubt in the word "barnaboy" (237.15).[25] This form is due to a corruption, and one which Joyce himself introduced. The original intention was apparently to write "baruaboy"—*barua* being Swahili for "letter." But Joyce misread his handwriting. The error has completely obscured the original "barua." Is the Swahili for "letter" present in the text as it now stands? If we decide that it is not, what is the meaning of "barnaboy"? Should we read, for example, Swedish *barn* ("child")? If Joyce misread "barna" for "barua" he probably thought of the pun on "barn." It is certainly coherent with "boy."

There are numberless "errors" of this type, introduced either by Joyce himself or by his printers and assistants. Joyce nevertheless approved the text after he had drawn up the "Corrections of Misprints"[26]—few of which touch on the sort of errors with which I am now concerned. When Joyce read and approved those corrupted passages, what did he think they meant?

Authorial irresponsibility, forgetfulness, lethargy, quirky laissez-faire, or a genuine desire to relinquish artistic control for an aesthetic purpose has thus led to a situation in which the rational methods of explication desired by Nathan Halper and (so far as one can tell) by Jack Dalton can be used to the full only when the heavy machinery of scholarship is applied to the manuscripts and proofs—and even then a deal of doubt remains. A reading of the text produced by such scholarship is, of course, thoroughly artificial, taking as its text a book written by an ideal Joyce who never existed.[27] What is the ordinary serious reader to do? We may postulate, as Robert Adams did for *Ulysses*, that the fractured surface is a part of the artwork rather than a flaw in it. Joyce's artistic methods, which include irresponsibility and the *ça marche* shrug, may not be attractive to all readers, but we need, I think, to take *Finnegans Wake* on its own terms. Sometimes the consistency of the text will lead to precise answers, separating the essential very clearly from the peripheral. Sometimes, on the other hand, no such precision is attainable, and we would do well to make what we can of the flux.

One of the commonplaces of *Finnegans Wake* commentary is a comparison of the book with a prose palimpsest, each layer of which is ultimately discernible, although some of the layers may be more readily apparent than are others. It is also commonly objected that the multiplicity of layers of meaning which Joyce added to his text has in many instances rendered some of the earlier meanings of his words so obscure as to detract from the richness and impact of the book. Walton Litz made the point in a commentary on "Anna Livia":

> "I warrant that's why she murrayed her mirror. She did? Mersey me!" [cf. 208.35–36]
> Here Joyce has introduced the Mersey and the Murray, a river in South Australia: but in doing so he has almost completely obscured the original (and more important) meaning of "muddied." Similarly, on the first carbon he inserted the Cher by converting "she must have turned" to "she must have charred"; changed "in which of her mouths" to "in whelk of her mouths," thus incorporating a "whelk" and the Elk river of Tennessee; and altered "nose" to "naze," the term for a headland or promontory. In each of these cases the original meaning was greatly obscured by the additional allusion.[28]

While I think that such criticism may often be justified, it is perhaps rather too cerebral and analytical as a general principle. Once again the idea of the fractured or distorted surface needs to be invoked. Like the universe, *Finnegans Wake* has weathered. As in descriptions of the universe, so with commentary on the book: we need to introduce a time factor. Some things that were once there are so no longer. Only an outline or an occasional fragment is left to witness to features which have been superseded. And, as I suggested above, sometimes Joyce carried out the weathering process himself, while at other times he allowed it to happen outside his control. I use this analogy because many critics argue, as Litz did, that "muddied," for example, is still present in "murrayed." I think, on the contrary, that it may no longer be there and that there is no call to criticize Joyce adversely for having let it wear away. The outlines and fragments of past forms may hint at the way the world of *Finnegans Wake* used to look, but the reader will be doing the book more justice if he immerses himself in what is there now (including the old fragments), instead of trying to reconstruct the past states. "Murrayed" means "murrayed" ("turned it into the river Murray"; "made it a little masculine"; "married it"; "compared it to a murrain"; "left it with a faint suggestion of mud.") In adopting this principle one nevertheless needs to be careful to take into account all ordinary meanings of the words.[29] "Charred," for example, is more analogous to the passage about "putty" that I discussed earlier. The meaning "she must have turned" remains fully intact. To char is to turn. That is what a charwoman does: she turns things over and around in the house. (See *OED*.)

I would advocate, then, a rational method of explication which deals with the surface of *Finnegans Wake* as it now lies, but always with the proviso that reason shades off into doubt and ambiguity where the text is imprecise and badly weathered. I would advocate this method because it seems to me to produce the most stimulating results.

Finnegans Wake invites analysis, probing, and rational discussion. It also, however, invites receptiveness and immediacy of response. Joyce's polyglot shorthand is worse than useless if the whole is not greater than the sum of the parts. While we may not be able to accept Joyce's half-enunciated theory that the book may communicate subliminally, independent of knowledge of the meaning of the words, we ought to be careful not to suppose that the task of understanding has been performed when all the details have been elucidated. *Finnegans Wake* is no coldly conceived deposit of human events. It is not a set of cultural annals in the David Jones sense. We should remember what Joyce himself said: "It's meant to make you laugh." Laughter is stimulated most immediately by the surface sense. In order to keep the balance right we should pay heed to the book's unique quality of tone and emphasis, created by its unparaphrasable juxtapositions. Perhaps that is what Joyce meant when he said "let the linguistic phenomenon affect one as such."

IV

I append a few comments on my sense of how, in recent decades, the issues seem to have changed. Most of my original article was concerned with the difficulty of reading *Finnegans Wake* at the atomic or molecular level. Along with many others in the fifties and sixties I made two tentative assumptions: first, that details of the text could be clarified by the exercise of sufficient scholarly effort and, second, that an understanding of the whole would readily follow. Recent discussions of *Finnegans Wake* have focused attention on the fashionable topics of uncertainty, openness, and multivalence. For many readers now, clarification of detail is not only not possible, but undesirable. The aim is no longer certainty but richness and diversity of meaning. While this has its charm it also creates difficulties. If most great literature is open in this way, most also has a strong thread of plain sense to act as a control. The exploration of rich implications in *Hamlet* is unproblematical because there is little doubt about the underlying thrust of the text. The first scene is about people waiting for a ghost, not about baking a cake. But in large parts of *Finnegans Wake* such simple certainties are, even now, wholly lacking. Some passages may well be about ghosts and cakes and many other things simultaneously, but they are not about anything and everything we may care to name—or, if they are, there is almost literally no book to read and nothing of interest to take us out of our own minds.[30] Before we can profitably explore the energy coming from *Finnegans Wake* rather than what we put into it ourselves, we need a better grasp of its finite core. The current fashion for "playing" with the detail brings with it the danger of our amusing ourselves in a land of fantasy.

Of course it may be that the only control we need should come not from molecular explication but from a grasp of the total gestalt. It might be proposed that, as with Hofstadter's anthill, the shape and significance of the whole are independent of the detail.[31] Two difficulties, however, arise from this analogy. First, we cannot see the anthill of *Finnegans Wake* at all unless we can see the ants, and the ants remain invisible until we attribute to the words of which they are constituted some sense allowing them to cooperate in making patterns. In the pursuit of perceptible patterns we have, in *Finnegans Wake*, far too wide a range of linguistic and referential systems on which to call; the establishment of patterns is crucially dependent on the cooperation of traces having a high degree of categorical similarity. Since, in the absence of guiding principles as to which categories to choose, traces of meaning rapidly cancel each other out, we find ourselves falling back on personal whim to avoid the signs' disappearing once again into invisibility. The traces by which the anthill communicates are thus too unstable to be truly independent of the whole composite organism.

Second, the search for a gestalt is, like the search for individual significance, profoundly unfashionable. One's response to these matters depends on one's understanding of the nature of a work of art. The ideal of coherence, and above all of a completed set of interlocking parts, has ceased to be universally attractive. The idea of an organic work, to some degree independent of the reader and protected from his manipulation, is understood to be threatening. Criticism generally has been imbued with a dislike of completion, of closure, a dislike stimulated, it seems, by fear of submission to a creating mind. The idea of closure is, however, too broad a category; we need to distinguish. There is doubtless a kind of closure which limits and stifles the imagination. Various so-called discoveries as to what *Finnegans Wake* is "all about" warrant this description. But there is another type of closure that liberates and opens up further worlds of inquiry. Successful scientific and mathematical theories are often of this kind, while in literature the outstanding example is doubtless Dante's *Commedia*. As wholeness and harmony, when conceived to have only a limiting effect, pose an emotional threat to freedom, their very possibility is tendentiously denied and texts are read in ways which guarantee the continuous generation of escape routes. Although the game can be fascinating, it also seems to me to be trivial. It leaves entirely unanswered, for example, the question why *Finnegans Wake* is a long book in four sections and seventeen subsections (or chapters). A generation ago many of us were fussing, unproductively it may be, with this and related questions. I was in search of such liberating answers—closures— when writing *Structure and Motif*, a book whose alarming wrongheadedness in detail is now noticed less often than are its unfashionable modes of inquiry, which I still find attractive.[32] Almost no one asks such questions now, and some are heard to say that they find the aims repellent or that they simply don't care. If the shape and rhythm of the book, the relationship of its parts, do not matter, what does? It would seem that the arguments about openness and multiplicity of meaning would remain unchanged if we had, say, no more than the first four subsections. The celebrations of the rich fun offered by *Finnegans Wake* take into account the kind of thing the book is made of, but say nothing about what the book *is*. Perhaps it isn't anything but a collection of such passages, held together by the tenuous presence of a nuclear family group with an emotional problem. I hope not, because, if that is true, so much the worse for *Finnegans Wake*. Speaking only for myself, what matters to me in most works of art is the illumination offered by the interrelationships of charged materials which the reader, viewer, or listener is led to juxtapose. With *Finnegans Wake* we know, as yet, neither how the materials may best be interrelated nor what charge they bear. A lot of work remains to be done at both microcosmic and macrocosmic levels.

Finally, it may be that, whether we seek it or not, we shall soon find in *Finnegans Wake* a more harmonious and coherent book than some of us have recently thought likely. Danis Rose, who has now (1991) completed his editing of the text, reports that in its restored state the book is very much more lucid, much easier to read, much more consistent than is the notoriously corrupt edition of 1939. When, in due course, it is published, many of the issues I have raised may cease to be relevant. We shall need to look at *Finnegans Wake* with entirely fresh eyes.

Notes

1. Drafted nearly thirty years ago, this article is very unlike anything I might now attempt to write on the subject. Finding it rather alien, I have reworked it in something like the spirit in which I might suggest revisions for a student essay. The first section, now outmoded and redundant, has been excised completely. Elsewhere, apart from trivial stylistic changes, I have rewritten only when the substance seemed to me to be grossly faulty. At the end I have added a short new section commenting very generally on the relevance of the present critical climate to an understanding of *Finnegans Wake*. I hope the hybrid result may prove of some interest.

2. Among the most outstanding examples is Frances Motz Boldereff's violently anti-British *Reading Finnegans Wake* (Woodward, Pa.: Classic Nonfiction Library, 1959). My own deeply held aesthetic and critical beliefs will be apparent throughout the essay.

3. See, for example, Richard Ellmann, *James Joyce*, rev. ed. (New York: Oxford University Press, 1982), 590.

4. *Letters of James Joyce*, 3 vols., vol. 1 (1957) ed. Stuart Gilbert, vols. 2 and 3 (1966) ed. Richard Ellmann (New York: Viking Press, 1966), I, 213; hereafter cited in text as *Letters*.

5. Heinrich Straumann, "Last Meeting with Joyce," in *A James Joyce Yearbook*, ed. M. Jolas (Paris: Transition Press, 1949), 114.

6. Samuel Beckett, "Dante . . . Bruno. Vico . . Joyce," in *Our Exagmination round His Factification for Incamination of Work in Progress* (Paris: Shakespeare and Company, 1929), 3–22.

7. Sven Fagerberg, "Finnegan och det öde landet," *Poesi* 3, no. 1 (1950): 11–40.

8. Stuart Gilbert, "Prolegomena to *Work in Progress*," in *Our Exagmination round His Factification for Incamination of Work in Progress* (Paris: Shakespeare and Company, 1929), 49–75.

9. *Times Literary Supplement* review, 6 May 1939, 265–66; D. S. Savage, *The Withered Branch: Six Studies in the Modern Novel* (New York: Pellegrini & Cudahy, 1952).

10. Clive Hart, "James Joyce's Sentimentality," *Philogical Quarterly* 46, no. 4 (October 1967): 516–26.

11. S. L. Goldberg, *Joyce* (Edinburgh and London: Oliver & Boyd, 1962); Joseph Prescott, *Exploring James Joyce* (Carbondale: Southern Illinois University Press, 1964); Francis Russell, "Joyce and Alexandria," in *Three Studies in Twentieth Century Obscurity* (Aldington, England: The Hand and Flower Press, 1954), 7–44.

I have omitted discussion of a number of early studies which have proved of great value to students of *Finnegans Wake*. These include Father William T. Noon's very scholarly account of Joyce's theology: *Joyce and Aquinas* (New Haven: Yale University Press, 1957), and the chapters on *Finnegans Wake* in Hugh Kenner, *Dublin's Joyce* (London: Chatto & Windus, 1955), which are among the most brilliant on the subject.

12. With some reservations this is my own view; see below.

13. J. S. Atherton, "*Finnegans Wake*: The Gist of the Pantomime," *Accent* 15, no. 1 (Winter 1955): 14–26.

14. Readers wishing to follow up the background of these intriguing matters might care to consult my *Kites: An Historical Survey*, rev. ed. (1967; Mount Vernon, N.Y.: Paul P. Appel, 1982), 33–60.

15. We might equally, of course, expect "mercy"; it may be possible to derive this sense by some other manipulation, in which case it would be difficult to demonstrate that "mercy" was less "correct" than "pity."

16. William York Tindall, *A Reader's Guide to James Joyce* (New York: Noonday Press, 1959), 265.

17.   Nathan Halper, "Notes on Late Historical Events," *A Wake Newslitter*, n.s., 2.5 (October 1965): 16.

18.   See Adaline Glasheen, *Third Census of Finnegans Wake* (Berkeley: California University Press, 1977), 146.

19.   Nathan Halper, "A Passage in Albanian," *A Wake Newslitter*, o.s., no. 14 (June 1963), 5–6.

20.   This still seems to me to be true in 1991.

21.   Clive Hart, "The Elephant in the Belly: Exegesis of *Finnegans Wake*," revised version, *A Wake Digest*, ed. Clive Hart and Fritz Senn (Sydney: Sydney University Press, 1968), 3–12.

22.   For an early discussion of the matter, now somewhat outdated, see Robert M. Adams, *Surface and Symbol: The Consistency of James Joyce's Ulysses* (New York: Oxford University Press, 1962). Recent explication and work on the text have shown *Ulysses* to be very much closer to full consistency than has sometimes been thought.

23.   See, for example, Fred H. Higginson, "Notes on the Text of *Finnegans Wake*," *JEGP* 55, 3 (July 1956): 451–56. The controversies over the text of *Ulysses* have raised the matter in still more acute form.

24.   See the the story about Beckett and "Come in," Ellmann, 649. (The details of this story are at present, however, in some doubt.) For further discussions of the state of the text, see Jack P. Dalton and Clive Hart, eds., *Twelve and a Tilly: Essays on the Occasion of the 25th Anniversary of Finnegans Wake* (London: Faber & Faber, 1966), 119–37.

25.   Jack P. Dalton, "Kiswahili Words in *Finnegans Wake*," *A Wake Digest*, ed. Clive Hart and Fritz Senn (Sydney, Australia: Sydney University Press, 1968), 43–47.

26.   "Corrections of Misprints in *Finnegans Wake*" (London: Faber & Faber, 1945).

27.   The difficulty is similar to that raised by the "Corrected Text" of *Ulysses*. See Philip Gaskell and Clive Hart, *Ulysses: A Review of Three Texts. Proposals for Alterations to the Texts of 1922, 1961, and 1984* (Gerrards Cross, England: Colin Smythe, 1989), ix–xvi.

28.   A. Walton Litz, *The Art of James Joyce: Method and Design in "Ulysses" and "Finnegans Wake"* (London: Oxford University Press, 1961), 109. It is not quite accurate to say that the Murray is "in South Australia."

29.   As I failed to do in my original comment on "charred." See *James Joyce Today*, ed. Thomas F. Staley (Bloomington: Indiana University Press, 1966), 164.

30.   As must be apparent, I have no sympathy with the critical solipsism which asserts reading to be indeed impossible for just such reasons.

31.   Douglas R. Hofstadter, *Gödel, Escher, Bach: An Eternal Golden Braid* (New York: Basic Books, 1979), 311–36.

32.   Clive Hart, *Structure and Motif in Finnegans Wake* (Evanston: Northwestern University Press, 1962).

Reading *Finnegans Wake*

Louis O. Mink

For anyone who has played its game until its rhythms sound in the pulse beat, *Finnegans Wake* provides an inexhaustible comic commentary on ordinary human situations. I hardly ever rise from a committee lunch, for example, without thinking (from page 17), "Gut aftermeal! See you doomed," or read papers by certain students without muttering (from page 281), "Translout that gaswind into turfish, Teague, that's a good bog." And the big black book contains its own introduction to every discussion of it, all prepared and ready to go: "As my explanations here are probably above your understandings, lattlebrattons, though as augmentatively uncomparisoned as Cadwan, Cadwallon and Cadwalloner, I shall revert to a more expletive method which I frequently use when I have to sermo with muddlecrass pupils. Imagine for my purpose that you are a squad of urchins, snifflynosed, goslingnecked, clothyheaded, tangled in your lacings, tingled in your pants, etsitaraw etcicero. And you, Bruno Nowlan, take your tongue out of your inkpot! As none of you knows javanese I will give all my easyfree translation of the old fabulist's parable" (152).

I

Now of course I don't know javanese either, and there is no easyfree translation of *Finnegans Wake*—although it is no joke that it is being translated into Polish (by Maciej Slomczynski), the only translation of the whole book ever attempted. The untranslatability of *Finnegans Wake* into any language but Polish is a fact about it known even to many people who have never tried to read a page of the book on which Joyce spent almost the last two decades of his life. *Finnegans Wake* is extraordinary in every way. It is certainly the only literary classic which professors of English and of comparative literature freely admit that they haven't read and don't even intend to read. Unlike the *Divine Comedy*, the *Canterbury Tales*, *Don Quixote*, *Faust*, *War and Peace*, and other blockbusters of Western literature, it has never been included in humanities courses or educational curricula and almost certainly never will

Reprinted from *Southern Humanities Review* 9 (Winter 1975): 1–16, by permission of the journal.

be. No theory of literary criticism dares to test itself against *Finnegans Wake*, and no College Outline Series summarizes it for students needing a quick term paper. The reason, of course, is that reading *Finnegans Wake* is a lifetime enterprise—a vocation for a handful of professional scholars and an obsessive avocation for a larger number of amateurs like myself. Thornton Wilder said many years ago that no one is qualified to say anything about *Finnegans Wake* who has not spent at least a thousand hours reading it. Professors of English don't have that kind of time. So the *Wake* is the only undoubted classic which belongs to a literary underworld, inside and outside the academy. It is to literature as cockfighting is to sport. Neither will appear on NBC-TV and be interrupted by commercials.

In accumulating a thousand hours of flying time in Joyce's lighter-than-air craft, one goes through several stages of technique and comprehension in reading. In the first stage there is a simple pleasure in the hilarious double meanings, the multilingual puns, the kaleidoscope of styles, the jumpcuts from scene to scene, and the feeling of being just on the verge of understanding it. In the second stage there are new pleasures in recognizing repetitions, like variations on themes; in discerning the ubiquitous allusions, like the garden of Eden and the fall, or the flood, the ark, and the rainbow; in recognizing through their disguises the theatrical family who play all the leads—Humphrey Chimpden Earwicker and his wife Anna Livia Plurabelle, their children Shem, Shaun, and Issy, and a cast of supporting players; and in the growing certainty of being just on the verge of understanding it. In the third stage, there are other pleasures, as the shape of the book begins to loom out of the mist, in riddling out the closer texture of the prose with the help of reference books, both those about the *Wake* and those which bring one closer to the *minutiae* of Joyce's personal and literary experience; in poring over histories and maps of Dublin and Ireland and finding unsuspected references on every page; in reading Ibsen, the Egyptian *Book of the Dead*, Madame Blavatsky, *Alice's Adventures in Wonderland*, and innumerable other books mined by Joyce for allusions; and in the comfortable conviction of being just on the verge of understanding it. In the final stage, one achieves what every book invites but only *Finnegans Wake* imperiously demands—the possession more or less of the book as a single whole, the reading of every sentence as echoing, corresponding to, alluding to other sentences and passages throughout the book, like a city whose map one could draw more or less accurately from memory although one must always go back to its streets to see whether a certain building is taller than its neighbor or whether the filigree on its façade is like that of a distant counterpart. And at this stage, which is the stage of *Wake* scholarship whether professional or amateur, there is still a simple pleasure in the feeling of being just on the verge of understanding it.

When I began reading *Finnegans Wake* almost twenty-five years ago, very little had yet been written about the book; a long essay by Edmund

Wilson and the *Skeleton Key* by Joseph Campbell and Henry Morton Robinson were about the only guides, and while they gave some idea of what goes on in its chapters they were of no help at all in decoding it page by page, sentence by sentence. So every reader could congratulate himself on discoveries; we were all prospectors in newly discovered territory, and every stream could be panned for gold. Since then the *Wake* has become a book for the amateur scholar rather than for the amateur reader. Clive Hart's *Concordance* to every word and symbol in the *Wake*, and Adaline Glasheen's *Census* of all the names in the *Wake*, together with James Atherton's book on Joyce's literary sources, and a whole library of exegesis and lexicography, have mapped the area and worked all the rich lodes. Yet the book is such a fantastic anagram that it still promises discoveries to every reader. Reading *Finnegans Wake* is something like playing charades, with the mounting excitement that goes with the recognition that one is getting warm and the certainty and triumph when the answer is finally guessed. Every paragraph, almost every sentence, and most phrases and even single words rise from the page, signalling and gesturing, acting out a hidden meaning with body English, appealing to every resource to hint at some arcane allusion. From this standpoint, *Finnegans Wake* is a virtually inexhaustible game of solitaire charades, ready to play whenever you are. And as in other forms of inquiry, every success generates a number of new puzzles not noticed before. To give a couple of examples: There are five places in the book where the initials "V. P. H." are connected with Earwicker, usually so subtly that one would not notice them unless he were looking for them. One looks for them only because in one case HCE's cloak is described as bearing the initials V. P. H. on the tailor's tab, and two hundred pages later an otherwise inexplicable footnote says "V for wadlock, P for shift, H for Lona the Konkubine" (284.F4). So you look for other occurrences of "V. P. H." to help explain the connection between these two, knowing that such repetitions are never accidental in *Finnegans Wake*. But I haven't guessed this particular charade, although I have discovered that other students of the *Wake* have noticed it and are just as baffled. I have spent a fair amount of time looking out of plane and train windows, turning over possible connections. Numerology, for instance: V. P. H. are the 22nd, 16th, and 8th letters of the alphabet. That adds up to 46, but 46 is not one of the important numbers in the book. Then there is the fact that those initials appear in contexts in which Earwicker is being hunted down as a man or as a fox; and one thinks too of any other possible group of three, such as the colors of the British or Irish flags. The most famous triple is of course the Trinity: and in German "V" could be "Vater" and "H" "[der] heilige Geist," but "P" isn't anything to complete that interpretation. And so on—every hypothesis seems to work for one or two of the initials but not for all three. So all that is left is serendipity. There is a 50-50 chance that some day, maybe tonight, I will read or hear something that will go *click* with "VPH," and that particular guessing game will be over. But the supply of games is inexhaustible. To mention another: Earwicker's putative ancestors are named as the "Glues, the Gravys, the Northeasts, the Ankers, and the Earwickers of Sidlesham in the Hundred of Manhood" (30.6–8). Now there is a Sidlesham near Chichester in England and it is in the ancient "hundred" or subdivision of a shire, once called "Manhood," where Clive Hart discovered that there are in fact Earwickers buried in the churchyard and some still living. Apparently Joyce found this out on a holiday in the neighborhood long after he had already given Humphrey Chimpden his cognomen, and he wove this local allusion into his book (as he inserted so many other happy accidents). But this leaves the Glues, the Gravys, the Northeasts and the Ankers still unexplained, and they are not unimportant because they appear together, more or less deeply hidden, in a number of other passages in the book which they would help to explain if we could explain them. But no one has. Mrs. Glasheen's *Census* suggests that Glue and Gravy could be the Blue and the Gray, or North and South in the American Civil War. And HCE's family lines might well be the points of the compass, but "Northeast" spoils the symmetry and "Anker" won't work at all. One summer in Zurich (Joyce lived many years in Zurich, and there are many local Zurich references in the *Wake*) I thought for a passing moment that I might have a clue when I noticed a sign advertising Anker beer, but then what does one do with "glue" and "gravy"? There are four points of the compass, four elements— earth, air, fire and water—four provinces of Ireland, four Viconian ages, four Evangelists, four historians of Ireland, and most importantly the Four Old Men who are usually present in the dream history of the *Wake*, watching and listening, and getting things mixed up. Joyce's symbol for the book itself was a square—four equal sides and angles. But no hypothesis or interpretation yet connects Earwicker's four family lines with any of these quadruples. One day, perhaps, someone who has failed often enough never to forget the Glues and the Gravys will remember them while reading or talking about something else entirely—an account of Cromwell's campaigns, or a recipe, or an article about something else in the 11th Britannica—and one more charade will have been guessed. The probability is, even so, that these names will turn out to be not importantly connected with each other except perhaps as words from an obscure ballad or tale, or as translations of some words in a language other than English. Even if the riddle is guessed, that is, the meaning of these names will not *transform* our understanding but will simply, by removing the mystery which now attaches to all the contexts in which the names appear, take away at the same time the possibility that a passage incompletely interpreted means more than it seems to mean. And this is characteristic of the *Wake*. What I mean to suggest by such examples and by calling the *Wake* a game of solitaire charades, is that it is not, as it has often been thought to be, an allegory of human life, with a single although complex meaning gradually coming into focus with the patient clarification of its astounding detail. It is rather the supreme verbal construction of Western literature. Its exploration is endlessly rewarding to anyone who is happy, at least sometimes, to be both *homo sapiens* and *homo ludens*; but its final meaning is a guffaw.

II

There are books, like *Moby Dick, The Brothers Karamazov,* and *Don Quixote,* which accompany one through life, changing like a landscape which changes as one travels through it. Both the *Odyssey* (not, I think, the *Iliad*) and *Ulysses* belong to this class; at least, since I first read them as an undergraduate, they have almost completely supplanted each other, Homer changing from the celebrant of epic imagination to the observer of common life, and Joyce making the opposite movement. But books remain books, however various and complex. As *Finnegans Wake* is unlike other books, so the experience of reading it comes to be unlike other experiences of reading—in fact, hardly like "reading" at all. It seems to me now much more like the experience of a scientist confronting nature (the "book of nature") or, in Bacon's phrase for scientific experimentation, trying to put nature to the torture, that is, to wring from it a confession of its own hidden forces and functions. As Anthony Burgess has remarked (in *Re Joyce*), "*Finnegans Wake* is as close to a work of nature as any artist ever got." I would go even further and say that Joyce has created a world, though it is a word-world, which like the natural world has indefinitely many levels of organization and patterns of relationship. And reading *Finnegans Wake* is like the scientific inquiry into nature, constantly driven forward by the dynamic of intellectual curiosity and the satisfaction of small discoveries. To understand this analogy one should not think of the vast and technologically sophisticated research projects of modern science, but of science in simpler and more optimistic days. In reading the *Wake*, I am often reminded, for example, of Henri Fabre, the French entomologist, who wrote an entire book about his patient observations of the burgeoning life in a single square-meter of his garden—the numerous species, their life-cycles and individual variations, their complex interrelations and changes over the seasons. Reading a single page or section of the *Wake* can be very much like Fabre studying his square-meter slice of life; what seems at first to be the aimless scurrying of ants turns out on inspection to reveal more and more complex differentiation of function and patterns of response and interaction with other species. But even Fabre's tireless and scrupulous observations missed much; for instance, he never observed the phenomenon of the biological clock—the capacity of his organisms to behave according to a time schedule quite independently of the changing stimuli of light and dark. Similarly, one can read a passage of *Finnegans Wake* following whatever narrative content it has, identifying many of its puns and allusions, and yet discover for the first time, on the tenth or twentieth or even thirtieth reading, that it is chockful of references to music, or to cricket, or to the names of Dublin streets; or that it contains in recessive form a whole series of words which are key words in another passage separated from it by hundreds of pages; or that some of its sentences have the rhythm of recognizable popular songs, although nothing resembling their lyrics.

Or for a different example of scientific inquiry, one could think of Lavoisier's attempt to isolate the common factor in all acids, which he proleptically and quite incorrectly named "oxygen" or "acidmaker." There are in the *Wake* a number of events of which we hear different versions, some more direct, some more oblique, but not wholly consistent with each other. There is an encounter between two men, roughly native and stranger, in which the stranger begins with a show of friendliness, holds the other up inexpertly, and ends by accepting a reluctantly offered loan. Or maybe it is the other way round. One of them carries a package containing a fender; is it a boat fender, a fireplace fender, or is it perhaps what defender and offender have in common? One of them carries a portable still, or perhaps it is a thermos bottle or a hot-water bottle. In one version of their encounter they are prehistoric men, in another St. Patrick and the Archdruid of pre-Christian Ireland, in still another Earwicker himself and the "cad with a pipe" who encountered him in Dublin's Phoenix Park. Why the fender? But why does aqua regia dissolve gold and sulphuric acid not? What do nitric, sulphuric, hydrochloric and acetic acid have in common? Are these irreconcilable versions, *different* stories, or is there a primal story of which these are systematically varied versions, differing with the story-teller? If there *is* a primal story, as the oxygen which Lavoisier sought to isolate *was* really there although not quite what he thought it was or everywhere he thought it to be, then it could be discovered if we could decide which of the clues lead *to* the story and which are irrelevant details. And every clue, and there are many others like the fender, leads to contexts all over the book. In some of these, connections with other clues are supported, in others such connections are severed—like experiments which disconfirm an hypothesis. But "hypothesis" here belongs to the language of experimental inquiry rather than to the language of hermeneutics, and the experience of reading the *Wake* is better explained by the philosophy of scientific inquiry than by any theory of literary interpretation. This is another way of recognizing that the *Wake* is unlike any other literary work—is, in fact, a unique and indescribably complex verbal artifice which stands over against us, as Burgess has said, like a work of nature, "massive, baffling, serving nothing but itself, suggesting a meaning but never quite yielding anything but a fraction of it, and yet (like a tree) desperately simple. Poems are made by fools like Blake, but only Joyce can make a *Wake*."

III

Nature has no theories about itself; neither does *Finnegans Wake*. Nor is nature a cipher of transcendent meaning, and no more is *Finnegans Wake*. I say this to dismiss without argument all fulsome tributes to the profundity of meaning of the *Wake*. Joyce invented a dream-language, it is sometimes said, which plunges beneath the surface of conventional consciousness to capture the universal human mysteries of dream and myth. Joyce realized more than anyone else, it is sometimes said, the relativity of time and space, and explained the cyclical rise and fall of human life and civilization by extracting and reexpressing for modern man the gnomic truths of the sacred scriptures of East and West and the theories of Vico, Nicholas of Cusa, Freud, and Jung. Joyce has taught us, it is sometimes said, that the meaning of language is silence. All this is nonsense. Joyce was not a seer or a magus or a shaman, but an artificer of language and complex form. Ideas were important to him only as literary material to be shaped, as structural devices, or as sources of verbal motifs. As his workbooks and manuscripts show, he built up his more elaborated text on an armature of fairly simple characters, events, and motifs, and within a scaffolding of structural principles which permitted him to work piecemeal with anticipation of where each piece would fit. As everyone knows who has had an elementary introduction to *Ulysses*, each chapter of that book is associated with a color, an art or science, and an organ of the body, not to mention the episodes of the *Odyssey*; but for the most part these correspondences were either used and then dismantled in the creative process, like scaffolding, or else they lie so deeply buried in the text that no one could conceivably respond to them even subliminally, or tease them out by any sort of critical analysis if Joyce himself had not slyly transmitted through Stuart Gilbert his ready-made handbook for exegetes. Covering his tracks and then tipping his hand was one of Joyce's favorite games. He stage-managed, through Samuel Beckett and others, the first critical and scholarly book of essays on *Finnegans Wake* when it was still being published in *transition* as draft installments of "Work in Progress"—and then made fun of this book and its authors in the final text of *Finnegans Wake* (496.35–497.03). The *Wake* often smacks its lips at the thought of the hermeneutical mess it is creating for literary scholars; not even the great American Ph.D. factories, if Joyce could have envisioned them, can cope with it: "List!" the book says of all its interpreters to come. "They will be tuggling foriver . . . They will be pretumbling forever. The harpsdischord shall be theirs for ollaves" (13.17–19). Again, *Finnegans Wake* contemplates its own obscurity with satisfaction: "And look at this prepronominal *funferal*, engraved and retouched and edgewiped and puddenpadded, very like a whale's egg farced with pemmican, as were it sentenced to be nuzzled over a full trillion times for ever and a night till his noddle sink or swim by that ideal reader suffering from an ideal insomnia" (120.09–14). Occasionally the book pats the despairing scholar on the head with a false show of sympathy: "You is feeling like you was lost in the bush, boy? You says: It is a puling sample jungle of woods. You most shouts out: Bethicket me for a stump of a beech if I have the poultriest notions what the farest he all means" (112.03–06).

A great deal has been discovered about *Finnegans Wake* in the last twenty-five years—quite a lot of which was never there to begin with. The day may never come when the relentless, slightly mad corps of *Wake* scholars no longer continue to find names of obscure people and words from exotic languages hidden in the language of the *Wake*. But it is already safe to say that all the secrets still withheld are little ones. There is no unplumbed wisdom in Joyce's achievement, not even for the kind of retrospective understanding which quite legitimately can discover that its subject wrought better than he knew. One of the fascinations of imaginative literature, I believe—and this may be the only definition of "genius" left to us—is the discovery that while no writer succeeds in saying as much as he intends, some succeed in saying more than they realize. Their work, so to speak, contains answers to questions which they never entertained and which we have not yet learned to ask. But Joyce is an exception on both counts. In *Finnegans Wake* he matched achievement to intention, and nothing more. Whatever answers lie still unextracted from *Finnegans Wake* are answers to questions not about the world, not about life, but only about *Finnegans Wake*.

An example of an encompassing theory which serves *Finnegans Wake* only as scaffolding and armature is Vico's theory of the history of civilization, which passes through three eras—the Age of Gods, the Age of Heroes, the Age of Civil Society, and then recycles to begin over again. Reference to Vico's theory is a commonplace of *Wake* interpretation, and it can—up to a point—easily be extracted from the text itself. The first sentence of the book, beginning in the middle to complete the unfinished sentence with which the book ends, introduces Vico both by name and by doctrine: "riverrun, past Eve and Adam's, from swerve of shore to bend of bay, brings us by a commodius vicus of recirculation back to Howth Castle and Environs" (3.01–03). The book's last explicit reference to itself is as "Our wholemole millwheeling vicociclometer" (614.27). But there may be more or less deeply buried allusions to Vico on every page of the book. The famous thunderwords—ten hundred-letter words (the tenth actually being 101 letters, presumably so that the total will add up to the 1001 Arabian Nights) derive directly from Vico's speculation that civilization begins when primitive men are driven into caves by their fear of thunder, perceived as a divine threat, unintelligible but menacing. References to Vico's three ages, with a fourth interlude or *ricorso* before the cycle begins again, abound in the *Wake*, often identified with the basic human cycle of birth, marriage, death and rebirth. As armature, the cycle may be "eggburst, eggblend, eggburial and hatch-as-hatch can" (614.32–33), or such a phrase as "Harry me, marry me, bury me, bind me" (414.31), or again, "a good clap, a fore marriage, a bad wake, tell hell's well" (117.05). The pattern of 3 + 1 is even in the title—a three-syllable plus a one-syllable word, which means both a ceremony for the dead and the return to consciousness after sleep—and it is also in the structure of the book, which consists of three parts divided into chapters plus a fourth part of one chapter whose final sentence returns to begin the first page. Plenty of material for a dissertation, in other words, but a dissertation about *Finnegans Wake*, not about history or cosmology. The form of Vico's theory was useful to Joyce, but its truth was of no interest, and the relevance of Vico's great *Scienza Nuova* to Joyce's word-world is of exactly the same order as the list of Dublin's Mayors, or a list of Tom Moore's songs, which one scans in order to identify their occurrence in the text (and there they are, as a matter of fact: some 200 Lord Mayors of Dublin, and 150 of Moore's *Irish Melodies*, not to mention almost all the names of Shakespeare's plays, of the books of the Old Testament, New Testament, and the Koran, of all the Irish counties, of more than 800 rivers of the world, and of everything that Joyce himself ever wrote).

My point is that *understanding* Vico is not necessary preparation or equipment for reading *Finnegans Wake*, although almost anything in Vico *might* be a key to some allusion—in about the same way that it is useful in a few places to know that there is actually a Vico Road in Dublin, around the circle of the bay from Howth Castle and Environs. And it is in this respect that the *Wake* is like a work of nature, or Nature itself, which has equal care for molecules and mountains—which is to say, indifferently, total care or none at all. It is we, not Nature itself, who sort out the important from the unimportant, the normal from the anomalous, the necessary from the contingent, that which supports human aspirations and gratifications from that which threatens them. Nature embraces death as readily as life, and is as blind to litter as to literature. How could a book hope to imitate such overwhelming indifference? Yet *Finnegans Wake* to some extent achieves just this. It embraces all meanings but has none of its own.

IV

Because *Finnegans Wake* is not about anything but itself it is, I believe, the most consummately nihilistic work in any literature. By "nihilism" I do not mean merely an extreme degree of skepticism, rebellion, or destructiveness, but rather the complete absence of the capacity to order the world by a scale of relative values, by *any* hierarchy of relative importance. It doesn't matter whether you believe that the joy and suffering of men are more important in the cosmic economy than the irritations and satiations of clams, or whether they are of equal importance as manifestations of life superior to the insentient being of stones and stars; it doesn't even matter whether you believe that stones and stars are of equal value with the Milan cathedral and the Aswan Dam insofar as all belong to the world of concrete and self-subsistent things as compared with the inferior images and abstractions of fantasy and conception. There is still *some* framework of value and importance, and it is hard to see how one could live a conscious life without *some* way of subordinating certain values to others, different as this way might be from conventional scales of value.

In the word-world of *Finnegans Wake*, however, everything is of equal value with everything else. Earwicker's hump and stammer are of no less importance than his archetypal role as builder of all the world's cities. A phrase from a forgotten music-hall routine is as important as the doctrine of the Trinity; a pub altercation yields no pride of place to the history-changing battles of the Crimea and Waterloo; a ballad by Percy French ranks with the plays of Shakespeare, an obscure Dublin street with the Appian Way [I didn't know, when I first wrote this, that there *is* an obscure Dublin street called Appian Way!], a teastain on a letter with the Liebestod of Tristan and Isolde, a letter of the alphabet with the world's literature, the sound of a snore with all of modern science. Part of the pleasure in reading *Finnegans Wake*, in fact, is the discovery at long last of a use for the inconsequential scraps of information which otherwise clutter and distract one's mind. The *Wake* is not merely stuffed with such shards; they are used as motifs, given significance by the way they are used as devices, but a significance which cannot be transported beyond the limits of the *Wake*'s world. If you happen to know that Oscar Wilde called fox-hunting "the pursuit of the uneatable by the unspeakable," you are entitled to the pleasure of discovering the many puns on this phrase. If you happen to know that George Bernard Shaw made fun of English orthography by saying that "GHOTI" spells "fish"—"gh" as in "rough," "o" as in "women," and "ti" as in "nation"—you can have the tiny thrill of understanding the otherwise cryptic line on page 299: "Gee each owe tea eye smells fish." If not, no matter; maybe you know instead the words to "Casey Jones" or "Tea for Two"—they are equally important with Machiavelli's *Prince* and Marx's *Capital*. And all these, individually and collectively, are no less and no more important than the story that General Cambronne, one of Napoleon's generals, when told that the battle had been disastrously lost, replied, "Oh, shit." The *mot de Cambronne*, in fact, becomes associated in the *Wake* with the Logos, the Word that was in the beginning, and unites the Divine Comedy and the human comedy by the clear suggestion that creation and defecation are equivalent. But Joyce's rather heretical theology illustrates my point about nihilism: no scale of value distinguishes between individual defecation and universal creation. A major organizing story and source of motifs in the *Wake* is a story originally told by Joyce's father about how Buckley shot the Russian general: an Irish sniper with the British army in the Crimean war, Buckley has the Russian general in his sights when the general lets down his pants to relieve himself. Touched by this reminder of their common humanity, Buckley can't squeeze the trigger, but when the general wipes himself with a sod of turf—a *green* sod of turf—Buckley is angered by this insult to Ireland and shoots him without a second thought. And this piece of mild Irish scatology, accompanied by the odor of sawdust, Guinness, and damp wool in the pubs where the elder Joyce told his stories, is as important in the *Wake*-world as Vico's story of the creation of human civilization.

Therefore, I say, nihilism. In a world where everything has equal value and importance with everything else, nothing has any value or importance in itself, since the concept of value is essentially comparative and a function of some relative scale. One can read *Finnegans Wake* as the supreme expression of the comic impulse, in which greatness is diminished to the mundane—Socrates a figure of fun in his elevated basket, General Grant staggering drunk and handing his own sword in surrender to the astonished General Lee, Einstein unable to balance his checkbook. Or one can read it as the perfection of the lyric vision, for which a feather, a pebble, or an earlobe can be uniquely celebrated and elevated to a totally preoccupying object of consciousness—something which at least while the vision lasts cannot be exceeded by any grandeur or sublimity. Each of these ways is legitimate if we forget the other; but taken together, the comic impulse and the lyric vision add up to the kind of nihilism I have tried to characterize, and *Finnegans Wake* is the supreme and possibly the only example of this formula.

The language of the *Wake* has more levels of meaning than anything else in literature; and it is almost totally successful in permitting the reader to respond intuitively to different levels simultaneously while yet inviting him to disentangle the levels intellectually, even if it means tuggling foriver and pretumbling forover. Were there time enough and to spare, we could repeat such relatively self-contained passages as the pastoral description of Dublin's Phoenix Park (which merges with the Garden of Eden, Valhalla, and the Elysian fields), a description which simultaneously reports a minute inspection of Earwicker's backside as he lies naked in bed. One line may give the idea: "The straight road down the center (see relief map) bisexes the park which is said to be the largest of his kind in the world." In many passages, *double entendre*—and triple, quadruple, quintuple and sextuple meaning—is so successfully integrated that one cannot point to words or sentences which accomplish the contrived ambiguity; a whole passage may be obscene although no part of it is, by a combination of rhythms, juxtapositions, allusions, and exploitation of established motifs and devices. And what more can one ask than prose which is hilariously funny because one responds to a juxtaposition of levels of meaning which one may be totally unable to analyze or discern separately?

But although "levels of meaning" is a standard cliche in the critical quiver, I mean to distinguish *Finnegans Wake* from other literary works, not to say that it resembles them in this respect even though it outdoes them. For in literature understandable in this way, I believe, levels of meaning correspond to levels of value or importance—as, to take the simplest case, the meaning of parable or allegory is intended to be of greater significance and moral value than the concrete narrative details which bear that meaning. There is, in other words, a hierarchy or at least a directionality of levels presupposed in any such work: from particular to universal, from concrete to general, from natural to moral, from human to divine, from the Steps of the Pentagon to the American Experience. In *Finnegans Wake*, on the other hand, there are levels and always more levels but no correspondence between levels of meaning and levels of importance. Earwicker's voyeurism in Phoenix Park is no more a symbol for the original sin of Adam than the other way round, but on the other hand Earwicker is no less important for being Adam, the father of us all—as he is—than for being the proprietor of the Mullingar pub in the Dublin suburb of Chapelizod. In the world of *Finnegans Wake*, everything and everyone metamorphoses continuously into everything and everyone else (even male and female are interchangeable) and therefore nothing has its own inviolable nature and value. Hence there is adumbrated a nihilist cosmology, which could not, I think, be stated as a coherent philosophical theory, or given expression in any literary or artistic form other than the unique word-world of Joyce's artifice.

One final example in the *Wake* of the self-cancellation of significance which I have chosen to call nihilism is the Letter, an event or theme which is one of the major motifs of the book. It is met with early in the book as a mysterious manuscript scratched up by a hen from the middenheap of history. It somehow encodes the lesson of history if only it can be deciphered. Most of an early chapter is devoted to a hilarious parody of scholarship, a learned lecture on paleography in which every physical detail of the manuscript is minutely scrutinized without giving anyone the least clue as to what the Letter is *about*. Later it appears that the Letter stands for all scriptures, in fact for all literature and all writing. It is nominally from Anna Livia and addressed to "Revered Majesty," but seems to have been written for her by Shem, the scapegrace prophet, poet, and grasshopper, and is eternally carried for delivery by Shaun, the hypocritical priest, politician, and ant. Let me quote from Clive Hart's *Structure and Motif in Finnegans Wake* to indicate the kind of cosmic symbolism which can be attached to Shaun's function as archetypal mailman-mediator: "As a 'deliverer of soft missives' it is his job to 'voyage round the world in forty mails' (237.14). His travels take him along one arm of the cross of the cardinal points of the compass, symbolized by the Christian cross and the Church which is built in its image. The representative of a worn-out Age, Shaun moves westward to the bottom of the cross where, a sun-god sinking below the horizon, he will rejoin the mute earth from which he sprang. . . . Shaun's spirit crosses the Styx-dateline in his journey around the globe and . . . he turns up again, 'After rounding his world of ancient days' (623.36), renewed in vigour by its lifegiving power, thinly disguised and prepared to begin again his fertilizing trip up the Liffey, travelling in a direction opposite to that of the female principle so as to keep the cycles rolling . . . etc." (114–115).[1] Now in all this—and it is only a sample—remember that what Shaun is carrying is the Letter, the Word, the Logos, all literature of both East and West. Not surprisingly, the fact emerges that there are at least two letters, one to Anna Livia, probably, from female relatives in Boston, Massachusetts, the other from Anna Livia to "revered majesty," or whoever is running things, defending her husband against scurrilous rumors. The letter to Anna Livia adds up to something like, "Dear Maggy: How are you? Hope you are well. All well here only the heat turned the milk for the cocoa. Thanks for the lovely parcel of cakes. Poor Father Michael's funeral is tomorrow. Sure, he was a born gentleman. Hope soon to hear from you. Well, must close now with love and kisses." And that's it. The full text of the letter from Anna Livia, finally revealed at the end of the book just before her dying soliloquy, is less banal but no less mundane. My husband is a good man, she says. The prick of his spindle gave me the keys to dreamland, she says. No matter what they say he never watered the milk he sold. McGrath, the butcher, has been spreading lies about him, but with what that snake in the grass charges for bacon he's a fine one to talk and besides he doesn't know what the solicitor is doing with his wife in the afternoons on the sofa. Signed, Alma Luvia, Pollabella.

So there is the Logos, or Logoi. The message whirls through space and time and across the dimensions and gyres of all cosmologies, composed by, addressed to, and delivered by great archetypal figures of humanity; and what the message says, variously, is: "I'm broke. Wire money," or "Thanks for the lovely present," or "The family is in good health," or "Hope to hear from you soon," or "I remember when your hair was red." The lyric vision of the *Wake* is that molecules of meaning like these are just as important as anything else. The comic corrosiveness of the *Wake* is the revelation that everything else consists of pretentious and hugely inflated transformations of these simplicities. The Wizard of Oz is a nondescript little man surrounded by his fantastic apparatus of amplification and projection. Yet this revelation may be taken by the reader as frustrating and insulting, or as joyous and liberating. As Lichtenberg said, "Such books are like mirrors. If an ape peers in, no angel will look back."

V

As I think about what observations like these must mean to someone who has not reached the second or even the first stage of reading *Finnegans Wake*, it seems that I have omitted to note the quality which makes its complexity and nihilism still humane: what makes the *Wake* unlike other books at the same time makes it like other kinds of art. Many people are drawn irresistibly into the *Wake* and sustained through every stage of reading by the fact that it is, for all its artifice, expressive. The music that sang in Joyce's head is there in the texture of his words, as the emotional meaning of many operas is in the music rather than in the simplistic and often inane libretti which the music transmutes. A friend once told me that when he read the plots of Greek tragedy he felt pity and terror, but when he read the plays themselves—in the English translations then available, of the "Methinks all is not well within the house" variety—he felt nothing at all. Reading *Finnegans Wake* is exactly the opposite. Joyce's first drafts are strangely flat and banal; synopses of the book's chapters by themselves seem merely strained and discontinuous. Even the final text must, like all poetry, escape the bondage of the eye (though not entirely) and sound in the ear. Joyce made a voice recording of the final pages of the "Anna Livia Plurabelle" chapter—those pages in which the two old washerwomen by the stream, gossiping about Anna Livia, turn into an elm and a stone as night falls. An underground classic of the 1940's and early 1950's, the recording has been easily available in commercial pressings since then. Hearing it (with a text for the eye to follow) is, like reading *Genesis*, one of the few experiences which could be said to be absolutely indispensable to the understanding of both language and imagination. Attentive listeners, knowing little of *Finnegans Wake* except its reputation for unintelligibility, invariably say something like, "Why, it's perfectly clear!—But don't ask me to explain it." Now this is the condition of response to music. For such an experience to be achieved through the agency of language is a kind of miracle, which justifies Joyce's reported boast, "I can do anything I want with language." It shows, I think, how much can be expressed beyond the limits of referential meaning. As Cubist painting says nothing about how things really look but expresses what it feels like to *see*, so *Finnegans Wake* says nothing about the world but expresses what it feels like to live.

Note

1. Clive Hart, *Structure and Motif in Finnegans Wake* (Evanston, Ill.: Northwestern University Press, 1962).

A Reading Exercise in *Finnegans Wake*

FRITZ SENN

Whatever innovations James Joyce has brought to literature, to remain there, to be assimilated by writers, to be studied by the critics, there is also something eminently novel, or so it seems, in the relation that his words have to ourselves as readers. Something happens to our reading habit; it will never be quite the same again, and the transformation may alert us to some reactions that are probably inherent in that mysterious way of communication, the written letters. The following remarks are an attempt to generalize from what is essentially a personal but continuous reading experience.

The first effect to notice is a slowing down of the process. *Ulysses* cannot be rushed through. A leisurely, ambling pace is much more to the purpose; we do well to pull up from time to time for pauses that are, in both senses of the term, re-creative, and we are compelled to treat ourselves to a privilege that was forbidden to Lot's wife—to satisfy our curiosity by turning back. One of the recurrent phrases in the book, about a "retrospective arrangement," seems to hint at this demand. Events and relations arrange themselves for us if we look, or turn, back, and this holds good in a much more retrospectacular way than it does in any traditional novel.

But it is *Finnegans Wake*, really, that makes us aware just how inadequate normal consecutive reading can become, starting at the top of a page and going from left to right (or, in a different culture, starting at some other end, which comes to the same thing), unreeling a linear semantic thread. This we still do with *Finnegans Wake*; a book is not to be read—literally—backward. But the rewards of that kind of serial advancement are limited. The restrictions can be counteracted, up to a point, by reiteration, by a theoretically interminable circular progress. Joyce's conspicuous device is to make the end fold back into the beginning and to have the reader recursing, if his patience lasts, eternally along a Viconian spiral. This still amounts to traveling along one road that happens to form a closed circuit.

From the very start the discerning reader of *Finnegans Wake* is aware that he finds himself traveling on two or more roads at the same time, roads

Originally published in *Levende Talen* 269 (1970):469–80; revised in Fritz Senn, *Joyce's Dislocutions: Essays on Reading as Translation*, ed. John Paul Riquelme (Baltimore: Johns Hopkins University Press, 1984) 85–95. Revised version reprinted here by permission of Wolters-Noordhoff, the Johns Hopkins University Press, and the author.

that may or may not appear to be interrelated, but somehow always manage to coalesce verbally in the one typographical line, for there cannot be anything except a single-track string of letters. There is, for a first example, a recognizable syntactical movement from beginning to end of:

Now eats the vintner over these contents . . .

(318.20)

The sense may be a trifle odd, but not really baffling. If we are familiar with the opening line of Shakespeare's *Richard III*, however, we can *hear* an entirely different semantic development: "Now is the winter of our discontent. . . ." We may not see the thematic connection of the two lines (the context would have to provide that). What matters here is that both of them can be followed independently, both are (syntactically, semantically) self-contained. We can learn to take them both in our (one) stride.

Similarly, "Bacchulus shakes a rousing guttural" (365.6) does not in itself confuse us. A clumsy phonetic effort seems to be going on ("Bacchus," an overtone, may hint at the cause for the uncouthness of the speech). A reader who has worked his laborious way as far as p. 365 of the book will have little trouble to catch one more echo of what is perhaps the most frequent phrase to come across, a reference to an episode in the Crimean War (Joyce's version): "Buckley shot the Russian General." This reader will probably also see how the manifest meaning somehow tallies with the latent one; the surface version is, perhaps, an illustration that suits the context. Another variation, for instance, spreads an air of philosophical calm about it: "Berkeley showed the reason genrously" (423.32). A first-comer opening the book at random on this page would not suspect a war incident here. This is not so different from what happens to the reader of any novel. If I know the whole series of events leading up to any given episode it will mean more to me than to the casual onlooker. In *Finnegans Wake*, however, the words themselves have acquired a new, often *entirely* new, meaning to the initiated.

The most attentive of first readers could not possibly discover the same hidden draft when coming upon the earliest occurrence of the phrase: "the bouckaleens shout their roscan generally" (42.11). Here the motif is sounded vaguely, but not at all clarified, for the first time in the book. When the traveler returns to this same passage on his second lap, he will have learned about the Crimean war and the Irish soldier aiming a gun at a Russian general, he will have become conditioned to be on the lookout for a name or noun with a consonant structure like "B-k-l" followed by a verb beginning with "sh-"; his ear will be attuned to the particular rhythm of the phrase. At one's first exposure to the sentence, there is just a noise that some persons make, a noise that may be felt to be obscure or to have an Irish ring about it. If we knew Gaelic, we might have noticed that the theme of war or strife is potentially present already: "roscan" is an inflammatory speech, a rallying song or a battle hymn. But even so, the full meaning would have escaped us. The experience is roughly similar to our perusing the opening scene of a detective novel again, with the revelations of the last chapter fresh in our minds—there too we would discover little traces that might have aroused our suspicion for the first time, but somehow did not, but in any case the whole and ghastly significance could not possibly be appreciated without the knowledge that only the whole book can provide. Some of the insights can only be arrived at by hindsight. In *Finnegans Wake*, hindsight, rather "culious an epiphany" (508.11), affects the linguistic structure, phonetically as well as semantically. The words themselves have changed their character.

It is this sort of experience that has given rise to our talk about the various "levels" of the book, a handy and useful comparison. But like a corresponding one, that of a musical score, or musical performance—many voices and several instruments in parallel melodic development—it cannot be kept up consistently, since in practice we shall hardly be able to follow the various levels right to the end, or to listen to the voices consecutively, as in a musical performance we could, even allowing for intervals. All analogies for *Finnegans Wake* seem useful at times, and all break down sooner or later.

It is certain that *Finnegans Wake* is to be absorbed slowly and, like any other medicinal poison, preferably in small doses, and in tranquillity. Pauses are necessary, to ruminate and to sort out the various itineraries that have been traversed, to glance around, backward and sideways. The reader of *Finnegans Wake* often feels himself in a world full of tricky *déjà vus*, of elusive voices uttering vaguely familiar sounds that get more familiar, if not always more clear, with each successive tour, guided or unguided, through the maze. As usual, Joyce, who has a way of indicating not only what happens in the book but also what happens to his reader, hints at this in his opening chords. "Sir Tristram," we learn, "had passencore rearrived from North Armorica" (3.4). Like Tristram, the reader is a passenger who has not yet (*pas encore*) arrived on the strange shore, or else who, in his passage, or his steps (*pas*), has rearrived once more (*encore*). This we know well enough by now. This is the path that goes round and round, circular but still linear. Yet there appears to be a different direction as well, not from front to back, but in reverse order, backward, arriving at the "rear" end. There is probably a physiological side to this, but, more prominently, a geographical one. We notice that the hero coming to Ireland is arriving both from North America in the West and, like Tristram, from North Armorica, Brittany, France, in the East. We too, the opening ambiguity implies, can travel in either direction.

This is all very well in geography and tourism, but we cannot, in actual fact, read a book backwards, from right to left. Well, sometimes we can a bit. "Cloudia Aiduolcis" (568.10) can be tackled from whichever end we prefer. There are also characters like "natsirt" (he is the Tristram, now Tristan, of the first page, whose traveling habits seem to have affected his name), or "Kram" (388.3/2), or we may find ourselves in "Nilbud" (24.1). Occasionally, *Finnegans Wake* is palindramatic or anagrammatical, and inversion abounds.

Even so, the general drift must be forward. But the text sometimes tempts us to go back, to retrace our steps, before we can advance again, and this literally, verbally. Some such movement backwards and forwards is alluded to in the first chapter: "furrowards, bagawards, like yoxen at the turnpaht" (18.32). This is the movement of the plough; it is also, in the history of writing and the alphabet being described at the same time, a feature of early inscriptions called *boustrophedon*, which Joyce obligingly translates for us, a turning of the oxen. It is also, I feel, the situation of the reader who, in ploughing through the pages, sometimes reverses his direction and at times bovinely wonders which path to take. In his characteristic way, Joyce goes beyond naming, to presenting the thing referred to. The next sentences read:

> Here say figurines billycoose arming and mounting.
> Mounting and arming bellicose figurines see here.

The path actually does turn back on itself, and we review the same sequence in exactly inverse order. What is interesting, from the point of view of communication, is that some changes have intervened in the meantime. The word "billycoose" (which admits of several readings, among them a menacing highwayman's club, *billy*, and some amatory billing and cooing), while continuing to mean, probably, beautiful things in Italian (*belle cose*), has been turned into something patently warlike. This is, of course, as we know, also the way of the world. And there appears a difference between what we "say" first and what we "see" later: hearsay gives way to closer inspection, as good a clue as any as to what we are to encounter in, and do about, *Finnegans Wake*.

The point elaborated here is that we sometimes really travel the opposite way, that, if we do not turn back, we inevitably miss a previous meaning. In its full linguistic impact this is fairly unique. The mind is stimulated by an uncustomary kind of impulse.

Assuming that in *Finnegans Wake* several meanings are often just "there" simultaneously, and even granting their occasional transparency, we, the readers, will hardly experience the two or more meanings at the same time, right from the start. At one particular moment (or never) the mind is startled and begins to apprehend luminously that more is at stake than at first met the eye. Take a few more simple phrases: "raising hell while the sin was shining" (385.10). I submit that before we come, at the earliest, to "sin," the secondary latent meaning has no chance to resound at all: "sin" may startle us, especially if followed by "shining." Sins do not normally shine, but suns do, and the emerging sun points its rays back to the preceding words, allowing the proverbial expression "to make hay while the sun shines" to penetrate our consciousness. Only when we have come to the end of the sentence can "hell" become "hay" in a semantic ignition delay. Semantic potential is released retroactively.

What is the meaning of "So all rogues"? Not, really, anything beyond what these words denote in any dictionary (a reader, in fact, is unlikely, at this point, to trouble about overtones). If we go on, "all rogues lean," we may or may not get on to the scent. The finishing words enable the click to occur: ". . . to rhyme" (96.3) evokes "All roads lead to Rome." Toward, or after, the end of the movement a jolt of recognition metamorphoses the rogues. The jolt of recognition may never come, as when we do not know the proverb or if we fail to respond. A large part of the irritation about *Finnegans Wake* is the certainty that we shall always remain deaf and blind to a great many potentialities of the text.

Among other things, it is this (retarded) transmutation of words that justifies a reference to Shem the writer as an alchemist—"the first till last alshemist" (185.34). Change, transsubstantiation, the metamorphoses of gods, men, animals (especially insects), protean transformation affect the words as well as the reader, the contents of whose mind are also subject to change.

The neat examples quoted above are atypical exceptions, selected for their relative lucidity; the glosses are didactical simplifications. What we are generally faced with is not such a system of tidily separable semantic curves, but rather a confusing crisscross, an apparently unpatterned welter of verbal matter, sometimes primeval, seemingly unarticulated, with a strong suspicion of a random assortment of rubbish. Some lines can usually be discerned, but statements about our perceptions, those systematic relations the rational mind is not satisfied without, stand in need of almost immediate qualification. The interpretative progress is not usually linear but consists of a haphazard zigzag and transverse leaps, the wind of inspiration blowing where, and if, it listeth. The movement, a succession of associative impulses, resembles the hop, step, and jump rather than a journey along a twisted road.

A more optical analogy would be that insights gained at one place help to illuminate some other part. By a jostle of ideas, like sparks setting off a series of mutual reflection, of interradiation, the darkness will gradually disperse.

I select two sentences from a passage of medium to light opacity to give a practical demonstration. The words are taken from Jaun's Sermon. One of the two rival brothers, Shaun, here transformed into Juanesque Jaun, delivers an edifying sermon to a circle of admiring girls. Before launching out he is at pains to find his bearings in the prescribed liturgical calendar:

I've a hopesome's choice if I chouse of all the sinkts in the colander. From the common for ignitious Purpalume to the proper of Francisco Ultramare, last of scorchers, third of snows, in terrorgammons howdydos.

(432.35–433.2)

Every reader will recognize a few features and, starting from what he thinks he knows, choose his own path. Let us start somewhere. Obviously, there is an ecclesiastical flavor about the whole passage. Even the layman is likely to understand "the sinkts in the colander" as the saints in the calendar that the Church has assigned for each day of the year. But why "sinkts"? One component part seems to be "sin." Saints contrast with sinners, and some saints were sinners first, and all of them (and priests too) concern themselves with sin. Perhaps—and here the guessing begins—we should hear and see "cinct" (girded) as well. Priests, among others, are girded.

How would we test the validity of the meanings saint/sin/cinct? There is no approved way. The priestly girdle, we might venture, is the symbol for continence and chastity (we can look this up). Priests have been voluble on this particular subject; unchastity is a favorite sin. There is a traditional relation between chastity and being cinct, wearing a belt (it dates from a time when priests had much to say and when saints were still at large). Chastity, thus implied, will also be an attractive topic in Jaun's sermon to come. Readings of this digressive kind will appeal to some readers, and not to others. They are offered here—and might be kept in mind—as possibilities. William York Tindall, an American commentator, has wittily combined "colander" and "saint," by grace of extraneous punning, remarking that a "colander is, of course, as holy as a saint." He arrives at a contrast that is not so very much different from that of saintliness and sinful unchastity.

A colander, as it is, belongs to the kitchen, and this may serve as a pointer to suggest the "sink" that occupies the busy housewife. The connection between "kitchen" and "Church" is not an isolated occurrence in Joyce's works. Readers will have various examples in mind, from Mrs. Kernan in "Grace," whose "faith was bounded by her kitchen," to "the church which was the scullerymaid of christendom" in A Portrait of the Artist as a Young Man. And on to the last page of Finnegans Wake, where the kitchen sink doubles with a gesture of humble worship: "I sink I'd die down . . . only to washup" (628.11). The female of the species has for a long time been relegated to kitchen and church, and these afforded predetermined careers for many Irish girls of the kind that Jaun is addressing.

There is also an odd scintillating character about the "choice" that is so tautologically expressed. It is hopeful and double, and yet—through the proverbial "Hobson's choice," originating from a real person who used to impress his own choice on his customers, whatever they wanted—it implies that there is no choice at all. So things are not what they appear to be. And of course "chouse" is not quite the same thing as (how it may have looked at a first hasty glance) "chose" or "choose." Its meaning is to cheat, to trick, to dupe—not a saintly occupation.

Since we are now prepared for saints, though perhaps a trifle distrustful, we shall see one or two of them in the second sentence. Francis (Francisco) leaps to the eyes. Many places were named after him, not only San Francisco in California; one of them, in Mexico, is even called S. Francisco do la Mar. It (and most of them) is beyond the sea, *ultra mare*.

In the radiating atmosphere of *Finnegans Wake*, saintliness can blaze from other words than capitalized proper names, and so it is easy to make out another saint, a prominent one, in "ignitious": St. Ignatius Loyola, the founder of the Society of Jesus. He has become assimilated to the Latin word for fire, and ignition is implied as well; and the same element seems to have infused itself into "Purpalume," which might remind us of French *"allumer"* or else Spanish *"alum*brare." These languages could have some relevance, for Loyola, of Spanish origin, was wounded when the French were attacking the Spanish city of Pampeluna, in French "Pampelune"—another rough approximation of "Purpalume." So the light spreading from the name (by Joyce's change, not etymology) may serve to illuminate the surroundings further. The analogy may be apt since spreading the light is also a saintly function and one of the aims of the Jesuit order. Moreover the place where, according to the biographies, St. Ignatius began to see the light, was the Pampeluna already mentioned.

"Purpalume" contains also "purple," a color rich in significance, also within the Church, and this may alert us to another color—"ultramarine," through 'Ultramare.' The emblematic and symbolic significance of color offers itself as a tempting but tricky subject; here it is enough to note that the two holy men of whom a glimpse has been caught so far, with respective colors, purple and ultramarine blue, seem to be part of a spectrum, a variant perhaps of the rainbow, which is so ubiquitous in the book. The circle of colors might then constitute an optical parallel (light being refracted into some of its parts) corresponding to the temporal cycle of the church year, which allots a day for each saint and is made up, as Jaun indicates himself, of the *"Common* of Saints" and the *"Proper* of the Saints."

If one saint is a Jesuit of common fame it is only proper for his partner to belong to the same order. There is a Jesuit saint of nearly equal brilliance, one of the first to join the new order, and one greatly adored in Ireland: St. Francis Xavier (Francisco de Yasu y Xavier), the Apostle of the Indies. He was a great missionary, baptizing numerous souls in India and Japan, dying before achieving his great aim of carrying the torch to China. His travels well warrant the epithet "Ultramare." Like Ignatius, his temperament was fiery, and both of them were canonized in the same year, 1622. And—just to show what use Joyce can make of hagiological coincidence—Francis Xavier was born in Pampeluna.

So a Jesuitical pair emerges, one of the many variations of a pair of complementary and often contrasting characters that we always connect with Shem and Shaun. Actually, St. Ignatius and St. Francis Xavier have been paired before, in *A Portrait* (which is colored by Joyce's own Jesuit education). In the first chapter, their two portraits are described hanging in the same long narrow corridor of Clongowes Wood College. But their joint saintly presence is invoked later, in the third chapter, before Father Arnall, also a Jesuit, launches into his sermon on the torments of hell, a regular feature during the annual retreat.

If we remember the hell sermon in *A Portrait*, we have some idea as to why one of the saints should be called "last of scorchers." It may refer to his temperament, but it calls to mind the evocation of hell with the meticulous description of each single torment: the fire of hell is one of the more memorable traits. (The torment of fire, in the sermon, incidentally, is second only to hell's "awful stench," and this might, by the sort of hindsight illumination mentioned a while ago, reintroduce the meaning of "stinks" into the already overglossed "sinkts"—a gratuitous addition, to take or to leave.) The hell fire sermon in *A Portrait* is closely modeled on a standard treatise on hell, written by a Jesuit father who in turn grounds his somewhat medieval vision firmly on St. Ignatius's teachings. In the *Spiritual Exercises of St. Ignatius* we are invited "to see with the eyes of the imagination those great fires, and the souls as it were in bodies of fire." And a few lines later we are referred to the smell (First Week, The Fifth Exercise). A scorcher indeed.

A biblical innuendo may be relevant: The fourth angel in "Revelations" "poured out his vial upon the sun; and power was given unto him to scorch men with fire. And men were scorched with great heat . . ." (Rev. 16:8–9). Seen in this particular light, the passage about "terrorgammons howdydos" may be understood, at least as far as terror is concerned. Perhaps "howdydos" corresponds in marked contrast to the casual greeting with which the preacher in *A Portrait* started off his sermon. Just such a contrast is set up by the opposition of fire and snow. Christ's coming, again in "Revelations," happens to unite the same two elements: "His head and his hair were . . . as white as snow; and his eyes were as a flame of fire" (Rev. 1:14). But fire and snow are common enough in legend, literature, and elsewhere to render this specific reference dispensable. It is mentioned here as a by-product of that combinative urge that readers find hard to resist, and also as an example of the groping that is part and parcel of the whole process.

The relation between St. Ignatius and hell fire, established in an earlier book by Joyce, may appear far-fetched, and as an attempt to explain "last of scorchers" it falls short of its aim. But we are, after all, still dealing with the saints as they are listed in the calendar. St. Ignatius Loyola is commemorated on the day of his death, 31 July. It is the last day of a hot month, the last of scorchers. A "scorcher," the slang dictionary tells us, is a very hot day. It is also a "severe person" (Loyola was that, no doubt), as well as "a scathing vigorous attack": this too would fit the context, and it is also what the girl audience is going to get from Jaun, who will give them hell in his own sweet way. That we are really given a date in the calendar is confirmed by the entry on St. Francis Xavier in any missal: his death and feast day is 3 December, a wintry month: "third of snows." (A "snow" is also a sailing boat, useful for a seafaring missionary.)

The presence of the two Jesuits is established several times over. They are invoked by name and they are fixed by their co-ordinates in space and time: the place of birth and of a decisive event and a terrestrial destination are named, and they are given their proper place in the calendar. Or, to put it another way, the pair of them plays at universality, comprising the temporal cycle of the Church year (at nearly opposite poles), and spanning the earth from Spain (their origin) to the far seas in the east and the west. Since the birthplace of one and the death dates of both are implied, the circle of human life and death is added to the picture. And, as we have seen, they also embody the spectrum of colors. On a different scale, or temperature, they range from the coldness of snow to scorching heat. Temperamental opposites are indicated too, as well as moral ones: what is common (in the sense of vulgar) is set off against what is proper (implied also in "pur" of the first place name and the traditional image of snow)—perhaps even the scorching blast of communism against traditional propriety and property. This is an aspect of the customary opposition between the two rival brothers, which again finds its equivalent in a man like Ignatius, a writer turning inward and mapping out processes of the human soul with great care, writing influential, even incendiary (ignitious) books; and the other one, Francis Xavier, a man of action and conspicuous achievements, making converts by the tens of thousands.

The two saints, in short, go a long way.

The luster of their presence sheds light on a wider context too. A few lines later we come across "farrier's siesta in china dominos" (433.7): *farrear* and *siesta* are Spanish words, the first meaning to celebrate a feast; and Francis Xavier wanted to bring the Lord (Dominus) to China. Another meaning is *"in coena Dominis"* from the feast of Maundy Thursday, another prominent day in the Church calendar. And the same sentence goes on to accommodate the militant organizer of the Jesuit order and sovereign author: "from the sufferant pen of our jocosus inkerman militant." Inkerman was a battle fought by temporal powers (where the Russian general keeps being shot). The jocosus wielder of pen and ink, however, may well be Joyce himself. In *Ulysses*, Buck Mulligan says of Stephen Dedalus, as no doubt was also said of James Joyce: "You have the cursed jesuit strain in you, only it's injected the wrong way." We know that Joyce learned a great deal from his Jesuit educators and confessed himself grateful to them for teaching him "how to gather, how to order and how to present a given material."

We have begun to see some of the order and the presentation of the material.

But, for all the order that can be imposed on the passage, enough muddle remains to give room for supplementary interpretations. The correspondence, for example, between Joyce himself, or his fictional projections, and St. Ignatius does not work out too neatly—they could also be viewed as being in opposition. Jaun is not perhaps quite on the side of Francis Xavier either. So the commentator's show of rigid order needs the qualification of other observers, which is another way of saying that interpretation is not likely to stop at any given point. And there is always the possibility of error (as the Jesuit saints would be the first to agree). Some parts, moreover, have not yielded to analysis.

"Purpalume," to give an instance, has not yet been satisfactorily accounted for. It is probably Pampeluna, essential station in both saintly careers; it contains "purple" as well as "pur." In the absence of the precise, clinching gloss (which may yet come to light), a bit of fumbling in reference works is usually resorted to. "Purpalume" resembles a cluster of Greek words, composites of *pyr* (fire, usually transliterated as *pur* in English), and *palame* (palm of the hand). A verb *purpalamao* means to handle fire, a related adjective is once used to describe a flash of lightning. A saint handling fire or manipulating a celestial flash might be appropriate. A development of the same verb and an adjective *purpalames*, for a crafty, cunning person or someone given to pranks, may remind us of the charges often made against the Jesuits, or the pejorative sense that the name of the order has acquired, or else of the cunning prankish writer Joyce. Actually the verb just cited is furthermore defined to mean "cheat" by means of sly and cunning ways. This would take up the meaning of "chouse" that we encountered before and would be in tune with the whole passage. To be in tune does not, however, prove that these meanings are actually present. Could we accept these Greek lexicographical finds as relevant when we know that Joyce was no Greek scholar? (He could fumble with a dictionary, though, just as we can.) I offer all these possibilities here with a large question mark. The question is a rather fundamental one in the discussion of the exegetical methods and the limits of interpretation. More attention might be devoted perhaps to the fact that Joyce's words do have the effect of urging us on a quest for meaning; they urge us to make up analogies ourselves, by a process of inventive extrapolation.

For the question is: Do *I* make this all up? And of course I do, at least in part. Some of the foregoing exfoliation is one particular reader's imaginative weaving of the textual threads, a development of what I think is there on the page. So while, on one hand, Joyce himself is obviously involved as author, I, as the reader, on the other side of the fictional work, find myself very much entangled as well. To the writer, the poet, the maker, the reader is joined as a maker-up. And our making things up seems to be part (to retain an analogy made up from the words of our jocosus inkerman) of our mission. *Finnegans Wake* seems to send us abroad into far away fields (linguistic, historical, here hagiographical) beyond the seas, to engage us in our own spiritual exercises.

Games are a combination of orderly rules, skills, and a touch of chance. An aleatory element may not always appeal to our reason, but it would be difficult to exclude it from the unruly jostle of verbal particles in the book. There is a game in our passage too. Gammon (also called backgammon) in "terrorgammons" is a game in which the throwing of dice determines the moves. It helps to know that the activity "to gammon" also denotes humbug, deceit, and feigning. In "terror" and "gammons" we may have the playful and the serious side of our mundane existence, another implied contrast.

The game of *Finnegans Wake*, at any rate, is an ignitious one, and once we become ignitiated there is no simple way to stop the process. Joyce's words activate us. The criterion in such exegetical sports then might well be whether there is a reasonable and meaningful relation between our secondary elaboration and the original creation.

It is the intriguing half-light of the book that tempts speculation and elaboration. And even a passage as thoroughly subjected to scrutiny as the quoted one still contains rather dark patches. Ignorance is part of the game too, and it is because of ignorance that I did not have much to say on the last part of the second sentence: the basic meaning of "in terrorgammons howdydos" still escapes me.*

And this interrogative is a suitable one to bring this inconclusive exercise to a close. Its exemplary aim was to display, by prolonged trial and instructive error (error/gammons perhaps), a reader's position in a fairly new kind of experience, and to show, by practical demonstration, that we, as readers, are induced to depart from ordinary, linear progression in favor of what is a series of (hopesomely) illuminated leaps.

1970

---

*When I first wrote the reading exercise I was about to end it on what looked like an appropriately interrogative note: "in terrorgammons" seems to contain *"interrogamus"*—something that is always true about our relation to any part of the *Wake*. At the last moment James S. Atherton answered one of my queries by pointing out that, as everybody would know, the phrase is built around an echo from the Litany of the Saints, often sounded in Church: *"te rogamus, audi nos."* "We sinners *{peccatores}*, beseech Thee, hear us" (compare "Loud, graciously hear us . . . hear the wee beseech of thees" [*FW* 258.26, 259.3] as further variations).

The intriguing, sobering thought is that all my extensive interrogations had not enabled me to hear the appeal to my ears *"audi nos."*

1983

Finnegans Wake, Page 185: An Explication

ROBERT BOYLE, S. J.

The artistic mirror of James Joyce, when he held it up to nature, reflected with the intensity of a Freudian age the hidden, festering corners of the human spirit. Like Chaucer's mirror and Shakespeare's and others of our greatest artists, Joyce's reflected sanctity only obliquely. Those critics who see Bloom as the embodiment of charity should, in my judgment, seriously check their critical mirrors. They err, I opine, almost as badly as those valiant few who believe that the stuffy Platonist representing Christ in *Paradise Regained* reflects divinity. Joyce's mirror, as I see it in mine, reflects evil far more profoundly than it directly reflects good, and, to his glory as an artist, he insisted upon expressing that evil in the matter of his art as perfectly as anyone has done it in English.

With extraordinary directness and courage, Joyce set out to turn vulgarity and scatology to his artistic purpose. He uses them in many ways, but the one principal way which will concern us in this paper is to explain and to justify his own artistic practice. He wants also to excoriate the work of artistic Philistines, some of whom used scatological terms in speaking of Joyce's work. But mainly, in *Finnegans Wake*, he wants to justify himself more effectively than Stephen Dedalus was ever able to do, and to do so in a pioneering use of Swiftian scatology turned effectively to an artistic end. His success, or lack of it, may perhaps be more objectively judged after a study of the page with which this paper deals.

Like most of the chapter in which it appears, the Latin passage of page 185 of *Finnegans Wake* deals with events in Joyce's artistic career. A literal translation of the Latin should make a helpful beginning to discussion:

> First of all, the artificer, the old father, without any shame and without permission (or, perhaps, pardon), when he had donned a cope and undone the girdles, with rump as bare as on the day of birth (literally: as bare as though it had been born), approaching himself to the viviparous and all-powerful land, weeping and groaning the while, defecated (literally: emptied) into his hand; and secondly, having unburdened himself of the black living thing (or, possibly, of the black air), while he beat out the battlesignal, he placed his

Reprinted from the *James Joyce Quarterly* 4 (Fall 1966):3–16, by permission of the *James Joyce Quarterly*, University of Tulsa.

own faeces, which he entitled his "purge" (possibly: the sinking of his star), in a once honorable vessel of sadness (or, once procuring honor for sadness), and into the same, under the invocation of the twin brothers, Medardus and Godardus, he pissed happily and melodiously, continuously singing with a loud voice the psalm which begins, "My tongue is the reed of a scribe swiftly writing." Finally, from vile crap mixed with the pleasantness of the divine Orion, after the mixture had been cooked and exposed to the cold, he made for himself imperishable ink.

The names at the top of Page 185, "Robber and Mumsell, the pulpic dictators," give us the setting for the Latin passage. George Roberts and Maunsel and Co., the Dublin publishers, frustrated the publication of *Dubliners* over a period of several years, an agonizing procedure for Joyce. Ellmann gives the whole story.[1] The legal advisers who cautioned against publishing a book with names of private concerns and of persons (shades of Notre Dame and *John Golfarb*!) are characterized in Latin terms which mean "book" and "anus." "Codex," however, lends itself easily to the punning "tail" or "penis," either of which goes ideally well with the second term and with the Latin passage to follow. "Father Flammeus Falconer" refers to the Dublin printer connected with Maunsel and Co., John Falconer, who, according to Joyce, burned the sheets of the book.

Joyce's first draft of this chapter, reproduced in David Hayman's invaluable *A First-Draft Version of Finnegans Wake* (Austin, 1963), pp. 108–112, contains the following relevant passages:

> boycotted, local publican refuse to supply books, papers, synthetic ink, foolscap, makes his own from dried dung sweetened with spittle (indelible ink) writes universal history on his own body (parchment) . . . Sings hymn: Lingua mea calamus scribae, veliciter scribentis. . . . Primum flens et gemens in manum suam evquacuavit (shit in his hand, sorry) postea stercus proprium, good appellavit dejectiones meas, exoneratus in poculum tristitiae posuit, eodem lentiter et melliflue minxit psalmum qui incipit *Ligua mea calamus scribae velociter scribentis* magna voce cantitans (did a piss, say he was dejected, asks to be exonerated) demumque ex stercore turpi cum divi Orionis, jucunditate encaustem sibi fecit indelibilem (speaking of O'Ryan, the devil's own ink)

One or two things relevent for my discussion of the finished text and the second draft, might be mentioned. "Dried dung sweetened with spittle," since it is to be used to open eyes, to bring light, possibly is based in part on the preparation Christ made to open the eyes of the man born blind in *John* 9:6: "With that, he spat on the ground, and made clay with the spittle . . ." Joyce drops this allusion, choosing instead his urine theme to develop the image of the artist's vocation. Secondly, "veliciter" looks like a portmanteau word combining "velociter" with "feliciter." Joyce knew Latin too well to write down such a mistake, I would judge. For example, in the second draft, Mr. Hayman notes "sic" after Joyce's a "appellaviat." I believe, as I discuss later in this article, that Joyce was working for the portmanteau effect in Latin as he does in English. Further, he can be extremely sophisticated in these Latin puns and double meanings. For example, in draft two, page 113 of *First-Draft*, among the answers to the riddle, "When is a man not a man?" one of the answers, not included in the final text, is, ". . . et enim imposuit manus episcopas fecit illum altissimis sacerdotem . . ." Thus a man is not a man when the episcopal hands have made him a priest to (or for) the highest (or the lowest). "Episcopas" is not a conventional form, however; "episcopales" would be the expected word. But neither is it a mere mistake. Joyce knows that "manus" is feminine, and in constructing an adjective of the noun "episcopus" he makes it possible to suggest that the ordaining bishop is an old woman. He dropped the clause, and I suspect he did it because it would distract from his later treatment of the artist as priest. Here the point would be that a priest is not a man. He wants no suggestion later, I suggest, that an artist, who is in an even higher sense a priest, is not a man.

The following answer in the riddle in draft two, "when pigs begin to fly," intrigues me with its proximity to the bishops since I think that Joyce, in his final draft, does tie up bishops and pigs in the word, "porporates."

The second draft of the chapter, which Mr. Hayman includes because the first draft is so fragmentary and confused, is more useful for my purposes. On page 118 of *A First-Draft Version*, from which page all further quotations of the second draft are taken[2], the passage under discussion appears thus:

Naturally he never needed such an ~~alcove~~ alcohove for his purpose and when George W. Robber, the ~~paper state~~ paper king, boycotted him of all stationery and muttonsuet candles for any purpose he went away and made synthetic ink ~~for~~ and unruled ~~foolscap~~ parchment for ~~it~~ himself ~~with~~ out of his wits' ends. How?

"Muttonsuet" already implied, I suppose, that the writers Roberts would print were sheepish followers of classical traditions. Joyce then, wishing to bring in also the Catholics, the *Pulpit* dictators, who objected to *Dubliners* on moral or religious grounds, substituted "sensitive" for "unruled" as an adjective for "parchment," so that he could add "romeruled" as the perfect adjective for "stationery." "Parchment" he changed, perhaps because, since it turns out to be his own skin, the word made too close a tieup with "muttonsuet." And "sensitive" both fits with his idea of the suffering and responsive artist and matches better with "synthetic."

The most significant addition, however, is the statement that Shem "winged away on a wildgoup's chase across the kathaftic ocean . . ." So Joyce as Icarus winged away to France, to become the exiled Irishman, or wild goose. His going across the "kathartic" ocean calls to mind the bitter ode he wrote during this period of difficulty, "the Holy Office." The title suggests his notion of the artist as priest of the eternal imagination, and the name he gives himself as artist is "Katharsis-Purgative." Aristotle's use of Καθαρσις leads Joyce to the bitter, scatological pun. He thus expresses his determination to deal directly with the human filth to which "that motley crew" hypocritically close their eyes:

> That they may dream their dreamy dreams
> I carry off their filthy streams . . .
> Thus I relieve their timid arses,
> Perform my office of Katharsis.

In his second draft, Joyce wrote:

> Let the manner and the matter of it for these our sporting times be veiled cloaked up in the language of ~~blushing~~ blushfed cardinals ~~lest~~ that the Anglican ~~cardinals~~ cardinal, not reading his own ~~words~~ rude speech, may always behold the scarlet brand on the brown of ~~the~~ her of Babylon and yet feel not the pink one of his own damned cheek.

Joyce's reference to the Sporting Times, a newspaper which attacked the "filth" of *Ulysses*[3], bolsters his resolve to explain in Latin his method of obtaining the proper ink and paper for his writing. Latin suggests the Church of Rome, and cardinals are the chief speakers of the tongue there. Cardinal suggests scarlet (bringing in the scarlet woman or the apocalyptic whore of Babylon) which suggests blushing. The shift from Latin into English calls in the Anglican clergy, who are here oddly cardinals, but less pronouncedly so, pink rather than scarlet. These presumably will either not understand the Latin or will read it with the comfortable assurance that its hideous vulgarity owes its existence to the Church of Rome. "Blushing" becomes "blushfed," which no doubt contributes to the change of the first "cardinals" to the final "porporates," derived from the purple of the cardinals and bishops, and suggestive of the disease attendant to too much food and drink. Perhaps we can also make out "porpoise," with its "fish," symbol of Christ, aligned with "pork," Mr. Casey's notion of "the tub of guts up in Armagh."[4]

The second "cardinal" becomes "ordinal," appropriately distinguished from "cardinal," as in numbers. The fact that one of Roberts' attorneys was English may furnish an added basis for concealing the description from the Anglican clergyman. "Speech" becomes "dunsky tunga," which, besides suggesting heaviness ("dunt") and English weather ("dun sky") and Eastern languages ("Tungus"), foreshadows the psalm to be loudly sung a few lines below, which in English goes, "My tongue etc." "Her of Babylon" ("her" in Dublin accent becomes "whore"), the ordinary Reformation designation for the Roman Catholic Church, has indeed a Codex of Canon Law in Latin. Furthermore, her writers of moral case books, when writing or translating into the vulgar tongues, used to leave in Latin those cases which dealt with violations against sexual morality, partly at least to spare the blushes of the innocent or prudish. Joyce, though, I am inclined to suspect, since on the next-to-last page of this chapter he becomes "unseen blusher in an obscene coalhole," here feels minutely closer to the "blushfed porporates" than to the "Anglican ordinal."

I will now take up the Latin passage phrase by phrase, indicating as well as I can what clearly appears in the text, and adding speculations of my own which seem at this time helpful.[5]

1) "Primum opifex, altus prosator . . ." Joyce here translates literally the terms with which *Portrait* ends, "Old father, old artificer," referring to his Father-in-Arts, invoked in the passage from Ovid which opens *Portrait* and called upon again in the final prayer which concludes it. Stephen, the Icarus figure, intends to grow into another Daedalus, the maker of art, the "opus-facio," and appeals to his "old father," his "pro-sator" or "before-sower," to give him the daily bread of art, experience transmuted into the radiant word. Both of the terms are additions to the second draft, which begins "Primum ad terram etc."

2) "ad terram viviparam et cunctipotentem . . ." Joyce might be referring here to his harried trips back to Ireland to see if he could there get *Dubliners* published and get some money; in that case, the adjectives are surely ironic, in the light of the paralysis and sterility which *Dubliners* so vividly portrays. He could, though, be referring to what he (and the young Stephen) hoped from the France to which he flew, which would fit well enough with the later invocation of the French saints Medard and Gildard. Line 33 of this page, "gallic acid on iron ore," may suggest that Joyce wrote: "ad terram viviparam et cunctipotentem," shifting from a negative to a positive attribution. If he had added the intended object of "ine," we could no doubt better judge whether he means to refer to Ireland or to France or to both. The adjectives fit well with the France described in the last act of *Henry V*; but Ireland is described in *Portrait* as the old sow that devours her young. The pun implied in the first syllable of "cunctipotentem" further tends to identify Ireland, as bitter young Stephen saw her.

3) "sine ullo pudore nec venia . . ." This phrase rather argues that he is thinking, at least primarily, of his return trips to Ireland, since the young Joyce would have no special shame in taking off for Paris, surely, and the "pardon," if that is the meaning to be taken, would not there be operative at all. On the other hand, he might be saying that he felt no shame at leaving paralyzed, deaf Ireland and that as a rebel he went without permission, ["exking noblish permish," asking nobody permission, p. 187] since "venia" also permits that meaning.

In the second draft, Joyce had written: "nec ullo pudori nec venia." His change to "sine" called for a change of the second "nec" to "vel," but he missed it or chose to let this stand for some reason. He went correctly from dative to ablative in changing to "pudore." He merely corrects the spelling of "venea." In that spelling, he may have been attempting to suggest venery or Venus. In several places, as I shall indicate, Joyce seems to have had in mind puns and double meaning in his handling of the Latin words, but when, as here, there was no operative function for the word in Latin, he dropped the attempt.

4) "suscepto pulviali . . ." To an ancient Roman, the word "pulvialis" conveyed the notion "of or belonging to rain, rainy." In the course of time, the word came to mean "raincoat, outer garment," and in ecclesiastical contexts, "cope" or "chasuble." Thus the word in the present context suggests rain, which as we shall see, is tied up with St. Medard and with Orion. Further, the word involves the activity of the priest. Stephen saw himself as "the priest of the eternal imagination," and his work as artist as the "transmuting the daily breath of experience into the radiant body of everliving life."[6] The Mookse of the previous chapter, embodying both Henry II and Pope Hadrian, after he had "vacticanated his ears" proceeded to "put on his impermeable," (152) which would correspond to this taking up of the "pluviali." This phrase recalls the opening of *Ulysses*, also, particularly in connection with the next phrase.

5) "atque discinctis perizomatis . . ." The word "perizoma" is most familiar in its use in the Vulgate for the "coverings" which Adam and Eve made for themselves after the fall (*Genesis*, 3/7). Hence the suggestion of a cosmic uncovering fits well with Joyce's (at least young Joyce's) idea of his vocation. As artist, he would tear away the false coverings of shame and hypocrisy from his race. And Buck Mulligan, on the first page of *Ulysses*, appears for his mockery of the Mass and the act of transsubstantiation in a dressing gown which is an obvious surrogate for a chasuable, and he is "ungirdled." In Buck's case, the suggestion surely involves his own lack of chastity as well as his blasphemy. In the present context, Joyce, I presume, wants to suggest the necessary frankness and clarity of the artist who dares to hold up his mirror to reflect a hypocritical society.

In correct Latin, the word should be "perizomatibus." This phrase and the one preceding it are additions to the second draft.

6) "natibus nudis uti nati fuissent . . ." Joyce changes the ordinary gender of "nates," no doubt for sound or to suggest the verbal connection here between "rear end" and "born." The imagery here and in the following lines recalls that of "Gas from a Burner":

> I'll burn that book, so help me devil.
> I'll sing a psalm as I watch it burn
> And the ashes I'll keep in a one-handled urn.
> I'll penance do with farts and groans
> Kneeling upon my marrowbones.
> This very next lent I will unbare

My penitent buttocks to the air
And sobbing beside my printing press
My awful sin I will confess.
My Irish foreman from Bannockburn
Shall dip his right hand in the urn
And sign crisscross with reverent thumb
Memento homo upon my bum.[7]

"Memento homo, quia pulvis es, et in pulverem reverteris," the priest says on Ash Wednesday, echoing the curse of God on the human race in *Genesis* 3/19, as he signs the cross in ashes on the foreheads of the faithful. The speaker of "Gas from a Burner" personifies Roberts, blended, as Ellmann points out,[8] with Falconer. The psalm, the urn, the writing material from the urn, the farts and the groans, and the writing upon the skin all appear on the page we are discussing.

In the second draft, Joyce wrote: "natibus nudix uti nudi fuissent." The coined word "nudix" is perhaps an effort to echo "Codex and Podex" above. No doubt Joyce dropped the effort because "nudix" is meaningless in Latin. Why he decided upon the subjunctive here is a mystery. I suspect that he had the rhythm of some other saying, a motto or proverb, in mind. He changes "nudi" to "nati" primarily, I suppose, to bring in a birth image.

7) "sese adpropinquans, flens et gemens . . ." At the top of the next page, Joyce speaks of Shem's deriving all history "from his own individual person." This, I suppose, is what "sese adpropinquans" may faintly, if considered by itself out of its context, suggest—his taking himself as his subject matter, as he thought he was doing in producing *Portrait*. As in "The Holy Office," he here, "myself unto myself," interprets himself. The weeping and groaning here contrast with the joy with which he micturates later. The answer to the difference, I suggest, might be found in the quotation from *Portrait* in Point 4 above, where the painful "daily bread of experience" is joyfully transmuted into what he in *Ulysses* calls "the word that will not pass away."[9] Shem makes his ink from experience, here as in "The Holy Office" imaged as defecation, mixed with artistic insight or skillful exercise of art, imaged as micturition.

8) "in manum suam evacuavit . . ." The word "emptied" may have had for Joyce some implication of the wholeheartedness of his dedication to his artistic vocation.

9) "highly prosy"—mistranslates, in the tonality of an almost illiterate and hasty reader, "altus prosator," taking "altus" in the sense of "high" and "pro-sator" as if it had something to do with "prose."

"crap in his hand"—the effect of the phrase in Point 8.

"sorry!"—suggested by the last part of the phrase in Point 7.

As his first effort to write this Latin passage, Joyce wrote, "Primum gemens in manum evacuavit." He added after that, "(shit in his hand,

." Thus, it appears, he first intended to translate the meaning of the passage, but after the complications had come in, he apparently to translate only the most important notions.

10) "postea, animale nigro exoneratus . . ." This I find to be the most puzzling phrase in the passage. Shem has been relieved of the burden of something black and living, unless "animale" here means "air." The bilious humor which produced *Dubliners*, according to its critics, might be involved in the "black." Joyce might be referring to the blackness in which the "nightmare of history" takes place, from which daily experience comes, black until made radiant by the artist. This might be tied up with the "black panther" of *Ulysses*, the frightening threat of the brutal and irrational. It could conceivably suggest that thus Shem relieved the frustrations which daily experience laid upon him. By a good stretch, it could be tied with the Black Mass of *Ulysses*, since "animale" does have a liturgical context in which it means a victim whose life is offered to the gods while the flesh is given to others; Joyce could conceive of his own work as a Black Mass through which the dark spirits of men could be brought to the light, dogs might become gods. Mercius does, on Page 193, call Justius (and presumably Ireland, whose womb bore him and paps gave him suck, a reference to *Luke*, 11/27) "one black mass of jigs and jimjams . . ."

"Animalis" does primarily refer to air and the movements of air, so that the phrase may basically tie up with the "farts" quoted above in Point 6, and mean that painful black gas has been voided with the faeces. The "animale" instead of the expected "animali" is puzzling, and if taken seriously, could yield a meaning like "having been unburdened of a living thing which lives by a black thing." Both this phrase and the one that follows are additions to the second draft.

11) "classicum pulsans . . ." Stephen's battlecry of "non serviam" comes to mind, and Joyce's proud words in "The Holy Office":

> And that high spirit ever wars
> On Mammon's countless servitors.

Joyce's attack on dead classical forms, as in the Aeolus chapter of *Ulysses*, might by way of pun be suggested, especially in the odd participle. Since the "classicum" was sounded on the trumpet, and "pulsans" means a striking or a plucking, some special meaning probably lurks in their connection. The "Nothung," Siegfried's battlecry which Stephen shouts out in the Circe chapter of *Ulysses* while he strikes the light from the world, inducing the Götterdammerung into Bella's house, may be echoed here.

12) "stercus proprium, quod appellavit deiectiones suas . . ." He called his faeces "things cast down," or "castings down," but I suspect he is thinking of good things coming from above, of the artist as god casting down his light, not desired by those who love darkness, the "pulpic dicta-

tors." They would call it ugly and evil. Or perhaps it merely means that his daily experience is ugly and worthless until through the process to be described he makes of it ink for artistic use.

In the second draft, Joyce wrote: "postea stercus proprium quod appellaviat dejectiones meae . . ." "Appellaviat" might have been some effort to introduce the notion of water into the word by stressing the "lav," and to suggest "alluvial." It is not likely, in the light of the first draft, as I indicated above, to have been merely a mistake. The "meae" should correctly be "meas," as Joyce correctly indicates in the first draft, and suggests, if it is not only the echo of some quotation, that Joyce was thinking of himself in writing the passage and not of Shem, or that he identified himself totally with Shem.

13) "in vas olim honorabile tristitiae posuit . . ." This suggests a funeral urn, containing the ashes of the honored dead over whom the survivors weep. In literary terms this might suggest the ode, at least a threnody. The phrase provides a good description of "The Holy Office," if we take "vas" to refer to the literary form and Joyce's content to refer to "stercus." Perhaps, however, Joyce is referring to the *Chamber Music* poems, songs in a form once popular with sad lovers. This would tie up better with what follows, and could better recall Bloom's musing on Molly's melodious micturitions, as well as the exhortations on Pages 21 and 571: "Lissom! lissom! I am doing it," and "Listen, listen! I am doing it."

In the second draft, Joyce wrote: "in poculum vasum olim honoribilem tristitiae posuit." His first notion was, apparently, "poculum tristitiae," "cup of sadness." "Poculum" he changed to "vasum," probably because this word can mean a container in a sexual context—even more so in the form "vas." "Honoribilem" looks like an effort toward a Latin portmanteau word, combining "honorabilem" and "horribilem." If so, the effort is abandoned in the final text.

14) "eodem sub invocatione fratrorum geminorum Medardi et Godardi . . ." The *Roman Martyrology* (The Newman Press, Maryland, 1962) includes the following pair of saints on the eighth day of June:

> At Soissons in France, the birthday of St. Medard, Bishop of Noyon, whose life and precious death were approved by glorious miracles. At Rouen, St. Gildard, Bishop, brother of the same St. Medard. Both brothers were born on the same day, consecrated bishop on the same day, and on the same day were withdrawn from this life, so that together they entered heaven.

Butler's Lives of the Saints, Vol. II (P. J. Kenedy & Sons, New York, 1956):

> St. Medard is a favourite with the peasants of northern France, and his *cultus* goes back to his death in the sixth century; it has been enhanced by the legends that have grown up around his name, as well as by his veneration as the patron

of the corn harvest and the vintage . . . St. Medard sometimes is depicted with a spread eagle above his head, in allusion to the tradition that once in his childhood an eagle extended its wings over his head to shelter him from the rain. This story may account for his supposed connection with the weather. The peasants say that if it rains on St. Medard's feast the 40 ensuing days will be wet, and that if, on the other hand, the eighth of June is fine, a spell of forty fine days is to be expected, just like our English St. Swithun. Occasionally the saint is represented with St. Gildard, who is erroneously described as his twin brother, and who as such is commemorated with him in the *Roman Martyrology*. St. Medard for some reason was sometimes depicted in the middle ages laughing inanely with his mouth wide open ("le ris de St. Médard"), and he was invoked to cure the toothache. Whether his association with dental troubles was the consequence or the cause of this representation, it is hard to say.

The connection of the twins, however legendary, Joyce would, in the light of his twin-patterns in *F. W.*, scarcely relinquish. St. Medard's connection with rain brings him into relation with the life-giving micturition,[10] and his position as canonized bishop of the Church of Rome ties him up both with the "porporates" and with the "pluviale." That last connection again involves him, like Orion below, with rain. His inane laughter fits with the tonality of the passage. And his name suggests the name of one of the persons involved in Joyce's life at the time of which the passage treats, Patrick Mead, editor of the *Evening Telegraph*, the model for Crawford in *Ulysses*, a heavy drinker, and friendly to Joyce. (Cf. Ellmann, pp. 297–8) St. Gildard's name becomes "Godardi," and as a twin to Mead, Gogarty, another heavy drinker and hazily friendly to Joyce, fits well. Thus the symbolic Mead and Gogarty smile upon the symbolic micturition of Shem-Joyce, as the real characters had no doubt often joined him in the literal act. As Joseph Wilson pointed out to me, Joyce had used the connection of micturition with literature in relation to Gogarty in *Ulysses* (197):

> Quickly, warningfully Buck Mulligan bent down:—The tramper Synge is looking for you, he said, to murder you. He heard you pissed on his halldoor in Glasthule. He's out in pampooties to murder you.
> —Me! Stephen exclaimed. That was your contribution to literature.

And it is perhaps relevant that in *Ulysses* both Crawford and Mulligan encourage Stephen's writing; both anticipate that he will produce something living from the experiences he is having in Dublin.

In the second draft, Joyce wrote: "eodem lente ac melliflue minxit . . ." That "lentiter" looks like another, and clever, attempt at a portmanteau word, combining "lentus" ("pliant"), "lente" ("slowly"), and "leniter" ("smoothly, gently"). Under the influence of the inanely smiling saints, however, all these meanings disappear, and are replaced by the psalmistic "laete" ("joyously").

15) "laete ac melliflue minxit . . ." In their farewell urination, Stephen and Bloom revealed their opposed attitudes toward reality, Bloom's phenomenology, Stephen's mysticism (*Ulysses*, 687–8). Here in *F. W.* urine becomes the means for producing ink from the raw material of experience. The water from outside, which Stephen feared and hated so much, is here replaced by the water which the artist himself produces, and which, in his hands, can become a baptismal channel of life.

16) "psalmum qui incipit: Lingua mea calamus scribae velociter scribentis: magna voce cantitans . . ." The psalm is *Psalm* 44, which begins, in English: "My heart overflows with a goodly theme; as I sing my ode to the king, my tongue is nimble as the pen of a skillful scribe." "Calamus," a reed, is not without some tonality of the pointing ash-plant which Stephen used, and surely close to the lifewand which Shem lifts at the end of this chapter. He lifts that wand, and those who were dumb cry, reiteratively, "quoi." Their cry goes with the wild-goose image. Stephen became a wild-goose in order to bring the dead to life. This goose-speech is the beginning of life. As the "quoi" of French, it would imply surprise and curiosity at the revelation of the artist, at the coming of life. This is the aim of the Icarus-figure of *Portrait*. Stephen mocks his own failure in *Ulysses*:

> Fabulous artificer, the hawklike man. You fled. Whereto? Newhaven-Dieppe, steerage passenger. Paris and back. Lapwing. Icarus. *Pater, ait*. Seabedabbled, fallen, weltering. Lapwing you are, Lapwing he.
>
> (208)

The dative "voci" of the second draft is corrected in this final version to the ablative.

17) "did a piss . . ." from "minxit"; "says he was dejected . . ." from "appellavit dejectiones"; "asks to be exonerated . . ." from "exoneratus . . . cantitans"

18) "demum ex stercore turpi cum divi Orionis iucunditate mixto, cocto, frigorique exposito . . ." The most relevant fact about the handsome and powerful giant Orion we find in *The Oxford Classical Dictionary*: ". . . Hyrieus, eponym of Hyriae, asked for offspring from three gods (their names vary) whom he had hospitably received. They made water (ομρησαν) on a bull's hide and bade him bury it; in time a child was born, which he called Urion, the name afterwards becoming Orion." Life, and even divine life (as the priest in the Christian tradition effects it through the sacraments), here emerges from the mixture of the bull's hide and the gods' urine. Joyce, or Shem, will produce life from the artist's defecation and his urine. In the case of Orion, urine produced a powerful man, beloved of the gods, who became

a constellation, a divinity. Hence, in Stephen's view of the artist's function as priest transmuting ordinary experience into the radiant body of everliving life, Orion serves as an excellent illustration of the artistic process.

Orion, like Medard, is closely connected with rain:

> The constellation of Orion set at the commencement of November, at which time storms and rain were frequent: hence by Roman poets is he often called *imbrifer, nimbosus*, or *aquosus*.[11]

No doubt the fact that the mixture in the urn is being mixed, cooked, and exposed to cold has far more significance than I now see in it, but at the moment all I can perceive is that the preparation takes time and suffering. The "denique" of the second draft is changed here to "demum," perhaps to echo "demon." As I will note later, Joyce removed the word "devil" from the final parenthesis of this passage as it appeared in the second draft, and he may have tried to retain some touch of the word in this rather distant echo. Perhaps more useful is the suggestion made to me by Michael Connelly, that since "mum" is a sweet strong beer,[12] Joyce might by the change be indicating that the activity being discussed proceeds "from beer."

19) "encaustum sibi fecit indelibile . . ." Joyce here corrects the "indelibilem" of the second draft. "Encaustum" is certainly ink, but not ordinary ink. It is the purple-red ink of the later Roman emperors (secular "porporates"), the color of royalty, and of blood. It comes from a word meaning "burned in." Only caustic writing, one infers, will follow from its use. If it is applied to the skin, as it is in the last line on the page, it will burn in "corrosive sublimation." But it produces, as the following page states, the "word that would not pass away." This ink is formed from the mixture of painful crap, low, earthy, death symbol; and from his pleasant piss, like rain, a life symbol. Literally, it is made from the ugliness of evil humans, the dead, hypocritical, paralyzed, vulgar, lecherous, classical; and from the artist's literary insight and skill, life-giving, honest, candid, moving, original. Thus the priest of the eternal imagination can bring the true eucharist to an otherwise dead world.

20) "faked O'Ryan's, the indelible ink . . ." from "fecit" and "Orionis." Fred Ryan, together with Eglinton an editor of *Dana*, rejected Joyce's earliest attempt to print a version of *Portrait* (cf. *Letters*, 98). His name, like the first one given to Orion in the myth quoted above, suggests urine without, in Joyce's treatment here, the elevated symbolic tonality noted in Point 19.

In the second draft, Joyce closed the passage with "(made O'Ryan the devil's own ink)." "Made" translates "fecit," and Joyce no doubt wished to suggest a parallel between making water and making ink. The printer's devil would work in well with Fred Ryan's relationship to Joyce. But apparently Joyce decided to stress the first name of Ryan and to echo more pointedly his treatment of "My unchanging Word is sacred. The word is my wife, to exponse and expound, to vend and to velnerate, and may the curlews crown our nuptias! Till Breath us depart! Wamen." (*F. W.*, 167).

This page of *Finnegans Wake*, then, sets forth the philosophy of art, the bitter vulgarity, the delight in word-play, the rebellious blasphemy, the determination to total honesty, the doubt of self, the hatred of hypocrisy, the straining idealism of the youthful Joyce.[13] It prepares us for the naming, on the two following pages, of every story in *Dubliners* ("for the deathfête of Saint Ignaceous Poisonivy, of the Fickle Crowd (hopon the sexth day of Hogsober, killim our king, layum low!)"—"Ivy Day in the Committee Room," 6th of October, Hynes poem and "Et tu, Healy," treating of the priests and crowd who laid low Parnell, "our uncrowned king"; "Petty constable Sistersen," "The Sisters"; "foul clay," "Clay"; "in little clots," "A Little Cloud"; "wrongcountered," "An Encounter"; "an eveling," "Eveline"; "boardelhouse," "The Boarding House"; "after the grace," "After the Race" and "Grace"; "the painful sake," "A Painful Case"; "his countryports," "Counterparts"; "the dead med dirt," "The Dead"; "arrahbejibbers," "Araby"; "two gallonts," "Two Gallants"; "his murder . . . What mother?" "A Mother."),[14] and for the listing of the chapters of *Ulysses* on Page 229 ("Ukalepe," "Calypso"; "Loathers' leave," "Lotus Eaters"; "Had Days," "Hades"; "Nemo in Patria," "Aeolus," in reference a) to Ulysses's adopted name in the cave of Polyphemus, "Nobody," here applied to Bloom—b) to the patriotism in the speeches read in the newspaper office—c) to Christ's statement in *Matthew* 13/57, "Non est propheta sine honore, nisi in patria sua et in domo sua"; "The Luncher Out," "Lestrygonians"; "Skilly and Carubdish," "Scylla and Charybdis"; "A Wondering Wreck," "Wandering Rocks"; "From the Mermaids' Tavern," "Sirens"; "Bullyfamous," "Cyclops," i.e., Polyphemus; "Naughtysycalves," "Nausicaa"; "Mother of Misery," "Oxen of the Sun," reference to the misery of Mrs. Purefoy and the name of the hospital near Bloom's house, the Mater Misericordia; "Walpurgas Nackt," "Circe"). It helps us to see the justice in the charge of Justius:

> . . . and now, forsooth, . . . you have become of twosome twiminds forenenst gods, hidden and discovered, nay, condemned fool, anarch, egoarch, hiresiarch, you have reared your disunited kingdom on the vacuum of your own most intensely doubtful soul. (188)

And it helps us to sympathize with the self-knowledge of the artist in our world,

> . . . to me unseen blusher in an obscene coalhole, the cubilibum[15] of your secret sigh, dweller in the downandoutermost where voice only of the dead may come . . . (194)

Notes

1. Richard Ellmann, *James Joyce* (New York, 1959), passim.
2. I do not attempt to reproduce all of Mr. Hayman's extremely valuable typographical guides to the development of the text, since for my purpose the crossed-out words give the most useful signals of the veerings of Joyce's intention.
3. Stuart Gilbert, ed., *Letters of James Joyce* (New York, 1957), pp. 183 and 201.
4. *The Portable James Joyce* (Viking, New York, 1955), p. 275.
5. I acknowledge here my considerable debt to my colleague, Father Daniel Costello, S. J., head of the Classics Department at Regis College. He has gone over the passage with me, noting the oddities of Latin construction, supplying connections from his knowledge of Latin and Greek myths and authors, and suggesting possible allusions and puns.
6. *The Portable James Joyce*, p. 488.
7. *The Portable James Joyce*, p. 662.
8. *James Joyce*, p. 346.
9. James Joyce, *Ulysses* (New York, 1946), p. 385.
10. Not until this paper had been written did I see Adaline Glasheen's *A Second Census of Finnegans Wake* (Northwestern University Press, 1963), where Medard is identified as a "6th century French bishop, patron of rain." Mrs. Glasheen also helpfully identifies another reference to Medard in which, in a passage dealing with micturition, he is specifically associated with St. Swithun: "Never christen medlard apples till a swithin is in sight" (**FW**, 433).
11. *A Smaller Classical Dictionary* (London, 1937), p. 359.
12. Cf. Joseph Campbell and Henry Morton Robinson, *A Skeleton Key to Finnegans Wake* (New York, 1960), p. 28. They identify "mum" in relation to "doublin their mumper" on the first page of *F. W.*
13. The page should certainly be added to the significant passages dealing with micturition which Clive Hart discusses in his excellent *Structure and Motif in Finnegans Wake* (London, 1962), pp. 202–208. And the page bolsters W. Y. Tindall's observation that for Joyce the act of micturition symbolizes an act of creation—see *Chamber Music* (New York, 1954), pp. 74 ff.
14. James Atherton, in *The Books at the Wake* (New York, 1960), pp. 106–109, lists these titles and gives other information valuable for placing in context the Latin passage I have attempted to explicate.
15. Another fascinating Latin-English portmanteau word, formed of "cubile," the ordinary meaning of which is a couch, a bed, a place to rest, and the English slang "bum," meaning buttocks. It suggests that the low work of Joyce, a resting place for the buttocks, might lead to the secret dreams of the longing spirit as inevitably as do the moonbeam-haunted banks where Shakespeare's Bully Bottom (bilibum) dreamt his dream, "past the wit of man to say what dream it was."

[The Peculiar Language of *Finnegans Wake*]

Derek Attridge

THE POWER OF THE PORTMANTEAU

Published responses to *Finnegans Wake* afford examples of . . . hostility [to punning] in profusion. That the last major work of one of the language's most admired and influential writers—the product of some sixteen painful years' labor—has remained on the margins of the literary tradition is an extraordinary but well-established fact. That the phenomenon is so evident does not mean that it requires no explanation; on the contrary, if we could properly account for it, we might throw light on the processes of reading and evaluation which determine the shape of the literary canon. Those who find little appeal in Joyce's earlier writing are unlikely to have a good word to say for the *Wake*, but what is more remarkable is that many of those who have written admirably about Joyce's other works testify to difficulties with his last book. Sometimes, as a result, an introductory text that one might expect to offer encouragement to the new reader in tackling Joyce's most ambitious work can have the opposite effect. Thus John Gross asks, in his volume on Joyce in the widely selling Modern Masters series, "What was Joyce's object in devising so outlandish a style?—always assuming, that is, that the entire book isn't best regarded as a hoax?" And he sums up his position as follows: "In the end the *Wake* seems to me a dazzling failure, the aberration of a great man. Viewed as a whole, I don't believe it is nearly worth the effort which it demands" (*Joyce*, 79, 89). S. L. Goldberg says of *Finnegans Wake* in another introductory book on Joyce's entire output: "The work itself seems to me an artistic failure; and despite the enthusiastic assertions of its admirers, the questions it prompts the ordinary reader to ask remain, I believe, still the most important—questions concerned less with its verbal 'meaning' or its machinery than with its value: why Joyce ever undertook it, why it seems so laborious and, more particularly, so unrewarding to read through" (*Joyce*, 103).[1] And A. Walton Litz, in his study *The Art of James Joyce*, comments that "at one and the same time the *Wake*

Excerpted and reprinted from Derek Attridge, *Peculiar Language: Literature as Difference from the Renaissance to James Joyce* (London: Methuen; Ithaca: Cornell University Press, 1988), 195–209. Copyright © Derek Attridge 1988. Reprinted by permission of Cornell University Press and Methuen & Co. Footnotes have been slightly altered.

is too abstract and too concrete. Paradoxically, it displays a detailed point-by-point fidelity to Joyce's early experiences without reflecting—as do *Portrait* and *Ulysses*—a full sense of the reality of those experiences. The result is an infinitely rich texture combined with a tedium of basic thought. That sense of 'felt life' which Henry James considered the essence of literary form infuses Joyce's artifice by fits and starts" (124). Litz goes on to use the same word as the other two critics, referring to "this failure I find in the *Wake*." Yet it is clear from his valuable discussion of Joyce's writing of the *Wake* that Litz's reservations do not arise from any lack of sympathy, sensitivity, or effort; he seems almost unwilling to reach the conclusion he feels he has to. In his later introductory book on Joyce one hears the same tone:

> I have spoken earlier of the triumphs and limitations of *Finnegans Wake*, which force me to conclude that it is a partial failure. Any set of standards that will account for the essential greatness of *Ulysses* must, I feel, find a certain sterility in *Finnegans Wake*. Even the comic spirit which, much more than the elaborate structural patterns, gives the *Wake* its unity, seems to me ultimately self-defeating. In *Ulysses*, parody and satire have direction because they serve a moral vision; but in *Finnegans Wake* they turn upon themselves and destroy their own foundations.
>
> (*James Joyce*, 118)

The many readers who find the *Wake* a source of great pleasure, the many teachers and students who find it a delight to discuss in a small class (once initial prejudices are overcome), will regret that comments like these, sincere though they are, put obstacles in the way of others who might find in the work pleasures similar to their own. But our present task is to ask what about Joyce's last book is so resistant to the efforts of many well-disposed and well-qualified readers to find enjoyment in it. There can be no doubt that a major reason for this negative reaction is the work's intensive use of the portmanteau word, which is what makes the style "outlandish," demands "effort" from the reader, renders the work "laborious" and "unrewarding," inhibits the communication of "felt life." The portmanteau word is a monster, a word that is not a word, that is not authorized by any dictionary, that holds out the worrying prospect of books which, instead of comfortingly recycling the words we know, possess the freedom endlessly to invent new ones. We have learned to accept novels without firm plots or consistent characters, novels that blend historical periods or submerge the authorial presence, even novels that pun and rhyme; but sixty years after it first started appearing, the novel—if it can still be called a novel—that makes the portmanteau word a cornerstone of its method remains a troublesome presence in the institution of literature.[2]

My argument so far suggests an explanation that goes beyond discomfort with the unusual and dislike of the difficult, understandable though these reactions are. The portmanteau word challenges two myths on which most assumptions about the efficacy of language rest. Like the pun, it denies that single words must have, on any given occasion, single meanings; and like the various devices of assonance and rhyme, it denies that the manifold patterns of similarity which occur at the level of the signifier are innocent of meaning. It does so with the pun's simultaneity of operation but more flagrantly and with less warning. There is no escape from its insistence that meaning is an *effect* of language, not a presence within or behind it, and that the effect is unstable and uncontrollable. Notice, too, that whereas the pun can easily be contained by being treated as the index of an imperfect language, allowing ambiguity where it should insist on univocity, the conclusion is harder to escape that the portmanteau can be nothing other than a defining feature of language itself, because the portmanteau derives from the fact that the same segments (letters, phonemes, syllables) can be combined in different ways to encode different meanings. A language in which portmanteau formations were impossible would be a language in which every signified was matched with a unique and unanalyzable signifier—that is, not a language at all.[3]

Not surprisingly, therefore, the portmanteau word has had a history of exclusion much more severe than that of the pun. Outside the language of dreams, parapraxes, and jokes, it has existed chiefly in the form of malapropism and nonsense verse—the language of the uneducated, the child, the idiot. (The very term "portmanteau word" comes from a children's story, *Alice Through the Looking-Glass*, and not a work of theory or criticism.)[4] And the literary establishment has often relegated *Finnegans Wake* to the same border area. How else can it avoid the claim made by the text that the portmanteau word, far from being a sport, an eccentricity, a mistake, is a revelation of the processes upon which all language relies? How else can it exclude the possibility that the same relation obtains between *Finnegans Wake* and the tradition of the novel, that what appears to be a limiting case or a parody, a parasite on the healthy body of literature, is at the same time central and implicated in the way the most "normal" text operates? It is the familiar logic of the Derridean supplement or *pharmakon* I have already discussed in relation to [George] Puttenham's writing: the "artifice" to be excluded from the category of "natural" literature (with its "felt life" and "full sense of reality") which nevertheless reveals the artificial character of literature itself.[5] In the *Wake*'s deconstruction of the oppositional structures of the literary tradition, the portmanteau word proves to be a powerful tool, but its very power has rendered it ineffective. (This is not, of course, to argue that those who find the *Wake* hard going are party to a conspiracy dedicated to the preservation of a metaphysical conception of language; we can never be fully conscious of the reasons for our preferences, and to attempt to explain the acceptance or rejection of a literary text is not to award praise or lay blame.)

To demonstrate the operation of the portmanteau and to explore the reasons why, for all their superficial similarity, the portmanteau and the pun are very different kinds of linguistic deviation, a specific example is needed. The following passage was chosen at random, and the points I make about it could be made about any page of *Finnegans Wake*.

> And stand up tall! Straight. I want to see you looking fine for me. With your brandnew big green belt and all. Blooming in the very lotust and second to nill, Budd! When you're in the buckly shuit Rosensharonals near did for you. Fiftyseven and three, cosh, with the bulge. Proudpurse Alby with his pooraroon Eireen, they'll. Pride, comfytousness, enevy! You make me think of a wonderdecker I once. Or somebalt that sailder, the man megallant, with the bangled ears. Or an earl was he, at Lucan? Or, no, it's the Iren duke's I mean. Or somebrey erse from the Dark Countries. Come and let us! We always said we'd. And go abroad.
>
> (620. 1)[6]

At the risk of seeming to posit the very things I have said the text undermines—themes, plot, characters—let me tender a bald and provisional statement of some of the threads that can be traced through the passage, in order to establish an initial orientation. The predominant "voice" in this part of the text—its closing pages—is what Joyce designated by Δ, the shifting cluster of attributes and energies often associated with the initials ALP and the role of wife and mother. The addressee is primarily the group of characteristics indicated by Π, the male counterpart frequently manifested as the letters HCE. Two of the prominent narrative strands involving this couple in the closing pages are a walk around Dublin in the early morning and a sexual act, and both are fused with the movement of the river Liffey flowing through Dublin into the sea. Contradictory tones and modes of address are blended, in particular the eager admiration of a young girl for her energetic lover and the disappointment of the aging wife with her now impotent husband. Here ALP is asking HCE to don his new, expensive clothes and go out with her on a jaunt, but she is also inviting him to demonstrate his naked sexual potency. (At first, the words are also those of a mother to her young son; they echo, too, a letter of Joyce's to Nora on 7 September 1909: "I want you to look your best for me when I come. Have you any nice clothes now?" [*Letters*, 2:251].) At the same time what we hear is the river addressing the city of Dublin (reversed in "nill, Budd"), with its green belt and modern comforts. The relationship is also reminiscent of that between Molly and Leopold Bloom in *Ulysses*. "Blooming in the very lotust" points to the earlier novel, especially the "Lotus-Eaters" chapter; Sinbad the Sailor ("somebalt that sailder") is also associated with Bloom as he goes to bed in "Ithaca"; and Molly's own closing chapter has something in common with ALP's final monologue. It includes, too, the exploitative relationship of England and Ireland ("Proud-purse Alby with his pooraroon Eireen": perfidious Albion and poor Eire or Erin). The passage enunciates a series of ALP's sexual memories, all of which turn out to be memories of HCE in one or other of his guises: as sailor (Sinbad, Magellan, and Vanderdecken, the captain of the *Flying Dutchman*); as military figure (the man with the bandolier, the duke of Wellington, and the earl of Lucan—whether the hero of the Williamite wars or the Lord Lucan who fought at Balaclava); and as the stranger (the man with earrings, the man from the Dark Countries) who is also an Irishman (not only Wellington but Lucan as a village on the Liffey, "Iren" as Ireland, and "erse" as Irish). That the exploits of these figures are partly sexual (or excretory, for the two are not kept distinct in the *Wake*) emerges from the "gallant" of "megallant," "erse" understood as "arse," and another echo of *Ulysses*, this time of Bloom's pamphlet advertising the "Wonderworker," "the world's greatest remedy for rectal complaints" (17.1820).[7] Once phallic suggestions begin to surface, they can be discovered at every turn: a few examples would be "stand up," "straight," "I want to see you" (an instance of the familiar synecdoche discussed in the previous chapter), *bod* (pronounced *bud*) as Gaelic for "penis," "cosh" (a thick stick), "bulge," the "wonderdecker" again (*decken* in German is to copulate), the stiffness of iron, and the Wellington monument. And the evident ellipses (reminiscent of those in the "Eumaeus" episode of *Ulysses*) can easily be read as sexual modesty: "a wonderdecker I once . . . ," "the Iren Duke's . . . ," "Come and let us . . . ," "We always said we'd. . . ." I have provided only an initial indication of some of the meanings at work here, and one could follow other motifs through the passage: flowers, sins (several of the seven deadly ones are here), tailoring and sailing (the two often go together in the *Wake*), and battles. All of these are associated in one way or another with sex.[8]

Let us focus now on one word from the passage, "shuit." To call it a word is of course misleading—it is precisely because it is *not* a word recognized as belonging to the English language that it functions as it does, preventing the immediate move from material signifier to conceptual signified. Unlike the pun, which exists only if the context brings it into being, the portmanteau refuses, *by itself*, any single meaning, and in reading we therefore have to nudge it toward other signifiers whose meanings might prove appropriate. Let us, first of all, ignore the larger context of the whole book and concentrate—as we would for a pun—on the guidance provided by the immediate context. We seem to be invited to take "shuit" as an item of clothing, one that can have the adjective "buckly"—with buckles—applied to it. Three lexical items offer themselves as appropriate: *suit, shirt, shoes*. The first two would account for the portmanteau without any unexplained residue, but "buckly" seems to point in particular to *shoes*, partly by way of the nursery rhyme "One, two, buckle my shoe." A writer employing orthodox devices of patterning at the level of the signifier might construct a sentence in which the separate words *suit, shirt*, and *shoes* all occur in such a way as to make the reader conscious of the sound-connections between them, thus creating what I called earlier a nonce-constellation, but it would be a rather feeble, easily ignored, device. "Shuit" works more powerfully because it insists on a productive act of reading, because its effects are simultaneous, and because the result is an expansion of meaning much more extensive than that effected by the pun. The pun . . . carries a powerful charge of satisfaction: the specter of a potentially unruly and ultimately infinite language is raised only to be exorcised, the writer and reader are still firmly in control, and the language has been made to seem even *more* orderly and appropriate than we had realized, because an apparently arbitrary coincidence in its system has been shown to be capable of semantic justification. But "shuit" and its kind are more disturbing. The portmanteau has the effect of a *failed* pun—the patterns of language have been shown to be partially appropriate but with a residue of difference where the pun found only happy similarity. And though the context makes it clear that the passage is about clothing and thereby seems to set limits to the word's possible meanings, one cannot escape the feeling that the process, once started, may be unstoppable. . . . No reference book or mental register exists to tell us all the possible signifiers that are or could be associated in sound with "shuit," and we have learned no method of interpretation to tell us how to go about finding those signifiers or deciding at what point the connection becomes too slight to be relevant. Certainly other signifiers sound like "shuit," and if similarities of sound can have semantic implications, how do we know where to draw the boundary?

The answer to this question may seem straightforward: like the pun, the portmanteau will contain as much as the verbal context permits it to contain and no more. But the answer brings us to a fundamental point about the *Wake*, because the context *itself* is made up of puns and portmanteaux. So far I have spoken as if the context were a given, firm structure of meaning which has one neatly defined hole in it, but this notion is of course pure interpretative fiction. The text is a web of shifting meanings, and every new interpretation of one item recreates afresh the context for all the other items. Having found *suit* in "shuit," for example, one can reinterpret the previous word to yield the phrase *birthday suit*, as a colloquial expression for "naked-ness," nicely epitomizing the fusion of the states of being clothed and unclothed which the passage implies—one more example of the denial of the logic of opposites which starts to characterize this text with its very title. Thus a "contextual circle" is created whereby plurality of meaning in one item increases the available meanings of other items, which in turn increase the possibilities of meaning in the original item. The longer and denser the text, the more often the circle will revolve, and the greater will be the proliferation of meanings. It is important to note, however, that the network of signification remains *systematic*: the familiar accusation that "there is no way of denying the relevance . . . of any meaning any commentator cares to find," to quote Goldberg again (*Joyce*, 111), is without substance. In a text as long and as densely worked as *Finnegans Wake*, however, the systematic networks of meaning could probably provide contexts for most of the associations that individual words might evoke—though an individual reader could not be expected to grasp them all. This sense of a spiraling increase in potential meaning is one of the grounds on which the *Wake* is left unread, but is this not an indication of the way *all* texts operate? Every item in a text functions simultaneously as a sign whose meaning is limited (but not wholly limited) by its context and as a context limiting (but not wholly limiting) the meaning of other signs. There is no escape from this circle, no privileged item that yields its meaning apart from the system in which it is perceived and which can act as a contextless context or transcendental fixing-point to anchor the whole text. The enormous difference between *Finnegans Wake* and other literary works is, perhaps, a difference in degree, not in kind.

The next word, "Rosensharonals," provides another example of the operation of contexts in the *Wake*. As an individual item it immediately suggests "Rose of Sharon," a flower (identified with crocus, narcissus, and others) to go with bloom, lotus, and bud and to enhance further the springlike vitality of the male or his sexual organ. It gives us a reference to the Song of Solomon (itself a sexual invitation), reinforcing the text's insistence that apparently "natural" human emotions are cultural products: love and sexual desire in this passage are caught up not only with the Hebraic tradition but also with Buddhism (both in the lotus and in "Budd"), with *Billy Budd* (a story whose concerns are highly relevant), with *Sinbad the Sailor* (as a tale from the *Arabian Nights* or as a pantomime), and with popular songs (*Eileen Aroon*—"Eileen my darling"—and phrases from "I will give you the keys to heaven"). (I suspect there may also be a song called "The Man with the Bandolier," though I have not been able to trace it; in fact the text problematizes that very urge to "verify" what offers itself as an "allusion.")[9] The sense of new beginnings is also heightened by a suggestion of Rosh Hashanah, the Jewish New Year. In the context of clothing, however, the name sounds more like that of the Jewish tailor who made the garment in question: "the buckly shuit Rosensharonals near did for you," bringing to mind the story of Kersse the tailor and the Norwegian captain from earlier in the book (311–32), a story that involves a suit with a bulge in it, apparently made necessary by a hunchback. But once we move to the context of the whole work, another story, from the same earlier chapter (337–55), comes into prominence: the tale of Buckley and the Russian general, which appears in the text at many points and in many guises. Buckley is a common Irish soldier in the Crimean War who comes upon a Russian general with his pants down, in the act of defecating, and either does or does not shoot at him. The story interweaves with other stories of encounters involving exposure and/or voyeurism, such as the much-discussed event in Phoenix Park involving

HCE, two girls, and three soldiers. It has to do with the attack by the younger generation on the older, and the older generation's fall from power before the younger, the drunkenness of Noah and the drugging of Finn MacCool by his young bride being other versions. (It is typical of the *Wake*'s method that an indecent anecdote which Joyce heard from his father is accorded the same status as religious myth and epic narrative.) So in the middle of a passage of praise for the virility of HCE comes a reminder of his loss of control, and "near did for you" becomes a reference not to tailoring but to an attempt at, or a resisted temptation to, murder. And our portmanteau *shuit* unpacks itself further, yielding both *shoot* and *shit*.[10]

PARIAH AND PARADIGM

My aim is not to demonstrate the plurality of meaning in Joyce's portmanteaux; that is easily done. It is to focus on the workings of a typical portmanteau to show both how crucial they are to the method of *Finnegans Wake* and how they help make the book conceivable as a central, rather than a peripheral, literary text. The portmanteau shatters any illusion that the systems of difference in language are fixed and sharply drawn, reminding us that signifiers are perpetually dissolving into one another: in the never-ending diachronic development of language; in the blurred edges between languages, dialects, registers, idiolects; in the interchange between speech and writing; in errors and misunderstandings, unfortunate or fruitful; in riddles, jokes, games, and dreams. *Finnegans Wake* insists that the strict boundaries and discrete elements in a linguist's "grammar of competence" are a neoplatonic illusion.

But the portmanteau problematizes even the most stable signifier by showing how its relations to other signifiers can be productive; we find that we can quite easily relate *suit* to *shirt* just as we do in fact relate *suit* to *suits* or *suited*. Instead of saying that in learning a language we learn to ascribe meaning to a few of the many patterns of sound we perceive, it may be as true to say that we learn *not* to ascribe meaning to most of those connections (Freud takes this view in his book on jokes)[11]—until we are allowed to do so again to a certain degree in rhetoric and poetry, and with almost complete abandon in *Finnegans Wake*. The result, of course, is that as we read the *Wake* we test for their possible associations not only the obvious portmanteaux but every apparently normal word as well. The phrase "bangled ears" does not present itself as a portmanteau, and in most texts it would be read as a somewhat odd, but semantically specific, conjunction of adjective and noun. But the context of the *Wake*'s portmanteau style encourages us, as I have suggested, to hear it also as "bandolier," to combine the attributes of the savage or stranger with those of the soldier. Even the most normal and innocent word will invite such treatment. As Jean-Paul Martin has said of *Finnegans Wake*, "the portmanteau word, but also every word, every fragment of a word or of an utterance, marks the interlacing of sinuous and diverse chains of associations which cross codes and languages" . . . Another theoretical distinction becomes blurred, that between synchronic and diachronic dimensions, because a pertinent meaning may be retrievable from the history of a word. "Erse," for instance, offers both a Middle English word for "arse" and an early Scottish word for "Irish." Here, too, the *Wake* heightens a process that operates in all language, in spite of the Saussurean enterprise of methodically separating synchrony and diachrony. . . .

The implications of the portmanteau word, or rather the portmanteau text, go further, however. The portmanteau undermines the notion of authorial intention, for instance, in a way quite foreign to the traditional pun. The pun in fact strengthens the illusion of intention as a presence within the text. . . . The careful construction of context to allow both meanings equal force and to exclude all other meanings is not something that happens by accident, we feel, and this feeling makes the pun acceptable in certain literary environments because there is no danger that the coincidence thus exposed will enable language to wrest control from its users. But the portmanteau word, though its initial effect is often similar, has a habit of refusing to rest with that comforting sensation of "I see what the author meant." To find *shirt* and *suit* in *shuit*, and nothing else, might yield a satisfying response of that kind: "clearly what Joyce is doing is fusing those words into one," we say to ourselves. But when we note the claims for *shoes, shoot*, and *shit* as well, we begin to lose hold on our sense of an embodied intention. If those five are to be found, why not more? The polyglot character of the text, for instance, opens up further prospects. If French ears hear *chute*, one can hardly deny the relevance of the notion of a fall (or of the Fall) to the story of Buckley and the Russian general or to the temptation of HCE in the park.[12] And why should any particular number of associations, in any particular number of languages, correspond to the author's intention? Joyce has set in motion a process over which he has no final control—a source of disquiet for many readers. Litz, for example, complains that "in reading it one does not feel that sense of 'inevitability' or 'rightness' which is the sign of a controlled narrative structure" (*The Art of James Joyce*, 62). Others are more willing to accept the vast scale of what the multilingual portmanteau opens up. In "Finnegans, Wake!" Jean Paris observes that "once it is established, it must by its own movement extend itself to the totality of living and dead languages. And here indeed is the irony of the portmanteau style: the enthroning of a principle of chance which, prolonging the intentions of the author, in so far as they are perceptible, comes little by little to substitute for them, to function like a delirious mechanism, accumulating allusions, parodying analogies, and finally atomizing the Book" (60–61).[13] But *every* text, not just this one, is ultimately beyond the control of its author, *every* text reveals the systems of meaning of which Derrida speaks in his consideration of the word *pharmakon* in Plato's *Phaedrus*: "But the system here is not, simply, that of the intentions of an author who goes by the name of Plato. The system is not primarily that of what someone *meant-to-say* [*un vouloir-dire*]. Finely regulated communications are established, through the play of language, among diverse functions of the word and within it, among diverse strata or regions of culture" (*Dissemination*, 95).

Similarly, the portmanteau word leaves few of the conventional assumptions about narrative intact: *récit* cannot be separated from *histoire* when it surfaces in the texture of the words themselves. When, for instance, the story of Buckley and the Russian general is woven, by the portmanteau method, into a statement about new clothing, it is impossible to talk in terms of the narration of a supposedly prior event. Rather, there is a process of fusion which enforces the realization that *all* stories are textual effects. Characters, too, are never *behind* the text in *Finnegans Wake* but *in* it; ALP, HCE, Buckley, and the Russian general have their being in portmanteau words, in acrostics, in shapes on the page—though this, too, is only a reinforcement of the status of all fictional characters. Finally, consider the traditional analysis of metaphor and allegory as a relation between a "literal," "superficial" meaning and a "figurative," "deep," "true" meaning. The portmanteau word, and *Finnegans Wake* as a whole, refuses to establish such a hierarchical opposition, for anything that appears to be a metaphor is capable of reversal, the tenor becoming the vehicle, and vice versa. In the quoted passage we might be tempted to say that a literal invitation to go for a walk can be metaphorically interpreted as an invitation to sexual activity. At the level of the word one might say that "lotust" is read literally as *latest*, a reference to fashion, but that the deeper meaning is *lotus*, with its implication of sensual enjoyment. But the only reason for saying that the "deeper" meaning is the sexual one is our own preconception as to what counts as deep and what as superficial. All metaphor, we are made to realize by this text, is potentially unstable, kept in position by the hierarchies we bring to bear upon it, not by its inner, inherent division into literal and figurative domains. . . .

The fears provoked by *Finnegans Wake*'s portmanteau style are understandable and inevitable, because the consequences of accepting it extend to all our reading. Every word in every text is, after all, a portmanteau of sorts, a combination of sounds that echo through the entire language and through every other language and back through the history of speech. *Finnegans Wake* makes us aware that we, as readers, control this explosion, allowing only those connections to be effected which will give us the kinds of meaning we recognize—stories, voices, characters, metaphors, images, beginnings, developments, ends, morals, truths. We do not, of course, control it as a matter of choice. We are subject to the various grids that make literature and language possible at all—rules, habits, conventions, and all the boundaries that legitimate and exclude in order to produce meanings and values, themselves rooted in the ideology of our place and time. . . . Nevertheless, to obtain a glimpse of the infinite possibility of meaning kept at bay by those grids, to gain a sense that the boundaries upon which our use of language depends are set up under specific historical conditions, is to be made aware of a universe more open to reinterpretation and change than the one we are usually conscious of inhabiting. For many of its readers *Finnegans Wake* makes that glimpse an experience of exhilaration and opportunity, and as a result the book comes to occupy an important place in their reading; but for many others it can be only a discouraging glimpse of limitless instability.[14] So the book is treated as a freak, an unaccountable anomaly that merely travesties the cultural traditions we cherish, and its function as supplement and *pharmakon*, supererogatory but necessary, dangerous but remedial, is thereby prolonged.

When the *Wake* is welcomed, however, it is often by means of a gesture that simultaneously incapacitates it, either by placing it in a sealed-off category (the impenetrable and inexpressible world of the dream) or by subjecting it to the same interpretative mechanisms that are applied to all literary texts, as if it were no different: the elucidation of an "intention" (aided by draft material and biography), the analysis of "characters," the tracing of "plot," the elaboration of "themes," the tracking down of "allusions," the identification of "autobiographical references," in sum, the whole panoply of modern professional criticism. The outright repudiation of the Joycean portmanteau, though it may one day seem as quaint an attitude as Johnson's rejection of the Shakespearean quibble, is perhaps preferable to this industrious program of normalization and domestication. Johnson's passionate lament for his flawed idol involves a fuller understanding of the implications of the pun than many an untroubled celebration of textual indeterminacy, and to be afraid of *Finnegans Wake* is at least to acknowledge, even if unconsciously, the power and magnitude of the claims it makes.

Notes

1. Goldberg's phrase "read *through*" suggests one reason for the problems he has with the *Wake*.
2. In *Adultery in the Novel*, Tony Tanner comments that "puns and ambiguities are to common language what adultery and perversion are to 'chaste' (i.e., socially orthodox) sexual relations. They both bring together entities (meanings/people) that have 'conventionally' been differentiated and kept apart; and they bring them together in deviant ways, bypassing the orthodox rules governing communications and relationships. (A pun is like an adulterous bed in which two meanings that should be separate are coupled together.) It is hardly an accident that *Finnegans Wake*, which arguably demonstrates the dissolution of bourgeois society, is almost one continuous pun (the connection with sexual perversion being quite clear to Joyce)" (53). As I have tried to show, the pun can constitute a thoroughly respectable coupling, which is why the *Wake* is not, *pace* Tanner, essentially a punning text. Tanner's remark is more appropriate to the promiscuous liaisons of words and meanings in the portmanteau.
3. The portmanteau exploits to the full the language's potential for what in chapter 5 I called "nonce-constellations": groups of words with similar sounds which create the impression of a particular appropriateness between those sounds and the dominant semantic content of the group. In the portmanteau the words in question are presented not as a sequence

but as a combined unit. Dwight Bolinger's discussions of sound and sense in *Forms of English*, referred to in that chapter, are highly relevant to the language of *Finnegans Wake*.

4. A text such as Francis Huxley's *The Raven and the Writing Desk*, which treats Carroll's portmanteaux with the comic brilliance they deserve, is equally likely to be overlooked by the literary establishment.

5. See ". . . That Dangerous Supplement . . . ," in *Of Grammatology*, 141–64, and "Plato's Pharmacy," in *Dissemination*, 61–171.

6. References to *Finnegans Wake* are to the standard Faber/Viking edition of 1939 and indicate page number and line number on that page. Where a quotation is of more than one line, only the first line number is given. In commenting on this passage I have made use of several of the standard reference books on *Finnegans Wake*, and I gratefully acknowledge the labors of their authors.

7. See *Ulysses* 11.1224, 15.3274, and 18.716 for further references to this invention, which "claims to afford a noiseless inoffensive vent."

8. Needless to say, the relation between shifts and indeterminacy in the language and intimations of sexual desire is not fortuitous.

9. Charles Peake has suggested to me a possible reference to the once-popular song "The Bandolero" (private communication). The word "bandolier" is also associated with Leopold Bloom: he is recalled as a school pupil in "Oxen of the Sun," "his booksatchel on him bandolierwise" (14.1047); and in "Circe" he appears with *"fieldglasses in bandolier"* (15.538). The French word "bander," to have an erection, is perhaps in the background.

10. Horne Tooke would have found these multiple associations unsurprising. For him they would have revealed the historical processes of the language.

11. Freud refers to a group of jokes ("play upon words") that make "the (acoustic) word-presentation itself take the place of its significance as given by its relations to thing-presentations" and observes, "It may really be suspected that in doing so we are bringing about a great relief in psychical work and that when we make serious use of words we are obliged to hold ourselves back with a certain effort from this comfortable procedure" (*Jokes*; 167–68).

12. For a discussion of the effects of Joyce's coalescing of languages which focuses on a single (and apparently simple) portmanteau from the *Wake*, see Derrida, "Two Words for Joyce."

13. See also the discussion by Jean Paris of the portmanteau word in "L'agonie du signe."

14. Someone who was able to go further than most in reading a wide range of literature against the grain of established codes, prefiguring the strategies required by *Finnegans Wake*, was Saussure; but he too took fright at the infinite possibilities he opened up, as Jean Starobinski documents in *Words upon Words*. Starobinski's comments have an obvious relevance to the anxieties and pleasures of reading *Finnegans Wake*: "If this approach [the theory of hypograms] had been further developed, it would soon have become a quagmire. Wave upon wave of possible names would have taken shape beneath his alert and disciplined eye. Is this the vertigo of error? It is also the discovery of the simple truth that language is an infinite resource, and that behind each phrase lies hidden the multiple clamor from which it has detached itself to appear before us in its isolated individuality" (122).

Raiding fur Buginners: *FW* 611.04–613.04

MICHAEL PATRICK GILLESPIE

Hugh Kenner's idea that Joyce devoted a great deal of space in *Ulysses* to instructing readers on how to approach his book has long been a critical commonplace. In an essay devoted to the compositional strategy of *Finnegans Wake*, David Hayman has implicitly developed a similar perspective of the relation between Joyce and his readers. Using post-modern critical methods Hayman offers a theory of interpretation that extends Clive Hart's ideas of the structure of *Finnegans Wake* to include a more elaborate scheme for identifying the stylistic and contextual framework that gives form to the work. In addition to illuminating aspects of Joyce's process of creation, I believe that Hayman's concepts also provide useful guidelines for a greater consideration of the role of the reader in the text.

> Hart's account of the "motif" demonstrates one aspect of Joyce's method (an aspect of what might be called the *Wake*'s micro-structure). But Joyce's practice suggests another approach which, rather than the individual motif, would focus the coherent clusterings of motif-like materials and might be called "nodalization." The key element here is the "prime node" or apex of the "nodal system," a passage where some act, activity, personal trait, allusion, theme, etc. surfaces for its clearest statement in the text, is made manifest, so to speak, and in the process brings together and crystallizes an otherwise scattered body of related material. This prime node is the generative center for lesser and generally less transparent passages devoted to its elaboration or expansion and strategically located in the text.[1]

In my sense of *Finnegans Wake*, the Hart-Hayman approach needs yet another extension to include the rhetorical dimension of the work.[2]

    While both Hart and Hayman have made important critical contributions to our comprehension of *Finnegans Wake*, strict adherence to the vocabulary of their methods can inhibit exploration of some of the most significant areas of inquiry that they highlight. One can infer from certain descriptive terms like prime node, apex, and generative center a series of dualisms and hierarchies—high/low, surface/depth, margin/center—in which one side of

Reprinted from the *James Joyce Quarterly* 24 (Spring 1987): 319–30. Reprinted by permission of the *James Joyce Quarterly*, University of Tulsa.

the dualism always benefits from an evaluative preference. I believe that the pattern of incremental repetition which they identify reflects efforts within the narrative at reforming conventional habits of interpretation brought to the text by many readers, and I propose to examine the paradigmatic significance of the debate between Paddrock and the archdruid Balkelly in terms of the directions it suggests for a general response to the work.

Before taking up that passage, however, I would like to offer a sample of some of the impressionistic statements on reading—what Hayman would term elements of the "nodal system"—scattered throughout *Finnegans Wake*. These observations, and others like them, loosely combine in a grammar of rhetoric guiding "that ideal reader suffering from an ideal insomnia" (*FW* 120.13–14) through the text.

> Thus the unfacts, did we possess them, are too imprecisely few to warrant our certitude.
>
> (*FW* 57.16–17)

> No, assuredly, they are not justified, those gloompourers who grouse that letters have never been quite their old selves again since that weird weekday in bleak Janiveer (yet how palmy date in a waste's oasis!) when to the shock of both, Biddy Doran looked at literature.
>
> (*FW* 112.23–27)

> He is cured by faith who is sick of fate. The prouts who will invent a writing there ultimately is the poeta, still more learned, who discovered the raiding there originally.
>
> (*FW* 482.30–33)

> For newmanmaun set a marge to the merge of unnotions. Innition wons agame.
>
> (*FW* 614.17–18)

The tenor of these remarks may appear at first marred by contradiction and even in some instances by an aura of malevolence, but, as one becomes accustomed to the linguistic fluctuations of the book, the persistent reader will find in these gnomic flourishes hints for perceiving the "metheg in your midness" (*FW* 32.04–05).

While the structure of *Finnegans Wake* overtly resists conventional interpretive approaches, Joyce's intrusive commentary, via the narrator(s), attempts to mitigate the frustration its form inevitably produces in readers accustomed to basing their responses to literature on the primacy of a single system of explication. The alternative method suggested by the text proposes abandoning the tyranny of cause and effect logic ("the unfacts") and overturning the hegemony of "those gloompourers" who advocate the dominance of orthodox critical systems. In their stead one must give oneself over to the work through an act of faith, depending not on any prescriptive system to release the pleasure of the text but on the polymorphic power of the book itself to push the border ("marge") of acceptance "to the merge of unnotions."

The rhetorical framework of *Finnegans Wake* testifies to the efficacy of such an approach. Through syntactic and grammatical constructions that systematically disrupt single-minded interpretations, Joyce compels readers intent upon discovering meaning to move away from linear approaches to comprehension and towards a dialectic acceptance of ambiguity: either/or questions give way to both/and answers which have stability and significance only to the degree conferred by the individual perceiver. Developing around the "nodal system" of narration identified by Hayman, the language of the text presents a particular concept, image, or situation from a range of perspectives and produces equilibrium from the tension of diverse perceptions held in suspension. This condition of balance, however, comes about only through the intervention of the reader willing to give equal authority to a range of potential meanings within the text. In a harmonious response to the work, no single meaning will achieve primacy over other interpretations, and any reading cut off from all others remains deficient in proportion to its degree of isolation. To counteract the impulses of Enlightenment empiricism which still influence our response to experience, Joyce urges the acknowledgment and even the pursuit of ambiguity as a means of opening one's consciousness to the mystery inherent in art. Ultimately in *Finnegans Wake* the problem does not turn upon a resolution of contraries but upon a reconciliation with them.

Joyce was able to derive the creative vocabulary that formed the prose of *Finnegans Wake* because by the time he began to write it he had achieved to his own satisfaction a full sense of the nature of the aesthetic experience produced by a work of art. His opinions evolved over his artistic career, and his own work often served as testing grounds for his ideas. Questions of creation and perception run through Joyce's canon, generally bound up with references to philosophical considerations of time and space. In *A Portrait of the Artist as a Young Man*, for example, Stephen Dedalus, perhaps stimulated by Donovan's fatuous reference to Lessing and the *Laocoon*, begins an explanation of his theory of art to the sulphurous Lynch by first distinguishing, along the lines laid down by Lessing, the means by which perceptions become impressions:[3]

The first phase of apprehension is a bounding line drawn about the object to be apprehended. An esthetic image is presented to us either in space or in time. What is audible is presented in time, what is visible is presented in space. But, temporal or spatial, the esthetic image is first luminously apprehended as selfbounded and selfcontained upon the immeasurable background of space or time which is not it.

(P 212)

Stephen's distinctions are impressionistic and artificial, but they reflect concerns to which Joyce's work continues to return in search of some sort of resolution of cruxes within the discourse.

In *Ulysses* one can see the increasingly assertive movement away from certitude and towards mutability. On Sandymount strand in the "Proteus" episode Stephen struggles to overcome the limitations of his oversimplified view of the relation of the comprehension of a work of art in time and in space, and of necessity he begins to confront the inherent ambiguity of his conclusions. Lessing's ideas again appear as Stephen centers his aesthetic meditations on the competition for attention generated by synchronic and diachronic perceptions, but now Lessing's theories must compete with temporizing ideas from Aristotle, Jakob Boehme, and Bishop Berkeley for Stephen's attention. (Both Weldon Thornton and Don Gifford cite the diverse allusions to these philosophers that appear in the chapter.)[4]

> Ineluctable modality of the visible: at least that if no more, thought through my eyes. Signatures of all things I am here to read, seaspawn and seawrack, the nearing tide, that rusty boot. Snotgreen, bluesilver, rust: coloured signs. Limits of the diaphane. But he adds: in bodies. Then he was aware of them bodies before of them coloured. How? By knocking his sconce against them, sure. Go easy. Bald he was and a millionaire, *maestro di color che sanno*. Limit of the diaphane in. Why in? Diaphane, adiaphane. If you can put your five fingers through it it is a gate, if not a door. Shut your eyes and see.

(U-G 75)

Late in the chapter Stephen returns to ideas of Berkeley with a more specific reference introducing a time/space association with an incipient rainbow image in which colors conform to natural laws both of time and of space. "The good bishop of Cloyne [Berkeley] took the veil of the temple out of his shovel hat: veil of space with colored emblems hatched on its field. Hold hard. Coloured on a flat: yes, that's right" (*U-G* 99).[5] Stephen's momentary illumination does not fully resolve the questions of perception with which he has grappled, but his allusion to the rainbow becomes an important feature of Joyce's continuing investigation of the problem.

Although he never completely erases the boundaries of the two dimensions in any of his works, in writing *Finnegans Wake* Joyce comes to present them in a way that encourages conjunction in the mind of the reader. In any given passage historical, cultural, and mythical allusions converge diachronically to underscore the perception of our civilization as developing through incremental progression. At the same time, through cyclical emphasis, they synchronically level the primacy of any reference making it congruent to familiar archetypal patterns. As temporal and spatial images present contrasting though not mutually exclusive perceptions, he moves readers toward a reconciliation, though not a synthesis, of these positions by encouraging one to form a stereoscopic vision of cumulative and simultaneous elements in *Finnegans Wake*.

The elements making up the debate over time and space occur in variant forms in a number of key passages (the meeting of the Mookse and the Gripes and the fable of the Ondt and the Gracehoper come immediately to mind), but the confrontation of Paddrock (St. Patrick) and the archdruid Balkelly (Berkeley) seems the clearest illustration of this process and the selection presenting Joyce's final statement on the question. In a letter to Frank Budgen written three months after the publication of *Finnegans Wake* Joyce drew attention to the paradigmatic significance of this passage and offered through inference a means of reading it. "Much more is intended in the colloquy between Berkeley the arch druid and his pidgin speech and Patrick the arch priest and his Nippon English. It is also the defence and indictment of the book itself, B's theory of colours and Patrick's practical solution of the problem" (*SL* 397–98).* Despite the polarities apparent in the episode, one would be mistaken to read this letter as a linear response to an either/or question. I believe that one finds "the defence and indictment" not in the opposition of one argument to the other but in the alternating emphasis throughout the passage on contrasting temporal and spatial methods of apprehension. Taken together, space and time demonstrate Joyce's manipulation of the episode's contextual and stylistic framework to impel readers towards accommodation of diachronic and synchronic approaches.

With its opening word—"Tunc," the title given to a famous and pivotal page in *The Book of Kells*—the paragraph devoted to the druid's ideas (beginning on *FW* 611.04) announces a familiar reference point of the nodal system that Hayman has described, for it recalls the lengthy evocation of *The Book of Kells* in the Hen chapter (*FW* 119.10–123.10) which contains a lingering description of the page itself (*FW* 122.22–123.10) and the cryptic remark from the Studies chapter: "I've read your tunc's dimissage" (*FW* 298.07). In *The Book of Kells* the muddy parchment background of the page, the circuitous intertwining of text (*Tunc crucifixerant XRI cum eo duos latrones*: Then two robbers were crucified with him—Matthew 27:38) and illumination, and the traces of script which have bled through from the sheet's verso side do indeed make the message appear dim but not, for Joyce's purposes, indecipherable.

The "Tunc" page also evokes a series of images informing our perception of Balkelly that blur the pagan/Christian dichotomy suggested by his opposition to St. Patrick. As early as Campbell and Robinson's *Skeleton Key*, critics

Selected Letters of James Joyce, ed. Richard Ellmann (New York: Viking Press, 1975).

remarked on the page's illuminations, "strangely suggestive of pre-Christian and oriental symbols."[6] Earlier in *Finnegans Wake* Joyce has introduced equally ambivalent interpretations of the passage from the Gospel of St. Matthew which appears there. The drawing ending the Studies chapter on *FW* 308 mimics the chi (X) of the tunc page while blending allusions to the two thieves and the *Dio Boia*.[7] Reference called up by "Tunc" to the death of Jesus associates the druid with the Judeo-Christian tradition of the scapegoat/ sacrifice and may obliquely allude to Balkelly's impending defeat by Pad-drock. The appearance, however, of "quoniam" early in the paragraph (*FW* 611.10) mitigates the tone of defeat. The word appears on another illuminated page of *The Book of Kells* (Luke 1:1), and its brilliant decoration and position announcing a beginning again, the start of St. Luke's gospel, reminds one of the final triumph of the Resurrection.

While *The Book of Kells*, derived from pagan and Christian aspects of Irish culture, emphasizes the complexity of Balkelly's nature, the word "Tunc" also underscores the central feature of his consciousness which will inform the debate: his association with time which brings about his downfall but also suggests the process of his redemption. As his argument makes clear, the druid approaches knowledge by a procedure emphasizing diachronic perception. His method for understanding bases its authority on its assimilation of his cultural and intellectual heritage, and he claims that his ability to "absorbere" prior learning has enabled him to progress to the esoteric realms of the "numpa one puraduxed seer in seventh degree of wisdom of Entis-Onton" (*FW* 611.19–20). To illustrate the efficacy of his system, the druid presents his theory of colors, a mixture of Aristotle, Berkeley, and Kant with an adumbration of Freudian psychology. By sweeping away the "all too many much illusiones through photoprismic velamina of hueful panepiphanal world spectacurum of Lord Joss" (*FW* 611.12–14),[8] he articulates the enhanced understanding one enjoys through directing perception to the "true inwardness of reality, the Ding hvad in idself id est" (*FW* 611.21).

This impulse to ingest the wisdom of the past, however, suffers the inevitable temporal consequence, and even as Balkelly attempts an explanation of his ideas the process of entropy sets in. As the druid speaks, increasingly diminishing renderings of the phrase "hueful panepiphanal world" appears parenthetically. When Balkelly finally reaches the "sextuple gloria of light actually retained, untisintus, inside them" (*FW* 611.23–24), he has ingested all but a trace of the accidents. The husk that remains after he has drawn off the substance, "(obs of epiwo)" (*FW* 611.24), suggests the desiccation of appropriative, solipsistic learning.

Despite the firmness of the druid's conviction, as the paragraph continues the obvious flaws under which his system labors become increasingly apparent. Balkelly's example of the colors illustrates how acquisitiveness internalizes knowledge, how hoarding cuts off intellectual exchange. Growth for the druid comes only through expropriation, but because he gourmandizes without discrimination his method lacks consistency and stability. When Paddrock fails to follow the explanation, "no catch all that preachybook" (*FW* 611.25), the druid again draws on his intellectual antecedents, rephrasing his theory in a conglomeration of Latinate and Oriental-sounding phrases, "with other words verbigratiagrading from murmurulentous till stridulocelerious in a hunghoranghoangoly tsinglontseng" (*FW* 611.28–30). To bolster his theory he attempts to demonstrate its application, but he cannot contain his nationalistic description of the greenness of King Leary. As he regurgitates his argument, one internalized color spills out over everything that he sees: "verdant readyrainroof . . . spit of superexuberabundancy plenty laurel leaves . . . like thyme choppy upon parsley, alongsidethat . . . olive lentil" (*FW* 612.03–10).

The debate shifts attention to the views of Paddrock, intellectually and temperamentally in diametrical opposition to those of the druid. Paddrock bases his response to Balkelly on a rudimentary but steadfast Christian faith. This belief is founded on an instantaneous moment of illumination and summarized spatially in the opening of his paragraph, "Punc" (*FW* 612.16). While the word lacks the cultural and religious overtones associated with the druid's temporal "Tunc," it draws force from Paddrock's synchronic approach to perception. His rigid devotion to a primitive form of Christianity stands as the immoveable antithesis of Balkelly's progressive digestion of secularized philosophy.

Despite the fixity of Paddrock's faith, he does not remain static when confronted with the druid's contradictory approach to perception. Beginning aggressively by dismissing opposing views, Paddrock bends—"refrects" (*FW* 612.16): refracts, reflects—the argument of Balkelly back against him, articulating a sense of the world based on Paddrock's faith in the limitless and incomprehensible power of God. He dismisses the druid's linear, either/or view of the world—"you pore shiroskuro blackinwhitepaddynger" (*FW* 612.18)—and Balkelly's attempts to gain understanding through *a posteriori* reasoning, which he labels "apatstrophied and paralogically periparolysed" (*FW* 612.19–20), abbreviated, shrunken, and paralyzed.

Paddrock instead advocates a dogmatic ("dogmad") reliance on a garbled version of St. Augustine's doctrine of the Trinity, with the same sort of supreme confidence with which Balkelly presented his beliefs.[9] Turning from logic to iconography, he brushes aside as a pagan delusion the image of the rainbow (fundamentally evanescent in its character)—"Iro's Irismans ruinboon pot" (*FW* 612.20)—introduced by the druid to illustrate his argument. Paddrock supplants it with another analogy to outline the central mystery of his faith, the Trinity, proposing the shamrock/handkerchief, "a handcaughtscheaf of synthetic shammyrag" (*FW* 612.24–25), plucked out of the ground (and thus putatively timeless, removed from the cycle of nature) as "the sound sense sympol in a weedwayedwold of the firethere the sun in his halo cast" (*FW* 612.29–30). Unlike the time-bound druid who acquires understanding from the past over a period of time, Paddrock relies on faith, instead of comprehension, to account for a mystery which operates outside temporal bonds.

As the passage closes, however, Joyce begins to shift emphasis away from the conflicting aspects of the views of the two men and towards complementary elements, introducing hints of amalgamation into Paddrock's declamation. As Robert Boyle has observed, Paddrock derives his Triune invocation, "saving to Balenoarch (he kneeleths), to Great Balenoarch (he kneeleths down) to Greatest Great Balenoarch (he kneeleths down quitesomely)" (*FW* 612.26–29), from an inversion of an "Italian word for 'rainbow,' 'arcobaleno.' "[10] In the manifestation of the Trinity through the citation of the same sign that he had just dismissed as Balkelly's "ruinboon," Paddrock's speech moves from denunciation and towards accommodation. The accession of all to this declaration, "[e]ven to uptoputty Bilkilly-Belkelly-Balkally" (*FW* 612.32), brings in a corresponding movement on the part of the druid. The passage's conclusion, with all bathed in twin reflection of the Pascal candle and the Celtic twilight of the "good safe firelamp" [God save Ireland] (*FW* 613.01), points to a redemption of saint and sage without a resolution of their differences or an unequivocal admission of hegemony of the one over the other. This finale has for me broad implications regarding the adjustments one must make in reading the passage and by extension the entire text.

St. Patrick's method of argument can overcome the logical inconsistencies that disrupt the druid's philosophy because of Paddrock's willingness to embrace the mystery of the Trinity without possessing the ability to understand it. In this approach he avoids the obligation of accounting for any of the apparent contradictions often appearing in empirical approaches. This procedure, however, is not without its drawbacks. While freeing him from the possibility of error (at least within the boundaries of the system he has articulated), St. Patrick's approach blunts inquiry, and, in his garbled rendering of the mystery that he embraces, he conveys to others no clear sense of where he places his faith. Although the struggle ends with Paddrock's triumph by popular acclamation, the *deus ex machina* resolution of the conflict over perception remains profoundly unsatisfying for the reader. Neither the theology of the saint nor the epistemology of the sage has produced completely satisfactory systems of perception, for "the unfacts . . . are too imprecisely few to warrant our certitude" (*FW* 57.16–17).

It seems to me, however, that as Joyce incites feelings of dissatisfaction and insufficiency as the natural, initial responses to the passage, he also suggests development beyond the cause and effect thinking informing those attitudes. Balkelly and Paddrock are both readers trying to articulate and to comprehend, to the limit of their abilities, the world around them. As such they form a paradigm and a conundrum for us as readers of *Finnegans Wake*.

Their efforts present strategies for interpretation that we may accept, reject, or modify. Their articulations test the efficacy of whatever method we adopt. The "nodal system" identified by Hart and by Hayman and the intricate decoration of *The Book of Kells* emphasize expansive, cyclical perception rather than linear, restrictive progression. The approaches of Paddrock and of Balkelly illustrate the inability of the human mind to forge a single means of perception perfectly suited to all experiences, and yet each method provides limited illumination of the worlds encountered by the priest and by the druid and of the work of art that Joyce has created. Like Balkelly, the reader must "set a marge to the merge of unnotions," drawing together what we encounter in the text into a conglomerate vision based on what we have previously absorbed. At the same time we must resist the impulse towards leveling lest, like the druid, we end with a monochromatic view. Paddrock, who has been "cured by faith," provides the encouragement necessary to make the leap toward the unknowable. His example makes clear that we must give ourselves over to the mysteries of the text, experiences evoking aesthetic satisfaction while resisting intellectual comprehension. Consequently, one must reach an accommodation with apparently contradictory conceptions, for Joyce encourages the reader to follow the example of King Leary, who "has help his crewn on the burkeley buy but he has holf his crown on the Eurasian Generalissimo" (*FW* 610.11–13).

Riana O'Dwyer, examining Stefan Czarnowski's book *Le Culte des Héros et ses Conditions Sociales: Saint Patrice, Héros National de l'Irlande* (Paris: Alcan, 1919) as a source for *Finnegans Wake*, draws attention to material in Czarnowski that seems to me to inform Joyce's intentions in the passage.

> [Czarnowski] goes on to use the example of early Christian Ireland to study phenomena of hero veneration in general, and uses Saint Patrick as a particular example of how a Christian saint was absorbed into the pre-Christian social framework.[11]

Throughout the examination in *Finnegans Wake* of *The Book of Kells* (*FW* 119.10–123.10) the narrative voice repeatedly suggests the general impulse of Christian and pre-Christian cultures to merge, "those superciliouslooking crisscrossed Greek ees awkwardlike perched there and here out of date like sick owls hawked back to Athens: and the geegees too, jesuistically formed at first but afterwards genuflected aggrily toewards the occident" (*FW* 120.18–22). These references prepare for the more direct confrontation and amalgamation of the opposing societies in the Paddrock/Balkelly debate touched on in chapter three of Czarnowski's book. There he asserts that the struggle between St. Patrick and the Druids "ont l'aspect de batailles entre puissances opposées et également divines,"[12] hinting at further blurring of roles. While O'Dwyer's study emphasizes the close relationship between the figure of St. Patrick and that of HCE, broader associations also suggest themselves. In light of the proclivity of ancient Irish culture to "absorbere" the impact of St. Patrick's faith, his victory over the druid becomes less conclusive while the aim of the passage becomes clearer. The reader must initiate this process of amalgamation, not by leveling differences but by embracing them.

In *Finnegans Wake* there is no height, depth, integrity, or central reference, except as these are created through perspectives, styles, and paradigms that direct the reader in describable and always disputable ways. One cannot adjudicate between dualisms such as those presented in the confrontation of Paddrock and Balkelly because Joyce wants the reader to reflect on the futile, endless, and thus illuminating and liberating format of any dualism. His loosened languages—eclectic, idiosyncratic, dense, bizarre—show words refusing to be tamed or regulated by the semantic patterns that create such oppositions. At the same time his discourses depend heavily upon such semantic designs or restrictions to give them consequence for the reader. Thus the nodal phases of the text both assert and withdraw their own authority, by giving heights that collapse, surfaces that recede yet without yielding any essence or depth. So the nodes are not as solid, real, or comforting as we readers would like to hope.

In presenting these contrasting figures, Joyce does not articulate the hopelessness of perceiving meaning in the text. Instead he offers a paradigm that encourages us to reconcile extremes of apprehension, not in a synthetic way that erases the uniqueness of each position but in a manner that conjoins where possible and accepts with equanimity what cannot be fit into a system for understanding. It emphasizes the subjectivity of all views. "What can't be coded can be decorded if an ear aye sieze what no eye ere grieved for" (*FW* 482.34–36).

Notes

I am grateful to my colleague John Boly for his perceptive criticism during the revision of this essay.

1. David Hayman, "Nodality and the Infra-Structure of *Finnegans Wake*," *JJQ*, 16 (Fall 1978/Winter 1979), 136. See also Clive Hart, *Structure and Motif in "Finnegans Wake"* (Evanston: Northwestern Univ. Press; London: Faber and Faber, 1962).

2. Hayman indicates that he would exclude the rhetoric of the text from consideration in the system of nodes (p. 149, n.2).

3. George Otte's "Time and Space (with the emphasis on the conjunction): Joyce's Response to Lewis," *JJQ*, 22 (Spring 1985), 297–306, explores in detail the links in Joyce's works between time and space. While pointing to several examples in *Finnegans Wake*, especially in "The Mookse and the Gripes" and "The Ondt and the Gracehoper" episodes, he does not examine the confrontation of Balkelly and Paddrock. I feel, however, that time and space stand as elements informing the conjunction of the two figures, although the link to Lewis is less explicit. William F. Dohmen has also examined the Joyce-Lewis relationship in detail in his " 'Chilly Spaces': Wyndham Lewis as Ondt," *JJQ*, 11 (Summer 1974), 368–86.

4.   Weldon Thornton, *Allusions in "Ulysses": A Line-by-Line Reference to Joyce's Complex Symbolism* (1968; rpt. New York: Touchstone, 1973), pp. 41–42. Don Gifford with Robert J. Seidman, *Notes for Joyce: An Annotation of James Joyce's "Ulysses"* (New York: E. P. Dutton, 1974), pp. 32–33.

5.   Pierre Vitoux, "Aristotle, Berkeley, and Newman [sic] in 'Proteus' and *Finnegans Wake*," *JJQ*, 18 (Winter 1981), 161–75, discusses Joyce's amalgamation of Berkeley's theories of perception with those of Aristotle. William T. Noon, S. J., in his *Joyce and Aquinas* (New Haven: Yale Univ. Press; London: Oxford Univ. Press, 1957), pp. 113–14, also takes up Berkeley's influence on Stephen's consciousness.

6.   Joseph Campbell and Henry Morton Robinson, *A Skeleton Key to "Finnegans Wake"* (1944; rpt. New York: Viking, 1973), p. 103.

7.   For a discussion of this see Robert Boyle's *James Joyce's Pauline Vision: A Catholic Exposition* (Carbondale: Southern Illinois Univ. Press, 1978), p. 41.

8.   Vitoux, in his essay holds that "if we overlook the un-Berkeleyan emphasis on the 'illusory' character of perception, [the allusion] is not inconsistent with Berkeley's concept of 'signs on a veil' " (170). He goes on to point out that the passage borrows even more from Newton's *Opticks* and from his theory of light and colors. My point is that this is exactly Joyce's intention, to blend apparently conflicting views into a single perception, to give up the pursuit of certitude. Vitoux's examination of the Paddrock and Balkelly seems to me quite perceptive, but I differ with him in the emphasis he gives to reconciling the picture of Balkelly with the concepts of Bishop Berkeley (170–74).

9.   For a full discussion of Patrick's corruption of St. Augustine's teachings and of Joyce's application of the doctrine of the Trinity, see Robert Boyle's "Worshipper of the Word: James Joyce and the Trinity" in *A Starchamber Quiry: A James Joyce Centennial Volume, 1882–1982*, ed. E. L. Epstein (New York and London: Methuen, 1982), pp. 109–51.

10.   Boyle, "Worshipper of the Word," p. 116.

11.   Riana O'Dwyer, "Czarnowski and *Finnegans Wake*: A Study of the Cult of the Hero," *JJQ*, 17 (Spring 1980), 282.

12.   Quoted by O'Dwyer in "Czarnowski and *Finnegans Wake*," p. 283.

The Last Epistle of *Finnegans Wake*

PATRICK A. MCCARTHY

One of the commonplaces of *Finnegans Wake* criticism is that the mysterious letter retrieved from the midden heap represents the book itself, so that the characters' various attempts to decipher the document constitute a self-reflexive commentary on the reader's encounter with the *Wake*. This might seem to give the letter passages a centrality not enjoyed by other parts of *Finnegans Wake*, granting them a privileged status as a key to the book's core meaning, and perhaps in some respects it is true that the discussions of the letter are crucial to our understanding of how the *Wake* operates. Working against the reader's expectation that the letter contains definitive answers to the meaning of *Finnegans Wake*, however, are these factors: 1) No two versions of the document are identical, although they typically include variations on such familiar phrases as "a born gentleman" and "for Father Michael." 2) Even within a single version of the letter, the ambiguity of the language often undermines the writer's apparent intention, so that what seems to be meant as a defense against baseless charges becomes instead an accusation. 3) The narrator's attention is constantly diverted from the epistolary text to the envelope, the handwriting, and other aspects of the letter's existence as a physical artifact. 4) Likewise, it is difficult to separate the text of the manuscript itself from the commentaries that spring up around it, yet the narrator-interpreter's attempts to pinpoint the meaning of the letter tell us more about the human tendency to embrace reductive interpretations than they reveal about the letter. (The same tendency might be seen in the catalogue of titles at the outset of I.5 [Book I, Chapter 5]: each title encapsulates some perspective on the letter, and none seems satisfactory because the letter itself can no more be reduced to a single name than to a single level of meaning.) 5) The damage sustained by the letter in the course of its burial and resurrection (not to mention the teastain, the holes made by the professor's breakfast fork, etc.) makes it difficult to reconstruct the original text. Finally, 6) even the letter's authorship is in doubt, although it is normally attributed either to Shem or to ALP.

The longest version of the letter, which runs for more than four pages

Reprinted from the *James Joyce Quarterly* 27 (Summer 1990):725–33. Reprinted by permission of the *James Joyce Quarterly*, University of Tulsa.

(*FW* 615.12–619.19), is reserved for last. Phillip Herring has called this rendition of the letter "as close to the original letter in prehenscratch and preteastain condition as we are ever likely to get," adding that "What Joyce intended here was presumably to draft the letter as a document to which he could frequently refer, but to keep it hidden until Book Four, a strategy of absence guaranteed to heighten reader interest."[1] This view of the letter, which assumes that it is an actual document that is first presented to us in truncated and distorted form and then finally revealed in its entirety with relatively little distortion, is one way of looking at the last epistle of the *Wake*, but it is equally reasonable to suppose that the form of the letter that we see in Book IV is an expanded text, a rebuttal to an earlier document, or perhaps a sanitized revision of the letter designed to replace the more incriminating statements that we have already encountered. My own supposition is that no single account of the letter is more accurate than any other, because there is no evidence that the letter exists as a single real document to which a textual editor—a fictional Gabler or Kidd, let us say—might appeal for authority.

One of the oddities of this "final" draft is that it both contains material that is not present in other appearances of the letter and omits motifs that we find elsewhere. The great bulk of its text, in fact, consists of language that does not echo other soundings of the letter. Much of this language, and almost none of the more familiar letter motifs, appears in an early draft of the letter that Joyce composed around the end of 1923, apparently intending to insert it after I.4; only in 1938 did Joyce move an expanded version of this text to Book IV.[2] Thus, a great deal of the material that Joyce used in his earliest draft of the letter comes, in the published text of *Finnegans Wake*, to be associated only with the final edition of ALP's mamafesta, where it forces us to reconsider events from a new perspective. In the first paragraph of this version (*FW* 615.12–616.19), for instance, only the salutation, the repetition of "well," and the Magrath references are clear indications of material associated elsewhere with the letter; on the other hand, phrases like "these secret workings of natures," "so denighted of this lights time," "a twohangled warpon," and "the man what never put a dramn in the swags but milk from a national cowse" (*FW* 615.14–27)—not to mention the various song references and allusions to "Goldilocks and the Three Bears," "Jack and the Beanstalk," and "Sleeping Beauty"—are new additions to the letter motif.

This newly introduced material could, of course, be interpreted as something that has been there all along but has been suppressed by the censoring function of the dreaming mind. If that is so, however, we need to ask why the dreamer's mind has been censoring language that generally praises him and condemns his detractors. A more difficult question to answer is why, if this is the definitive text of the letter, it fails to include familiar phrases from the account of the letter in I.5. One such phrase is "all she wants," which is first compressed into "All schwants (schwrites) ischt tell the cock's trootabout him" (*FW* 113.11–12) and is later transformed into "All we wants is to get peace for possession" (*FW* 378.21–22). Likewise, the apparently significant phrase "the hate turned the mild" (*FW* 111.11–12), which refers simultaneously to the hot weather turning mild (but not before it has "turned," i.e., spoiled, the milk) and to the lessening of hatred, disappears after its statement on *FW* 111, although there is a distant echo at *FW* 116.23. If we expect the ambiguities of this statement to be cleared up in Book IV, we are disappointed by the absence of any reference to it, unless we want to connect the soured milk of *FW* 111 with the "milk from a national cowse" (*FW* 615.27). Nor are these the more significant omissions from the final statement, since variations on such phrases as "fondest love" (*FW* 111.17, 458.02, 489.11, 601.02), "Stop. Please stop" (*FW* 18.17–18, 124.04–05, 232.18–19, 272.09–14, 367.05–06, 379.05–06, 421.13–14, 560.16–17, 609.06–08), and "Well, how are you?" (*FW* 111.16, 280.13–14, 364.12) surface frequently in passages associated directly or implicitly with the letter, yet none of these motifs is to be found in the letter's ultimate text.

Among other elements omitted from the letter draft on *FW* 615–19 are aspects of the physical description of the letter. The use of four ampersands in the letter draft on *FW* 111.05–24 is striking precisely because these are the only ampersands in *Finnegans Wake*, if the *Concordance* can be trusted on this point.[3] Are these merely abbreviations for the conjunction which is spelled out in full in the complete, definitive letter? Hardly, for the commentator in I.5 gushes about the beauty of "the four shortened ampersands under which we can glypse at and feel for ourselves across all those rushyears the warm soft short pants of the quickscribbler" (*FW* 121.36–122.03). Likewise, the teastain specified at *FW* 111.20 (and alluded to elsewhere—28.28–29, 112.30, 369.32) is missing in Book IV, although we might account for this by supposing that we have here only the text of the letter, not a description of the manuscript's condition. If that assumption explains the absence of the stain, it is much more difficult to rationalize the omission of the four X's that represent kisses in the conclusion to most variants of the letter (*FW* 11.27, 111.17, 424.13, 458.03; cf. 19.20, 42.08–09, 114.11, 172.08–10, 280.27, 625.02). These "crosskisses" (*FW* 111.17), which resemble the four X's at the end of Martha Clifford's letter in *Ulysses*, certainly appear to be a reliable part of earlier forms of the letter which stress the written quality of the missive; since X is the siglum for the Four Old Men, the frequent recurrence of the four X's might also signal the presence of the Four, either as master annalists who are responsible for an edition of the letter or as scholarly commentators on the text of the document. On one level, then, omitting the X's from the final letter removes it from the domain of the historians who are last seen less than a page before the letter begins, where they are described as "the 'Mamma Lujah' known to every schoolboy scandaller, be he Matty, Marky, Lukey or John-a-Donk" (*FW* 614.28–30); on another level, the deletion of the kisses helps to change the tone of the letter from one of intimacy to the public letter in defense of Earwicker that it becomes in Book IV.

It is perhaps in its transformation of motifs directly associated with the letter that the final version most clearly reveals its character. Take, for example, Maggy, who in her multiple incarnation as the Maggies is, I assume, associated with the "jinnies" of the Willingdone episode. In the statement of the letter on *FW* 111, Maggy is the recipient of the correspondence, although she might also be its subject, since the letter begins "Dear whom it proceded to mention Maggy well & allathome's health well" (*FW* 111.10–11). Maggy is also a variant on Madge, Issy's mirror image (*FW* 459.04), and in II.2 one of Issy's footnotes takes the form of a message to Maggy, her other self (*FW* 273.n.6). That the letter addressed to or concerning Maggy is generally associated with Earwicker's guilt seems reasonable since the *Wake's* earliest reference to Maggy comes in an allusion to the Phoenix Park incident: HCE is buried "by the mund of the magazine wall, where our maggy seen all, with her sisterin shawl" (*FW* 7.31–32). Maggy also has a sexual significance in her role as Margareen, the object of the boys' romantic interests in the Burrus-Caseous episode (*FW* 161–67).

One of the Maggy references in the final version of the letter comes just after a denunciation of the Magraths: "If we were to tick off all that cafflers head, whisperers for his accomodation, the me craws, namely, and their bacon what harmed butter! It's margarseen oil. Thinthin thinthin" (*FW* 615.29–32). I have trouble with the literal sense of "bacon what harmed butter," which evolved from such earlier drafts as "and his bacon not fit to look at never mind butter" and "their bacon what priced butter,"[4] although if Glasheen and Cheng are correct in associating the bacon here with Francis Bacon, supposed author of Shakespeare's plays, the butter may represent Brutus (as in the Burrus and Caseous story), and the charge may be that Bacon let Brutus come to harm in "his" play, *Julius Caesar*.[5] Margareen is present here, and the dairy theme, which begins a few lines earlier with the reference to "milk from a national cowse," seems to lead from butter to butter-substitute (margarine), which will keep us "thinthin thinthin." Yet the more significant overtone here is undoubtedly the echo of "maggy seen all" and other variants on the Magazine Wall references, which often accompany the sort of repeated syllable that we see here. (See, for example, *FW* 13.14–16: "By the mausolime wall. Fimfim fimfim. With a grand funferall. Fumfum fumfum.")

The overtones of "It's margarseen oil. Thinthin thinthin," therefore, suggest the Park incident in two different ways: by recalling the story directly through the references to Maggy and the Magazine Wall and by hinting at the sons' overthrow of the father through the allusion to the Burrus-Caseous-Margareen incident. Yet the Park references are sufficiently obscured to protect Earwicker from confronting an accusation which, in any event, is directed against his enemies. The other Maggy references in the letter and its immediate vicinity are even more innocuous. For instance, a few lines before the opening of the letter, in a parody of the Quinet sentence, Maggy is given her formal designation as "Margaret" (*FW* 615.03), a name that most certainly does not equate with "the social revolution," as we were assured in I.5 (*FW* 116.08), since the flower imagery in the passage hints that French *marguerite*: daisy is intended. Daisy is in fact a common nickname for English girls named Margaret, according to the *OED*, and the traditional use of the daisy as an emblem of "innocence and purity"[6] makes the designation "Margaret" in the letter seem chaste enough, and unthreatening. The context of the passage focuses on the disintegration and recombination of elements in the cyclic dream—"Our wholemole millwheeling vicociclometer" in which "heroticisms, catastrophes and eccentricities [are] transmitted by the ancient legacy of the past, type by tope, letter from litter, word at ward, with sendence of sundance" (*FW* 614.27–615.02). Insofar as this refers to the construction of the letter out of litter, it suggests that ALP ("the *a*ncient *l*egacy of the *p*ast") picks up the pieces of HCE ("*h*eroticisms, *c*atastrophes and *e*ccentricities") and restores his reputation through the letter.

The third "Maggy" reference occurs in the salutation to the letter: "Dear. And we go on to Dirtdump. Reverend. May we add majesty?" (*FW* 615.12–13). In I.5 the commentator hazards the opinion that "Maggy's tea" translates into "your majesty" (*FW* 116.24), a suggestion that would be more persuasive if the phrase "Maggy's tea" actually appeared in any version of the letter that we see. This apparently is the way "majesty" comes to be part of the salutation—through the interpreter's attempt to account for "Maggy's tea," presumably the combination of Maggy and the incriminating teastain. If the conjunction of a Boston address and a teastain on *FW* 111 adds up to a reference to the Boston Tea Party, as has been supposed, then "the general's elections" (*FW* 111.12) gives us the aftermath to the American Revolution, the election of the general, George Washington.[7] The antiroyalist sentiment implied in the early statement of the letter is then countered by the conservatism of the last epistle's address to "Dear . . . Reverend . . . majesty," a salutation that incorporates both church and state and may indicate that the letter is really addressed to God, or at least to a divinely appointed king. (This interpretation is quickly reinforced by the parenthetical remark, "thanks ever for it, we humbly pray"—*FW* 615.14–15.) The appeal, in any event, is to higher authority, the friendly Maggy of the original letter having been transformed into the force which ALP hopes will restore her husband's reputation.

Remembering that "majesty" entered the letter motif through a scholar's attempt to decipher the meaning of "maggy's tea," however, we might also note that the letter's saluation in Book IV indicates the extent to which the document appears to have been altered by commentary on it.

Another phrase comes directly out of the historical discussion of the letter's origins: the scholar's phrase "About that original hen" (*FW* 110.22), used in I.5 as part of the introduction to the text of the letter, becomes in Book IV an integral part of the letter itself—"About that coerogenal hun and his knowing the size of an eggcup" (*FW* 616.20–21).[8] Both in I.5 and in IV the phrase begins a paragraph, indicating a change of direction: in I.5 the discussion shifts to the actual discovery of the letter, and in IV a paragraph that praises Earwicker is succeeded by one that inadvertently opens up his scandalous past. The chicken has switched sexes, changing from a *hen* to a *Hahn* (German for rooster), and it is Earwicker himself rather than Biddy who is described here, but the fact that he is identified as a Hun—a "coerogenal" one at that—lends credence to the rumors of his misconduct. The overtone of "Original Sin" might suggest that the problems discussed in the letter can all be traced back to a specific source, but the phrase also undermines the search for origins through its oblique reference to the problem of whether the chicken or the egg came first.

Having entered the letter through the commentary on it, the "original hen" motif becomes transformed once again into an "urogynal pan of cakes" (*FW* 619.02), the hen who found the document having become intertwined with the "wedding cakes" mentioned in it (*FW* 111.14; cf. 11.23–24, 116.09, 116.21–22, 131.14–15, 279.n.1, 280.15–16, 365.02, 619.24). The whole sentence in which the original hen makes her final appearance in the letter is a marvelous example of language operating at cross-purposes: "While for whoever likes that urogynal pan of cakes one apiece it is thanks, beloved, to Adam, our former first Finnlatter and our grocerest churcher, as per Grippiths' varuations, for his beautiful crossmess parzel" (*FW* 619.02–05). On the surface, this seems to be little more than a note thanking Adam Findlater, grocer and churchgoer, for supplying the cake and dividing it up; sharp-eyed readers might also note that the purported date of the letter, given as "the last of the first" (i.e., 31 January—*FW* 111.10), has been converted into an attribute of our hero, "our former first Finnlatter." Former and latter make Finn comprehend all times within the cyclic dream, and as Adam he is also Everyman.

What seems to me most obvious about the passage, however, is its declaration of the *felix culpa* theme: ALP thanks Adam for the "urogynal pan of cakes"—Original Sin—that leads to the "beautiful crossmess parzel," a Christmas parcel in the form of Christ as redeemer. Typically, all allusions to Earwicker's crime in the final statement of the letter are essentially favorable, a matter either of shifting the blame to someone else or of suggesting a compensating factor. Here, the sin is specifically associated with women's urine ("urogynal"), which connects the passage to the teastain on the earlier letter and also to the suggestive "P.S." of this version (*FW* 619.17; cf. "pee ess"—*FW* 111.18). As urine is a fertility symbol in the *Wake*, the "urogynal pan of cakes" leads to the birth of the Christmas baby; on another level, the sin in the park generates the letter, a "crossmess parzel" whose apparently chaotic form defies our attempts to decipher it by providing the sort of exact equivalents called for by a crossword puzzle.

Although the letter briefly concludes with the signature "Alma Luvia, Pollabella" (FW 619.16), there is also a brief postscript in which Issy, the "wee one" (FW 619.15) referred to at the end of the letter proper, becomes "Soldier Rollo's sweetheart" (FW 619.17). Whether ALP adds the postscript to her own letter or Issy scribbles the note at the bottom in the manner of her footnotes in II.2, the P.S. announces a change of tone that will carry over to the final monologue: fed up and worn out, ALP is "still her deckhuman amber too" (FW 619.19), a phrase that suggests not only continuity but also rebirth, since Decuma, one of the Roman Fates, was associated with birth.[9] In connection with the letter motif, the most important overtone here may be "Document No. 2," which signifies not only de Valera's alternative to the 1922 treaty of partition but an alternate form of the letter, one that blames Earwicker rather than excusing him. In III.4 (FW 588.21–25), numbers one and two are both alternative letters or treaties and also the two girls in the park, and in that passage number two is explicitly associated with Issy. I assume that the association carries over into the postscript to ALP's letter, and that "she's still her deckhuman amber too" indicates that the youthful form of ALP is still inside her, waiting to be reborn as the book recycles back to its inception.[10] The dominant tone of the postscript, however, is one of resignation (and, to the extent that Issy and ALP are the same person at different phases, self-absorption) rather than the indignation and amazement that characterized much of the letter itself; and this change of tone carries over to the final monologue.

That monologue, a welter of words, soon buries the letter and its contents, which will be exhumed for our inspection as Biddy, or perhaps Kevin, will once again unearth the document. Scholars inside and outside Finnegans Wake will examine it closely, analyzing it from various angles, as I have done here. While other issues might abide our question, however, the letter is free—that is, irreducible to a consistent level of meaning, or even to a definitive text. In this, as in other respects, it is a model of the mysterious, compelling, kaleidoscopic work of which it is a microcosm.

Notes

1. Phillip F. Herring, Joyce's Uncertainty Principle (Princeton: Princeton Univ. Press, 1987), p. 201.
2. David Hayman, ed., A First-Draft Version of "Finnegans Wake" (London: Faber and Faber, 1963), pp. 24, 81–83, 281–84, 293–94, 329.
3. Clive Hart, A Concordance to "Finnegans Wake" (Minneapolis: Univ. of Minnesota Press, 1963), p. 344.
4. Hayman, pp. 81, 282.

5. Adaline Glasheen, *Third Census of "Finnegans Wake"* (Berkeley: Univ. of California Press, 1977), pp. 21–22; Vincent John Cheng, *Shakespeare and Joyce: A Study of "Finnegans Wake"* (University Park: Pennsylvania State Univ. Press, 1984), p. 190. The food references here—bacon, butter, and margarine, and possibly ham in "harmed"—make sense in the dream logic of *Finnegans Wake*, since the Shaunish Professor Prenderguest stood accused of damaging the letter by trying to read it at breakfast (*FW* 124.08–12) and since the final version of the letter is written on eggshells (*FW* 615.10). The egg theme is also relevant because, as Mink notes, "The crash (Fimfim Fimfim, etc) which usually appears with refs to the Magazine Wall is the fall of Humpty Dumpty and of HCE." Louis O. Mink, *A "Finnegans Wake" Gazetteer* (Bloomington: Indiana Univ. Press, 1978), p. 394. On "Shakespearean Breakfasts" in the *Wake*, see Cheng, pp. 101–06.

6. J. C. Cooper, *An Illustrated Encyclopaedia of Traditional Symbols* (London: Thames and Hudson, 1978), p. 49.

7. Bernard Benstock, "Concerning Lost Historeve," in *A Conceptual Guide to "Finnegans Wake,"* ed. Michael H. Begnal and Fritz Senn (University Park: Pennsylvania State Univ. Press, 1974), p. 38. The presence of George Washington in the letter might also be inferred from one of the proposed titles to the mamafesta: *"As Tree is Quick and Stone is White So is My Washing Done by Night"* (*FW* 106.36–107.01).

8. For another element of the letter's text that appears to be derived from earlier commentaries on the letter, compare "Impossible to remember persons in improbable to forget position places" (*FW* 617.08–09) with the treatment of the (im)possible and (im)probable at *FW* 110.11ff. The manner in which the letter is changed by commentary on it is consistent with Susan Sontag's observation that "Interpretation is a radical strategy for conserving an old text, which is thought too precious to repudiate, by revamping it. The interpreter, without actually erasing or rewriting the text, *is* altering it. But he can't admit to doing this. He claims only to be making it intelligible, by disclosing its true meaning." *Against Interpretation and Other Essays* (New York: Dell, 1981), p. 6.

9. Manfred Lurker, *Dictionary of Gods and Goddesses, Devils and Demons* (London: Routledge and Kegan Paul, 1987), p. 275.

10. See also John Gordon's observation that " 'Document number two,' apart from being a phrase from Irish history, describes the *Wake* when in a few pages we will commence a second reading of it—another document altogether." *"Finnegans Wake": A Plot Summary* (Syracuse: Syracuse Univ. Press, 1986), p. 273.

MEANDERTHALLTALE:
DREAM AND STRUCTURE
IN THE *WAKE*

◆

L. Boom as Dreamer in *Finnegans Wake*

BERNARD BENSTOCK

It has taken a relatively short time for critics to become convinced of the basic continuity of James Joyce's entire body of work, despite Joyce's own protestations while in the process of creation that he had forgotten each previous effort in favor of the one in progress. While concerned with Leopold Bloom, Joyce impatiently asserted that "Stephen no longer interests me. He has a shape that can't be changed," and when writing *Finnegans Wake*, he contemptuously shrugged off *Ulysses*: "*Ulysses!* Who wrote it? I've forgotten it."[1] It was imperative for him as an artist to concentrate on his new effort, and since he acted as his own publicity agent, it was necessary for him to call attention to it; but a retrospective appraisal should take note of the manner in which each work overlaps with one another: the child in the first three stories of *Dubliners* is very much the child Stephen in the first chapter of *A Portrait of the Artist*, Richard Rowan in *Exiles* is a projected image of the mature Stephen, and Shem the Penman is a caricature of both. *Finnegans Wake* in fact is a summation of all that Joyce had previously written: it recapitulates themes and motifs, reworks many of the same characters, and puns every previous Joyce title into its fabric. The Dreamer in the *Wake* is more than just a single individual, even if one assumes that on the literal level we are viewing the dream of publican H. C. Earwicker.

When Leopold and Molly Bloom fall asleep head-to-foot toward dawn on 17 June 1904, they form a circular pattern of the combined unconscious of Everyman and the Eternal Woman, containing the residue of the collective unconscious of the race of mankind. From the self-interrogation of Bloom in the penultimate chapter to the night-thoughts of Molly in the ultimate one, there exists a single logical step into the dream technique of the *Wake*. We had previously witnessed the non-naturalistic way in which Stephen and Bloom shared a mutual hallucination in the Circe phantasmagoria, and there is little difficulty then in accepting the composite form that the night's dream would take. The general confusion of that dream is precisely anchored in the particulars of the *Ulysses* day, which in turn had been based upon the "nightmare of history" which it culminated. Even within *Ulysses* itself a

Reprinted by permission of the Modern Language Association of America from *PMLA* 82 (March 1967):91–97.

projection into the future takes place to anticipate the *Wake* dream: when Stephen meets the friendless, jobless, homeless Corley (himself an extension of the Corley of "Two Gallants"), when Molly conjures up a scholarly Stephen as her future lover, but most important when Bloom reads about his day in the evening newspaper at the cabman's shelter. Staring back at him from the *Evening Telegraph* is the spectre of *"L. Boom"* (*U*, p. 609),[2] and he winces at the typographical error that has metamorphosed him. Both Bloom and Stephen had had dreams the night before, dreams that they see being reenacted, verified, and explicated by the day's events, while Molly had laid out the cards that morning in her forecast of the future. Several years earlier, in *A Portrait*, Stephen had watched the birds from the steps of the National Library and wondered about what they augured. Those birds have now come back to roost, as all past leads into future (and back again), all of Joyce's books moving toward the compilation and new prophecy of *Finnegans Wake*.

The prophetic newspaper provides a valid link into the larger pattern of Joyce's canon: not only does Bloom find himself distorted into "Boom," and not only is the mysterious man in the macintosh coat listed as *"M'Intosh"* (*U*, p. 609), but Stephen and McCoy are included, McCoy by dint of Bloom's courtesy, although neither was at the funeral. Stephen Dedalus, B.A., was of course absent from the interment of Paddy Dignam, having been noticed by Bloom from the funeral carriage. When Simon Dedalus' attention is called to his son, he assumes that Stephen had been at his aunt Sally's, but Stephen had not been there either: having conjectured about what would happen during a visit there, he settles for the hypothetical in lieu of the actual event and passes the house without stopping. The elusive Stephen Dedalus is a multiple projection of the tangible Stephen Dedalus: he is reported to be where he never is; he is on his way to avoid a scheduled appointment with Mulligan; and he is seen by others when unaware that they are observing him. Like Spencer Brydon of Henry James's "The Jolly Corner," or like Ebenezer Scrooge, he is being presented with alternate images of himself, should he be willing to read the writing on the wall. The priest who emerged from the sea in the first chapter of *Ulysses*, a substitute for the drowned man whose body is expected to wash ashore, is just that sort of image of the hydrophobe Stephen (who has not bathed in eight months) had he become the Reverend Stephen Dedalus S. J. that he envisioned in *A Portrait*. In *Exiles* a newspaper is brought to Rowan for him to read an article about his return to Ireland (*his* emergence on Irish land from the sea). Sporting a Joycean sense of whimsy, he pretends to mistake another headline for his story: "Death of the Very Reverend Canon Mulhall" (*E*, p.99).[3] "Is that it?" he asks, and in an odd and oblique way it is. The death of the Reverend James Flynn in "The Sisters" had been an important event to the sensitive boy who narrates the story: Father Flynn had hoped that the boy would follow him into the priesthood, but with the circumstances of his death came disillusionment, the death of the boy's interest in a clerical vocation.

In *Ulysses* the newspaper obituary plays an important role: Bloom notices that an advertisement for *"Plumtree's Potted Meat"* (*U*, p. 67) has been placed beneath the obituary column of the *Freeman's Journal*. At Dignam's funeral he muses that a corpse is "Ordinary meat" for rats, "meat gone bad" (*U*, p. 106). When he uses his newspaper to hide his letter-writing to Martha in the Ormond bar, his eye is again caught by the obituaries: "Callan, Coleman, Dignam" (*U*, p. 265). Explaining to Richie Goulding that he is just answering an ad, he pretends to address his letter to "Messrs Callan, Coleman and Co, limited" (*U*, p. 266). This is his letter to the dead, a love letter from which no live issue will ensue, written at the precise moment of Boylan's arrival at the Bloom house for the seduction of Molly, a much livelier affair. An hour later, the Citizen reads the list of names in the births, marriages, and deaths columns of the *Irish Independent*, inadvertently summarizing past, present, and future, the continuum of time in Joyce's works.

Just as the paper records Bloom's day in *Ulysses*, its counterpart sums up Earwicker's dream in the *Wake*. Newspapers had played their role throughout the dream, but the most important instance occurs in the dawn scene of the last chapter, which opens with the reports of seven news agencies ("Tass, Patt, Staff, Woff, Havv, Bluvv and Rutter"—*FW*, p. 593.6),[4] where the "Durban Gazette" (*FW*, p. 602.20) offers a spate of headlines for its lead story:

> From a collispendent. Any were. Deemsday. Bosse of Upper and Lower Byggotstrade, Ciwareke, may he live for river! The Games funeral at Valleytemple. Saturnights pomps, exhabiting that corricatore of a harss, revealled by Oscur Camerad. The last of Dutch Schulds, perhumps. Pipe in Dream Cluse. Uncovers Pub History. The Outrage, at Length. Affected Mob Follows in Religious Sullivence. Rinvention of vestiges by which they drugged the buddhy. Moviefigure on in scenic section. By Patathicus.
>
> (*FW*, p. 602.20–27)

These are the headlines and credits of the story (a technique of condensation familiar to the reader of the Aeolus chapter of *Ulysses*), and in themselves they contain the germ of the guilty dream. The story that follows dissolves into a cinematic narrative, a Pathé newsreel (*Movie-figure on in scenic section. By Patathicus*) which veers off subject to present a deceptive scene of the household at its tranquil breakfast. But the menacing headlines tell a different tale: the great man has fallen (*Bosse* stands for God, as witness "gosse and bosse"—*FW*, p. 325.16—Son and Father, since *gosse* is French argot for "brat"—and *Father and Son* was "fathered" by Edmund Gosse). The fallen titan is Earwicker (anagrammed *Ciwareke*), and the funeral games are in progress, suggesting the burial of the hero in the *Iliad*. These Games appear at various times: in the Tavern scene we are told that the *Boston Evening Transcript* will carry the story ("A trancedone boyscript with tittivits by.

Ahem. You'll read it tomorrow, marn, when the curds on the table"—*FW*,
p. 374.3–5), but the final defeat is recorded in the "Tara Tribune" (*FW*, p.
375.24) and sounds like a radio broadcast: "Good for you, Richmond Rover!
Scrum around, our side! Let him have another between the spindlers! A
grand game! Dalymount's decisive" (*FW*, p. 375.21–23).[5] Humpbacked
Earwicker is again being trounced by his enemies, in this case Richmond,
the overthrower of humpbacked Richard III. In the *Durban Gazette* headlines
the "outrage" of Earwicker's indiscretion in the park is being revealed by the
soldiers, personified in *Oscur Camerad*, the newspaper photographer who
records the dark deed. In this account the crime is public exposure (*exhabiting
the corricatore of a harss*); since Earwicker is God, he is exposing his backside
to Moses (as in Exodus xxxiii.23). The guilty publican dreams of his demise
as the gangland slaying of an underworld overlord, *Dutch Schulds—schuld* is
Dutch for guilt.

Earwicker's guilt, like Bloom's, is essentially sexual, and it is the
persistence of this unhappy fault that is presented in the conscious mind of
the daytime Odysseus and the nighttime God-Adam-Caesar-Richard III figure. The Thursday that was 16 June 1904, the *Ulysses* day, haunts the
Dreamer's mind as he frets about "that tragoady thundersday this municipal
sin business" (*FW*, p. 5.13–14), "a trying thirstay mournin" (*FW*, p. 6.14).
The evidence supports the contention of Clive Hart that the dream takes
place on a Friday night,[6] and that the sinful event took place on the previous
day, a Thursday like Bloom's. Yet Bloom's Thursday was a remarkably
uneventful one, giving rise to the popular characterization of *Ulysses* as the
depiction of an ordinary day in the life of an ordinary man. Bloom does not
see himself as being quite so run-of-the-mill, however, and for him the
events of 16 June 1904 are highly charged. Yet from our objective viewpoint
the typical bourgeois can be seen at his typically bourgeois occupation, and
in the *Wake* we find an appropriate catalogue of the monotony of just such
a day: "business, reading newspaper, smoking cigar, arranging tumblers
on table, eating meals, pleasure, etcetera, etcetera, pleasure, eating meals,
arranging tumblers on table, smoking cigar, reading newspaper, business;
minerals, wash and brush up, local views, juju toffee, comic and birthdays
cards; those were the days and he was their hero" (*FW*, p. 127.20–25).[7]
Even more germane to Bloom's condition is the riddle which asks:

if a human being duly fatigued by his dayety in the sooty, having plenxty
off time on his gouty hands and vacants of space at his sleepish feet and as
hapless behind the dreams of accuracy as any camelot prince of dinmurk,
were at this auctual futule preteriting unstant, in the states of suspensive
exanimation, accorded, throughout the eye of a noodle, with an ear-sighted
view of old hopeinhaven with all the ingredient and egregiunt whights and
ways to which in the curse of his persistence the course of his tory will had
been having recourses . . . whiles even led comesilencers to comeliewithhers

and till intempestuous Nox should catch the gallicry and spot lucan's dawn
. . . then *what* would that fargazer seem to seemself to seem seeming of,
dimm it all?

(*FW*, p. 143.4–27)

Here is Bloom, fatigued from his day in the city, asleep at Molly's feet, from
night until dawn dreaming the dream of the *fargazer*, back into his past (and
particularly that previous day) and forward into the future. What the stars
hold in store for him had been of concern to him just an hour before going
to bed, when he mused over "the monthly recurrence known as the new
moon with the old moon in her arms: the posited influence of celestial on
human bodies: the appearance of a star (1st magnitude) of exceeding brilliancy
dominating by night and day," and so forth (*U*, p. 661), while the *Wake*
Dreamer, before being cautioned to "steep wall!" (*FW*, p. 26.24)—sleep
well!—notes: "Your heart is in the system of the Shewolf and your crested
head is in the tropic of Copricapron. Your feet are in the cloister of Virgo.
Your olala is in the region of sahuls. And that's ashore as you were born"
(*FW*, p. 26.11–14).

Yet what exactly troubles Bloom's sleep? We know what troubles Earwicker: his nocturnal encounter in Phoenix Park with two maids was witnessed by three soldiers, and he assumes that the incident is being gossiped
about after his accidental confession-denial to the Cad. But Bloom has committed no great offense and has no reason to believe that he is the subject of
any really malicious rumors. He had served his wife breakfast in bed, been
to Paddy Dignam's funeral, scurried about for an advertisement in his occupational capacity, played the good samaritan in aiding Paddy's orphans, had
an unpleasant argument with the Citizen, visited the maternity hospital for
news of Mina Purefoy's delivery, saved Stephen from several difficulties and
taken him home for cocoa. Of these only the encounter with the Citizen
bothers him: he gives Stephen a self-inflating version of it and completely
avoids mentioning it to Molly. It plays its part, however, in the dream,
paralleling Earwicker's conversation with the Cad. The "midwesterner" who
shouted abuse at Earwicker and "drunkishly pegged a few glatt stones, all
of a size, by way of final mocks for his grapes, at the wicket in support of
his words" (*FW*, p. 72.26–28) is the Citizen who hurled the biscuit tin
"like a shot off a shovel" (*U*, p. 329) at Bloom, so that Ulysses-Noman and
Polyphemus are labeled "nobodyatall with Wholyphamous" (*FW*, p. 73.9).[8]

Far more traumatic for Bloom are the sexual activities of the day, limited
as they were. He received a letter from Martha Clifford and answered by
return mail in perpetuation of his semi-sordid correspondence, which developed from the advertisement he had placed. The letters and the advertisement
figure importantly by day and by night. The letter, in fact, is a major motif
in *Finnegans Wake*, assuming historical and archetypal levels of significance,
finally emerging as the Woman's vindication of the Man. Martha's letter,

however, merely excites, embarrasses, and frightens poor Bloom. Her grammatical errors ("my patience are exhausted"—*U*, p. 70—and "I have never felt myself so much drawn to a man as you") and her slip-of-the-hand ("I do not like that other world"—*U*, p. 70) constantly grate against Bloom's sensibilities, reminding him how tawdry his pen-pal affair actually is. During the initial proliferation of the gossip concerning Earwicker's crime, we find: "the small p.s. ex-ex-executive capahand in their sad rear like a lady's postscript: I want money. Pleasend" (*FW*, p. 42.8–10)—Bloom had gratuitously sent Martha a money order with his reply—the guilty stammer creates an elision between the P.S. and the X's at the bottom of a letter into SEX. Bloom, alias Henry Flower, gave the Westland Row post office as his mailing address, so that it is not surprising when the letter in the *Wake* goes undelivered, having been stamped: "No such parson. No such fender. No such lumber. No such race" (*FW*, p. 63.11–12). Martha's postal address at Dolphin's Barn crops up often in the *Wake*: "the nusances of dolphins born" (*FW*, p. 275, n. 6), "tenpounten on the pop for the daulphins born" (*FW*, p. 211.20–21), "to joy a Jonas in the Dolphin's Barncar" (*FW*, p. 434.27), and "Jambs, of Delphin's Bourne" (*FW*, p. 513.9).

But it is the transformation of World for Word that is of particular significance: Bloom has apparently chosen the tangible World in lieu of the spiritual Word. Having a choice of all three of the basic Western creeds, he has turned his back on the Judaism of his grandfathers, the Protestant substitute of his father, and the Catholicism of his marriage to Molly. Yet the world of which Bloom is very much a part has not proved to be a kind one to him, and the end of his chance to perpetuate himself in it through a male child is a painful cancellation to him of his only immortality. He remembers, however, the Valentine poem he had written to Molly during their courtship: the last line reads, *"You are mine. The world is mine"* (*U*, p. 639), and of course neither one is. The world-word pun carries over into the *Wake* as well: in the question concerning the letter ("What subtler timeplace of the weald than such wolfsbelly castrament to will hide a leabhar from Thursmen's brandihands or a loveletter, lostfully hers, that would be lust on Ma"—*FW*, p. 80.12–15), and in the author's address to the reader regarding his book—the macrocosmic letter—"(Stoop) if you are abcedminded, to this claybook, what curios of signs (please stoop), in this allaphbed! Can you rede (since We and Thou had it out already) its world?"—*FW*, p. 18.17–19).

Two other letters arriving on the morning of 16 June 1904 also play their part in Bloom's life—the one to Molly from her lover-of-the-day, Blazes Boylan, and the other to Bloom from daughter Milly. Throughout the day Bloom broods over Molly's affair with Boylan and worries about Milly's coming-of-age (a fear which culminates with Bloom learning about the probable seduction by Alec Bannon). Milly's childlike letter and Martha's childish one merge in Bloom's mind. Sexually estranged for over ten years from adequate relations with his wife, a silent partner to her escapade with

Boylan, and concerned that daughter may emulate mother, Bloom is tortured and half-hearted in his affair with Martha, refusing her request for an actual rendezvous. The role of the nubile daughter Milly is recreated in the *Wake* by Issy, the daughter that dreaming Earwicker lusts after, seeing her as a carbon copy of his wife when she had been young. Issy, in turn, writes lascivious footnotes in the Lessons chapter (e.g., "Improper frictions is maledictions and mens uration makes me mad"—*FW*, p. 269, n. 3), and outdoes herself with two erotic letters (*FW*, pp. 143.31–148.32, and *FW*, pp. 457.25–461.32).

The advertisement itself is of lesser importance, but it is an interesting corollary to the letter. "Wanted smart lady typist to aid gentleman in literary work" (*U*, pp. 148–149), Bloom muses as he passes the offices of the *Irish Times*. Bloom's "literary work" is of course a subterfuge, although that morning he did contemplate a sketch for *Titbits* to be submitted under the byline of "By Mr and Mrs L. M. Bloom" (*U*, p. 62), which ironically returns him to his position as faithful husband to Molly. His thoughts frequently involve him with his wife, just as Earwicker's dream centers often about Anna Livia, recognizing that Issy is merely a latter-day version of her mother. Mock advertisements intrude at various instances in the *Wake*: "Tip. Take Tamotimo's topical. Tip. Browne yet Noland. Tip. Advert" (*FW*, p. 599.23–24). One gives us a travel suggestion in four languages (*FW*, p. 540.9–12), while another is Shaun's advertisement for himself as a butcher (*FW*, p. 172.5–10), in contrast with Shem's, which echoes Bloom's:

> Jymes wishes to hear from wearers of abandoned female costumes, gratefully received, wadmel jumper, rather full pair of culottes and onthergarmenteries, to start city life together. His jymes is out of job, would sit and write. He has lately commited one of the then commandments but she will now assist. Superior built, domestic, regular layer. Also got the boot. He appreciates it. Copies. ABORTISEMENT.
>
> (*FW*, p. 181.27–33)

The major pattern can be seen in terms of sexual guilt, which, although it manifests itself primarily in action or at least in contemplation, becomes a signed confession in the form of a piece of literature (letter, newspaper, advertisement, even the book itself that contains all of these, and the larger Joycean volume that is the history of mankind).

Yet in dozens of small ways as well, the persistence of a memory is transferred from *Ulysses* to *Finnegans Wake*. What Joyce calls "the steady monologuy of the interiors" (*FW*, p. 119.32–33) is the technique of *Ulysses*, while the central twelve chapters of that book have punned titles included in the later one (*FW*, p. 229.13–16): "Ukalepe" (Calypso), "Loathers' leave" (Lotus-eaters), "Had Days" (Hades), "Nemo in Patria" (Aeolus), "The Luncher Out" (Lestrygonians), "Skilly and Carubdish" (Scylla and

Charybdis), "A Wondering Wreck" (Wandering Rocks), "From the Mermaids' Tavern" (Sirens—the Ormond bar), "Bullyfamous" (Cyclops—Polyphemus), "Naughtsycalves" (Nausicaa), "Mother of Misery" (Oxen of the Sun—Mater Misericordiae), "Walpurgas Nackt" (Circe—*Walpurgisnacht*). Minor details of the day appear in the dream: Bloom has left his house key in his other trousers ("Ask Kavya for the kay"—*FW*, p. 93.22–23); he noted the advertisement he wrote for *"Kino's 11/-Trousers"* (*U*, p. 142): "11/-in the week" (*FW*, p. 70.1–2); he assisted the drunken Stephen through the streets of Nighttown, an experience now attributed to Shem: "reeling more to the right than he lurched to the left, on his way from a protoprostitute . . . just as he was butting in rand the coyner of bad times under a hideful between the rival doors of warm bethels of worship through his boardelhouse fongster" (*FW*, p. 186.25–31). The besotted Stephen is then confronted by equally besotted soldiers who attack him for his effrontery to the king; these two soldiers expand into three in the *Wake* (subsuming Stephen-Shem), just as drunk and just as abusive: "they had, chin Ted, chin Tam, chinchin Taffyd, that day consumed their soul of the corn" (*FW*, p. 34.16–18). But Bloom rescued the fallen Stephen from the Watch (while Shem is arrested for his own protection by "Petty constable Sistersen . . . the parochial watch . . . who had been detailed from pollute stoties to save him"—*FW*, p. 186.19–22); Stephen is taken to the cabman's shelter, reputed to be run by the notorious Skin-the-Goat (*U*, p. 583)—known in the *Wake* as "Scape the Goat" (*FW*, pp. 329.36–330.1)—where a seaman named Murphy[9] (a name used for the twelve customers in the *Wake*: "The Morphios!"—*FW*, p. 142.29) insists that he knows Stephen's father and attributes to him the feat of shooting "two eggs off two bottles at fifty yards over his shoulder" (*U*, p. 585), which in the *Wake* is "executing with Anny Oakley deadliness . . . empties which had not very long before contained Reid's family . . . stout" (*FW*, p. 52.1–6).

Such coincidences could be easily dismissed, or at best passed over as repetitions of elements that persisted in interest for Joyce, were it not for the convenient clusters into which they logically assemble. Bloom's sexual preoccupations have already been mentioned, but even so minute an event as following the peasant-hipped servant out of the porkbutcher's (*U*, pp. 52–53) has left a permanent deposit ("the losel that hucks around missivemaids' gummibacks"—*FW*, p. 66.12–13), while his attempt to see a woman's ankles when she boarded a carriage (*U*, p. 66) earns him the title of "Mr Anklegazer" (*FW* p. 193.11–12). His concern regarding his wife's affair with Boylan has its echo in the awarding of a "jauntingcar for Larry Doolin, the Ballyclee jackeen" (*FW*, p. 210.19). His relationship to his wife is apparent in the juxtaposition of "she, the lalage of lyonesses, and him, her knave arrant" (*FW*, p. 229.10–11) and "She knows her knight's duty while Luntum sleeps" (*FW*, p. 12.4–5). But the important change forecast for the Blooms as a result of the day's action is that Molly may well reverse the procedure and serve Leopold his breakfast in bed; we have seen the husband providing such service for the wife on the morning of 16 June, so that in the *Wake* the dreamer is told: "Walk while ye have the night for morn, lightbreakfastbringer, morroweth whereon every past shall full fost sleep" (*FW*, p. 473.23–24).

The Bloom we have come to know wanders through the city of Dublin as an alienated individual, suspected of being a Freemason ("freemen's maurer"—*FW*, p. 4.18–19), a cuckold, a tightwad, and a "perverted jew" (*U*, p. 321). The anti-Semitic Citizen in particular makes much of his antagonism toward Jewish Bloom, but Bloom's Jewishness is as ludicrous as his Christianity. His ignorance of Catholicism is handsomely displayed both in his brief stroll through St. Andrew's and at the interment of Dignam (viz., "The priest took a stick with a knob at the end of it out of the boy's bucket and shook it over the coffin"—*U*, p. 96), and he innocently lists among Protestant hymns "*Bid me to live and I will live thy protestant to be*" (*U*, p. 622) of Robert Herrick. His ties with Judaism are equally absurd: he is able to pinpoint Denis Breen as "Meshuggah" (*U*, p. 148), which he colloquially translates as "Off his chump" (*U*, p. 148), and in the Circe hallucination he displays what probably amounts to his total knowledge of Hebrew: "Aleph Beth Ghimel Daleth Hagadah Tephilim Kosher Yom Kippur Hanukah Roschaschana Beni Brith Bar Mitzvah Mazzoth Askenazim Meshuggah Talith" (*U*, p. 463), a compendium of holy days, the alphabet, dietary strictures, religious paraphernalia, and such. This is undoubtedly the composite of Bloom's Jewish residue and indicates a second aspect of guilt in his regret regarding a lost heritage. The deracinated Dreamer in *Finnegans Wake* collects this same sort of flotsam and jetsam of a Hebraic past; his dream is riddled with "Olives, beets, kimmells, dollies" (*FW*, p. 19.8–9)—the alphabet; "sherif Toragh" (*FW*, p. 29.17)—the Torah; "the Dumlat" (*FW*, p. 30.10)—the Talmud backward; "Yuddanfest" (*FW*, p. 82.36)—Hebrew festivals; "his Sheofon" (*FW*, p. 83.8–9)—the ram's horn; "new book of Morses" (*FW*, p. 123.35)—the Pentateuch;[10] "Hanoukan's lamp" (*FW*, p. 245.5)—Hanukah, festival of lights; "Kidoosh!" (*FW*, p. 258.5)—*kaddish*, prayer for the dead; "To Mezouzalem with the Dephilim" (*FW*, p. 258.8–9)—*mezuzah* and *tephilim*, doorpost prayer-box and phylacteries (Bloom confuses one with the other—*U*, p. 361); "*roshashanaral*" (*FW*, p. 340.27)—Rosh Hashana, the New Year; "Meschiameschianah" (*FW*, p. 358.19)—literally, an ugly fate ("misha mishinnah"—*U*, p. 408); "it shall come to pasch" (*FW*, p. 594.17)—the Passover; "Sukkot" (*FW*, p. 612.15)—Sukkoth, feast of tabernacles.

In the light of this dual guilt and alienation, an important epiphanic moment occurs for Bloom as he stands alone on the Sandymount beach after his auto-erotic experience during the fireworks. He reviews the day's events ("Long day I've had. Martha, the bath, funeral, house of keys, museum with those goddesses, Dedalus' song. Then that brawler in Barney Kiernan's"—

U, p. 363), seeing himself as a literary character of his own creation, *"The Mystery Man on the Beach*, prize titbit story by Mr Leopold Bloom" (*U*, p. 359), and recognizing at the end of the day (but the beginning of the Hebrew day) the circular nature of past, present, and future: "So it returns. Think you're escaping and run into yourself. Longest way round is the shortest way home" (*U*, p. 360). (Intellectual Stephen has already harbored this thought: "We walk through ourselves, meeting robbers, ghosts, giants, old men, young men, wives, widows, brothers-in-love. But always meeting ourselves"—*U*, p. 201.) The culmination for Bloom comes when he writes in the sand: "I. . . . AM. A." (*U*, p. 364), commenting, "No room. Let it go" (*U*, p. 364). His unfinished testament, like his run-down pocket watch, attests to his incomplete life: the rupture with the past, the inability to live in the present as a sexually normal male, and the lack of a male heir to assure him of a future. His tone of resignation is typically Hebraic, as his role of Moses, vouchsafed a glimpse of the promised land but not permitted to enter, leads him to record his own version of God's "I am what I am" (Exodus iii. 14). God's role is fixed and certain, but Bloom's is indefinite, and we are left with the tempting blank to fill in. The epiphanic *ricorso* chapter concluding the *Wake* provides a Joycean version of God's statement to Moses, "I yam as I yam" (*FW*, p. 604.23)—the misspelling proves significant when *I yam* is read backward as an interrogative *may I?*

Even more apt, however, is the part played by the decisive woman in contradistinction to the vacillation of the sexually timid male. Like the God Who Is, Molly continually makes her complete and positive statement, her drowsy thoughts ending in the repeated "yes I said yes I will Yes" (*U*, p. 742). That *Yes* is echoed often in *Finnegans Wake*, as in the cataloguing of items in the Shem house, ending: "war moans, special sighs, longsufferings of longstanding, ahs ohs ouis sis jas jos gias neys thaws sos, yeses and yeses and yeses" (*FW*, p. 184.1–2). Anna Livia's manifesto has as one of its projected titles: *"He Calls Me his Dual of Ayessha"* (*FW*, p. 105.19–20). And that same paragraph in the last chapter that contains God's declaration begins: "Oyes! Oyeses! Oyesesyeses! The primace of the Gaulls, protonotorious, I yam as I yam" (*FW*, p. 604.22–23). Head-to-foot the married couple sleep: the male wanderer of the day is the male wanderer of the dream, a neurotic compound of his fears, inabilities, destroyed roots, and frustrated hopes, while the wife remains the solid rock of certainity, security, and absence of shame or regret, for whom the last words in both *Ulysses* and *Finnegans Wake* are reserved.

Bloom is indeed that *"Hoebegunne the Hebrewer"* (*FW*, p. 104.12) that is Anna Livia's designation for Earwicker. Yet he is a combined Catholic-Protestant-Jew without God, whose thoroughly secular thinking is capsulized in his repeated reliance upon the theory of "natural phenomena" (*U*, pp. 289, 377, 635, 643). Whatever else the rubbed-out "T" in his hatband may mean ("Plasto's high grade ha"—*U*, p. 49), it certainly indicates the Cross missing from Bloom's existence. In the same sense, the missing "L" in his printed name in the newspaper is the loss of the Hebraic God, El, from his life. Bloom is a wanderer, the Wandering Jew, exiled from Beth El. When the newspaperman at the funeral approached Bloom and asked, "What is your christian name. I'm not sure" (*U*, p. 103), the response was: "—L, Mr Bloom said. Leopold" (*U*, p. 103). The mysterious thirteenth person, the man in the macintosh coat who is so often credited by commentators with being a spiritual emanation, arouses the reporter's curiosity, and he asks Bloom if he knows him. Bloom of course does not, and in the confused exchange the type of coat becomes mistaken for the name (the ineffable name of God which may not be uttered, for which surrogates must be found, represented by the Tetragammaton: notice that the "shout in the street" that is God reads, "Hooray! Ay! Whrrwhee"—*U*, p. 32). So the Man in the Macintosh is metamorphosed into the M'Intosh of the funeral notice. When Bloom next searches for the mysterious stranger, he cannot find him: "Where has he disappeared to? Not a sign. Well of all the. Has anybody here seen? Kay ee double ell. Become invisible. Good Lord, what became of him?" (*U*, p. 104).

Notes

1. Richard Ellmann, *James Joyce* (New York: Oxford University Press, 1959), pp. 473, 603, n.
2. Page numbers are to the 1937 Bodley Head edition of *Ulysses*, designated hereafter by "*U*."
3. Page numbers refer to the Compass edition of *Exiles*.
4. Page numbers (followed after the period by inclusive line numbers) are to the Viking Press edition of *Finnegans Wake*, hereafter prefaced by "*FW*"; Ch. x footnotes are designated by "n." and the footnote number. Corrections have been made from Joyce's *errata*.
5. Other significant instances of the intrusive newspaper in the *Wake* are found in: "the moaning pipers could tell him to his faceback" (*FW*, p. 23.30–31); "reading her Evening World. To see is it smarts, full lengths or swaggers. News, news, all the news. Death, a leopard, kills fellah in Fez" (*FW*, p. 28.20–22); "the hakusay accusation againstm had been made, what was known in high quarters as was stood stated in Morganspost" (*FW*, p. 36.4–5); and the four Dublin dailies of 1904; "Christ in our irish times! Christ on the airs independence! Christ hold the freedman's chareman! Christ light the dully expressed!" (*FW*, p. 500.14–16).
6. *Structure and Motif in Finnegans Wake* (Evanston, Ill.: Northwestern University Press, 1962), pp. 70–71.
7. The cigar neatly links Bloom with Earwicker: in the Cyclops chapter Bloom declines a drink, "saying he wouldn't and couldn't and excuse him no offence and all to that and then he said well he'd just take a cigar" (*U*, p. 288), while Earwicker gives one away: "he tips un a topping swank cheroot . . . suck that brown boyo, my son, and spend a whole half hour in Havana" (*FW*, p. 53.22–26).
8. See two other instances in the *Wake*: the initial encounter between H. C. E. and the Cad (*FW*, p. 35.1–38.8) and the summation of events (*FW*, p. 580.23–36), where the Citizen and his dog are combined into "the fenian's bark" (*FW*, p. 580.28).
9. Joyce toyed a good deal with the morphous-Morpheus-Murphy pun, both in the

Wake and in *Ulysses*. As the answer to the question regarding the customers, the triple pun exists in the one word, while the punning in *Ulysses* covers several portions of the chapter: "in the arms of Morpheus" (*U*, p. 600) modulates into "the arms of Murphy" (*U*, p. 622). See also "andrewpaulmurphyc" (*FW*, p. 31.35) and "a dozen of the Murphybuds" (*FW*, p. 161.28–29).

10.   James S. Atherton, *The Books at the Wake* (New York: Viking Press, 1960), finds every book of the Old Testament mentioned at least once in the *Wake*; see his listing, p. 180.

Finnegans Wake and the Nature of Narrative

MICHAEL H. BEGNAL

The answer to the question is there a plot in *Finnegans Wake* is an ambiguously Joycean yes, and no. Joyce never has been very much for plot—not much really happens in *Dubliners*, perhaps a little more in *A Portrait*, perhaps a little more or less in *Ulysses*. Some commentators speak confidently about the Earwickers (or is it the Porters?), their relationships and trials and tribulations, but where do we actually get to see them in action? Some recent studies assert that there is no plot in *Finnegans Wake*, or, if there is, it is so amorphous or treated so scantily that it cannot be perceived in any conventional fashion. HCE becomes "a goal, a thing sought, a retort to the enigma of creation,"[1] and "all events in the *Wake* are merely stories, and it is impossible to determine whether they represent history or fiction."[2] "Only by abandoning the novelistic approach to *Finnegans Wake* can readers free themselves from waking conventions and logic enough to enjoy the wholly imaginative reality of a dreamwork."[3] Yet still we continue to speak of HCE, ALP, Shem, Shaun, and Issy, and the reason for this is that they are characters, of a sort, and *Finnegans Wake* does have a plot, of a sort.

In attempting to describe his mammoth work, Joyce said that *Finnegans Wake* was a night-piece, and that what he wanted to describe "cannot be rendered sensible by the use of wideawake language, cutanddry grammar and goahead plot."[4] The structure of the novel bears this out, since there is no "goahead plot" to speak of in the whole of Book I. What we get instead is a lengthy catalogue or picture album of the central characters, the heredity and history of HCE, Anna Livia described by a pair of gossipy washerwomen, a mature Shaun chastizing a mature Shem, and a series of puzzling questions whose answers describe the *Wake* itself. Nowhere is there plot as we conventionally know it.

As we move through the novel we notice that, not only are several different characters speaking, but also that different narrative techniques are used from chapter to chapter, and within individual chapters, just as they were in *Ulysses*. Wake speech itself is not consistent, since some passages are relatively easy to deal with while others are almost impossible. In II, i [Book II chapter 1], the children's games are cast in the form of a dramatic

Reprinted from *Modern British Literature* 5 (Spring and Fall 1980):43–52, by permission of the journal.

119

production, complete with playbill; in II, ii, the twins' studies are described as the pages of a scholarly tome, with sidenotes and footnotes; in III, iv, the Earwickers' house is a stage set, presumably described by the Four Old Men as the four bedposts, and so it goes.

Yet still there is a plot to *Finnegans Wake*, but it is a plot which is being told in a completely new and experimental way. In a conventional novel virtually all of the action takes place on one level; that is, we follow the experiences of Raskolnikov, for example, from their beginning to end in one period of time and on one level of space. There may be variations on this (the narrator of *Tristram Shandy* may decide to comment to the reader or to play a trick on him with a blank page), but basically conventional narrative or storytelling occurs on one fairly comprehensive level. A realistic presentation of time and space provides the boundaries of this level, with variations such as flashback or stream of consciousness, all tied together with a cause and effect unfolding of events. If a novel begins with some form of once upon a time, we expect it to end with they all lived happily, or unhappily, ever after.

Finnegans Wake sometimes does tell a story on this one level, but it is also operating on several other levels simultaneously, moving from one to another with effortless ease, and leaving a reader in boundless confusion unless he recognizes the technique. In a conventional novel, time and space are limited; here all potentialities of time and space are present at the same time. The narrative technique of the *Wake* is quite similar to that of the "Circe" chapter in *Ulysses*. There Leopold Bloom has absolutely no control as a character over what is happening, as the bounds of time and space disappear. Bloom can be a young boy explaining how he tore his trousers, the Lord Mayor of Dublin, a woman giving birth, or a prostitute displayed for the benefit of potential customers. We know that there is a literal narrative somewhere behind all this—Bloom enters Nighttown looking for Stephen Dedalus, finds him at Bella Cohen's, helps him through some scrapes, and eventually gets him out of there. But this literal narrative fades behind the multiplicity of potentiality which Joyce is presenting, as Bloom's character is dramatized and revealed.

Conventional time is destroyed. As Bloom banters with Zoe: "The mouth can be better engaged than with a cylinder of rank weed," he is told: "Go on. Make a stump speech out of it" (*U*, p. 478). Suddenly this level dissolves; Bloom is elected Lord Mayor, proclaims the new Bloomusalem, falls, becomes the womanly man, gives birth, and is finally eulogized by the Daughters of Erin. Twenty-one pages later not a second has been lost, as Zoe says: "Talk away till you're black in the face" (*U*, p. 499), and the narrative resumes on its previous level. Joyce has taken the reader on a quick trip through Bloom's psyche, without Poldy's permission or awareness, and has then set him back again on course. The shifting levels of reality, or of possibility, operate in "Circe" in much the same way as they do in the "Mime of Mick, Nick, and the Maggies," or anywhere else in *Finnegans Wake*. In both cases, all is controlled by the narrative consciousness which picks and chooses as it, and not reality, sees fit.

In actuality, the levels of reality which we see in both "Circe" and the *Wake* are always at least one remove from normality. Joyce noted in his famous, or notorious, schema that the technique of "Circe" is hallucination, and the very dramatic structure itself places Bloom and all the other characters at one remove away from us. The same is true for the whole of the *Wake*. Joyce never attempts to lull the reader into a suspension of disbelief; here and elsewhere the style of *Ulysses* insists upon its own artificiality. In *Finnegans Wake*, from beginning to end, it is again the style that consistently indicates the presence of the narrator, the puppeteer, the punster. Unravelling the pun possibilities of Wakian prose necessitates the conscious functioning of the pun-anagram solving aspect of the reader's intellect, the conscious drawing back from the action, so that, first, we will not be linguistically ambushed, and, second, we can grasp where we are and continue on. If Dreiser uses language in an attempt to immerse us in the real, Joyce uses language to fend it off.

To return to plot, then, one might ask with Mamalujo: "as we there are where are we are we there?" (*FW*, p. 260.01). The basic plot of *Finnegans Wake* is a level of narration which is interlaid, or sandwiched in, among several other levels. In brief, it unfolds like this: Book II, chapter one—the children are outside, playing a game after school until their parents call them in at nightfall. Book II, chapter two—Shem and Shaun do their homework, while Issy sits on a couch, knitting and kibitzing. Book II, chapter three—Earwicker presides in the pub until closing time, finishes off the drinks left around, falls down drunk, and staggers up to bed later. Book III, chapter four—the Earwickers are awakened by the cries of Shem-Jerry; they soothe him, return to bed, make love, fall asleep as dawn is breaking. Book IV, chapter one—Anna Livia awakens, and her thoughts form the monologue which concludes the book. This may not be much, but, at least, as Robert Frost said: "For once, then, something."

Progressing along with this narrative level are at least four others: an archetypal level, a fable or anecdotal level, a projected, children as adult level, and a level on which the narrator converses with the reader. To Joyce, all these levels tell the same story, or at least flesh out the central narrative. What is most important is what the characters *are*, not what they do, and each of these plot levels is connected to, and buttresses, the others. These other levels, all self-contained and at the same time interrelated, seem to me to be these:

Archetypal level: the hero Finn, for example, in his grave, Tim Finnegan at his Wake, HCE and ALP as mountain and river, Shem and Shaun as tree and stone.

Fable or Anecdotal level: the invented stories or tales whose characters are analogues of the Earwickers, the Prankquean and Jarl von Hoother, the Ondt and the Gracehoper, Burrus and Caseous.

Projected Age level: the children as mature and sexual beings, Issy in the footnotes of the Lessons chapter, Shaun in the first two chapters of Book III, Shem in parts of the "Mime of Mick, Nick, and the Maggies."

Narrator-Reader level: the myriad points in the novel where the action stops and the reader is ridiculed or urged on: "You is feeling like you was lost in the bush, boy?" (FW, p. 112.03).

My purpose in establishing these levels is not limitation (an individual reader may reject one or all of these levels, and offer one or more of his or her own), but is rather to give a reader a starting point, a place to begin the assault, and to assert again that there is some kind of story being told here, though it is being told at least five different ways at the same time. Where a conventional novelist would be concerned with the *result* of the plot, Joyce focusses on the potentiality of plot and characterization as they unfold on many levels at once. As Mamalujo remind Shaun: "There are sordidly tales within tales, you clearly understand that?" (FW, p. 522.05). The events or the levels of *Finnegans Wake* are not connected causally, but they are controlled novelistically. They are not psychoanalytic free associations, but are distorted mirror reflections of each other. In actuality, it seems that Joyce completely rejected psychoanalysis, and Frank Budgen warns that if one thinks that Joyce: "adopted the theory and followed the practice of psychoanalysis in his work as did the Dadaists and the Surrealists, nothing could be farther from the truth. . . . Joyce was always impatient or contemptuously silent when it was talked about as both an all-sufficient *Weltanschauung* and a source and law for artistic production."[5]

Despite the fact that Joyce may be the most radical experimenter with prose fiction that the genre has ever known, he remains at heart a traditionalist, working with the basic components of novel construction. Rightly or wrongly, he hoped and expected that *Finnegans Wake* was a book which could be read by everybody, and his letters to Harriet Weaver are full of explications and helpful hints. In 1926 he asked her: "Will you let me know whether the 'plot' begins to emerge from it at all? Between the close of Δ [I.8] at nightfall and $\wedge$a [III.1] there are three or four other episodes, the children's games, night studies, a scene in the 'public,' and a 'lights out in the village.' "[6] All indications are that Joyce did think of the *Wake* in terms of plot—not necessarily "one thing follows another," but plot just the same.

All these plot levels are controlled, and, in this new sense, plot functions essentially as exposition of character, deriving from possibility rather than from logicality or necessity. If HCE, for example, can best be understood as a concept, a sigla, as Roland McHugh has asserted, then these overlaid, simultaneous plot levels in the *Wake* serve to present the E in potential, rather than in actuality. As the narrator describes his manipulations of HCE and ALP, he will: "guide them through the labyrinth of their samilikes and the alteregoases of their pseudoselves" (*FW*, p. 576.32).

And so the initial difficulty arises in the *Wake* when the reader tries to splice all these plot levels together in a horizontal, rather than in a vertical, way. If once these levels can be isolated, traced to their individual conclusions, or non-conclusions, and then wrapped cable-like together, the design of the narrative becomes clearer, as do our conceptions of the characters. An examination of the multiple reports or descriptions of the Sin in the Park will never allow a reader to pick a "correct" one, but will instead, when all are taken together, enlarge our perception of Wakian sin and guilt. Right or wrongheadedly, Joyce feels that a single, conventional narrative level would limit the artist's freedom of action, and this is his alternative to goahead plot.

The same thing happens with character. For quite some time now we have been aware of the Joycean technique of strings of identification to broaden the scope and significance of individual characters. In this sense, Shem is Shem, but he is also Cain, the Archdruid Berkeley, Jacob, Castor, and many others. One glance at Mrs. Glasheen's "Who is Who When Everybody Is Somebody Else"[7] should confirm this, and Elliot Paul noted in 1929 that: "If one can consider all events as having a standing regardless of date, that the happenings of all the years are taken from their place on the shelf and arranged, not in numerical order, but according to a design dictated by the mind of Joyce, then the text is not nearly so puzzling. For example, if Noah, Premier Gladstone and 'Papa' Browning are telescoped into one, because of common characteristics, no violence is done to logic."[8] But another thing which makes the narrative difficult to deal with is Joyce's collapsing and expanding of the time levels on which the members of the Earwicker family operate. To say that one fall is all falls is one thing, but to explain or to understand how Shem can be a young boy playing a children's game at one moment, a Joycean-Wildean artist writing a novel at the next, and a child once more immediately after, is something else again.

The *Wake* contains several overlying, structural symbols or metaphors, such as the Letter, the Sin, the Fall, and another which might help with this problem is the Telescope. Certainly the initial or primary function of a telescope is to see something which is far away more clearly. The Willingdone spies on the Jinnies with a telescope of "Sexcaliber hrosspower" (*FW*, p. 8.36), and Shem does much the same later: "he did take a tompip peepestrella throug a threedraw eighteen hawkspower durdicky telescope" (*FW*, p. 178.26). Buckley uses one to catch sight of the Russian General, and the narrator says that we could use one ourselves in our inspection of the Letter: "the farther back we manage to wiggle the more we need the loan of a lens to see as much as the hen saw" (*FW*, p. 112.01). The action of the *Wake* is far away, or at least separated from us by shifting dream fogs, so that we would probably agree with Shem's comment in the "Lessons" chapter: "When I'm dreaming back like that I begins to see we're only all telescopes" (*FW*, p. 295.10).

In the same chapter, the twins' attempt at solving the mystery of their mother's sexuality, as well as their homework, is described as: *"Two makes a wing at the macroscope telluspeep"* (*FW*, p. 275.L). Here the telescope becomes a microscope as well—they are trying to see from near and far at the same time—but the essential statement is that if we, or they, will only look, "peep," something will be revealed, something will "tellus" what we want to know. The primary emphasis then is upon focussing, upon magnification, sometimes to the benefit of the scientist and sometimes to the benefit of the Peeping Tom. Knowledge is knowledge, no matter to what purpose it is put.

Looking at the Telescope image from another angle, its meaning as a verb can help to explain how and why Joyce is manipulating timeshifts within the somewhat realistic portions of the narrative. To telescope something is to elongate it or to shorten it, as the instrument is expanded or contracted. (The sexual possibilities here are obvious.) If the main point is to see something in its totality, then it must be seen both from near and from far. The Twins, for example, cannot appear only as boys of about fifteen years old (*FW*, p. 483.21). They must also function as young children, as in III, iv, or as mature adults, as in III, i. Even better, they must be allowed to appear in varying phases of age in a single episode, as they do in II, i, the "Mime of Mick, Nick, and the Maggies." Joyce accomplishes this by concentrating or elongating the segments of their ages as one would a telescope. In *A Portrait*, Stephen Dedalus participates in the Christmas dinner argument, but does not really understand it; we can never see how he might have reacted then had he been the Stephen of the novel's final chapter.

In *Finnegans Wake*, age, like time, is fluid, can be telescoped, and characters reveal themselves to us from many different points at the same time. Joyce is not interested here in time as development, as in a *Bildungsroman*, but rather he examines time as immediate and simultaneous. As Marcel Brion commented: "he creates his own time, as he creates his vocabulary and his characters. He soon elaborates what he receives from reality by a mysterious chemistry into new elements bearing the marks of this personality."[9] The macrocosm and the microcosm are one, just as the various potentialities of each member of the Earwicker family form a unity. To paraphrase Beckett, the novel is not *about* the characters, it *is* those characters themselves. Joyce, to a certain degree, continues to use fairly realistic plot description—that is, at least individual incidents do have a certain logic, cause, a beginning, middle, and end—but realistic character analysis has been superseded by a truly new technique in the writing of fiction.

Interestingly enough, such time telescoping takes place only when the Earwicker children are present, and when the narrative has begun progressing on a close to realistic level. HCE and ALP, adult already, are never transformed into children, though their youths may be recalled in reminiscence and flashback. Mamalujo remain the same, as do Kate the Slops and the Man of All Work. For Joyce it appears that the adults have realized their character potentiality, and are no longer in a state of becoming. Characters within the fables or the interpolated tales, as well, never fall into Joyce's time tunnel.

The reason for this latter procedure seems to be that these fable characters exist on a level separate from the Earwickers, a level several steps below the quasi-realistic. They are in actuality part of the strings of identification, and serve to relate the Earwickers to the general and the archetypal, while the time telescopings operate on personal and specific levels, amplifying the nature of an individual character. We are given two definitions which apply to what is going on here. For archetype: "we are recurrently meeting em, . . . in cycloannalism, from space to space, time after time, in various phases of scripture as in various poses of sepulture" (FW, p. 254.25). But with the characters of the Earwickers it is the simultaneity of time which is primary: "The allriddle of it? That that is allruddy with us, ahead of schedule, which already is plan accomplished from and syne" (FW, p. 274.02).

The time transformations are immediately apparent with Shem and Issy in the "Mime." Intent on guessing the riddle in a children's game, Shem is a defeated youngster jeered by the Flora Girls. In anger and frustration, he lashes out at the other children: "childhood's age being aye the shameleast" (FW, p. 227.34), and fantasizes about running away from home. At this point, the narrative broadens, and Glugg-Shem becomes a grown man resembling James Joyce himself. He will: "Go in for scribenery with the satiety of arthurs" (FW, p. 229.07), and become a writer in exile. He: "would jused sit it all write down . . . rate in blotch and void" (FW, p. 229.26), as the child Shem vanishes. A message from Issy brings him back to the contest, and once back he is a child again. These oscillations serve to present us Shem as a unity, as an achieved potentiality. These age stretchings occur throughout the episode, and they describe Shem as child and adult at one and the same time.

This same sort of temporal expansion and contraction occurs with Issy, as well as with Shem, in the chapter, but she seems more aware, if not in control, of it. The narrator introduces her as an adult: "If you nude her in her prime . . . she'll prick you where you're proudest with her unsatt speagle eye. Look sharp, she's signalling from among the asters" (FW, p. 248.03). Issy speaks as temptress or seductress, and seems to imply that not only can she understand the telescope trick, but she can also make sense out of it and use it: "I see through your weapon" (FW, p. 248.15). She rues the fact that young Shem is as inept a riddle guesser as older Shem would be as a lover, but she finds the time transitions fascinating: "when he beetles backwards, ain't I fly? Pull the boughpee to see how we sleep" (FW, p. 248.18). (An aside to the narrator: make us children again so that we can show ourselves charmingly in bed.) And again: "here who adolls me," adores me, turns me into a child, "influxes sleep. But if this could see with its backsight he'd be the grand old greeneyed lobster. He's my first viewmarc since Valentine. Wink's the winning word" (*FW*, p. 249.01). If he (Shem) could look back now and see me, if he could see my behind, he would be as lustful and jealous as his father and could take his place. Certainly there are Tristan-Mark-Isolde echoes here too, but her immediate focus is on Shem, her telescoper: "My bellyswain's a twalf whulerusspower" (*FW*, p. 248.21). She will wink and play this game because it is fun. What she and the narrator know will not hurt anyone else. Through the telescoping, she can see: "where there's a hitch, a head of things" (*FW*, p. 248.14).

We can see the telescoping at work in a different way in Shaun's major appearance in the novel, the first three chapters of Book III. Certainly, Joyce's comment is fascinating that this: "is a description of a postman travelling backwards in the night through the events already narrated. It is written in the form of a *via crucis* of 14 stations but in reality is only a barrel rolling down the river Liffey,"[10] but ultimately it does not seem very helpful in terms of what is actually going on. We can find barrels in the text, and speculate about where the various stations occur, but what then? More to the point is to see that Shaun is moved from an immediate, realistic level to a mythic, archetypal one. He is all potential and possibility. At the beginning of the chapter which concludes his appearance, iii, the narrator says: "His dream monologue was over, of cause, but his drama parapolylogic had yet to be, affact" (*FW*, p. 474.04). His final appearance will be above and beyond a single, clear view. In other words, his manifestation is cast on three levels in the Book: the first as Shaun the Post (what he would actually seem to be as an adult); the second as Jaun (the figure of authority and romance he would like to be); the third as Yawn (what he is comprised of, his archetypal nature). The narrator describes these shifts in age and role as the process of becoming: "They are to come of twinning age so soon as they may be born to be eldering like those olders while they are living under chairs" (*FW*, p. 562.18).

Progressively, as Shaun moves from level to level, he more and more loses control. He says in chapter i of Book III that his goal is: "to isolate i from my multiple Mes" (*FW*, p. 410.12), but the reader soon realizes that this is impossible. Just as Joyce telescopes time in one way in Book II, to capsulize a character from youth to age, he telescopes various projections of the sum of Shaun's personality in Book III. By chapter iii of this Book, Shaun is all multiple me's. He is a sleeping personification of all the members of his family, of all people, speaking as himself, Shem, Issy, Earwicker, and Anna Livia. So it is impossible then for Shaun to isolate an I from the multiple me's, since, in Joyce's view of characterization, any I must be formed of a combination of me's. The reader must accept and digest all the levels of presentation of a single character if the character is to be comprehended.

One of the many places where Joyce demonstrates this position explicitly is III, iv, with the Earwickers in their bedroom, and four views of their goings on given to us by Matthew, Mark, Luke, and John. Matt's: "Side point of view. First position of harmony" (*FW*, p. 559.21) gives us the parents awakened by the child's crying. Mark's: "second position of discordance . . . rereway" (*FW*, p. 564.01) describes Anna Livia attempting to calm the child Shem. Luke's: "Third position of concord! Excellent view from front" (*FW*, p. 582.29) is the Earwickers' making love, a positive act in the Joycean scheme of things.

These three closeup views of the Earwickers at different critical moments are followed by Johnny's sweeping panoramic perspective of resolution: "Fourth position of solution. . . . Finest view from horizon. Tableau final" (*FW*, p. 590.22), as HCE and Anna Livia fall back to sleep. The four views have followed the Earwickers from harmony, through stress, to concord, to solution, and all four positions, taken together in both a physical and emotional sense, serve to capsulize the Earwicker relationship. (We might be reminded here of the four progressive emotional states which Bloom experiences as he settles into sleep at 7 Eccless Street: Envy, Jealousy, Abnegation, Equanimity [*U*, pp. 732–733].) The narrator has told us that there is: "Scant hope theirs or ours to escape life's high carnage of semperidentity by subsisting peasemeal upon variables" (*FW*, p. 582.14)—that is, sooner or later the various alter egos of personality must be unified to achieve character and resolution, and this is what is accomplished in III, iv. The four pictures of the Earwickers blend to form one. Dawn breaks on HCE and ALP: "while the queenbee he staggerhorned blesses her bliss for to feel her funnyman's functions" (*FW*, p. 590.27). These four views of the Earwicker parents carrying out their primal, archetypal roles in existence are, for Joyce, all we know, and all we need to know, of mankind. There are no guilt and sin here. The final tableau is a view from the horizon, a solution achieved by an acceptance of all that the Earwickers are, a fusion of levels of narrative and characterization.

Thus my basic point is that the various levels and incidents in the *Finnegans Wake* dreamstream are not random, but are in actuality bound together like the various sheets in a piece of plywood. Each of the levels of plot and time segments of character can and should be understood on its own terms, and then cemented together with the others. As Marcel Brion saw: "if the recent books of Joyce are considered hermetic by the majority of readers it is because of the difficulty which the latter experience in falling into step, in adapting themselves to the rhythm of each page in changing 'time' abruptly and as often as this is necessary."[11] Every presentation of Wakean characters, if we can call them that, is an integral part of these characters' personalities, as are their excursions down the time tunnels. When asked what he thought of simple works of literature, Vladimir Nabokov replied that art at its greatest is fantastically deceitful and complex. Perhaps *Finnegans Wake* can qualify on both counts.

Notes

1. Roland McHugh, *The Sigla of Finnegans Wake* (Austin: U. of Texas Press, 1976), p. 12.

2. Margot Norris, *The Decentered Universe of Finnegans Wake* (Baltimore: Johns Hopkins U. Press, 1976), p. 11.

3. Norris, p. 22.

4. *Letters of James Joyce* ed. Richard Ellmann, 3 (New York: Viking Press, 1966), 364.

5. *James Joyce and the Making of Ulysses* (Bloomington: Indiana U. Press, 1967), p. 320.

6. *Letters of James Joyce*, ed. Stuart Gilbert, 1 (New York: Viking Press, 1957), 241.

7. *A Third Census of Finnegans Wake* (Berkeley: U. of California Press, 1977), pp. lxxii–lxxxiv.

8. "Mr. Joyce's Treatment of Plot," *Our Exagmination* (Paris: Shakespeare and Co., 1929), p. 132.

9. "The Idea of Time in the Work of James Joyce," *Our Exagmination* (Paris: Shakespeare and Co., 1929), p. 29.

10. *Letters*, 1, 214.

11. "The Idea of Time in the Work of James Joyce," p. 31.

Nodality and the Infra-Structure
of *Finnegans Wake*

David Hayman

Joyce's last book is most remarkably a play of structures, a game the reader exerts himself to play and which in turn vigorously plays the reader. Whereas most texts incorporate the figure Genette has called the *narrataire* (or "ideal reader"), implicitly, *Finnegans Wake* manipulates and teases in the reader's name and virtually in his person. But, for this to be so, for the experience of reading to be one of making, the *Wake* must give the appearance of randomness when in fact it is organized down to its least unit. In demonstrating such order we can, of course, point to various macro-structures, beginning with the Viconian 3 + 1 of the sections, noting, for example, that part of Book One divides neatly into four male chapters and four female which can be doubled over to make an equivalence:

1-2-3-4	or	45
8-7-6-5-		3 6
		2 7
		1 8

Clive Hart's *Structure and Motif* shows how we can impose yet other schemes (circles, crosses, counterpoint, etc.) upon the larger matrix of the *Wake* without distortion.[1] Such schematization, perceived generally by hindsight, is what stands in for broad narrative development in the *Wake*, making its huge bulk more manageable. It certainly helped Joyce erect his wall of words.

If the macro-structure is the most accessible of the *Wake*'s devices, its infra-structure tends to be even more pervasive, more immediately relevant to the dynamic of reading, better integrated into the texture of the *Wake*. Hart's account of the "motif" demonstrates one aspect of Joyce's method (an aspect of what might be called the *Wake*'s micro-structure). But Joyce's practice suggests another approach which, rather than the individual motif, would focus the coherent clusterings of motif-like materials and might be called "nodalization." The key element here is the "prime node" or apex of

Reprinted from the *James Joyce Quarterly* 16 (Fall 1978/Winter 1979):135–49. Reprinted by permission of the *James Joyce Quarterly*, University of Tulsa.

the "nodal system," a passage where some act, activity, personal trait, allusion, theme, etc. surfaces for its clearest statement in the text, is made manifest, so to speak, and in the process brings together and crystallizes an otherwise scattered body of related material. This prime node is the generative center for lesser and generally less transparent passages devoted to its elaboration or expansion and strategically located in the text. The latter are reinforced by more numerous but briefer allusions to one or more of its attributes. As the units diminish in size, their distribution becomes increasingly, though never truly, random. Taken together, all of these components constitute a single nodal system though on occasion one prime node may generate more than one system and though such systems always tend to be interrelated. As in more conventional narratives some nodal systems are thematic, constituting centers of signification, but the category and its attendant principles are structurally more important than the term theme or even the term motif would suggest, since they constitute a major source of interest and coherence and take precedence over any vestiges of or allusions to narrative and plot.[2]

Joyce's manuscripts and letters provide us with clues to the history and function of what I am calling his nodal systems. They indicate that early in 1923 he composed from his own notes a group of non-narrative or minimally narrative episodes, evoking carefully culled shards and husks of a dormant culture. When he had sent drafts of these sketches to his benefactress Harriet Weaver, he wrote her: ". . . these are not fragments but active elements and when they are more and a little older they will begin to fuse themselves" (*Letters I* 205). The importance of Joyce's remarks should not be underestimated. The main struts of the *Wake* are indeed those early passages, the *Wake*'s focal nodes, which portray in a variety of burlesque conventions crucial instants in the male cycle, suggesting stages in the history of Ireland, of mankind, and of the individual. Dating from the first six to eight months of 1923, they constitute along with the ALP Letter the only existing structural paradigm of the *Wake*—Joyce's approximation of an outline, written before the advent of the puns or the Vico structure at a time when the book was to portray simply (!) the "nightmare of history" from which mankind, like Stephen Dedalus, is striving to awake.

In terms of mode, the early sketches recall the pastiches-parodies of "Cyclops," the chapter of *Ulysses* most transparently concerned with history. The difference here, an important one, is that Joyce does not propose these sketches as adjuncts to narrative and to meaning, as surreal or mock-commentary on a seemingly coherent text. Rather these snapshots function as texts or pretexts to which the rest of the *Wake* will be added as commentary, or shadow text. Instead of telling tales, establishing perspectives, eliciting suspense, these narrative fragments become contexts, centers of significance. It would appear, therefore, that their function and nature were fixed virtually from the start, that is, even before the final structure of the book had been established. But this is a matter which can be left to conjecture. More important is their ultimate placement and function.

Originally, there were five sketches, in order of composition: "Roderick O'Conor" (*FW* 380–82), "Tristan and Isolde" (*FW* 383–99, but interlaced with a slightly later "Mamalujo"), "St Patrick and the Druid" (*FW* 611–12), "St Kevin's Orisons" (*FW* 604–06), and the "Here Comes Everybody" passage which was originally to have opened the book (*FW* 30–34). To these we should add the earliest version of the ALP Letter, which was probably written in December 1923 before Joyce began to compose Iv [Book I, Chapter 5]. It is now located near the end of Book IV where it serves to introduce the concluding monologue (*FW* 615–19).

Significantly, these passages mark the beginning, middle, and end in good mock-Aristotelian fashion. But even more importantly, with the exception of the "HCE" which was published as part of chapter Iii in 1927, none of them saw print before 1939 and none of them grew much either in length or complexity. Perhaps, like the title, about which Joyce made such a fuss, these pieces were felt to be keys to the book and hence aspects of overall suspense structure. Even when inverting the norms of fictional discourse Joyce was conscious of himself as belonging to a timeless tradition of tale-telling and mystification.[3]

These are not true tales, unless we think of the "shaggy dog tale" as a conventional narrative, a tale which is all tail, one completely lacking in point and punch line. In another sense, like *Ulysses, Dubliners*, and the epiphanies, these vignettes, in terms of their narrative content, convey pauses in the action, stills, anticlimaxes which bring into focus the moment as a transparency through which significance may shine. They characterize Joyce's view of history as not so much a continuous sequence of significant action/ reaction as an impasto of activities breeding and feeding upon one another, producing nothing but more of the same in a slightly different order: "Yet is no body present here which was not there before. Only is order othered. Nought is nulled" (*FW* 613.13–14).

In the infra-structure, which is the *Wake* experienced most directly by the reader, the sketches help compose and flavor with specificity the life cycle of mankind. They constitute primal moments, strategically placed reference points for those who feel themselves "lost in the bush" (*FW* 112.03). Thus, they bridge the gap between the macro-and infra-structures and contribute to readability. Further, for all their remarkable range of parodic styles and materials, they established early on the dominant pantomine-farce mode of the text, being its broadest statement in the sense that the clowning and gesticulation is most readily available on first reading. Together, they compose what might be called a primary structure to which everything else is at least secondary in terms of accessibility and/or strategic placement.

Since the book is circular and subject to multiple readings (none of which is truly the first, though each may have the impact of a first reading thanks to the density and variety in the text) it makes no difference, theoretically, where the sketch or prime node falls. The fact that a node has been stated early alters only slightly the suspense or interest generated by the nodal system since the fleshing out of a system is itself a source of interest. Once nodality, the existence of a focused nodal system, has been discovered, it inevitably contributes to the structure of interest. If the prime node falls in Book IV as do the St. Kevin, the St. Patrick, and the ALP Letter, it both illuminates earlier passages and provides light for later readings.

The nodal systems guarantee the constant presence of varieties of narrative experience if not a developing thread of narrative discourse. References to the Letter of ALP or to the romance of Tristan and Isolde or to the fall of the great man are filled with predictive mystery, subject to fulfillment which will satisfy our craving to know, much as would the evolving action of a romance, a melodrama, or a tragedy. The dawn implications of St. Kevin (whose construction of a nine circled island-womb is a birth metaphor) or St. Patrick's bringing light to the gentiles by plucking a green trinity from the ground, evoke and condense and focus elements of utopic and pastoral narrative, to say nothing of hagiography. Thus the tradition of narrative-dramatic genres is at once conserved as an aura in suggestive contexts and destroyed by a text which refuses sequential presentation.

This is perhaps best understood in relation to two major nodal systems, both based in the early passages: The Tristan and Isolde tale, and the Letter of ALP. The former is crystallized in IIiv during the voyeuristic narrative of the four old men, the gospellers, the chroniclers. The Letter is not fully aired until Book IV where we finally read what ALP said in defense of HCE to Shem and what was contained in the letter delivered to HCE by Shaun.

The Tristan and Isolde system is patterned rather strictly after Bédier's reconstruction which Joyce suggested Miss Weaver might read for background. Both the approach he took and the material he used were already available in notes dating from 1922–23 (under the *Exiles*).[4] Even the uninitiated reader may, once he has been alerted by the text, pick up and retain certain familiar details from a well-known narrative. But if the recognition of such details arouses interest, their random and achronological distribution obviates conditional suspense.

By contrast, the tale of the writing and delivery, and the account of the contents of the Letter will be new to him, requiring a good deal of piecing together and ultimately yielding the illusion of narrative progression. As we might suspect, Joyce plays coyly with this suspense element throughout. In Chapter Iv where the theme is first developed, we have the questions what, how, and who applied to the Letter's genesis through scholarly detective work. A second treatment occurs during the children's lessons in IIii when Issy writes a practice letter, reproducing the tired format but revealing nothing (*FW* 279–80). In IIiii, HCE returns from the outhouse having perused and used a "sacred" text (*FW* 356–57):

> I have just (let us suppraise) been reading in a (suppressed) book—it is notwithstempting by measures long and limited—the latterpress is eminently legligible and the paper, so he eagerly seized upon, has scarsely been buttered in works of previous publicity wholebeit in keener notcase would I turf aside for pastureuration. Packen paper paineth whomto is sacred scriptured sign.
>
> (*FW* 356.19–25)

In IIIi Shaun is questioned concerning the Letter's content (*FW* 412–14, 419–24). Finally, the mystery is solved, in a text which is both exceptionally brief (a bit over four pages in the published version) and remarkably clear. What has been a major narrative development and what is certainly a major nodal system have come simultaneously to their climax. Here, for the first time, the voice of ALP is heard clearly and without interference, a voice which holds itself up to ridicule as does that of Winifred Jenkins in *Humphry Clinker*, one of Joyce's principal models. But then the letter is not ALP's true medium as we see when the "Soft Morning" monologue wipes the slate clean, giving us a person as vigorous, articulate, and delightful as Molly Bloom herself (though not as bawdy) and illustrating a principle of balance in the *Wake*, where compassion vies with ridicule and frequently wins.

Ultimately, the narrative development climaxed by the presentation of the Letter is of less moment than the Letter as a prime node in a nodal system; for the suspense generated by this motif is not dissipated by the revelations in Book IV. Neither is suspense at any point crucial to the reader, who hardly needs to solve the mystery of the pre-text when the text itself remains a source of endless surprises and everchanging vistas. Rather, the Letter tends to coalesce with other motifs, themes and narrative elements to fascinate by the proliferation of its implications. The Professor's question "who in hallhagal wrote the durn thing anyhow" (*FW* 107.36) is importantly beside the point, being precisely the question one does not ask of the *Wake*.

As suggested above, the Letter read to us (by us) in Book IV has as its secondary nodes four longish and elaborate passages: 1) the description of the manuscript, its discovery and its presumed origins; 2) a treatment of Issy as the young ALP practicing writing the Letter; 3) HCE telling the pub(lic) his reactions to the document he has wiped himself with; 4) Shaun telling a Shemish questioner about the Letter and his obligation to deliver it. These secondary nodes are not chronologically ordered in the text, a fact which reinforces the essentially antidiegetic nature of the nodal systems. Further, though in both Chapter Iv and Chapter IIii we find what Clive Hart calls "major statements" of the Letter motif (see *FW* 111, 113, 116 and 279F1, 280),[5] these "statements" do not constitute the substance of any of the secondary nodes.

Each of these secondary nodes is itself the source of at least one further nodal system. For example, the professorial account given in Iv, points up among other things the sacred book analogy, turning the text dug up from a dung heap by a neighborhood hen and rescued by a schoolboy into a fragment of the lost past, a mysterious scripture. It also illuminates a stage in the development of religions, the moment when scholarship brings rumor and superstition into rational focus and begins the process of evolving a code of belief and practice. Further, using a male voice to describe *the* female event, it introduces the subdominant nocturnal force, which hides its subjective energy behind a mask of scientific (male) objectivity. Or, again, we have the metaphor both for the creation of this book and for aesthetic creation in general, a mystery which haunted Joyce from the very start of his career. Thus a subordinate node is itself the base for further systems subject in their turn to elaboration. Such systems are also secondary in respect to the overall structuration of the *Wake*, though the reader need not perceive this organization. They are all, however, clearly generated by the primary node established in the early days of the *Wake's* history, and they must be seen as modifying and elaborating upon it.

The interrelatedness of these secondary nodes is supported by manuscript evidence, as is the primacy of the nodal system. To the completed first draft of the Letter Joyce added:

Alone one cannot [know who did][6] it for the hand was fair. We can suppose it that of Shemus the penman, a village soak, who when snugly liquored lived, so[7]

Unclear and unpolished though it may be, this passage must be seen as the source of Chapter Iv. It also generated Ivii, the Shaunish description of and condemnation of Shem in his role as counterfeiter/writer. The second bit of evidence is a longish passage written after the drafting of Iv. In it we find a description of Shaun delivering the Letter in his "emptybottlegreen jerkin," a discussion of his "qualifications for that particular post," a paragraph on ALP's reasons for writing her "petition," and one on HCE's reactions.[8] Here, though the sequence is not quite chronological, we are somewhat closer to a conventional narrative development in the manner of a chronicle or at least of a reportage. What interests us is the fact that in these short passages Joyce outlined the secondary level of the nodal system, that both were generated by the previously written Letter, and that they formed a pendant to the Letter from the very start.

With this in mind we can point to the components of the tertiary level of the Letter system, passages which, while significant and relevant, are somewhat more oblique in their rendering of the nodal subject, and function mainly as brief asides. Usually, they garble the message, presenting it in a more sublimated form; yet, as Hart's listings indicate they are recognizable by virtue of the number of key allusions worked into their texture and by their dominant subject matter.

For example, on pages 11 and 12 in Chapter One, we find a description of the "gnarleybird" scavenging on the field of battle, an avatar of the hen Biddy Doran who scavenged the Letter from the dung heap. It is normal that scraps of Letter find their way into such a passage, but an extended treatment would be out of place. Thus the catalogue of detritus ends as do certain versions of the Letter "With Kiss. Kiss Criss. Cross Criss. Kiss Cross." This is followed by a macabre salutation (a play on the name Anna Livia Plurabelle) and signature: "Undo lives 'end. Slain." Since this passage treats the salvaging of the lost, hence the mending of reputations, we need not be surprised to find the next paragraph ending with a reference to the enigmatic tea stain ("the tay is wet") with which the Letter examined by the Professor in Chapter Iv is signed.

The treatment on pages 301–02 of Shaun's reaction to Shem's account of the truth about his mother is a stronger example of the tertiary node. Indulging in a bout of self-pity Shaun contemplates, among other things, writing a letter to his lady.

> Dear and he went on to scripple gentlemine born, milady bread, he would pen for her, he would pine for her . . . And how are you, waggy?
>
> (FW 301)[9]

Allusions to the Letter occupy only a fraction of the published passage, but in the first draft where the subject was more clearly enunciated, we find mixed in with the aftermath of the Geometry Lesson an account of Shem's letter-writing lesson leading directly to an attack on him by his desperately confused brother. The present version, though over three pages long, submerges the letter motif and introduces references to a number of other nodes including the Tristan and Isolde. On the other hand, it joins the Letter to the secondary system Letter/literature which relates directly to HCE's account of his reading in the outhouse (see the secondary node in IIiii, 363–66).

Three other tertiary nodes can be listed briefly: the "Nightletter" which concludes IIii (FW 308), a ghoulish juvenile spoof; the account of ALP as secretary bird/scavenger which briefly interrupts the pub-jury's deliberations to summarize schematically the Letter's history and mark the decline of the hero (FW 369–70), and a few lines from Issy's response to a departing Jaun in IIIii during which her gift handkerchief (a reference to Veronica's cloth) is identified as a letter and signed with "X.X.X.X." (FW 457–58). It should be clear from this partial listing that while none of these passages adds significantly to our sense of the nodal subject, each of them furthers the system by connecting the Letter to other facets of the night world increasing its physical presence and range. Further, the location is in each case fitting, pointing up some aspect of the nodal subject which has been developed elsewhere.

The three strata of the system outlined above suggest at least two further levels which will broaden the base of the pyramid. Thus on the fourth level we find a strongly marked allusion to the Letter hidden in an account of the growth of the alphabet (*FW* 18.30). Somewhat less accessible, at the base of the structure, is an isolated allusion to the catch phrase "it begins to appear" somewhat randomly pasted onto a passing allusion to *Ulysses*'s critical and publication history: "it agins to pear like it" (*FW* 292.08). Such flitting references are probably the most numerous, but they are also the hardest to locate and chart. They will be found in appropriate places but more widely scattered and quite unaccented. We may think of them as constituting a large if tenuous fifth nodal level, one which may slip beyond the range of Hart's motifs, blending into the allusive subsoil of the text.

The Tristan and Isolde nodal system is of a different order and magnitude, though it too is based in a rather conservative principle of plot. The primary node of this system falls near the middle of the book in IIiv where the seduction of Isolde (or by Isolde) is witnessed by the senile four. The immediate source of Joyce's account is the first act of Wagner's opera, but the treatment owes much to Jules Laforgue among whose mock-*Moralités* we find revisions of *Hamlet, Herodias*, and *Lohengrin*. Like the other primal nodes, the account of the seduction is remarkable for the clarity of its presentation and, despite the intrusive comments of the "four," for its logical development. Joyce has managed to meld two distinct sequences while retaining the rhythms of both and without significantly altering the texture of the early Tristan skit to which he added many of his early *Scribbledehobble* notes:

> It brought the dear prehistoric scenes all back again . . . and after that now there he was, that mouth of mandibles, vowed to pure beauty, and his Arrah-na-poghue, when she murmurously, after she let a cough, gave her firm order, if he wouldn't please mind, for a sings to one hope a dozen of the best favourite lyrical national blooms in Luvillicit, though not too much, reflecting on the situation, drinking in draughts of purest air serene and revelling in the great outdoors, before the four of them, in the fair fine night, whilst the stars shine bright, by she light of he moon, we longed to be spoon, before her honeyoldloom, the plaint effect being in point of fact there being in the whole, a seatuition so shocking and scandalous and now, thank God, there were no more of them . . . listening, to Rolando's deepen darblun Ossian roll, (Lady, it was just too gorgeous, that expense of a lovely tint, embellished by the charms of art and very well conducted and nicely mannered and all the horrid rudy noises locked up in nasty cubbyhole!)
>
> (*FW* 385–86)

The seduction is a high point in the book's development, a seemingly satisfactory and delightfully explicit mating sequence. But it also mediates between the much more obliquely rendered mating of earth and water (mountain and stream, HCE and ALP) in Iviii, and the grotesque and explicit intercourse of Mr. and Mrs. Porter in IIIiv, a passage which comically turns the aging couple into a landscape of love, a map of the Phoenix Park, and hence a symptom of renewal out of bitter ashes. Thus the central love sequence contributes to a second nodal system, one that is tributary to the elaborately developed Tristan and Isolde.

The primary system resonates throughout the book developing allusions to chapters and incidents in Bédier's version of Tristan and Isolde. If the most explicit sequence is the Wagnerian kiss-philtre episode in IIiv, secondary sequences recount more or less clearly other adventures. A passage in Chapter Iiv (FW 94–96) deals with king Mark of Cornwall (an avatar of HCE). The irreverent narrative voice lets the senile four ("fourbottle men, the analists"— FW 95.27) extend their vicarious or voyeuristic experience without once mentioning Tristan and Isolde by name (except in terms of "dear Sir Armoury, queer Sir Rumoury" and "trickle trickle trickle triss"). The role of Mark ("old markiss their besterfar" and "marcus") is only one of several roles played here by HCE, the deceived father/husband. He is also Sinbad ("Singabob, the bedfather") and Pantaloon, the Commedia dell' Arte father figure ("Dirty Daddy Pantaloons") and identified as "that old gasometer with his hooping coppin and his dyinboosycough," with a "big brewer's belch." The intratextual reference to Mark and the events of chapter IIiv are unmistakable, but the ship has been replaced by a field and forest, Issy has become identified with a flirtatious Molly Bloom, and the seducing hero coalesces with the pub-crawling dun of "Cyclops," and even with Lenehan, the aging parasite:

> O breezes! I sniffed that lad long before anyone. It was when I was in my farfather out at the west and she and myself, the redheaded girl,[10] firstnighting down Sycomore Lane. Fine feelplay we had of it mid the kissabetts frisking in the kool kirkle dusk of the lushiness. My perfume of the pampas, says she (meaning me) putting out her netherlights, and I'd sooner one precious sip of your pure mountain dew than enrich my acquaintance with that big brewer's belch
>
> (FW 95.18–26).

This passage continues with a reference to the babes in the woods and the sly adultery aspects of the Tristan myth (see their exile in the wood of Morois) as the four discuss

> her whosebefore and his whereafters and how she was lost away away in the fern and how he was founded deap on deep in anear,[11] and the rustlings and the twitterings and the raspings and the snappings and the sighings and the paintings and the ukukuings and the (hist!) the springapartings and the (hast!)

the bybyscuttlings and all the scandalmunkers and the pure craigs that used
to be . . .

(FW 95.28–35)

As so often happens with well-developed secondary nodes, the passage has
taken on its own vitality, and fallen by associative linkage within a number
of other nodal systems. But if we sort out those elements which refer us to
the Tristan myth, we find them to be preponderant. Hence the passage
belongs to a system generated by a sequence the reader will not encounter
for 300 pages.

 We may speak of IIIiv as belonging to the same family as other chapters
(Iiv, Iviii, IIiv) telling of the fatal love encounter. Though the central event
(after the parents have been awakened by a crying Shem) is the unsuccessful
lovemaking of the aging couple, a bosky love encounter between Tristan and
Isolde by the pine in the garden constitutes an interlace secondary action and
a prelude to the parents' act. The sequence of allusions follows this pattern:
p. 556, Issy-Isolde and the forest theme; p. 561, Issy-Isolde and the philtre;
p.562, Shaun as Tristan the opportunist; p. 563, Shem as sad romantic lover
of Isolde; p. 564, Shem as Tristan by the pine and carving messages in wood
chips; pp. 570–72, a map of love recording the erotic zones of the parents
conceals, among other things, the trysting lovers.[12]

> This place of endearment! How it is clear! And how they cast their spells
> upon, the fronds that thereup float, the bookstaff branchings! The druggeted
> stems, the leaves incut on trees! Do you can their tantrist spellings? I can lese,
> skillmistress aiding. Elm, bay, this way, cull dare, take a message, tawny
> runes ilex sallow, meet me at the pine. Yes, they shall have brought us to the
> water trysting, by hedjes of maiden ferm, then here in another place is their
> chapelofeases, sold for song, of which you have thought my praise too much
> my price. O ma ma! Yes, sad one of Ziod? Sell me, my soul dear! Ah, my
> sorrowful, his cloister dreeping of his monkshood, how it is triste to death,
> all his dark ivytod! Where cold in dearth. Yet see, my blanching kissabelle,
> in the under close she is allso gay, her kirtles green, her curtsies white, her
> peony pears, her nistlingsloes! I, pipette, I must also quickingly to tryst myself
> softly in this littleeasechapel
>
> (FW 571)

The passage from Bédier farcically distorted here is the assignation made by
Tristan who sets cleverly carved chips afloat in the stream that passes through
the royal palace, asking Isolde to meet him by the pine. The names of
the lovers are cunningly disguised and distributed throughout the passage:
"tanttrist . . . trysting . . . sold . . . sad one of Ziod . . . my sorrowful
. . . triste . . . blanching kissabelle . . . tryst . . ." It is precisely this sort
of distribution of variously broad and subtle hints and particularly the allu-

sions to proper names which marks the secondary nodes to which we have been alluding.

We may begin to see how Joyce completed or gave an aura of integrity to the secondary level of the Tristan and Isolde system. If IIiv has a couple orientation, focusing more or less equally on Tristan *and* Isolde, and Iiv focuses mainly on king Mark, IIIiv emphasizes the Isolde role. Joyce seems to have worked out the permutations of focus which are completed by an extended parenthetical reference to "Dolph, dean of idlers," in IIii, an avatar of Shem, in which Tristan's voyages to Ireland are discussed along with those of St. Patrick. That passage interrupts the boys' Geometry Lesson, so the emphasis on the young male is as appropriate as the Isolde orientation is in IIIiv where a description of the female genitalia follows an extended description of HCE/Porter's Wellington Monument. Like all the other secondary nodes, it is recounted from the perspective of the "four." By including it in a central chapter, Joyce has achieved a semblance of formal balance on the secondary level while preparing for the fuller treatment in IIiv.

The Tristan and Isolde system proliferates throughout the text, taking on different colorations in different contexts, frequently blending with other systems but achieving exceptional coherence and consistency. We can point to six fairly distinct levels: 1) the central statement of the myth in IIiv; 2) tributary statements where the theme is elaborated (Iiv, IIii, IIIiv); 3) extended passages where, despite allusions to the personae and aspects of the myth, the myth itself is subdominant; 4) passages of a line or two which coherently evoke "Tristan and Isolde" but in an alien context; 5) passages containing allusions to correlative myths like the Dermot and Grania tale or the various Arthurian legends; 6) brief and generally unsupported references to the chief personae or to some central attribute. By far the largest category is number six in which we find items like "Chapelldiseut" (*FW* 236.20) whose spelling emphasizes both the French origins of this village name and the character of our heroine, but whose context while suggestive of young maidenhood or girlhood is one of several versions of the famous Edgar Quinet passage. If we look carefully in the vicinity of this allusion and of others in this category, we frequently find passages which belong to categories 4 or 5. On page 238 in a context that bristles with allusions to Oscar Wilde's career and which foreshadows Jaun's sermon in IIii, there are three clear references to Isolde of Britany and fidelity: "isapell . . . ishibilley," "for sold long syne"; and one veiled reference to Tristan who died at Penmark. To this same category (4) belong relatively coherent allusions like this one to the bath given Tristan by Isolde: "An they bare falls witless against thee how slight becomes a hidden wound? Soldwoter he wash him all time bigfeller bruisy place blong him" (*FW* 247.22–24). On the very next page we find an item from category 3, an allusion both to the kiss and to the adventure in the forest which includes references to Isolde and Mark but which also alludes to St. Kevin and to Arthur Rimbaud in his role as *le voyant* (*FW* 248.23–249.04).

Not all Joyce's early sketches generated systems as full and elaborate as those relating to the Letter and the Tristan and Isolde. But statements of HCE's vulnerable eminence, his mature vigor, and his mysterious crime all devolve from and refer back to the "Here Comes Everybody" sketch. The fall from eminence along with aging and impotence are most clearly stated in the "Roderick O'Conor." From the "St Kevin" we may trace not only references to the Kevin myth but also Shaun's (false and sentimental) piety, his youthful innocence, and his identity as a solar being. Similarly, there is the large and virtually unexplored system of allusions to St. Patrick, to the confrontation of brothers, to victories won by sleight of hand. As indicated earlier, these systems frequently overlap and interlace to complicate the texture of the book. Inevitably, like everything else in the *Wake*, they contribute to a single overriding system of allusions to the fate of post-fall man as subject to the daily, seasonal, life cycles and to the vicissitudes of history and human relations.

The interlocking systems, so sketchily outlined here, are only gradually unveiled by the process of the text; they are probably never fully perceived by any reader. Further, these primal nodal systems seen in context constitute only the first of at least eight categories which I shall list in something like their order of importance but not attempt to discuss here:

1. The early sketches plus the Letter.
2. Passages devoted to character exposition: the profiles and monologues.
3. Symmetrical passages like the three brother-confrontations and the fables.
4. Expositions of major themes: the fall, the flood, the crime, historical decay, sexual deviation, writing, etc.
5. Developments of aspects of the landscape: river, mountain, ocean, tree, stone, city, park, etc.
6. Allusive parallels drawn from history, religion, and literature: Oscar Wilde, Shakespeare, Ezra Pound, Humphry Clinker, Christ, Buddha, etc.
7. Key rhythms or rhythmic clusters: the tonality of the river, the legalistic "tion" passages of the twelve patrons/judges, the Quinet passage, HCE's stutter, the thunder words, song tags, etc.
8. Foreign language word clusters.

Clearly, we may add to this list and elaborate on the categories. Further, just as the two systems analyzed above deviate from each other, we may expect to find considerable variation among systems on all levels. Readers may differ over the precedence and content of certain categories, but the fact remains that a complex or hierarchy of nodal systems governs our (subliminal) perception of the *Wake*. It makes little difference whether or not the systems focused by the early sketches are *perceived as* more important than those in categories 2, 3, and 4. The principle established by Joyce's decision to build around them has controlled the organization of the rest of the book.

In composing *Finnegans Wake* over a period of eighteen years Joyce was not simply filling in the blanks of a structural plan or indulging in free association. The process was more like running after one's own language, adding allusions or picking them up in an effort to gain and regain mastery over a text which aimed for at least a semblance of comprehensiveness, an all-bookness similar to the one posited by Stéphane Mallarmé. His effort was partly to make language obey *his* rules rather than its own, partly to exploit the givens of language. It is the result of this process which the reader reacts to and experiences in his mirror struggle to master the "proteiform graph" that has immeshed him. Like the writer's, his is an effort to assert a self (by imposing a pattern or a flux of patterns) or rather to win a self back from the language over which he repeatedly gains and as often loses mastery. To this process the "proteiform" network of nodal systems contributes importantly through its imposition, on the very texture of the text it now permeates, of rhythmic orders with recognizable if unfixed dimensions.

In pointing to such an infra-structure we are approaching the essence of the *Wake*'s contribution to subsequent forms, one which may even surpass the contribution of its language to the liberation of the word.

Notes

1. *Structure and Motif in Finnegans Wake*, (Evanston: Northwestern University Press; London: Faber and Faber, 1962).

2. Clive Hart's "Leitmotif" overlaps with and foreshadows our concept of nodalization, but it functions in very different ways. Though he deals with several longer "complexes," Hart focuses mainly on brief allusions which would be placed low on any nodal scale. His practice of building up from the minimal evocative marker or motif to the larger cluster leads him to posit the "motif agglomeration" of which there are two sorts, the first a simple grouping of disparate motifs, the second and more important the "true interacting *leitmotiv*-complex, of which the Letter is the most outstanding example." (*Ibid.*, p. 180.) I would suggest that this sort of "complex" is more handily viewed as a primal node, that it is used in *Finnegans Wake* far less "sparingly" and with more system than Hart claims, and that it should be seen as generating as well as bringing together motifs. Hart also makes use of the term node. But for him "nodal point" occurs when in his catalogues Joyce halts the "narrative for a moment . . . filling the pause with . . . concentrations of motifs" so that the "reader can contemplate the primary materials at his leisure." (*Idem.*) For our purposes nodes are effectively primary materials and the prime nodes halt, not the narrative (which they may in fact constitute in its purest form), but the flow of the rhetoric before they once again break down into their component parts. I believe that this distinction is crucial if we are to understand how the nodes help structure the book.

3. Significantly, one of the more coherent series of early notes in the *Scribbledehobble*

notebook for *Finnegans Wake* concerns the oral tale and its conventions: the notes under "The Sisters," first of the *Dubliners* tales. *Scribbledehobble*, ed. Thomas E. Connolly (Evanston: Northwestern University Press, 1961), pp. 25–27.

4. *Ibid.*

5. *Scribbledehobble*, p. 232.

6. We can only approximate these words.

7. *A First-Draft Version of Finnegans Wake*, ed. David Hayman (Austin: University of Texas Press, 1963), p. 81. For a fuller account of the process by which not only book III but also Iv and Ivii were generated see my introduction and consult the text of the *James Joyce Archive* volume containing facsimiles of chapters Iiv–v (New York: Garland Press, 1978).

8. *Ibid.*, pp. 90–91.

9. This sentence is annotated with a letter to "Erosmas" from "Grunny Grant" but all of the footnotes are in the hand of Issy.

10 Isolde in IIiv has "nothing under her hat but red hair and solid ivory" (*FW* 396.09–10).

11. This is a clear enough reference to ALP's origins as a brook in the hills of county Wicklow (see Iviii) and to HCE as the Norwegian Captain, an avatar of the sea (see IIiii).

12. In this latter passage we find as a secondary subject a reference to Oscar Wilde and sodomy. The emphasis is reversed on page 588, where a passage devoted to Wilde's crimes, trials, and incarcerations includes references to "Issy's busy down the dell" and to a variety of trees.

The Identity of the Dreamer

JOHN BISHOP

HOW TO FIND A GOOD TAILOR

At the center of *Finnegans Wake*, in the darkest hours of its night, the story of a conflict between "Kersse the Tailor and the Norwegian Captain" occurs to our hero (II.ii, 311–30; cf. *U*, 61). As Ellmann explains it, the story is based on one that Joyce's father was fond of telling, "of a hunchbacked Norwegian captain who ordered a suit from a Dublin tailor, J. H. Kerse of 34 Upper Sackville Street. The finished suit did not fit him, and the captain berated the tailor for being unable to sew, whereupon the irate tailor denounced him for being impossible to fit" (*JJ*, 23). Though Ellmann goes on to note that the unpromising subject "became, by the time John Joyce had retold it, wonderful farce," its potential for sheer buffoonery has never been satisfactorily explained in writing on the *Wake*. It emerges, however, in a variant of the story according to which the captain, returning to pick up the suit he ordered, flies into a torrent of invective for the shoddy workmanship he discovers. The tailor looks at him with taxed professional calm, tugs at the garment, and says patiently, "Well, you're not wearing it right! If you just hold your arms like this [the arms twist up like mutant pretzels], if you hold your head like this [the head glues itself to the shoulder], and if you walk like this [the teller staggers off, doubled over and pigeon-toed], it fits perfectly."

What all this has to do with "a reconstruction of the nocturnal life" will become evident if, "by a commodius vicus of recirculation" (3.2), we "rearrive" at the first page of *Finnegans Wake* and the paragraph containing the phrase "in bed"—now to note that the two sentences forming that paragraph are internally linked by the garish homophony of the verbs "retaled" (3.17 [properly, "retailed"]) and "entailed" (3.19). Only a very craftless or a very canny writer would ever have paired them so loudly. Through "sound sense" (109.15, 121.15), Joyce is calling attention to the essential relation of these two "tailwords" (288.3 ["detail," a third]), which derive together with "tailors" from the Old French *taillier* ("to shape by cutting,"

Reprinted from *Joyce's Book of the Dark: "Finnegans Wake"* (Madison: University of Wisconsin Press, 1986), 126–45, 415–20, by permission of the publisher.

"to determine the form of"). The common element linking all these terms has to do with the idea of "tailoring"—formal alteration—it, too, made thematic from beginning to end of *Finnegans Wake*, though most notably in the "tail" (324.5 [or "retailored" "tale"]) of "Kersse the Tailor," which lengthily engages the dark questions "Who fits?" and "Who is suitable?" If the first sentence of that paragraph on the opening page tells us that a "fall" has happened "in bed," it adds by way of verbal qualification that this fall has been "retailed" there—"rendered piecemeal" in this way of telling ("retailing"), and necessarily "retailored" to suit the new and altered conditions of "the Evening World."

Now tailoring, in any form, simply involves the formal alteration of investments—articles of clothing—so that they come out fitting the body more comfortably. It works exactly like sleep if, "letting punplays pass to ernest" (233.19–20), we take "investments" or any of a whole array of related terms in the more abstract senses that have evolved from them. By day the hero of *Finnegans Wake*, something of "misfit," has a great many "vested" interests in "the factionable world" (285.26) represented in the map of Dublin, even though he sometimes feels not "cut out for" (248.17) and "unsuited" to its "fashions," and though sometimes in turn, "fearing for his own misshapes" (313.32), he finds its "modes" unsuitable and "unfitting" (165.25, 127.4). Often they "rub him the wrong way" and afflict him with "wears and tears" (116.36). Survival in the "fashionaping" Daily World (505.8), where being "fascinating" is indistinct from "fashion-aping," requires a kind of "wearing" "uniformity," though nobody ever quite fits the swell-looking "uniform" or lives up to his "model" (191.25; see 127.4). It also demands both a keeping up of "appearances," with "apparel," and the maintaining of "habits" that ultimately "run him ragged" and "wear him down." Clearly, a person so "worn out" needs to be "redressed," and in both senses of that word: on the one hand, he needs to be compensated for afflictions, but on the other, he simply needs a new set of "investments." Relief Map B, then, shows "the Wreck of the Ragamuffin" (290.F5) whose sustained residence in the Daily World of Map A has left him in "Rags! Worns out" (619.19)—the submerged reference to "the Wreck of the Hesperus" (306.26–27), here as throughout the *Wake*, reminding us that the "hole affair" takes place after nightfall (Gr. *hesperos*, "evening", cf. 321.14–15, 387.20, 557.6). In reconstructing this "wrecked ragamuffin's" passage through a night, the *Wake* now issues a general invitation to "Come to the ballay at the Tailors' Hall" (510.14)—where the rhythm of the line and the paragraph it opens evokes a song entitled "The Night of the Ragman's Ball" (510.13–30 [*Annotations*]), and therefore suggests that this night will entail the wholesale "formal alteration" and "redressing" of a badly "worn out" "misfit": "Name or redress him and we'll call it a night" (514.17; cf. 232.20, 489.22–23).

As it turns into his body in sleep, accordingly, the "old worold" (441.18–19)—the "worn" out "old" "worryld" (59.10)—is retailored, so to become "whirrld" (147.22) and to undergo a series of "formal alterations" for which the *Wake*, fond of the prefix of renewal, generates many terms. As it turns into his body in sleep, "willed without witting, whorled without aimed" (272.4–5), it is "recorporated" (228.20), "regrouped" (129.12), "recompounded" (253.35), "remassed" (358.13), "reformed" (361.4), "rearrived" at "from scratch" (3.5, 336.18), and at bottom "recreated" so completely (606.7)—"rereally" (490.17)—that it comes out "rassembling" the reassembled "whorl" shown in Relief Map B (373.14, 6.24), where our hero's "own fitther couldn't nose him" (322.12–13 ["fitter"]). And especially not "his own father," whose "model" no son ever quite "fits": "we drames our dreams tell Bappy returns. And Sein annews" (277.17–18 [Fr. *Sein*, "bosom"]); "the same renew[s]" (226.17). The relief map accordingly illustrates "the Benefits of Recreation" in two senses of the latter word (306.22). Sleep, as a "solstitial pause for refleshmeant" (82.10), is in one sense simply a form of recreation or refreshment that enables our "worn out" hero to return to the world, after undergoing extensive "formal alterations," "finefeelingfit!" (431.1). But in another sense, because it entails a wholesale "dismantling" of the "fabric" of things, sleep re-creates the "worold" completely, retailoring it precisely by "re-fleshing" it, in the form of the body (hence "refleshmeant").[1]

In Carlylean terms, "sartor's risorted" (314.17 [L. *sartor resartus*, "the tailor's retailored"])—at "One Life One Suit (a men's wear store)" (63.16–17). And our worn-out hero, as "besuits" the "ragged," is now simply *"suiting himself."* The orthodox way of putting this would be to say that in "sewing a dream together" (28.7), he is getting his wishes fulfilled— "nett sew?" (312.16). Tailoring, in *Finnegans Wake*, operates much like the "ingenious interweaving process" that Freud calls the dreamwork (*ID*, 317); for that, too, simply involves the "formal alteration" of "investments"— now construed as psychic ones—so that they fit the body more comfortably. It results in the production of that "weaver's masterpiece," the dream (*ID*, 319), where, "as the baffling yarn sail[s] in circles" (320.35), everything is formally altered to suit "our talorman" perfectly (see 375.34–35).

By "redressing" him, the dreamwork enables our hero to bid "sew wrong" (322.8 [and "so long"]) to a world characterized by "uniform matteroffactness" (123.10)—"Love my label like myself" (579.18)—and also to "curse the tailor" who taught him to "Respect the Uniform" (319.27, 320.2, 579.14 [hence "Kersse the Tailor"]). Since he harbors a great deal of bottled-up animosity for this "uniform," "he'll want all his fury gutmurdherers to redress him" (617.18–19); the wording here suggests that it will take a whole army of "fairy godmothers" to spin out the "baffling yarns" necessary to redress the "fury" and "murderousness" rising from his "gut," but at the same time to keep those forces comfortably concealed. As the *Wake* acknowledges in the play of these terms, the formal alterations that transform the Daily World of Map A into the Evening World of Map B make it difficult to know "how comes ever a body in our taylorised world to selve out thishis" (356.10–11 ["how can anybody ever solve out this thesis"])—where the line in part calls attention to the puzzling nature of meaning in dreams, but also latently reveals that HCE, the dreamer himself, inevitably "selves out" "this, his" world, and again, as it "suits" his body ("ever a body"). Passages in *Finnegans Wake* that allude to the story of "Kersse the Tailor" (23.10–11, for instance) operate in cipher to indicate that its hero is undergoing redress and a change of investments at the moment in question (e.g., at 22.30–23.15).

Now of all the properties formally altered in this wholesale retailoring of the world, one particularly bears note here: "telling," since Joyce has retailored the English "retail" into a neologistic "retale" on the first page of the book, and since a running play on words blurs together the meanings of "tailor" and "teller" throughout the *Wake* as a whole (cf. 317.27, 319.8, 319.24). The extended pun calls attention to problems of evident centrality in *Finnegans Wake* by inviting the simple question of how anyone can "tell" when he falls, or has fallen, asleep. As memory will attest, one largely does not, because "telling" is in every way antithetical to the condition of sleep. A Germanic equivalent of the Latinate derivative "rationality" (< L. *ratio*, "reckoning, calculation"), "telling" in even its most quotidian and feeble forms implies the ability deliberately to put two and two together. At root, "to tell" simply means "to count," as in "telling" time or in working as a bank "teller"; but beyond that, it means "to take account," recognitively, as in "telling" what is going on. Finally, in this escalating calculus, "to tell" is to provide a coherent "account," as in "telling a story." The man "tropped head" at the *Wake* cannot "tell" in any of these senses. At the instant he "falls to tail" (285.11)—suffers that "knock out" and "falls to his tail"—he also "fails to tell" in every way possible. He cannot tell a story; he cannot tell what is going on; and he cannot even tell himself apart from the figures in his dreams, who in turn, after his example, can "not rightly tell their heels from their stools" (476.31 [their heads from their toes]). The whole matter of "telling," therefore, is necessarily "retailored" and formally altered in *Finnegans Wake*.

One way of seeing how extensively these formal alterations sweep through the *Wake* would be to examine very closely the syntax of that paragraph on page three containing the verbs "retaled" and "entailed."[2] A broader perspective on the matter would emerge from a consideration of the "tail" of Kersse the Tailor itself, which cannot be read as a narrative involving distinct characters, no matter how hard one tries, because the *Wake*'s "worn-out ragamuffin" simultaneously plays the parts of the misfit and of the dream-weaving "talerman" who suits himself (319.8). The episode reconstructs not a discrete sequence of real-world encounters, but a general process of unconscious "redress" that reaches its climax in the murderous story of the shooting of the Russian general (who is at once our hero's father and our hero himself in the role of a father under attack by two sons). As this example in turn suggests, an ultimate way of seeing how radically the *Wake*'s "telling" is retailored to suit the conditions of the night would be to begin inquiring into the identity of the man who sleeps at *Finnegans Wake*, and all the more essentially because the question, "Who is he?," is central to a coherent reading of the book (261.28). The strangeness of this question emerges fully if we simply bend it back into "our own nighttime": how does anyone sleepily "knock[ed] out" and unconscious "tell" who he is?

"Righting His Name"

As will have become evident in passing, and as many passages in the *Wake* make clear, both the "nomen" (L. "name") of the "noman" who sleeps at *Finnegans Wake* (546.4) and "the facts of his nominigentilisation" (31.33–34) constitute an ongoing problem in the book, rather than a dislodgeable point of information:

> Here line the refrains of. Some vote him Vike, some vote him Mike, some dub him Llyn and Phin while others hail him Lug Bug Dan Lop, Lex, Lax, Gunne or Guinn. Some apt him Arth, some bapt him Barth, Coll, Noll, Soll, Will, Weel, Wall but I parse him Persse O'Reilly else he's called no name at all.
> (44.10–14)

Given these mutually contradictive and ridiculous choices, and considering that the ostensibly privileged name "Persse O'Reilly" fails to appear in "The Ballad of Persse O'Reilly" at all, we should incline toward the culminative item in this catalogue ("he's called no name at all")—and all the more particularly because the phrase "here lie the refrains of" reminds us that we are sharing the "eyewitless foggus" of somebody "dead to the world" in a dimension void of objects, whose "tropped head" contains only the "remains" of "lines" and "refrains," and not alertly arranged and ordered letters. Of necessity the man asleep at *Finnegans Wake* "remain[s] topantically anonymos" throughout the whole book (Gr. *to pan*, "the whole") because he has "tropped head" (34.2–6), concomitantly jettisoning the orderly stuff that ordinarily fills it, not least of which is a knowledge of his own name. As Joyce remarked in an interview of 1936, "there are, so to say, no individual people in the book—it is as in a dream, the style gliding and unreal as is the way in dreams. If one were to speak of a person in the book, it would have to be of an old man, but even his relationship to reality is doubtful."[3]

Anyone's "blank memory" of the night will attest that no one fully unconscious has a retrievable grip on his name, social security number, facial appearance as it most recently gelled in the mirror or the ego, or other such accoutrements of "identity" as enable him, in waking life, to know himself as familiarly as a third person. The *Wake*, accordingly, responds only with positive negativity to continually raised questions about the "indentity" (49.36 [the negated "identity"]) of its sleeping protagonist, as is suggested by the parenthetical answer to the question "Who was he to whom? (O'Breen's not his name nor the brown one his maid)" (56.32–33). By reference to Thomas Moore's lyric "Oh! Breathe not his name," the line indicates that the "naym" of this "nobodyatall" (29.19, 73.19)—where the "nay" negates the "name"—cannot be "breathed" at all, and for reasons lengthily spelled out in Moore's poem.[4] The chain of patently absurd names cited above, then—itself only representative of the string of names that runs through the book as a whole—constitutes only one of many "a long list (now feared in part lost) . . . of all abusive names he was called" (71.5–6), where these "abusive names" might be understood as the products of nomenclatural "misuse" and "abuse" both. Like many "a word often abused" in *Finnegans Wake* (149.34)—"abuse" included—they should not be taken at face value because each of them shows our hero "under the assumed name of Ignotus Loquor" (263.2–3 [L. *ignotus loquor*, "I am talking about the unknown"]).

Though the thousands of variable names patched around the "topantically anonymos" "belowes hero" of the *Wake* serve ultimately to cancel one another out—"In the name of the former and of the latter and of their holocaust. Allmen" (419.9–10)—so to emphasize his essential unnamability, they also serve the crucial purpose of capturing him obliquely, in the manner of "nicknames" (32.18, 46.1; 59.16, 98.27), "bynames" (29.31), "agnomen[s]" (30.3), "moniker[s]" (46.21), and "assumed names" and "ill-assumed names" both (49.8, 263.2; 86.12). They work associatively, that is, like the dreamwork's condensed and "composite structures," to reveal underlying states and conflicts that befall "this most unmentionablest of men" in his drift through the night (320.12–13).[5] The nickname "Timb" or "Tomb" (139.10 ["Finnegan"]), for instance, shows our hero laid out dead to the world. While some may call him "Gunne or Guinn" (44.12), he is surely, as a "Gunnar, of The Gunnings, Gund" (596.15), "Goney, goney gone!" (306.F2). As "Finn," by contrast ("some dub him Llyn and Phin" [44.11]), his "spatiality" (172.9 ["speciality"]) is the containment of space (hence the enclosure of "Dublin" in "dub him Llyn"). And since "some apt him Arth" (44.12), an "apt" composite name might be "Arser of the Rum Tipple" (359.15–16), which designates neither "Arthur of the Round Table" exactly nor a "blackedout" "rummy" whose "tippling" has landed him "on his ars" either (514.34), but their point of convergence, together with the sleeper's, in a once-and-future figure who will "rise afterfall" (78.7).[6]

As the example of these particular "bynames" and the *Wake* itself suggests, the trick to answering the excellent question posed and tackled by Adaline Glasheen in her *Censuses*—"Who's Who When Everybody is Somebody Else?"[7]—is simply to untangle, as in dream analysis, the "condensed" and "displaced" figures that have been "traduced by their comedy nominator to the loaferst terms" (283.6–8). Beneath the whole of *Finnegans Wake*, underlying all the "samilikes" and "alteregoases" and "pseudoselves" in the book (576.33), there lies only a singular "comedy nominator," the "one stable somebody" (107.30) whose nightlife generates the "comic denominations," distorting (or "traducing") them in the process, but who is finally the only real "common denominator" underlying them all. Given any name in *Finnegans Wake*, then, the reader should reduce it "to the loaferst terms"— where the appearance of the book's omnipresent and tell-tale "loafer" in this "lowest" suggests that such a reduction would best be accomplished simply by asking how the name reflects on its hero's "lofetime" (230.19 [nocturnal "lifetime"]).

If, "by a commodius vicus of recirculation," we "rearrive" at the vicinity of the opening page containing the phrase "in bed," all the strange nominal evocations surrounding it now turn out to reveal a little more about the constitution of "Arser's" "knock[ed] out" and "tropped head" at this particular moment in the night. Like Humpty Dumpty ("the fall," "offwall" "humptyhillhead," "humself," "prumptly," "tumptytumtoes"), he has fallen, although asleep, so to enter a state of mind "scrambled," "addled," "cracked," infantilely regressive, and elusive of capture in the King's English (47.26). Like anyone rubbled "after [the] humpteen dumpteen revivals" of a lifetime's mornings (219.15 [who counts them?]), our hero has been "eggspilled" (230.5 ["expelled"]) from the wakeaday reality represented in Map A and transformed, from *homme* to "homelette" (59.29–32), into the scrambled "eggshill" (415.9–10 ["exile"]) depicted in Relief Map B, where he lies "embedded," a Finnegan of sorts, in the night's "seemetery": *Hombly, Dombly Sod We Awhile* (415.14–15). As "a once wallstrait oldparr," comparably, "to name no others, of whom great things were expected in the fulmfilming department" (398.24–26), our hero resembles the legendary "Old Parr" simply in being an "old pa" or *père* (Fr. "father"), burdened with a "scraggy isthmus" (3.5–6 [Gr. *isthmos*, "neck"]) and a "body you'd pity" (381.15), but also with desires difficult of fulfillment in the day.[8] In the night, however, where this "old pa's" wishes get furtively "fulmfilmed," the term "Old Parr"—"to name no others"—in a way "names" "no others," but only the old man himself: since to be an "Old Parr" would be any old man's dream, the term shows our hero wishfully dissolving conflicts that arise from a waning virility. "Reduced to the loaferst terms," then, even particular "nicknames" like "Humpty Dumpty" and "Old Parr" turn out to describe states of unconsciousness and unconscious conflict endured in the sleep of the book's heroic "loafer"—though in their self-eradicating contradictiveness, again, they leave the *Wake*'s "knock[ed] out" nobody "called no name at all." And to the essential question, "Who is he?" (261.28)—"whoishe whoishe whoishe?" (499.35–36)—there are two primary kinds of answer. For as "someone imparticular" (602.7), our "belowes hero" is "someone in particular" whom the night has rendered indistinct.

"IN THE HEART OF THE ORANGEFLAVOURED MUDMOUND"

As readers of *Finnegans Wake* have long noted, Joyce incessantly likens "our mounding's mass," as depicted in Relief Map B, to a vast "dump" (110.26), or "DUNGMOUND" (276.R1), or "kikkinmidden" (503.8)—where the Danish archaeological term *kikkenmidden* (Eng. "kitchen midden") designates a heap of bones marking the site of a prehistoric dwelling, *midden* itself deriving from the Da. *møg dynge* ("dung hill" or "refuse heap"). "A sort of heaps" (596.18), "our mounding's mass" constitutes a "dump" of this nature because his rubbled and "deafadumped" body (590.1), now dead to the world, marks the site of a past life (yesterday's, for instance) and because matters deriving from his past, including letters, are buried inside of it. One way of discovering what lies "in the heart of the orangeflavoured mudmound" (111.34)—the "orange" makes our hero a Protestant—would be to *"Dig him in the rubsh!"* (261.L2 ["dig in the rubbish," or "dig him in the ribs" and wake him up]).

We might see the image of this "dump" particularized by "rearriving" at the book's first page and the vicinity of the phrase "in bed," now to consider "the great fall of the offwall" that it describes (3.18–19). Since the odd compound "offwall" evokes the German *Abfall*, the Danish-Norse *affald*, the Dutch *afval*, and the English *offal*, all generally meaning "refuse or scraps," the paragraph that we have been examining might now be construed as a dense trash heap compacted of things let fall: "oranges . . . laid to rust upon the green," a "dumptied" "Humpty Dumpty" (17.4), a badly contused Finnegan, letters that may have become "litters" (17.28), and finally, containing them all, our "scrapheaped" hero himself (98.17), a "dustman" of sorts (59.16 [Br. "garbage collector"]). "What a mnice old mness it all mnakes! A middenhide hoard of objects!" (19.7–8 [and a "midnight hoard of objects" internalized]).

These details suggest in particular what the paragraph shows more generally if considered as a formal whole. On the evident verbal surface, it reads like a scrap heap of conceptually disconnected words, fragments, references, and quotations: "it's like a dream." For in the psychoanalytical account of dream formation, the manifest content of any dream is much like the manifest content of this paragraph, in being particled together of "residue"—"the day's residue"—or, in Freud's German, *Tagesreste*, where the German *Reste*, literally meaning "remains" or "dregs," would figuratively give the dream the surface structure of a mnemonic dump. Through its ongoing reference to "dumps" and "middens," in part, the *Wake* is concretely conveying the orthodox insight that dreams are compacted of immense networks of scraps and fragments salvaged from the past.[9]

Another way of reading *Finnegans Wake*, then, would be to see any one section of it as a chaotic trash heap of mnemonic bric-a-brac, scraps, trivia, personal memories, and particles of information gathered from such places as the *Encyclopaedia Britannica* and Dublin's papers and lore. Rather than examining the "infrarational" connections that coherently link these particles of residue together in the "Evening World," it would be possible to trace them back to their sources in the Daily World, to see where they came from and to infer things about "the days when Head-in-Clouds walked the earth" (18.23–24 [as opposed to his nights, when he does not]). Studies of the *Wake* that identify the "facts" constituting its manifest content do just this, and they accordingly serve the important purpose of putting our hero's "nightlife" into a concrete, real-world context and milieu. The richness of these studies enables us to work backwards from the *Wake*, to establish a sense not of our hero's nightlife, but of his life in the day; and they allow us to begin seeing "this very pure nondescript" as a Bloom-like "ordinary man" (64.30), "somebody mentioned by name in his telephone directory" (118.12–13).

Although we have so far regarded "Sir Somebody Something" as a stupefied anyman (293.F2), an "imparticular" "Here Comes Everybody" (32.18–19), the sheer density of certain repeated details and concerns allows us to know that he is a particular, real Dubliner. The nature of these recurring concerns, moreover, enables us to see that most of what Joyce leaked out to his publicists and much of what the criticism has inferred is largely true. Our hero seems to be an older Protestant male, of Scandinavian lineage, connected with the pubkeeping business somewhere in the neighborhood of Chapelizod, who has a wife, a daughter, and two sons. Since the subject of his dreams is *not* these people or places as objective entities, however, but the more complex matter of his "investments" in them, a great deal about his factual life in the Daily World is hard to reconstruct with any certainty. *Finnegans Wake* offers less a factual "family history" than a "family histrionic" (230.29).

What emerges from an examination of the details is the sense of someone as singularly unsingular as Leopold Bloom. As "the herewaker of our hamefame" rises from the vacuum of his sleep toward a reacquired knowledge of his "real namesame" in the last pages of the book (619.12–13), his spectacular lack of distinction becomes more and more evident (and notably in III.iv). "One of the two or three forefivest fellows a bloke could in holiday crowd encounter" (596.15–17), he could not stand out in a crowd if he tried. Repeated indications suggest that he is "a man of around fifty" (506.34), roughly "fiftytwo heirs of age" (513.23), "anything . . . between fiftyodd and fiftyeven years of age" (380.13–14) or, more elaborately:

> a man in brown about town . . . picking up ideas, of well over or about fiftysix or so, pithecoid proportions [Eng., "apelike"], with perhops five foot eight, the usual X Y Z type . . . not in the studbook by a long stortch . . . always trying to poorchase movables by hebdomadaries for to putt in a new

house to loot [to let], cigarette in his holder, with a good job and pension in Buinness's, what about our trip to Normandy style conversation . . . seeking relief in alcohol and so on. . . .

(443.20–444.2)

Reference both to the draining activity of "poorchase" ("purchase") and to a "hebdomadary" ("weekly") salary earned in a "business" involving "Guinness's" (hence "Buinness's") tells us something about this man's income, as does reference to the "movables" that his harried "poor chase" takes as its objects ("movables," sl. for "small objects of value," also suggest the Fr. *meubles*, "furniture"). It is through countless details like these that we gradually amass the sense of a life as heartwrenchingly drab as Bloom's, a life of dispiriting modern routine whose quotidian highlights seem to be:

> business, reading newspaper, smoking cigar, arranging tumblers on table, eating meals, pleasure, etcetera, etcetera, pleasure, eating meals, arranging tumblers on table, smoking cigar, reading newspaper, business

(127.20–23)

As the mirrorlike structure of this little catalogue implies, the alpha and omega of the whole arrangement is "business," which brackets everything else so stolidly that "pleasure" can only dissolve in a listless blur of ill-defined "etceteras" somewhere in the middle of things. This happens because when our hero does get away from "business, reading newspaper, etcetera," "pleasure" takes singularly limited and unimaginative forms:

> minerals, wash and brush up, local views, juju toffee [a real treat!], comic and birthdays cards [on special days of the year]; those were the days and he was their hero.

(127.24–25)

Passages like these evoke a quotidian tedium much of the sort that our hero himself foresees in the late hours of the *Wake*, as he grows dimly conscious of the imminence of another day-in-the-life of this quality and so sinks resolutely back into sleep:

> Retire to rest without first misturbing your nighbor, mankind of baffling descriptions. Others are as tired of themselves as you are. Let each one learn to bore himself. It is strictly requested that no cobsmoking, spitting, pubchat, wrastle rounds, coarse courting, smut, etc, will take place amongst those hours so devoted to repose.

(585.34–586.3)

These details also suggest why Joyce, rather than writing another novel like *Ulysses*, sought in *Finnegans Wake*, with a Protestant publican rather than a Jewish ad-canvasser as a hero, to provide an account of the "alternate night-joys" (357.18) that lavishly open in the unharnessed imagination of this "very pure nondescript" and in the dreams through which he is "redressed." What he is unconscious of is precisely his own potential, and the possibility that life could be so much more.

The reader will notice that each of the passages examined above contains a reference to liquor ("Buinness's"), to barkeeping and bottlewashing ("arranging tumblers on table"), to pubs ("pubchat"), or to the sordid glory of the barroom ("wrastle rounds, coarse courting, smut, etc"). These are only representative instances of details whose continual recurrence compels us to see our hero as a "large incorporate licensed vintner, such as he is, from former times" (580.23–24 [like yesterday]). Though the wishfully inflated terms here elevate him into a better businessman than he seems to be, they inevitably suggest, together with an unending stream of references to a barroom ambience evoked through song fragments and gossip, that our hero is a "headboddylwatcher of the chempel of Isid" (26.17 ["head bottle-washer of Chapelizod"]). All such references as these would constitute vestiges of "the day's residue," too, allowing us to see the barroom as our hero's sphere of operation. "Arranging tumblers on tables" is his life.

One would be hard pressed to find a page in *Finnegans Wake* that did not name a variety of kinds and brands of alcohol and in part because these items are our hero's occupational tools; alcohol in general is part of his days' residue.[10] But if, on the one hand, these references allow us to work backwards from the manifest content of the text to draw inferences about "the days when Head-in-Clouds walked the earth," meanings in dreams are "overdetermined," so that these references also operate symbolically, to help describe the nights when "Head-in-Clouds" just lies there. Since alcohol has the power to "black out" and render him "alcoh alcoho alcoherently" "absintheminded" (40.5, 464.17; see 380.7–382.26), it invariably operates in the *Wake* as a cipher for the opiating powers of sleep: "poppypap's a passport out," but so are sleep and heavy drinking (25.5; cf. 84.17–18, 475.9–10). Because alcohol does to the brain much what sleep does, blotting out rationality and lifting inhibitions, the move "From Miss Somer's nice dream back to Mad Winthrop's delugium stramens" (502.29–30 ["midwinter's delirium tremens"]) is an inevitable one. "Arser of the Rumtipple," then, has "boomarpoorter on his brain" (327.33–34 [wishful delusions of Napoleonic grandeur because of strong-spirited "water on the brain"]), and also "a boodle full of maimeries" in both his "boozum" and his "hoagshead" (348.7, 449.16, 15.31 ["bottlefull"]); the reference here, to a "Howth head" with all the internal properties of a "hogshead," invites us again to inspect the "tropped head," of the figure shown "evidently under the spell of liquor" in the relief maps (43.16) and to ask the question, sustained in the *Wake*,

—Wisha, is he boosed or what, alannah? . . .
—Or he's rehearsing somewan's funeral.

(477.5,9)

Since the person "knock[ed] out" never knows what hit him, questions like this one, as far as he can "no," can have no answer: "it may half been a missfired brick" that "conk[ed] him" out (5.26, 170.14), or perhaps "he had had had o'gloriously a'lot too much hanguest or hoshoe fine to drink" (63.21–23 [Gael. *thoise fíon*, "fill of wine"; "had had had" yields " 'had' one too many"]). Alcohol, at any rate, saturates Joyce's "alcohoran" (20.9–10) for an overdetermined variety of reasons.

So too do references to names of pubs and inns, which drift through our hero's "nightlife" because he is concerned about his work and anxious about the competition.[11] But at the same time, meanings in dreams being over-determined, many of these pub-names also serve latent, sleep-descriptive functions. Etymologically, an "inn" is a place where one is not "out," and our "innermost" "innerman," (194.3, 248.32, 462.16) in the "duskguise" of "Here Inkeeper," (376.10 [not "innkeeper"]), does a very good job of "keeping in." As an "innvalet" (320.15), he is not simply a public servant ("innvalet"), but one asleep in bed (hence "invalid"). "Malthus is yet lukked in close" throughout the *Wake* (604.7), comparably, partly because this "Inkeeper's" "malthouse" is closed for the night, but also because, simply by sleeping, he is practicing a form of birth control (hence "Malthus"). Pub names like "The Old Sot's Hole" (41.32, 147.5), the "Halfmoon and Seven Stars" (59.1–2), the "Blackamoor's Head" (59.2), and the "Black and All Black" (59.4) accordingly help to evoke the blacked-out head of a benighted man who "is not all there, and is all the more himself since he is not so, being most of his time down at the Green Man" (507.3–4); and while this "Green Man" seems simply to name another pub, it also suggests that this man "keeping in" at "the Mullingcan Inn" (64.9), "mulling" as best as he "can," will rise from the dead in the morning (like "the green man" of folklore).[12] Attention to subliminal meanings like these, layered everywhere under the *Wake*'s verbal surface, now leads us back into a consideration of our hero's "imparticularity" in the night.

HCE

One of many passages in the *Wake* that clarifies our hero's "*Unmentionability*" (107.7) explains that

> . . . there is said to have been quondam (pfuit! pfuit!) some case of the
> kind implicating, it is interdum believed, a quidam (if he did not exist it
> would be necessary quoniam to invent him) . . . who has remained topantically
> anonymos but . . . was, it is stated . . . seemingly . . . tropped head. . . .
> (33.33–34.6)

These tangled words (note the six passive constructions) require some sorting out. They tell us that while the "topantically anonymos" man who sleeps at *Finnegans Wake* is largely only "a quidam" (L. "a certain unnamed person") with a "quondam" identity—"it used to be there" when "he was" (L. *quondam fuit*), but now it simply isn't—Joyce had to find a way of designating the central presence of his hero throughout the book; for "if he did not exist (and it is not at all clear that anyone "dead to the world" does) it would be necessary quoniam to invent him" (L. *quoniam*, "because," "for this reason"). While "allauding to him by all the licknames in the litany," then (234.21–22), Joyce draws on the inventive "sigla H.C.E." (32.14) less to "allude to" than to identify the "one stable somebody" who sleeps (107.30), unnamable because unconscious, at *Finnegans Wake*. Operating between lines (481.1–3), within words (421.23 ["HeCitEncy"]), in reverse order (623.9 ["ech?"]), but primarily in acrostic formations, the "normative letters" HCE (32.18) permeate *Finnegans Wake*, moving through the body of the text with supple protoplasticity, so to convey the continuous presence of a specific "Homo Capite Erectus" (101.12–13) within whom the "hole affair" unfolds. "A family all to himself" (392.23–24), "he is ee and no counter he who will be ultimendly respunchable for the hubbub caused in Edenborough" (29.34–36 [as for everything else in the book]). Like "Punch," in other words, "all the charictures in the drame" (302.31–32) are mere puppets invisibly controlled by HCE—a "puppetry producer" of sorts (219.6–8)— who alone is "responsible" for their motions (hence "respunchable"). Only interior to "the heavenly one with his constellatria and his emanations" (157.18–19) do all other manifestly differentiated "characters" like ALP, Shem, Shaun, and Issy appear, as "constelled" products of his dreaming mind, in the manner of the Kabbalah's sephirotic emanations (see 29.13–15, 261.23–24).

Consider, for example, "Shaun the Post," who seems to attain the status of an independent character in the third book of *Finnegans Wake* and whom the criticism customarily treats as a discrete agent. Not simply Joyce's remark that "there are no characters" in *Finnegans Wake*, but countless details in Book III itself reveal that Shaun's evidently "uniform" appearance is really "fumiform" (413.31 [L. "made of vapor"]); that he "weigh[s] nought" (407.5), like any phantom; and that his "autobiography," a nonexistent "blank," is "handled . . . in the ligname of Mr van Howten" (413.30–414.3). Since this "ligname" designates a body dead to the world (Ger. *Leichnam*, "corpse"), and since the "nickname" "van Howten" moves us into "Howth" ("HEAD"), the details show that Shaun is only a figment in HCE's "tropped head," representative of a letter-carrying and letter-conscious state of mind into which the dreamer ascends as he moves toward wakening.[13] The notoriously strange "barrel" in which Shaun appears ("I am as plain as portable enveloped" "care of one of Mooseyeare Goonness's registered andouterthus barrels" [414.10–12]) is therefore simply a cipher for the imperceived and "unknown body" of HCE (96.29), within which the "fumi-form[ed]" Shaun and all kinds of letters are in fact "enveloped": etymologi-cally, the English word "body" derives from the Old English *bodig* ("a cask" or barrel) and is cognate with the Middle Low German *boddig* ("a tub for brewing") because then as now the body was perceived as a container of better things ("spirits"). While Shaun's barrel seems to be one of "Msr. Guinness's," then, the spelling "Mooseyeare Goonness's" also suggests that beneath all appearances, Shaun is simply a diffuse aggregate of "spirits," a being with all the palpability of a fairy tale figure (hence "Mother Goose"), who appears inside of HCE.

It is impossible, of course, not to wonder why Joyce chose "the sigla H.C.E." to designate his hero, although these "initials majuscule," strictly speaking, mean nothing and are "meant to be baffling" (119.16–17). In the form explored by Roland McHugh, the "chrismon trilithon sign ⊓, finally called after some his hes hecitency Hec" (119.17–18), stands outside of all familiar alphabetic systems;[14] while its acrostic equivalent, "the sigla H.C.E.," "means" something independently of phonetic systems. The two formations constitute, like the letter M in Beckett's *Unnamable* trilogy, a sign without signification, a human formation closed to any referential exte-rior, and so come to carry, in *Finnegans Wake*, the weight of the Biblical Tetragrammaton, the unnamable name, in evoking only "a rude breathing on the void of to be" (100.27), "the allimmanence of that which Itself is Itself alone" (394.32–33 ["rude breathing" suggests the formative breath or "spirit" of YHWH in Genesis]). Still, since the characters in the acrostic *are* Romanic, and since Joyce was hardly a practitioner of the arbitrary, it seems inevitable that a rationale should underlie his choice of the trigrammaton HCE. The configuration clearly works better than HIM or IAM, either of which would hardly have been obscure enough to conform to anyone's sense of sleep (see, however, 166.18–19). But why HCE?

Readers who have engaged this question seem to have arrived at a sketchy consensus, commonly detecting somewhere beneath HCE an evoca-tion of the words of consecration in the Roman Catholic Mass (incidentally the longest wake on record): *Hoc est enim corpus meum* ("For this is my body").[15] The reading is difficult to disregard once it is pointed out because it enables HCE always to verge on signifying, without ever fully doing so, *hoc corpus est*—"This is the body," stripped of pronominal definiteness and caught at the transubstantiative moment in which "word is made flesh," and primarily only flesh. It enables HCE to mean nothing, in other words, in much the same way that the body "means" nothing. Whether or not one buys a reading this definitive is finally not crucial because its purport is everywhere evident anyway. Sleep is absolutely transubstantiative in force: turning the whole world into the body of the sleeper, it incarnates everything (see relief map). If the text periodically warns us that "it is a slopperish matter, given the wet and low visibility," "to idendifine the individuone" of which it treats (51.3–6 ["to identify" and "define" the "one" "individual"]), it adds by way of parenthetical explanation that the whole business is "slopperish" because the "sword of certainty which would indentifide the body never falls" (51.5–6). The wording here, for all its cultivated vagueness plainly "identifies the body," even as it "hides" it (hence "indentifide"), and in much the same way that the cipher HCE simultaneously "identifies" and "hides" the *Wake*'s central figure, "the presence (of a curpse)" (224.5–6). While "allauding to him by all the licknames in the litany," then (234.21–22)—by all such "nicknames" as "Finnegan," "Arser," "Old Parr," "etcicero" (152.10)—Joyce draws on "the sigla H.C.E." less to "allude to" than to "indentifide" the "Great Sommboddy" lying "dead to the world" at the *Wake* (415.17 [Fr. *somme*, "sleep"]), and to identify it largely as some "*body*"; for underlying all the *Wake*'s allusive "licknames" one finds only a body "let drop as a doombody drops" (289.15): these "licknames," too, "indentifide" the Ger. *Leichnam* ("corpse").

As HCE, then, the "belowes hero" of *Finnegans Wake* is not at all a "character," possessed of reified properties like "personality," "individuality," and "identity," but a body, inside of which, "tropped head," there is no consciousness of anything much outside, except as it has been cargoed and reformed in memory; on top of and throughout which, in wakefulness, the man-made constructs of character, personality, individuality, identity, and ego have been layered. This is the case not simply because all of these concepts and terms are arbitrary constructions entertained in consciousness to describe conscious agents, but also because they are parochially modern and narrow fictions, and not transhistorical or innate human properties. Developed in that period of historical upheaval that saw, with the rise of the novel, the evolution of a sense of selfhood compatible with the urgencies of capitalism, terms like "character" and "personality" harness the human into kinds of self-"possession"—ones heavily invested with a sense of the "proper" and "propriety," of "ownership" and one's "own"—that ensure adaptive survival within a system structured on the values of "possession" and "property."[16] The artificiality of these "fibfib fabrications" (36.34) enables us to see from yet another perspective why Joyce would have spoken of *Finnegans Wake* as a work breaking with a certain form of Cartesianism. It is not simply that no one asleep has the least consciousness of objective reality, or of the manifold objects of which it is constituted. In a world void of objects, "if I may break the subject gently" (165.30 [and this last time in a philosophical sense]), we also find the complementary property of the "subject," in whose eyewitness focus those objects congeal, "disselving" (608.5 ["dissolving"]). Insofar as the *Wake* has a psychological "subject," that "sopjack" is simply "an unknown body" (96.29).

If, then, we "rearrive" at the opening page of the book, we might see that "Howth Castle and Environs" (3.3)—an odd locution, when all is said and done—does not straightforwardly designate "Dublin," but Dublin as it has been transubstantiated and incarnated inside the all-absorbing cipher HCE; or, in Freudian terms, Dublin as it has been introjected and incorporated; or, in Joycean terms, Dublin as it has been swallowed "schlook, schlice and goodridhirring" (7.18–19 ["hook, line, and sinker"]), interior to a body that has "disselv[ed]" under "the Helpless Corpses Enactment" of sleep into the elements of "hallucination, cauchman, ectoplasm" (423.31, 133.24). If the first two of these elements evoke the familiar province of the dream and the nightmare (Fr. *cauchemar*), the last evokes only the less accessible eventfulnesses passed out in a body fallen "under heaviest corpsus exemption" and submitted to the "changed endocrine history" of night (362.17, 136.28): "ectoplasm," in the discourse of spiritualism, is the "nomatter" that forms the bodies of ghosts; in embryology, it is the primal matter from which, "later on life," all surfaces of the body that negotiate contact with the external world—sensory organs, skin, brain, "brainskin" (565.13)— eventually evolve. As a phrase, then, "Howth Castle and Environs" merely accomplishes in small what that paragraph at the bottom of page three does more elaborately. Like every other construction containing "the sigla H.C.E.," it shows our hero "hiding the crumbends of his enormousness" "to the hidmost coignings of the earth" (102.6, 118.36–119.1); for concealed beneath every manifest appearance in the *Wake*'s nocturnal universe ("hidmost") is the unconscious body of its sleeper, "himself in the flesh" (79.2), within whose "cremains" (hence "crumbends") all landscapes hallucinatorily or ectoplastically arise.

These considerations will enable us to begin filling in the vast "blank memory" we all have of the night by allowing us to see that what must take place in parts of sleep void of dreams is the body itself, which has to be there in the "Real Absence" of everything else for one "to be continued." This in turn will suggest why the opening pages of *Finnegans Wake* will conform, as "representation," to anyone's experience of the night, though not to a conventionally conceived dream. Since the content of our "knock[ed] out" hero's "tropped head" here is largely "his own body" (185.36)—"an unknown body" as dead to the world as Finnegan's—what is ultimately being represented is less a dream than the fertile ground of dreams; and if in wakefulness HCE "has" a body, in the night he simply "is" one. *Finnegans Wake*, in other words, is a representation of a human body. This is only what we might expect of a work entitled the *Wake*, where, as at all wakes, the body is the life of the party. *Finnegans Wake* now becomes a "vivle" of sorts (110.17), a form of "secret stripture" whose subject is "the supreme importance . . . of physical life" (293.F2, 35.22–23).

Ten years before *Finnegans Wake* was published, in that collection of essays entitled *Our Exagmination*, for which Joyce claimed responsibility, Marcel Brion spoke of *Work in Progress*, predictably enough, as an enterprise seeking to convey "a reality true and whole in itself," "obey[ing] its own laws and appear[ing] to be liberated from the customary physical restraints." But he added:

> I imagine that [Joyce] could write an unprecedented book composed of the simple interior physical existence, of a man, without anecdotes, without supernumeraries, with only the circulation of the blood and the lymph, the race of the nervous excitations towards the centres, the twisting of emotion and thought through the cells.[17]

Ten years later, presumably, Joyce had realized what in 1929 lay yet undone. A number of gathering energies in Joyce's literary career make it plausible that the *Wake* should move toward this end—not least the evidence of *Ulysses*, which ends where *Finnegans Wake* merely begins, *inside* a human body on the verge of sleep; and whose real structure (retrospectively elicited as Joyce revised and drew up the Gilbert-Linati schemata) turned out to be that of the human body, an organism Bloom-like in its adaptive energies, rather than an organization foreplanned. The body is, to some ways of thinking, a Catholic prepossession—the "cloacal obsession" of H. G. Wells's phrase—though by the time Joyce had passed through *Ulysses* into *Finnegans Wake* he had found it as catholic in its understructuring impingements on the real as had Freud ("One life is all. One body. Do. But do" [*U*, 202]). If by 1937 Joyce had taken to demeaning *Ulysses* as "a little prelude to WIP [*Work in Progress*]"—and in some sense, rightly—he clarified the preludic relation of his "day book" to his "night book" by calling *Ulysses* "more an epic of the body than of the human spirit," going on to observe impatiently that "for too long were the stars studied and man's insides neglected. An eclipse of the sun could be predicted many centuries before anyone knew which way the blood circulated in our own bodies."[18] Both the context in which Joyce made these remarks, and his tell-tale reference to an "eclipse of the sun"—one way of saying "night"—lets us know that he was explaining, obliquely as always, *Finnegans Wake*.

Already one can see why the English word "body," unlike the enveloping signifier "HCE," is hardly an adequate term for the "one continuous present tense integument slowly unfolded" through "all . . . moodmoulded cyclewheeling history," within which *Finnegans Wake* takes place (185.36–186.2). For this is not the body taken literally, or the body as we in any way consciously bring it to mind, in the process converting it into exactly what it is not (mind). It is above all not the body construed as an object—a thing through whose instrumentality a headier, *Britannica*-reading subject wedged in somewhere behind the eyes and between the ears can look down on the paltry "tumptytumtoes" to which it is attached and comprehend its relation to them by seeing them visibly "out there," in outer space, on a categorical parity with his shoes and the furniture. No, "(the best was still there if the torso was gone)" (291.14–15).[19] Nor is this the organic body of romantic ideologies; for as both a reading of *The New Science* and close study of "gradual morphological changes in our body politic" will show (165.26–27), HCE's is the "body politic" of "someone imparticular" (602.7), a body instilled with discrete laws by parents localized in a real historical situation and disciplined into polish, politeness, and other such self-policing laws as are entrenched in the "Hoved politymester" of the head to insure its survival in the polis (324.20 [the underlined words are etymologically related]).

The "local busybody" lying at the center of the *Wake*, then (438.16), has affinities with the body as treated in Foucault, in being "an effect of power," and "institution" humanly made and organized by subjection to extended disciplinary practices, within which a "micropolitics" is immanent. And it certainly has affinities with the body as treated by Freud, the body conceived as a field of emotions, attitudes, and symptomatic knots susceptible to discursive unravelling, whose structures unfold in dreams and whose formation is the story of a life held taut in unconscious conflicts of "wills gen wonts" (4.1). The body lying dead to the world at the *Wake* is the form outside of which nothing known to humanity ever happens and inside of which everything ordinarily set apart as external in fact only ever comes to life, in the form of sensationalistic impressions, memories, stamps, welts, and symptoms. Above all, this "unknown body" has affinities with the bodies of Vico's earth-founding giants, of which all other things are evolved forms.

What is true of the boozy, symposial crowd gathered at "Finnegan's Wake" holds equally true of much of the commentary on *Finnegans Wake* and of a platonically prepossessed Western culture generally: "they just spirits a body away" (289.F2); or, more conspiratorially, "(. . . we purposely say nothing of the stiff, both parties having an interest in the spirits)" (82.8–9). That so little has been said about the stiff at the *Wake* is only one sign of the unconsciousness to which consciousness repressively relegates the body;[20] but the oversight affects as well much commentary on dreams. Freud's insistence on the sexual grounding of dreams might well be regarded, in this Joycean light, as a determination not to see dreams foliating out of anything other than the living body which is the site of their origination and their driving cause. Dreams only hold out the manifest illusion of taking place, for instance, in Dublin or in any other locale that one might investigate "out there." In fact, they take place in sleep, in bed, inside of and because of the body of the dreamer. By putting us "back in the flesh" (67.5) the *Wake* returns us to "some precise hour which we shall again agree to call absolute zero or the babbling pumpt of platinism" (164.9–11). All things in the *Wake* start here, "in the flesh."

Notes

1.   Somewhere at issue in the *Wake*'s extended play with tailors and tailoring is the whole question of sleep's relation to "fitness." Everyone has heard the story of the energetic octogenarian who bounces out of bed every morning having required only an hour or two of sleep; and everyone knows the darker counterstory of the depressive teenager who cannot keep his eyes open anywhere, for anyone. To these stories one adds the legends—of Napoleon, for instance, who believed that a child needed six hours of sleep a night, a woman five, and a real man only four; or of Schopenhauer, who found it impossible to think unless he got a solid twelve hours a night. Stories like these raise questions of what sleep accomplishes that enables sleep requirements to vary so widely from individual to individual. And they are complicated by others that show how greatly people tailor sleep to suit themselves and their needs. Why is it that some people waken out of beds that look as crisp and unwrinkled as if they had hardly been slept in, while others crawl out of spaces that look as if they had been sacked? What happens down there?

People who have studied these things invariably note that the restorative powers of sleep have little to do with any such "healing processes" as folklore attributes to a changed metabolism. Though body temperature falls slightly in the night (see 597.32–34), the heartbeat decelerates (see 608.10–11), and the musculature relaxes, the most dramatic of the night's alterations sweep through the head, where distinctions between the purely physiological and the purely psychological grow very hazy indeed: both the evolved need for sleep and sleep's ability to reinvigorate originate in the brain. It would of course be extreme to claim, as some have, that the need for sleep is purely psychological (or physiological), because the whole area is one in which distinctions between the mind and the body break down entirely. Perhaps the only thing of which we can be certain is that by "redressing" one, sleep "will make a newman if anyworn" (596.36–597.1ff. ["of anyone" "worn"]): "after a goodnight's rave and rumble . . . he [is] not the same man" (41.14–15).

For further discussions of the subject, see Andre Tridon, *Psychoanalysis, Sleep and Dreams* (London: Kegan Paul, Trench, Trubner, 1921), pp. 11–15; Ernest Hartmann. *The Functions of Sleep* (New Haven: Yale Univ. Press, 1973), p. 68; and Luce and Segal, *Sleep*, pp. 21–29, 108–9.

2.   Like every other element in the paragraph, its syntax is retailored in order to "describe the night itself." Its first sentence, like the state of sleep, is passive and void of identifiable person ("The fall . . . is retaled"); while in the second ("The great fall . . . entailed . . . the pftjschute"), the object is just a foreign and blurred version of the subject (Fr. chûte = Eng. "fall"). Since we find "the fall" entailing a version of itself, moreover, rather than a distinct effect, causal relations have also clearly disintegrated "(for was not just this in effect which had just caused that the effect of that which it had caused to occur?)" (92.33; cf. 482.36–483.1). At every level, the grammar is elaborately replicating the perceptual character of dreams.

We know that these syntactical niceties are deliberate because other passages in the *Wake* self-consciously discuss them. *Finnegans Wake* is more thickly riddled with passive constructions—or "deponent[s]" (187.30)—than any teacher of writing would ever care to point out, because "passivism" (137.33) together with "being sinned" and "being been," is a condition of the night ("being been" would signify a purely passive form of being). "Has it become to dawn in you yet that the deponent, the man from Saint Yves, may have been (one is reluctant to use the passive voiced) may be been as much sinned against as sinning?" (523.7–10). A "deponent" in the legal sense since he alone emits all the conflicting evidence over which he refuses to budge, the *Wake*'s "pacific subject" is also a "deponent" in the grammatical sense, since in sleep he takes a form outwardly passive though internally active, at least until "dawn dawns" in him. He is also entirely like "the man from St. Ives" in lying at the heart of a riddle of apparently stupefying insolubility whose resolution, as here and as throughout *Finnegans Wake*, turns out to be very simple. As the recurrent rhythm of "As I Was Going to St. Ives" reminds us throughout the *Wake* (e.g., at 12.29–31, 215.15–17, 330.1–4), all the dizzily proliferating appearances in the dream finally reduce to a single "one," and he is simply sleeping.

Reference to the "relief map" will clarify some choice instances of the passive voice in *Finnegans Wake*: "it was attempted by the crown" (86.6–7 [sl. for "head"]) feebly and unsuccessfully; and "as if that were not to be enough for anyone" (85.20–21), "little headway, if any, was made" (85.21–22). This is the case, "it was felt by me" (537.22–23), because the owner of the head "to whom reference has been made had been absent" (39.28–29), although "it was not unobserved of those presents" (92.22–23). The passive voice in *Finnegans Wake* in general replicates the "passivism" of the "tropped head."

3. Vinding, "James Joyce in Copenhagen," p. 149. On the identity of the sleeper, see Edmund Wilson, "The Dream of H. C. Earwicker," *The Wound and the Bow* (New York: Oxford Univ. Press, 1947), pp. 243–71; Ruth von Phul, "Who Sleeps at *Finnegans Wake?*" *James Joyce Review* I (June 16, 1957):27–38; James Atherton, "The Identity of the Sleeper," *A Wake Newsletter*, n.s., 4 (Oct. 1967):83–85; Hart, *Structure and Motif*, pp. 81–83; Bernard Benstock, "L. Boom as Dreamer in *Finnegans Wake*," *PMLA* 82 (March 1967):91–97, and *Joyce-Again's Wake* (Seattle: Univ. of Washington Press, 1965), p. 215; Robert Martin Adams, *James Joyce: Common Sense and Beyond* (New York: Random House, 1966), pp. 178–81; and Michael Begnal, "The Dreamers at the *Wake*: A View of Narration and Point of View," in Begnal and Grace Eckley, *Narrator and Character in "Finnegans Wake"* (Lewisburg, Pa.: Bucknell Univ. Press, 1975), pp. 19–123.

The views expressed in these places, representative of those circulating in the criticism, fall into four main groupings, according to which: (1) the dreamer is a single sleeping man; (2) the dreamer is Joyce himself; (3) the dreamer is a "universal mind"; and (4) there is no single dreamer, but actually ten or several. Of these views, the first is most consistent both with Joyce's remarks on the subject and with the remarks of Joyce's co-workers and publicists (Budgen, Gillet, and all the writers represented in *Our Exagmination*). Not simply Joyce's reading of the *Wake* makes this the most sensible approach to the book, however, but repeated indications given everywhere in the text itself. There we read, for instance, that all "the traits featuring the *chiaroscuro* coalesce, their contrarieties eliminated, in one stable somebody" (107.29–30). That this "one stable somebody" (not ten) is identified as "our social something" humanizes and particularizes him.

4.   Oh! breathe not his name, let it sleep in the shade,
        Where cold and unhonor'd his relics are laid;
        Sad, silent, and dark be the tears that we shed,
        As the night-dew that falls on the grass o'er his head.

        But the night-dew that falls, though in silence it weeps,
        Shall brighten with verdure the grave where he sleeps;
        And the tear that we shed, though in secret it rolls,
        Shall long keep his memory green in our souls.

Thomas Moore, *Moore's Irish Melodies* (Boston: Oliver Ditson Co., 1893), rev. ed., p. 80.

Hodgart and Worthington (*Song*, pp. 9–10) have pointed out that Joyce incorporated into *Finnegans Wake* the titles of all but two of Moore's 124 *Irish Melodies*, together with the names of the original Irish airs to which they were set (Moore wrote "Oh! Breathe Not His Name," for instance, to the tune of "The Brown Maid"). While many readers apprised of this discovery have seen in Joyce's subsumption of "Moore's melodies" (439.9–10) an instance of a mechanical list-making tendency presumed to inform the *Wake* as a whole, the example of "Oh! Breathe Not His Name" will suggest that this is not the case at all. Like other works to which Joyce alludes in the *Wake*, the *Melodies* appear in the book because they develop many of the same themes as those that Joyce necessarily plumbed in his "reconstruction of the nocturnal life"; they deepen the senses of passages in which one finds them. Born of a late Romanticism already accustomed to finding the dream superior to reality, the *Melodies* could not have been written without the words *"night"* ("Oft in the stilly night, / Ere slumber's chain has bound me"), *"sleep"* ("When daylight was yet sleeping"), *"dream"* ("Twas one of those dreams"), *"death"* ("When in death I shall calm recline") or variants of these terms, one or another of which occurs in every other of Moore's lines: if one strings together enough phrases from the *Melodies*, a protoversion of *Finnegans Wake* emerges. Joyce would have found in "tummy moor's maladies" a parallel, native, if somewhat soupy version of his own work (492.34).

5.   "The composite structures which occur in dreams in such immense numbers are put together in an equal variety of ways. . . . Their strangeness disappears completely when once we have made up our minds not to class them with the objects of our waking perception, but to remember that they are the products of dream condensation and are emphasizing in an effectively abbreviated form some common characteristic of the objects which they are thus combining. Here again the common element has as a rule to be discovered by analysis. The content of the dream merely says, as it were, 'all these things have an element x in common' " (Freud, *On Dreams*, trans. James Strachey [New York: Norton, 1952], p. 47; see also *ID*, 327–30, 354–61).

6.   Freud likens the condensing power of the dreamwork to a "procedure by means of which Galton produced family portraits: namely by projecting two images on to a single plate, so that certain features common to both are emphasized, while those which fail to fit in with one another cancel one another out and are indistinct in the picture" (*ID*, 328). A procedure exactly of this kind generates all the names assigned to the *Wake*'s dreamer. Readers skeptical of Freud might turn to Aristotle to find confirmed the same understanding: according to Aristotle, "the most skillful interpreter of dreams is he who has the faculty of observing resemblances," not differences (*De Divinatione Per Somnum*, 464[b], *The Basic Works of Aristotle*, ed. Richard McKeon [New York: Random House, 1941], p. 630; quoted in *ID*, 130 n.1, 355 n.1).

7.   Glasheen, *Third Census*, p. lxxii.

8.   Thomas Parr, a Shropshire farmer, earned cultural fame not simply by living to the age of 152 (1483–1635), but by purportedly getting a girl into trouble when he was well over 100 and by taking a second wife when he was 122. His virile example seems to have inspired the aging rakes of the court of Charles I to have the old man carted to London in a special litter so that he could be put on exhibition before the king. Unfortunately, Old Parr died during the trip. Buried in Westminster Abbey along with the great figures of English history, he became a kind of local Adam in the English imagination: and the term "Old Parr," not at all an idiosyncratic invention of Joyce's, became a long-lasting synonym for a "very old man." One still finds it in twentieth-century thesauruses.

9.   In one way of thinking, everything that has ever gone into our hero's mind has stayed there, the vast bulk of it sorted out and relegated to the trash heap of amnesic obscurity because of its irrelevance, its uselessness, its triviality: still, "we keeps all and sundry papers" (147.24–25), and "each, every, all is for the retrospectioner" (265.5–6). An immense accumulation of "litterish fragments lurk dormant" in "our mounding's mass" (66.25–26, 8.1), and they make him something of a vast personal "museomound" of memories (8.5), many of which lie in his unconscious. Where by day the items in this "museomound" are retrieved

and brought to mind according to a reality principle, in order to suit the exigencies of the present, by night, as a dim "musing" moves through the "mound" (hence again "museo-mound"), they are stirred into new and exotic configurations—in much the same way that real particles of broken glass, torn paper, and other scraps are stirred into new and exotic configurations in "a collideorscape" (143.28 ["kaleidoscope"]). All of these terms are ciphers for our "scrapheaped" hero's "deafadumped" body, within which the "dummpshow[s]" of dreams take place (120.7–8). On the hypermnesia of dreams, see *ID*, 45–51.

10. In the opening pages of the book, for example, one finds "pa's malt," "brewing," "Jhem or Shen" (3.12–13 ["John Jameson's Whiskey"]); a "jiccup" (4.11 ["hiccough"]); "rushlit" (4.19 ["rushlight" is sl. for "liquor"]); "yeasty" (4.21); "guenneses" (4.24 ["Guinness's"]); "Toper's Thorp" (4.27 [a community of heavy drinkers]); the "craythur" (4.29 [whiskey]); "balbulous" (4.30 ["bibulous"]); "the alltitude and malltitude" (4.33 ["malt," and the sl. "in one's altitudes," meaning "drunk"]); "liquor" (4.34); "Wassaily Booslaeugh" (5.5–6); "Hootch" (5.9); "vine" and soured wine "vinegar" (5.11); "tippling full" (6.8); "thirstay" (6.14); "Fillagain" (6.14 [as a bartender must]); "agrog" (6.19); "filling" (6.22); "tap up his bier" (6.24 ["beer"]); "bock" (6.26); "finisky," "barrowload of guenesis" (6.27 ["fine whiskey," "barrel-load of Guinness's"]); "the tootal of the fluid" and "the twoddle of the fuddled" (6.28 [the "total of the fluid" generating "twaddle" among the "fuddled")—not to mention the heavily sustained evocations of "Finnegan's" major "blackout." What rises out of the play of these terms is a sense of our hero's life in the day. Comparable networks of references pertaining to Dublin, to luminaries of "the homely protestant religion" (530.28), to "Scandiknavery" (47.21), and to five recurrent family members would allow us to see the *Wake*'s protagonist as a Protestant Dubliner and family-man of Nordic lineage.

11. Since he is not particularly successful (589.12–590.3), he dreams, like Bloom, of better things. The names of private estates in his neighborhood preoccupy him (264.15ff.), as do the success stories of "wine and spirit merchants" who have thrived. Adam Findlater intrigues him as greatly as he intrigued Bloom in *Ulysses* (*U*, 58), and since some call him "Gunne or Guinn" (44.12), we can infer that he finds himself in competition with businesses operated by Michael Gunn, whose Gaiety Theatre was a place of entertainment, and with the Guinnesses, who made a fortune selling alcohol. In the night, where his inadequacies are wishfully redressed, the nicknames "Gunne or Guinn" reveal our hero's "investments" in these people.

12. For more on pub-names in the *Wake*, see the *Gazetteer*, passim, and Benstock, *Joyce-Again's Wake*, pp. 32–37.

13. Joyce spoke of the Shaun section of the *Wake* as "a description of a postman travelling backwards in the night," adding cryptically that "in reality it is only a barrel rolling down the River Liffey" (*L*, I, 214). Shaun's "work [at] postal night duty" (*L*, III, 107) has to do with the dreamer's *literacy*—his ability to carry and deliver letters.

14. Roland McHugh, *The Sigla of Finnegans Wake* (Austin, Texas: Univ. of Texas Press, 1976).

15. Henry Morton Robinson, "Hardest Crux Ever," *A James Joyce Miscellany*, Second Series, ed. Marvin Magalaner (Carbondale, Ill.: Southern Illinois Univ. Press, 1959), pp. 195–207; Philippe Sollers and Stephen Heath, "Joyce in Progress," *Tel Quel* 54 (June 1973):10–11 n. 3; Philippe Sollers, "Joyce and Co.," trans. Stephen Heath, *Tel Quel* 64 (Winter 1975):11; and Jean-Louis Houdebine and Philippe Sollers, "La Trinité de Joyce," *Tel Quel* 83 (Spring 1980):51–55, 69–76, and 80–81.

16. The terms are finally demoralizing because they consign to growth-capable people the status of fixed objects. For an excellent discussion of the histories of these words, see the entries on "Individuality" and "Personality" in Raymond Williams, *Keywords: A Vocabulary of Culture and Society* (New York: Oxford Univ. Press, 1976), pp. 133–36 and 194–97; for a discussion of their relation to the novel and the social reality of which it is a manifestation,

see Ian Watt, *The Rise of the Novel* (Berkeley and Los Angeles: Univ. of Calif. Press, 1957), pp. 9–27.

17. Marcel Brion, "The Idea of Time in the Work of James Joyce," *Our Examination Round His Factification For Incamination of Work in Progress* (1929; rpt. New York: New Directions, 1962), pp. 33, 31.

18. Mercanton, "The Hours of James Joyce," p. 237; Jan Parandowski, "Meetings with Joyce," in *Portraits of the Artist in Exile*, p. 159. Compare also Joyce's remarks to Arthur Power on Turgenev: "he is like all the classical writers who show you a pleasant exterior but ignore the inner construction, the pathological and psychological body which our behavior and thought depend on. Comprehension is the purpose of literature, but how can we know human beings if we continue to ignore their most vital functions" (Power, *Conversations with James Joyce*, p. 56).

19. Knowing one's "tumptytumtoes" through one's eyes, to illustrate the contortions that consciousness can perpetrate on the body, is to relocate one's "twoe nails on the head" (110.14–15) and also to ignore the vast underground that *Finnegans Wake* explores in its treatment of "matters that fall under the ban of our infrarational senses" (19.36–20.1). One way of comprehending these "infrarational senses," which involve no knowing at all, would be simply to move those "tumptytumtoes," which tend to vanish, on the principle "out of sight, out of mind," at the first appearance of a line of print. "You'll feel what I mean" (468.18). "I fee where you mea" (295.36–296.1).

20. For representative exceptions, see E. L. Epstein, "James Joyce and the Body," in *A Starchamber Quiry: A James Joyce Centennial Volume, 1882–1982*, ed. E. L. Epstein (New York: Methuen and Co., 1982), pp. 73–106; Solomon, *Eternal Geomater*; Benstock, *Joyce-Again's Wake*, pp. 267–82; and Norman O. Brown, *Love's Body*.

THE WHIRL, THE FLASH
AND THE TROUBLE:
WAKE-PERSPECTIVES

◆

Finnegans Wake and the Girls from Boston, Mass.

ADALINE GLASHEEN

In *Finnegans Wake* much is made of the sexual crime that H. C. Earwicker committed at the magazine wall in Phoenix Park, Dublin, a crime that is at once the misdemeanor of a private citizen and the fall of Adam. Joyce thus redeems Stephen Dedalus's promise of rewriting *Paradise Lost*, although it is possible to feel that God's ways toward man are less mysterious than Joyce's. For, among other eccentricities, Joyce provides his Adam with two tempting young Eves, who go by a score of names: sometimes they are Wellington's "Dear Jenny," sometimes Swift's Esthers, sometimes Napoleon's two wives. Most often they are the Maggies, after Magdalene and the magazine wall.

The Maggies melt into all the temptresses in *Finnegans Wake* and are ultimately to be identified with Earwicker's daughter Issy and Issy's "grateful sister reflection in a mirror" (*FW* 220.9), whose name is "sester Maggy" (*FW* 458.10) or "Madge, my linkingclass girl" (*FW* 459.4). The relation between the Maggies, on the one hand, and Issy and her image, on the other, has bothered critics of *Finnegans Wake* because the temptresses are two Maggies while a single Maggy is addressed in the wonderful letter from Boston, Mass. As Mr. Edmund Wilson observes: "The letter comes from Boston . . . and seems to have been written by some female relation. . . . One feels that there is a third woman in the story, and that something important depends on this."

Like Mr. Wilson, I was plagued by the feeling that there was a third woman in *Finnegans Wake*, intimately connected with Anna Livia, the mother, and Issy, the daughter, but not precisely identified with either one of them. I felt that the clue lay in the personality of Issy, who destroys her father and—as the new generation—gives him eternity.

Issy is identified with Anna Livia because she is her mother's past and future, but mother and daughter are distinct, positively opposed, in the present. Issy is profane, Anna Livia domestic love; Issy is diversity, the leader of the seven rainbow girls among whom Earwicker "spenth his strenth" before he married the unified Anna Livia (*FW* 102.22–27, 215.19–24). The

Reprinted from *The Hudson Review* 7, no. 1 (Spring 1954):89–96, by permission of the journal. Copyright © 1954 by The Hudson Review, Inc.

rhythm of Anna Livia's speech is calm, deeply integrated; Issy's is nervous, jerky, and tense. Here she is, speaking to her image, who plays Isolde of the White Hands to Issy's Isolde of Ireland.

> Listenest, meme mearest! They were harrowd, those finweeds! Come, rest in this bosom! So sorry you lost him, poor lamb! Of course I know you are a viry vikid girl to go in the dreemplace and at that time of the draym and it was a very wrong thing to do, even under the dark flush of night, dare all grandpassia!
>
> (FW 527)

Joyce surrounds Issy and her reflection with references to *Alice Through the Looking-glass*. The Alices who are "yung and easily freudened" (*FW* 115.22–23) are Issy-Maggy; and one character observes: "Nircississies are as the doaters of inversion. Secilas [Alices] through their laughing classes becoming poolermates in laker life" (*FW* 526–27). Another agrees that this is the way with Issies, too.

Alice, however, has no mirror image; and in certain passages of *Finnegans Wake*, notably 457–461, it seemed to me that Issy goes beyond narcissism and speaks of her image as separate from herself, a rival on whom she plays nasty little tricks. Further, she often says that it is "sester Maggy," not Issy, who does naughty things.

It occurred to me that Issy might well be one of those girls with a multiple personality, and I was led, therefore, to read Dr. Morton Prince's *The Dissociation of a Personality* (Boston, 1905, 1908), a study of the young woman known as "Miss Christine L. Beauchamp."

In *The Dissociation of a Personality* I hoped to find evidence that Joyce used Miss Beauchamp as a model for Issy and referred to or echoed Prince in *Finnegans Wake*; for I felt this would prove that Issy was indeed meant to be a multiple personality. I found the echoes and references, but I also found out why the wonderful letter of *Finnegans Wake* comes from Boston.

Miss Beauchamp (pronounced Beecham) was a cultivated New England girl whose personality was rocked on its foundation one stormy night when she saw an old friend, William Jones ("the embodiment of the spiritual") peeping from the top of a ladder[1] into the hospital where Miss B. was in nurse's training. Jones followed this up by attempting to make love to her at the hospital door, whereupon the decisive split in her personality occurred. She eventually became the patient of Dr. Morton Prince, a Boston neurologist, who hypnotised Miss B. and summoned from her depths, first one and then another distinct personality.

The first of these, B III or Sally (B II was the self in hypnosis) is most important in relation to *Finnegans Wake*. Prince identifies Sally as the subconscious self. Sally was an entrancing girl—gay, unconventional, witty, impish, and sweet—the sort of girl that male writers have hopefully been creating since the beginning of literature. Joyce borrowed a good deal of Sally's behavior for Issy, but he did not borrow her personality, for Issy is an uneasy whole with conflicting parts; Sally, a part wrenched from the whole, was marvelously integrated. In any case, Sally was lovable and merry, but Prince was obliged to be "severe" with her because Sally, who claimed always to have coexisted with Miss B., had always disliked her. Miss B. went in for good books, domestic tasks, and prayer; Sally was active, adventurous, liked men and—what horrified Miss B.—adored the abominable Jones, wanted to "stay with him and love him for always." Jones-the-spiritual had bored Sally, but Jones-the-ladder-climber was infinitely attractive. The act that morality and law condemn caused Sally to love.

She was far from loving Miss B. and tormented her constantly with spiteful tricks and disturbing letters:

> I am positively ashamed of you, my sainted Christine, that you should pretend to be shocked because I choose to go to ---with poor dear W. . . . Your prayer book is in the salt-box, covered way up, if you want it. Perhaps you'd better rescue it so you can pray out of it. . . . The Margaret Margaret [some paper work of Miss B.'s] is all gone too. I made cigarette papers out of it. . . .
>
> (Prince, 126–27)

Sally made Miss B. stutter, sent her hallucinations, jumbled her letters, tore them up (see FW 307 note 5), tried to cut off her hair so she would "look a guy." But she would quickly repent and write notes like the following to Prince, who gradually replaced Jones in her affections:

> Know all men by these presents that I, Sally, being of sound mind . . . do hereby solemnly promise to love, honor, and obey Morton Prince, M.D . . . of Boston, state of Massachusetts, from this time forth, *toujours*.
> *Toujours* is French, you know.
>
> (Prince, 138)

Some time after Sally appeared, Prince summoned up another personality, B IV, who was a kind of mirror image of Miss B. Prince has a list several pages long, showing how Miss B. was patient, IV impatient; one liked oysters, the other didn't; one wore her hair high, the other low, etc. (Prince 288–294). These three females had a very trying social life. On one occasion:

> B IV, in a depressed . . . angry frame of mind was looking at herself in the mirror. She was combing her hair. . . . Suddenly she saw, notwithstanding the seriousness of her thoughts, a curious, laughing expression—a regular diabolical smile—come over her face. It was not her own expression, but one that she had never seen before . . . (This expression I recognized from the description to be the peculiar smile of Sally. . . .) IV . . . seemed to recognize

it as the expression of the thing that possessed her. She saw herself as another person in the mirror and was frightened. . . . It suddenly occurred to her to talk to this . . . "other person" in the mirror. . . .

(Prince, 360–61)

Now here is Issy, talking not to, but about her image:

. . . nurse Madge, my linkingclass girl, [*Miss B. was a nurse and Sally a looking-glass girl—see also FW* 556] she's a fright, poor old dutch, in her sleeptalking [*Sally witnessed, like a spectator at a play, Miss B. acting and speaking in her dreams*] when I paint the measles on her and mudstuskers to make her a man. [*Sally played this kind of trick on Miss B., but the idea of a man existing within a woman is probably derived from Jung*] We. We. Issy done that, I confesh. . . . Simply killing, how she tidies her hair! [*Miss B. and IV found each other's hair dress absurd and always rearranged it*] I call her Sosy because she's sosiety for me and she says sossy while I say sassy and she says will you have some more scorns while I say won't you take a few more schools and she talks bout ithel dear while I simply never talk about athel darling [*The opposition of Miss B. and IV*] she's but nice for enticing my friends. . . .

(FW 459)

The words "Issy done that, I confesh" also echo Prince. He had concluded that the "Real Miss Beauchamp" could be achieved by integrating Miss B. and IV. Indeed, he found they were already integrated in B II, the self in hypnosis; but whenever he told II to awake, she behaved like a "dement." Finally, he persuaded Sally to let him put her out of existence, and Sally, wanting to be helpful, told him that she believed that II was the "Real Miss Beauchamp":

I reminded Sally that that had been my theory . . . but . . . when I told II to open her eyes and awake . . . she went into a condition of mental disintegration . . . became rattled and the victim of hallucinations. . . . Sally laughed and a look of mischief came over her face. Finally, *she confessed, "I did that* [italics mine], I did it to make you think it wasn't she, and to prevent your getting her."

(Prince, 519)

Sure enough, this is the solution, the happy ending that rings down the curtain on a more or less integrated Miss Beauchamp, cured of the split that Joyce calls the "Royal Divorce," and with "all her myriads of drifting minds in one" (FW 159.7). Miss B. was integrated but she had no recollection of herself as Sally, and indeed had never known Sally except by her letters.

The letter from Boston, Mass. haunts the pages of *Finnegans Wake*. This letter is described by Joyce as "selfpenned to one's other" (FW 489.33–34), and he says slyly that a really close inspection of the letter would reveal "a multiplicity of personalities" (*FW* 107.24–25). The letter gets nearly as much attention in *Finnegans Wake* as the crime in the park, and it is concerned with the crime, always reiterating "Maggy well," "Well Maggy." Moreover, Shaun, one of Earwicker's sons, declares that the letter, among other things, tells "How they wore two madges. . . ." (*FW* 420.7).

The letter is continually written, read, yearned for, discovered, mulled over. It was:

> . . . carried of Shaun, son of Hek, written of Shem, brother of Shaun, uttered for Alp, mother of Shem, for Hek, father of Shaun.
>
> (*FW* 420)

Shem, another of the Earwicker boys, is most often mentioned as author, but always with the proviso that he wrote at his mother, Anna Livia's dictation, and wrote not to, but *for* his father. Near the end of her life, however, Anna Livia claims authorship. "Sometime then, somewhere there, I wrote me hopes and buried the page . . ." (*FW* 624.3–4). Actually there is nothing contradictory in these claims since Shem is James Joyce, the artist, who gives form to his mother's secrets. It is her letter, she wrote it when she was the young, multiple Issy, and as the mature unified Anna Livia, she cannot just lay her hands on it. It was buried sometime, somewhere.

The letter comes to light on a winter's day when a little hen digs it up from a manure pile (*FW* 110). Its interment had done it no good, and only bits and fragments can be made out (*FW* 111) and these vary from time to time. Nevertheless, the letter always comes from Boston, Mass. and repeats "Well Maggy." It is treated as a document of high importance, a promise of spring to a wintry world. Certain commentators have taken the Boston address and the letter's mention of "tea" to be a reference to the Boston Tea-Party and concluded that the message is one of democratic hope from the new world. Nothing could be less in keeping with Joyce's thought, for he was not given to equating hope with political experiments, and throughout *Finnegans Wake* he follows Ibsen's early play *Love's Comedy* and equates tea and sexual love.

It was in Boston that Sally wrote many letters to her "other," and when Prince persuaded her to leave Miss B., she was writing the story of her life, "The Autobiography of a Subconscious Self." At the prospect of extinction, Sally refused to give Prince the ending of this story:

> She was ready to . . . give up . . . the sunshine of life, but her sorrow should be her own. . . . People, before they died, wrote their "last will and testament" . . . so she must write hers. . . . I never saw it, but I heard about it from IV who was puzzled by what she read. . . . Then Sally wrote a number of letters, stating her opinions about people. These and various other papers, the last pages of the "auto," letters from her friends . . . and presents given

her . . . all these she gathered together and put into a box. Then going far
out into the country, in a secret place in a wood, she buried her box of
treasures. . . .

(Prince, 487–88)

A footnote to this passage says:

In later days this buried box of letters was a source of great anxiety to IV,
who feared that some one might accidentally come across it—and what might
it not reveal!

Anna Livia's letter was also once part of a larger hoard of spoil which,
like Sally, she collected and buried.

. . . sing the day we sallybright. She's burrowed the coacher's headlight the
better to pry . . . and all spoiled goods go into her nabsack . . . boaston
nightgarters and masses of shoesets and nickelly nacks and foder allmicheal
. . . and midgers and maggets . . . and the last sigh that come fro the hart
. . . and the fairest sin the sunsaw. . . . With Kiss. Kiss Criss. Cross Criss.
Kiss Cross. Undo lives 'end. Slain.

(FW 11)

Here the mention of Sally, Boston, Criss (Sally's usual name for Miss Beauchamp was "Chris"),[2] and the suggestion that she who buried the treasure
was "slain," tie this passage to Prince's book.

"All the world's in want and is writing a letters," Joyce says. On p.
279 Issy writes a letter to her professor that sounds a good deal like those
that Sally wrote to Prince. Like Sally, Issy accuses her mentor of "severity";
like Miss Beauchamp, she is thinking of "putting an end to myself and my
malody"; and again, like Sally she says near the end of her letter "Amum.
Amum. And Amum again," an echo of Sally's commonly used "Amen,
amen, amen." (See also FW 495.33.)

And on the very next page, 280, the child Issy practices, as from a
model letter-writer, composing the letter from Boston that it will one day
be her prime business to write. She ends it:

With best from cinder Christinette if prints chumming, can be when desires
Soldi. . . .

Combined with Cinderella,[3] herself a girl of two personalities, this practice
letter is signed by little Christine Beauchamp (chumming . . . be). It says:
with best from the sender, Christine, who, chumming with Prince (or
charming Prince), can be Soldi (Sally) when she wants to be (or when she
feels desire). "Soldi" is, of course, an anagram of Isold, whose name is often

scrambled or written backward in *Finnegans Wake* in imitation of mirror-writing. Another anagram, "peethrolio" follows closely on "Soldi" and suggests that Joyce is imitating Sally's fondness for scrambling letters in the notes that Miss. B. wrote to Prince. Issy remarks elsewhere that she will be the "mort" of her "prince" (*FW* 460.12, 22).

The dual Issy, the twin Eves, very nearly are the death of Earwicker. They lure him to his fall in Phoenix Park, a fall that sets the citizenry against him in hate and derision, that delivers him into the hands of an angry God, that riddles him with the guilt which is manifest in his betraying stutter and the hump he carries on his back. But the letter that one young temptress wrote to her "other" can save him. To her, it was "the fairest sin the sunsaw."

The discovery that there is no expression of man's sexual energy that can displease the essential woman was apparently the great revelation of Joyce's life. Both *Ulysses* and *Finnegans Wake* are resolved by the cry of the eternal female, *"O felix culpa!"* Molly and Anna Livia are vessels of the cosmic secret and much possessed of Nature. They stand outside the moral and theological schemes that man erects to his torment. Joyce called Molly's soliloquy "Leopold Bloom's passport to eternity." The letter from Boston, Mass. is just such a passport. The dying Anna Livia, who knows that "all men has done something," says to her husband:

When the moon of mourning is set and gone. Over Glinaduna . . . Ourselves, oursouls alone. At the site of salvocean. And watch would the letter you're wanting be coming may be. And cast ashore. That I prays for. . . . Scratching it and patching at with a prompt from a primer. And what scrips of nutsnolleges I pecked up me meself. Every letter is a hard but yours sure is the hardest crux ever. . . . But once done, dealt and delivered, tattat, you're on the map. Rased on traumscrapt from Maston, Boss.

(*FW* 623.27–36)

Notes

1. "Stiltstunts on Bostion, Moss" (*FW* 347.13), Joyce calls it.
2. "Chriesty" also appears in the letter, 111.14. References to Sally are to be found on: 11.17 and 35; 144.34; 200.19; 204.15; 272.10; 280.23; 281.21; 293 note 2; 359.18; 364.30; 609.12.
3. Prince, 412: "As Cinderella, when the princess's robes were stripped from her, found herself suddenly in rags, so did IV, when her own emotions and thoughts—her own individuality—were stripped from her, find herself in the rags (as she thought) of her other self."

Dividual Chaoses: Case Histories of Multiple Personality and *Finnegans Wake*

Morris Beja

The theme of the dissociation of personality was of central importance to Joyce's concerns and techniques throughout his career, from Stephen's "theory of dualism which would symbolise the twin eternities of spirit and nature" (*SH* 210) through Stoom-Blephen to *Finnegans Wake*. By the time he wrote the *Wake*, Joyce clearly knew about case histories of "multiple personality" which provided fascinating corroboration for some of his most deeply felt assumptions and convictions about human character. It is my intention in this essay to take seriously the suggestion within the *Wake* about the *Wake*: that, "Closer inspection of the *bordereau* would reveal a multiplicity of personalities inflicted on the . . . document" (*FW* 107.23–25).

About one such case history I need not go into detail, for ever since the publication of Adaline Glasheen's important essay, "*Finnegans Wake* and the Girls from Boston, Mass.," there has been a general recognition of the significance of the famous Christine Beauchamp case.[1] But there has been no corresponding exploration of the possibility that—if one case is so important in the *Wake*—there may well be other allusions to similar case studies which it would be helpful for the reader to know about. A quick summary of the main features of the various Beauchamp personalities might help in providing us with an initial orientation; for although there are of course variations of importance and interest within all histories of multiple or "split" personalities, many of the better known ones do tend to fall into similar patterns. For example, the majority of them—and certainly the majority of the most complex and mysterious ones—for some reason or other involve women, as in the most famous ones in the years since the publication of the *Wake*, those of "Eve" and "Sybil."[2] In the Beauchamp case itself, which was studied and reported by Morton Prince, a noted psychotherapist of the late nineteenth and early twentieth centuries, a woman whom Prince names Christine L. Beauchamp developed several "selves" or "personalities." Each had "a distinctly different character" and "different views, beliefs, ideals, . . . tastes, habits, experiences, and memories." The "normal" Miss Beauchamp—called

Reprinted from the *James Joyce Quarterly* 14 (Spring 1977):241–50. Reprinted by permission of the *James Joyce Quarterly*, University of Tulsa.

"B I" (or, sometimes, "the saint")—was a serious young woman, with a strict moral consciousness. In addition to this "primary" self (according to Prince's words, "the self that was born and which was intended by nature to be"³), there were: "B II," the hypnotic state of "B I" and perhaps therefore not properly speaking a "different" personality; "B III," a free, gay, uninhibited girl at first called Chris, but named Sally when she ceased appearing only in a hypnotic state; and "B IV," who first appeared in 1899, over a year after Miss Beauchamp had come under Prince's care.⁴

Glasheen's essay explores the influence of the Beauchamp case on *Finnegans Wake* (especially in regard to Issy and the letter from Boston, Mass.) with such impressive results that after reading her discussion one can readily see why James S. Atherton includes a section on Morton Prince among "The Structural Books" in *The Books at the Wake*. Atherton also wonders about the possibility that "other sources for the theme of dissociation are being used."⁵ Surely his hypothesis is supported by the importance in all of *Finnegans Wake* of that theme—of the dissociation, duality, indeed multiplicity of human nature. It was precisely this "kind of dualism" that was Bruno's central contribution to the *Wake* (*Letters I* 224). And among the many conceivable answers to Shem's "first riddle of the universe: . . . when is a man not a man?" a reply we are given immediately is, "when he is a . . . Sham" (*FW* 170.4–5, 23–24)—suggesting that he is not a man when he wears a mask, another identity: that is, when he is a "nother man, wheile he is asame" (*FW* 356.13–14), a "secondary personality" (*FW* 38.27). But everything in the *Wake* points to the fact that this response is at least as incorrect as correct, for to be a human self is to be a divided one. The self is, then, what Shaun accuses Shem of being in his writings: "a dividual chaos, perilous, potent, common to allflesh, . . . doriangrayer in its dudhud" (*FW* 186.4–8). Indeed, so important is this general theme that it is hard *not* to suspect that Joyce read in or of some of the other "classic" cases of dissociation and split personality. I shall attempt here some conjectures in regard to several well-known or once well-known cases of multiple personality, but because of the notorious problems in determining the limits of association in regard to passages in the *Wake* I shall restrict myself to contexts which make allusions to multiple personalities seem especially appropriate or significant—as well as, of course, to cases which could have come to Joyce's attention by the time of the composition of the relevant passages of "Work in Progress" or the *Wake*.

The phenomenon which Prince's title refers to as the dissociation of a personality, and which is most commonly called nowadays multiple personality, has had many terms attached to it through the years: split personality of course, or dissociated personality, or coexisting or alternating personality, or unconscious or subconscious or intraconscious personality, or dual or double personality—and so on.⁶ Or "secondary personality"—the only such term Joyce uses in *Finnegans Wake* without distortion (*FW* 38.27), and the one favored by William James in his accounts of various case histories. For despite James's refusal to recognize the possibility of unconscious mental states—"There is only one 'phase' in which an idea can be, and that is a fully conscious condition. If it is not in that condition, then it is not at all"[7]—he extensively studied and reported cases of secondary personalities. As he explained it, *"we must never take a person's testimony, however sincere, that he has felt nothing, as proof positive that no feeling has been there. It may have been there as part of the consciousness of a 'secondary personage,' of whose experiences the primary one whom we are consulting can naturally give no account"* (p. 211). The "unconscious," then, is in effect the consciousness of a second self—" *a secondary consciousness"* in James's term (p. 203).

Probably the most famous of the cases with which James was himself directly involved was that of the Rev. Ansel Bourne. In *A Second Census of "Finnegans Wake,"* Adaline Glasheen lists eight references under the figure of "Bourne," but has next to the name an asterisk, her symbol indicating she does not know who he is.[8] Well, as far as that goes neither do I, with any certainty . . . but I suspect that the reference in at least a few passages is to Ansel Bourne—as when, during the lessons, doubles like "jemmijohns" cudgel about problems like "Browne and Nolan's divisional tables," while we hear in regard to Issy's grammar that "all is her inbourne": "if there is a third person, mascarine, phelinine or nuder, being spoken abad it moods prosodes from a person speaking to her second which is the direct object that has been spoken to, with and at" (*FW* 268.17–22). Joyce uses the phrase "secondary personality" with particular reference to "Mr Browne" (*FW* 38.26–27); Bourne's secondary personality was named A. J. Brown. Joyce's Mr. Browne is a "priest . . . disguised as a vincentian" (*FW* 38.26); the Rev. Ansel Bourne was a minister, an "itinerant preacher" from Greene, Rhode Island, who on January 17, 1887, withdrew $551 from a bank and then disappeared. On March 14, he awoke in Norristown, Pennsylvania, frightened at not knowing where he was or what he was doing there. It turned out that he had arrived in that town six weeks earlier, had given his name as A. J. Brown, and had rented a small shop which he had been running as a candy store. Several years later, in 1890, James induced him under hypnosis to assume the memory and character of Brown, but otherwise that personality never came back, and no similar attacks occurred (James, *Principles*, pp. 390–93). Cases such as Bourne-Brown's suggest why one technical name for multiple personalities has been "continued amnesias" ("the aphasia of that heroic agony of recalling a once loved number leading slip by slipper to a general amnesia of misnomering one's own"—*FW* 122.4–6). Incidentally, James departed from usual practice in giving the actual name of the patient, Ansel Bourne, in his account. Nevertheless, almost thirty years later Robert Howland Chase for some reason used a pseudonym in his summary of the case in *The Ungeared Mind*,[9] Silas Pronge:

"Save me from those therrble prongs! Two more. Onetwo moremens more" (*FW* 628.5–6).

The name or color Brown often appears in the *Wake* in contexts suggesting multiple personalities, as when Shaun-Justius says "to himother," "Brawn is my name and broad is my nature" (*FW* 187.24–25). The letter from Boston, Mass., is a "brown study" which has "importance in establishing the identities in the writer complexus (for if the hand was one, the minds of active and agitated were more than so)" (*FW* 114.31–35). In at least one passage there is a direct connection between Brown and the Beauchamp case ("Browne umbracing Christina"—*FW* 537.6). But of course Mr. Brown's "secondary personality as a Nolan" (*FW* 38.27–28) is the one that receives the most stress. For Browne and Nolan are "a doblinganger" (*FW* 490.17), and "Browne and Nolan's divisional tables" (*FW* 268.8–9) pervade the *Wake*. They are Dr. Jekyll and Mr. Hyde ("a jackal with hide for Browne but Nolan"—*FW* 211.31–32), although somehow "Browne-Nowlan" is also a "heavenlaid twin," "either prexactly unlike his polar andthisishis or procisely the seem" (*FW* 177.20–21, 32–33). In one passage, Glugg and Chuff are fighting:

> For these are not on terms, they twain, bartrossers, since their baffle of Whatalose when Adam Leftus and the devil took our hindmost, gegifting her with his painapple, nor will not be atoned at all in fight to no finish, that dark deed doer, this wellwilled wooer, Jerkoff and Eatsoup, Yem or Yan, while felixed is who culpas does and harm's worth healing and Brune is bad French for Jour d'Anno.
>
> (*FW* 246.26–32)

Brune and Jour d'Anno of course refer to Giordano Bruno, the Nolan. But I wonder if "d'Anno" could also suggest Gabriele D'Annunzio, whose work Joyce knew well, and who in his autobiographical *Notturno* (1921) gave an account of visions of his double.[10]

When we are told that Mr. Browne has a "secondary personality," he is referred to as a "poul soul" (*FW* 38.27–28). The word "poul" of course refers primarily to the hen who found the letter from Boston, Mass., and thereby to the Beauchamp case, particularly Sally, who buried a number of letters and papers in a secret spot, as Glasheen observes.[11] However (although without absolute conviction about its relevance), I would like to point out in regard to "poul" that the one case of an Irish person with a "split" personality to have received any notoriety or even attention of which I am aware was that of John Charles J. Poultney, whose secondary personality was named C. J. Poulting. This case, which has been grouped with those of Christine Beauchamp and Eve White-Eve Black as one of "the classical cases in the literature,"[12] was recounted in a popular 1933 book by Shepherd Ivory

Franz, a prominent American psychologist, under the nicely trinitarian title, *Persons One and Three* ("The same. Three persons"—*FW* 478.29).[13]

The case of Poultney-Poulting involved a fugue state rather like Bourne's, only one more prolonged and persistent. Poultney, a Dubliner who had been born in 1888, disappeared in 1914. When he was found by the Los Angeles police, dazed, in 1929, he called himself C. J. Poulting. At first he recalled nothing, but soon he could remember events as far back as February 1915. Then, in 1930, Poultney, the primary personality, reappeared—under the impression it was September 1914. (The time between September 1914 and February 1915 was never fully explained; Franz conjectures that there may have been still other personalities during that period.) Eventually, a third or combined personality ("Jack") retained memories of both selves. However, several relapses occurred before Poultney returned in 1931 to Ireland—to a wife and two sons he had left there in 1914. Of his other personality's name, incidentally, Poultney once remarked, "They made a Jew out of an Irishman. . . . I know Poultings, they're Jews" (p. 84).

Thus far I have brought up only male cases, aside from that of Christine Beauchamp; however, for reasons not fully understood, the majority of cases in the psychological literature have been women. For example, there was Léonie, whose history was reported by Pierre Janet and also recounted by William James (*Principles*, pp. 387–88). In her, the secondary states occurred only under hypnosis; normally serious and solemn, when hypnotized she became a gay, noisy, humorous woman known as Léonie 2 or Léontine; in a still deeper trance, there was a grave, quite personality called Léonie 3 or Léonore ("Loryon the comaleon"—*FW* 136.27?). In *Finnegans Wake*, just before the passage I have quoted where we read of "Yem or Yan," and "Brune" and "Jour d'Anno," we are told that "Leonie" has "the choice of her lives":

> A palashe for hirs, a saucy for hers and ladlelike spoons for the wonner. But ein and twee were never worth three. . . . Et la pau' Leonie has the choice of her lives between Josephinus and Mario-Louis . . .
>
> (*FW* 246.14–17)

"Saucy" suggests "sosie," the French for *Doppelgänger*, or double—though in this case "ein and twee were never worth three." Josephine and Marie Louise were of course Napoleon's wives, but here they are given masculine names, while Napoleon as "la pau' Leonie" becomes androgynous (or perhaps really hermaphroditic). Sexes are switched again with the overtone of Paul Léon, noted in Glasheen's *Second Census*.[14]

The likelihood that Janet's Léonie is one of the referents is increased not only by the contexts of doubles and multiple personalities I have already shown, but by other contextual elements as well. For example, "palashe" and "worth," and a discussion on the next page of an "invaded personality" (FW 247.8–9), may all combine to suggest Patience Worth, a very famous case in the early part of this century, in which a seventeenth-century Englishwoman was said to have invaded, or been reincarnated in, or at least appeared in the body of, a modern American woman as a second self. In the *Wake*, in addition to the passages I shall discuss, see: "a plurity of bells [belles, plurabelles]: Have peacience . . ." (FW 568.5); "Parish worth . . . durmed adranse [dreamed a trance]" (FW 199.8–10); and perhaps "peningsworths" (FW 548.23) and "solly [Sally?] well worth your pilger's fahrt" (FW 248.13–14).

The case of Patience Worth represents the type of "alteration in the present self" which William James grouped under the category of "mediumships or possessions" (*Principles*, p. 375). Pearl Lenore Curran was born in 1883 in Illinois, and was raised in Texas and then St. Louis, where she lived with her husband when, apparently in 1913 at the age of thirty-one, she began to show signs of receiving messages from some other force by means of a ouija board. After a while the ouija board yielded to automatic writing, but it took some time and confusion before the other force made itself known as "Patience Worth," a woman who had been born in England during the seventeenth century and had emigrated as an adult to America, where she was killed by Indians not long after her arrival. As an automatic writer, Patience Worth was prolific, and her poetry and fiction—including two long novels, *The Sorry Tale* (New York: Henry Holt, 1917) and *Hope Trueblood* (New York: Henry Holt, 1918)—received serious critical attention and praise.

In 1927, Walter Franklin Prince (no relation to Morton Prince) published *The Case of Patience Worth: A Critical Study of Certain Unusual Phenomena* (Boston: Boston Society for Psychic Research, 1927). The volume reprints an interesting essay by Charles E. Cory, originally published in the *Psychological Review* (Sept. 1919), in which Cory discusses the fascination of the case, and never doubts Mrs. Curran's sincerity, but does not so much reject Patience Worth's claim to be a spirit as dismiss it, as "an illusion" (p. 435). After reprinting this ten-page essay, Prince attacks it in his own twenty-eight page "Comments Upon Professor Cory's Article": for Prince's volume is presented straightforwardly as a demonstration of the argument for taking Patience Worth's claim to be a spirit at its face value. Prince, a Ph.D. but not a physician, neurologist, or trained psychologist, also studied other cases of multiple personality (including the Doris case, the next one I shall bring up). He accused Morton Prince of withholding information in regard to the Beauchamp case that would have indicated that "the most logical way" of explaining Sally "would be by assuming her to be a spirit" (p. 7). All this is relevant to *Finnegans Wake* insofar as most of the more important of what seem to me to be references to Patience Worth occur in Book III, in which spiritualism and seances play a pervasive role.

Prince informs us (with unconscious humor) that early in the ouija board sessions with Mrs. Curran:

> A new name and an unknown one seemed to be struggling to come through, at first understood to be "Pat-C, Pat-C, Pat-C" (the first three and seventh letters of "Patience"). Naturally it was thought that some Irishman was trying to communicate. According to my theory, it was the strong suggestion of this supposition, stimulated by many leading questions, which induced various ouija board remarks, at this and subsequent sittings, appropriate to an Irishman.
>
> (p. 31)

In Book III of the *Wake*, Yawn is confronted by the four inquisitors, and is accused of being an "idealist leading a double life" and of having "a doblinganger much about your own medium" who "stands pat for you before a direct object in the feminine" (*FW* 490.6–17).

Two of Pearl Lenore Curran's nicknames were "Pearlycue" and "ram's head" (Prince, *Patience Worth*, p. 12). Issy is described as a "queenly pearl" (*FW* 556.12; cf. "pearlagraph"—*FW* 226.1). The name "ram's head" is more interesting. Jeremy is described as "ramming amok" while his "lasterhalft was . . . operating the subliminal of his invaded personality" (*FW* 247.6–9). And in the confrontation between Yawn and the four old men that I have already cited, one of the inquisitors asks:

> What sound of tistress isoles my ear? I horizont the same, this serpe with ramshead, and lay it lightly to your lip a little. What do you feel, liplove?
> —I feel a fine lady . . . floating on a stillstream of isisglass . . .
> (*FW* 486.20–24)

Campbell and Robinson interpret the ramshead as "a mystic symbol intended to stir his memory of the past."[15] I would go further and say that it is meant to stir up memories of a previous life, as the old man's continuing questions show: "did it ever occur to you, *qua* you, prior to this, by a stretch of your iberborealic imagination, when it's quicker than this quacking that you might, bar accidens, be very largely substituted in potential secession from your next life by a complementary character, voices apart?" (*FW* 486.35–487.4). Yawn's reply includes an intriguingly enigmatic remark, "You knew me once but you won't know me twice" (*FW* 487.32–33).

Walter Franklin Prince also wrote about another well known dissociated personality—Doris Fischer. His massive study, *The Doris Case of Multiple Personality*, takes up two large volumes (IX, 1915 and X, 1916) of the *Proceedings of the American Society for Psychical Research*, not to speak of the even larger third volume by James H. Hyslop (XI, 1917), on Doris' role as a medium.

A conveniently brief excerpt from the 1915 volume, slightly altered, and providing an overall view of the case, was reprinted in 1929 in a Modern Library book.[16] Doris—who became Prince's foster daughter after coming under his care—had a loving mother but a violent, drunken father. When Doris was three years old, her father threw her on the floor—and the physical and emotional shock very quickly produced, Prince later believed, two secondary personalities, both named Margaret—two Maggies, as it were. One, called simply Margaret, played a role very much like Sally's in the Beauchamp case, or Léonie 2's (or Eve Black's, much later). The other Margaret was known as Sleeping Margaret and was felt by Prince to be the most unusual aspect of the entire case; she spoke and manifested herself only during sleep—the sleep, that is, of the primary personality, called Real Doris.

In *Finnegans Wake*, of course, among Issy's dissociated personalities are the Maggies—including the rainbow girl, the "arch girl, Arcoiris, smockname of Mergyt" (*FW* 186.28). Sleeping Margaret especially calls to mind Issy's *sosie* or "linkingclass girl," "nurse Madge," who is "a fright, poor old dutch, in her sleeptalking. . . . I call her Sosy because she's sosiety for me and she says sossy while I say sassy . . ." (*FW* 459.4–11).

When Doris was seventeen, her mother, whom she greatly loved, died; the resulting trauma seems to have created still another personality, an infantile one with no memories or background, who came to be known as Sick Doris (contrast "Maggy well . . . & Muggy well" and "Well, Maggy," and similar phrases repeated in references to the contents of the letter found by the hen, Belinda of the Dorans: *FW* 111.11,15–16; 273.F6; 280.20). Actually, the last self to be revealed to Prince was the so-called "normal" personality—Real Doris. Sick Doris alternated with Real Doris and in fact was at first dominant, but after five years she was almost completely gone, and eventually she disappeared. Margaret did so as well; occasional manifestations of Sleeping Margaret continued to persist. Prince regarded Sleeping Margaret as a spirit—and the Real Doris as a medium. In addition to *The Doris Case of Multiple Personality*, Prince wrote a book about the Real Doris as *The Psychic in the House*—"our psychous of the Real Absence," "a disincarnated spirit . . . with messuages from my deadported" (*FW* 535.36–536.6).[17]

In practically all the famous cases of multiple personality, those reporting them assume that whether or not we may say that they have ended "happily" depends on whether the various selves have merged into one. Accordingly, perhaps, those who have inspected the "multiplicity of personalities" have tended to find that "the traits featuring the *chiaroscuro* coalesce, their contrarieties eliminated, in one stable somebody . . ." (*FW* 107.24–30). But relatively few of the cases I have discussed involved a complete "cure" or total "integration"—indeed, in a recent interview "Eve White" has revealed that she has had many personalities in the years since the publication of *The Three Faces of Eve*.[18] Whether the divided self can be entirely united or reunited in either life or the *Wake* is no doubt undetermined at best. "You knew me once but you won't know me twice."

Notes

1. "*Finnegans Wake* and the Girls from Boston, Mass.," *Hudson Review*, 7 (Spring 1954), 89–96.

2. Corbett H. Thigpen and Hervey M. Cleckley, *The Three Faces of Eve* (New York: Popular Library, 1957); Flora Rheta Schreiber, *Sybil* (Chicago: Henry Regnery, 1973). The study of Eve White-Eve Black, written by her therapists, is much the more interestingly and cogently presented. In Schreiber's book the interpretations seem formulaic, and the handling of material seems sloppy: for example, pseudonyms of two of the people I shall deal with, Fischer and Pronge, are given incorrectly, and Schreiber is unaware that the latter is not a different case from that of Ansel Bourne, but the same one.

3. Morton Prince, *The Dissociation of a Personality: A Biographical Study in Abnormal Psychology* (1905; New York: Longmans, Green, 1925), p. 1.

4. Readers who wish more details may consult Glasheen's essay, or of course Prince's own massive volume, *The Dissociation of a Personality*. A somewhat shorter but still adequately detailed account is given in his "Miss Beauchamp: The Theory of the Psychogenesis of Multiple Personality," first published in 1920 in Prince's *Journal of Abnormal Psychology* (vol. 16), and reprinted in his *Clinical and Experimental Studies in Personality* (Cambridge, Mass.: Sci-Art, 1929), pp. 130–208. This essay has special virtues: it attempts, as its subtitle indicates, to explore the theoretical and psychological issues raised by the case, and while it is still frustratingly reticent about certain matters—notably the role of sex and the feelings of the various personalities toward "William Jones" ("W. J.")—it is less so than the original 1905 volume. Interestingly, it was this sort of self-censorship (as well as a feeling that Prince was "rather stupid") that led Sigmund Freud to have little regard for him—although it is also intriguing that Freud believed Prince to be guilty of "bad intentions veiled by friendly speaking": in other words, one may say, of duplicity. See Ernest Jones, *The Life and Work of Sigmund Freud* (New York: Basic Books, 1955), II, 62.

5. *The Books at the Wake: A Study of Literary Allusions in James Joyce's "Finnegans Wake"* (1959; rev. Mamaroneck, New York: Paul P. Appel, 1974), pp. 40–41. Atherton suggests as one such source Abram H. Dailey's *Mollie Fancher: The Brooklyn Enigma* (Brooklyn: Eagle, 1894). The revised edition of Atherton's study, incidentally, has a slightly expanded entry for Prince in the Appendix of "Literary Allusions," p. 279.

6. In addition, to be sure, there are such *literary* terms as double or *Doppelgänger*, which I cannot go into here, but which have been discussed in several full-length studies. See: Otto Rank, *The Double: A Psychoanalytic Study*, trans. and ed. Harry Tucker, Jr. (1925; Chapel Hill: University of North Carolina Press, 1971); Ralph Tymms, *Doubles in Literary Psychology* (Cambridge: Bowes and Bowes, 1949); Robert Rogers, *A Psychoanalytic Study of the Double in Literature* (Detroit: Wayne State University Press, 1970); C. F. Keppler, *The Literature of the Second Self* (Tucson: University of Arizona Press, 1972). For a briefer discussion, see the section on "Dissociation" in my own *Psychological Fiction* (Glenview, Ill.: Scott, Foresman, 1971), pp. 275–80.

7. William James, *The Principles of Psychology* (New York: Henry Holt, 1890), I, 173; cf. p. 164 ff.

8. *A Second Census of "Finnegans Wake"* (Evanston: Northwestern University Press, 1963), p. 33; see p. 1.

9. "Strange Case of Silas Pronge," in *The Ungeared Mind* (Philadelphia: F. A. Davis 1918), pp. 151–56.

10. For a discussion of D'Annunzio's "autoscopic" experiences as "aspects of his narcissism," see John Todd and Kenneth Dewhurst, "The Double: Its Psycho-pathology and Psycho-physiology," *Journal of Nervous and Mental Disease*, 122 (July 1955), 48.

11. "*Finnegans Wake* and the Girls from Boston," p. 94.

12. Ernest R. Hilgard and Richard C. Atkinson, *Introduction to Psychology*, 4th ed. (New York: Harcourt, Brace and World, 1967), p. 480.

13. *Persons One and Three* (New York: McGraw-Hill, 1933). The passages I have quoted do not occur in any portions of "Work in Progress" known to have been written before 1933. Nor does the coupling of "multiplest manner" and "pouly" in a passage I find it difficult to follow, *FW* 322.10–12.

14. *A Second Census of "Finnegans Wake,"* p. 147. Incidentally, in the same issue of *transition* in which appeared the "Work in Progress" version of this passage from the *Wake*, Eugene Jolas published an essay entitled "The Primal Personality," which discusses economic and political aspects of "the scissions in the human personality," *transition*, no. 22 (Feb. 1933), 78.

15. Joseph Campbell and Henry Morton Robinson, *A Skeleton Key to "Finnegans Wake"* (New York: Harcourt, Brace, 1944), p. 298.

16. Gardner Murphy, ed., *An Outline of Abnormal Psychology* (New York: Modern Library, 1929), pp. 221–48.

17. Walter Franklin Prince, *The Psychic in the House* (Boston: Boston Society for Psychic Research, 1926). In the context of the passages about metempsychosis I have already discussed, cf. the reference to "psychosinology," *FW* 486.13.

18. My source is a UPI wire story on Mrs. Chris Sizemore, carried in the Columbus *Citizen-Journal*, Sept. 15, 1975, p. 22.

Sexuality and Survival in *Finnegans Wake*

Shari Benstock

In handing down a decision on the possible obscenity of *Ulysses*, Judge John Woolsey remarked that "whilst in many places the effect of 'Ulysses' on the reader undoubtedly is somewhat emetic, nowhere does it tend to be an aphrodisiac."[1] Indeed, Judge Woolsey held that the book was not "pornographic" because he did "not detect anywhere the leer of the sensualist." The common reader in search of a sensual thrill probably lacks the patience, if not erudition, to make *Ulysses* the instrument of his pleasure. And if this be true of *Ulysses*, what of *Finnegans Wake*? By most accounts it appears to be a dirty book, where even a Judge Woolsey might find an occasional "leer of the sensualist" (belonging to a Dante Alighieri, a Jonathan Swift, a Charles Dodgson, or a Daddy Browning), and there certainly seem to be a number of nubile young women available as the objects of affection, disporting themselves for their own and others' pleasure. But is there sex in *Finnegans Wake*? And, if so, is it pleasurable?

Perhaps the prejudices of my own reading of this text should be revealed at the outset. From what I can tell, all the sex there is in *Finnegans Wake* (and there's not much, really) happened in the past and is rather foggily remembered in the present, making assessments of pleasure or pain a bit difficult to support; what sex there is in the present is unsuccessful, presuming a less than ecstatic estimate of its joyfulness. Indeed, more seems to rest in the sensual leer or the provocative come-on than ever gets itself actualized, and what's "dirty" about the book exists in dream, revery, fantasy, and memory. Depending on what limits of the narrative one subscribes to, all events may be displaced into the past, even those which seem to be happening in the present. And perhaps this displacement was important to Joyce, who certainly chose to keep the crucial events at 7 Eccles street on June 16 offstage of *Ulysses*, and whose linguistic encrustations in the *Wake* give the sense that all events hold sexual potential without the necessity of committing them to fact. The *Wake* seems premised on the notion that sex is the downfall of man ("First we feel. Then we fall"),[2] and all action conspires to sexual implication: brothers' battles, children's lessons, sister's make-believe,

Reprinted from *The Seventh of Joyce*, ed. Bernard Benstock (Bloomington: Indiana University Press, 1982), 247–54, by permission of Indiana University Press.

mother's worries, father's drinking. And history serves as well as the family: from Wellington's monument to Nelson's pillar, the landscape of Ireland offers the potential for a sexual mapping, from the humptyhill-head of Finnegan himself down to his tumptytumtoes.

There is at least one scene in the *Wake*, however, where most readers agree that copulation progresses, and perhaps a look at this most unusual of Wakean events could shed some light on the joyousness of its sex. The scene opens foggily in a voice heavy with sleep, questioning both surroundings and events as though they belonged to a past time: "So, nat by night by naught by naket, in those good old lousy days gone by, the days, shall we say? of Whom shall we say?" (55.5–6). Slowly we move from room to room in this scene of "whenabouts," discovering members of the cast: the four old men, the young twins, the baby Isobel, a manservant, a maidservant, twelve good men and true, twenty-nine flowergirls, and, finally, "in their bed of trial, on the bolster of hardship, by the glimmer of memory, under coverlets of cowardice," a man and a woman: "he, Mr of our fathers, she, our moddereen rue arue rue." Evidence for the actual events taking place in the bed of trial must be deduced from linguistic artifice. Hardship is bolstered, finally, into a "mace of might mortified," an oblique suggestion that the male is erect; meanwhile, the woman is described as a "beautifell" waterfall, whose "dinny drops into the dyke." But the scene is interrupted by "A cry off," and the storyteller must begin again: "Where are we at all? And whenabouts in the name of space?" The awaited answer is a description of the bedroom itself, where there is a "Bed for two . . . Chair for one. Woman's garments on chair. Man's trousers with crossbelt braces, collar on bedknob" (558.26–559.9). The narrative shifts so that its appearance is of drama rather than a "once upon a time" story, and the dramatis personae must be enumerated again.

A time.
Act: dumbshow.
Closeup. Leads.

(559.17–19)

This story/play seems to be having a very difficult time getting itself told. Perhaps there is something in its subject that makes its teller uneager to advance the plot. Again, the scene is set: "Man with nightcap, in bed, fore. Woman, with curlpins, hind. Discovered. Side point of view. First position of harmony." At long last, there is little doubt what the "dumbshow" constitutes, but there seems to be little joy in the act. "Man looking round, beastly expression . . . exhibits rage. Business . . . Woman, sitting, looks at ceiling . . . exhibits fear" (559.20–28).

At the second "Cry off," the woman leaps out of bed followed by the lumbering male, "Promiscuous Omebound to Fiammelle la Diva" (560.1). This unproductive scene is brought to a quick close by a "blackout." This most frustrating of narrative methods is typical of the *Wake*, where no scene is allowed to play out its drama without constant interruptions and digressions, which may eventually bring us back to Howth Castle and Environs, but not without venturing to farther lands. While sex seems to be at the center of what the *Wake* is all about, it is a subject that is constantly eluded and elided with multiple linguistic and semantic delay tactics.[3]

This particular scene is singularly unattractive. The opening glimpse of the bedroom strewn with garments suggests a homey enough atmosphere (and may well remind us of a similar scene at 7 Eccles street), but marital intimacy bears the stamp here of the all-too-familiar. Its effect is not unlike the "rumpled, shiny sole" of Molly's stocking looped over the bedrail (*U* 63): there is a hint of the sordid in these details of everyday life. And, indeed, the ensuing description confirms the worst—the man with his "beastly expression" and "fishy eyes," the woman with her "haggish expression" and "peaky nose." This scene of possible seduction is not romanticized by dewy-eyed anticipation, or dramatized by an insistent lechery, or even sentimentalized through revery. Rather, it brings "reality" into sharp focus: it offers the single opportunity in the *Wake* to pierce the surface of its structure, to meet Earwicker and Anna Livia as their human counterparts, the Porters. But one is relieved that the "Play!" is interrupted by the "cry off," since the characters as described are so disagreeably unaesthetic. The call of motherhood (to a son who has wet his bed) delays perhaps our only chance to observe "the act" that by its very mystery rests at the center of the Wakean universe.

To say that sex in Joyce's fiction is either remembered from the past or anticipated in the future denies us access to the facts we are led to expect. Do Molly and Leopold make love? How often? To what degree of mutual enjoyment? Under what circumstances? *How?* Well, we have Molly's word that she and Boylan made love on June 16, but her account is reconstructed several times over in the space of her one-hour monologue. And as her loyalties shift, so do her facts, so that she inflates the number of times they made love and exaggerates (perhaps) her satisfaction with her partner's performance. But then this is a performance that Molly had long anticipated (with a "someone," if not specifically Boylan); she arranged its details and set the stage for herself as a joyous cuckolder of her husband. Her afternoon matinee with Boylan, and its early evening reprise, are *not* standard fare for Molly. And it may be that the anticipation of it, the unusualness of its occurrence, the retrospective sense of its daring are of greater significance to Molly than the act(s) as such. If Joyce's fiction seems to argue that sex constitutes no moral fall, it does not go so far as to suggest that sex represents redemptive powers. James Joyce is neither John Milton nor D. H. Lawrence.

What the *Wake* suggests is that sex is a family affair, whether or not it always takes place within the confines of the family. The multiple displacements of the Wakean dream offer a cast of thousands, each somehow involved in the "sin" that serves as the dark center of the narrative. But when all the double-distancing of guilty dreams collapses into the "present" we discover a family of five, each linked to the other by sexual (as well as familial) design. And when we are introduced to Mr. and Mrs. Porter (560.23–26), we learn "They care for nothing except everything that is allporterous." They are subsumed by themselves, each appearing under the auspices of the other. When the present scene opens, the father is in bed with the mother but dreams of the daughter—who sees her father's "blade drawn to the full" in erection when he appears at her doorway (566.22)—while the sons war for the sister's affections. The mother is all the while more mother than mistress, attentive to her children's needs and speedily answering Jerry's nighttime cry. She is both the source of sexual interest for her husband (by her reincarnation in the daughter) and the agent of its frustration (by her responsibilities to her children).

At the level of the family, *Finnegans Wake* presents the inversion of sexual tension *chez* Bloom. Molly is less mother than mate. Her husband still commands the focus of her attentions and psychological energies, in large part because of her sexual frustration with him. Rudy has been displaced by time, existing in the "now" only in odd moments of regret; Milly has been removed in space, but existing even in her letters as an implied threat to her mother's sexuality. Molly thinks of herself as a mistress and eventually lives out her own fantasy. (Bloom, of course, lives out another fantasy with a lover who is present only in her letters.) Although Molly's intended adultery forms the backdrop to Bloom's day—determining his activities, his movements about Dublin—his thoughts return often enough to his children. His concern for his adolescent daughter is fatherly (almost motherly), but certainly is not predicated on sexual interest—except as it acknowledges her developing sexuality ("Sex breaking out even then"—*U* 63).

In the night world of the *Wake*, these roles reverse themselves. Bloom/Earwicker confronts in his dreams the possibility of incestuous longing, and Milly/Issy is present as a knowledgeable young temptress: "Undershift, by all I hold secret from my world and in my underworld of nighties and naughties and all the other wonderwearlds" (147.26–28). The dream provides multiple revisions of the scene in the park where the old man and young girl(s) play out a scene of seduction/masturbation/micturition, at the center of which seems to be the mutual desire of the old man for the young girl. A similar vision occurs to Bloom in "Circe" (*U* 542), when under Bello's spell Bloom plays a lustful Rip Van Winkle, dreaming of a young woman who turns out to be Milly Bloom (*U* 542). The youthful sexuality of the mother, meanwhile, is revealed through the daughters, recalled by Molly and Anna Livia in their reveries that close *Ulysses* and *Finnegans Wake*. Female sexuality exists here in its youth—in stolen kisses and remembered embraces—and is essentially absent from the present, adult marriage. Molly's sexual interest is in men other than Bloom (although her affections remain with him, and the defense of him against other men in Dublin—*U* 742—

is a testament to the solidity of their relationship apart from the purely sexual). Anna Livia seems to have lost interest in sex. She leaves this aspect of womanhood to her younger generation, to the "daughterwife" who is even now "Swimming in my hindmoist" (627.2–3). Anna Livia looks forward to her death, an embrace with her "cold mad father" who "makes me seasilt saltsick and I rush, my only, into your arms" (a vision of sexual seduction involving father and daughter), while Molly looks back, to the moment by the Moorish wall when she was fifteen and with Mulvey, and to Bloom's long kiss on the Hill of Howth when she was eighteen.

This repositioning of the sexual act occurs on various levels in Joyce's fiction, not the least important of which is constituted by memory, revery, fantasy, and dream, all of which alter the sexual perspective. The subject of sexual interest (Molly, Milly, Anna Livia, Issy, Gerty, etc.) is always at some remove from the would-be seducer. The twilight encounter between Bloom and Gerty offers a striking example of this displacement. By their positioning on the beach, these two are able to see each other—but only dimly. The narrative facade of flowery nineteenth-century women's fiction filters the scene for the reader as the two participants gradually lose sight of each other in the evening darkness. What Gerty and Bloom know of each other they know by inflection, by supposition: "Nausicaa" offers one of the most difficult exercises in establishing fact in *Ulysses*, precisely because its linguistic forms are so opaque. (We assume, for instance, that Gerty MacDowell is lame, but by what evidence do we know? By Bloom's supposition: "Tight boots? No. She's lame! O!" Bloom's observation is corroborated only by Gerty's thoughts, which are formed so self-consciously and obliquely as to further the mystery about her "deformity.") But the narrative perspective of *Ulysses* at its most obscure is nonetheless consistent within the boundaries of its various styles; the *Wake*, in contrast, is a kaleidoscope, constantly shifting the perspective.

The scene that begins in the Porter bedroom at page 555 suffers the major interruption of Jerry's awakening and the opportunity to retell the story of Humphrey Chimpden Earwicker before returning the parents to the conjugal bed on page 582. We have progressed from the "First position of harmony" (559.21) to the "Third position of concord" (582.29–30) and through the narrations of Matthew and Mark to Luke, as the bedposts recount the night's events. The scene is described in terms of male games: wars and naval battles, horse races (with Anna Livia as the "bucky brown nightmare"), and cricket. The description of coition is thus viewed through male eyes and told from the perspective of the male environ; Anna Livia, whom we have assumed to be a somewhat unenthusiastic sexual partner, shows herself rather full of life: "Kickakick. She had to kick a laugh. At her old stick-in-the-block" (583.26–27). Earwicker has his "waxened capapee . . . wick-in-her," and his game is strenuous enough to cause some concern that "he'd tyre and burst his dunlops and waken her bornybarnies making his boobybabies" (584.13–14). In the midst of this free-for-all, Anna Livia's voice may be heard as she chooses sides in the cricket match, rooting for Earwicker's opponent and the champion cricketer: "Magrath he's my pegger, he is, for bricking up all my old kent road. He'll win your toss, flog your old tom's bowling and I darr ye, barrackybuller, to break his duck! He's posh. I lob him" (584.5–8). The signals seem clear enough that Anna Livia, like Molly Bloom before her, is desirous of sexual activity that is athletic, uninhibited, and joyous, and that HCE (like Bloom) may not be up to her expectations any longer, "as he studd and stoddard and trutted and trumpered" (583.36–584.1). The game motif suggests that Anna Livia's hero, Magrath (the neighbor and cad, Earwicker's trickster enemy) wins the match: "(how's that? Noball, he carries his bat!) nine hundred and dirty too not out, at all times long past conquering cock of the morgans" (584.23–25). Sexual fulfillment is at the brink of satisfaction, spurred by Anna Livia's mental lovemaking with the neighbor in fulfillment of her physical duties to her husband. Her methods are psychologically sound and well known to both sexes when the interest and excitement of youthful sex has turned perfunctory and sour after years of practice with one's partner. Ironically, Anna Livia's moment of climax (signalled by the "Cocorico!" of the cock crowing) ends Earwicker's efforts. While she basks in the relief of orgasm ("her contractations tugowards his personeel"), Earwicker is still trying for "exclusive pigtorial rights of herehear fond tiplady his weekreactions" (584.33–585.1). As "dawn drags nearing nigh," the marriage bond "repeals an act of union"; Earwicker withdraws his member (585.26); and Anna Livia discovers that he "never wet the tea."

The long-awaited lovemaking is unsuccessful except that Anna Livia has managed through mental disguise to achieve her pleasure. The narrative condemnation of Earwicker's poor showing ("You never wet the tea!") may suggest impotency, a fear that Earwicker has harbored in a secret that is safe with his wife: "Never divorce in the bedding the glove that will give you away" (586.5–6). Anna Livia knows too much (as does Molly Bloom), and if she were to play the role of sexual accuser, her evidence could be even be more damaging than the circumstantial supposition that surrounds the scene in the park. But the point is that Anna Livia is not and will never be Earwicker's accuser, just as Molly Bloom will never say publicly what she thinks privately about Bloom's peculiar sexual habits. Indeed, both wives are the defenders of their husbands' honor in the face of a public that little understands or appreciates these men. While sexual tensions abound in the two works, and while sexual mystery lies at the center of "events" in *Ulysses* and *Finnegans Wake*, marital relationships survive by bonds of loyalty rather than sexual fulfillment. The sexual interests of these characters have changed over the years, altered by the responsibilities of parenthood and middle age: the moment by the rhododendrons on Howth Head will never occur again; Earwicker will never return the conquering hero to sail up Anna's river Liffey. Sexual capacity (if not desire) has been displaced.

If the process of sexual anticipation or remembrance—the vision that avoids the present by looking either backwards or forwards in time—makes Joyce's characters voyeurs of their own sexual lives, then the reader becomes a voyeur at second remove. We peep through the blinds and peer through the mists, our curiosity piqued by the sexual tensions appearing in the text by way of family relationships. And we suffer the worst frustrations of the voyeur, disappointed at the critical moment when the curtain is drawn and the sexual act itself is hidden from view. But the voyeur with the slightest bit of imagination can draw for himself, for his own sexual needs, the vision on the bed. And imagination is frequently more satisfying than the cold, factual thing itself. Having been denied the facts of Molly's tryst with Boylan, of Earwicker's first seduction of Anna Livia, of Milly's encounter with Bannon, of Bloom's misadventure with Bridie Kelly, the actual events between Stephen Dedalus and the prostitute, or of anything approaching sexual consummation in Bella Cohen's brothel, the reader surmises the real state of events shadowed by these various possibilities. Our minds play over the scarce remnants of the liaison between Molly and Boylan, plotting the progression of that relationship from first introduction, to the night of the bazaar dance when they walked along the Tolka, to the planned tour in Belfast in the "future." We speculate on the causes and consequences of Rudy's death, on the reasons for Milly's absence from 7 Eccles street, on Bloom's sexual potency and competency, on the frustration and gratification of Molly's sexual existence. But our fondest desires (like those of the characters we watch) are constantly frustrated. Even when we think we are viewing the "scene" itself, even when it appears that the cricket game that is being played out in *Finnegans Wake* is in fact the Porters making love, the scene is dimly lit and "we had only our hazelight to see with" (587.3): all rests in speculation.

In assessing these events seen dimly, I suspect that sexuality as such is only one aspect of the human survival in *Ulysses* and *Finnegans Wake*, and that the capacity for sexual experience that in and of itself is purely joyful exists only in youth, perhaps only in the first sexual encounter, and that it lives in the present through memory.

Notes

1. Reprinted in James Joyce, *Ulysses* (New York: Random House, 1961), pp. vii–xii. All parenthetical references to *Ulysses* are to this edition.

2. *Finnegans Wake* (New York: The Viking Press, 1947), 627.11. All further references are included parenthetically.

3. For a rather complete listing of all the various versions of the Phoenix Park incident, see Bernard Benstock, "Every Telling Has a Taling: A Reading of the Narrative of *Finnegans Wake*," *Modern Fiction Studies* 14 (Spring 1969): 3–26.

"See ourselves as others see us": Joyce's Look at the Eye of the Other

Kimberly J. Devlin

In memory of John Hannay, mentor and friend

*U*lysses has a curiously hesitant opening, and like hesitancies elsewhere in Joyce's fictions, this one functions to betray. Buck Mulligan steps up onto an open-air stage of sorts, carrying his shaving equipment; he intones a Latinate phrase from the Mass—and then suddenly halts. The extra motive behind this pause remains ambiguous. Does Mulligan start his mock ritual for the benefit of a wholly imaginary eye, only to realize that an actual eye is preferable and readily available? Or does he interrupt his theatrics when he realizes that the actual eye he has posited from the start is in fact wholly imaginary, that he has no audience, that he must summon his weary tower mate to watch the show? The second explanation seems more likely, but in either event the significance of that halt is largely the same: the gestural hesitancy betrays Mulligan's interest in the eye of the other, his desire for an other to witness and, he hopes, to appreciate his early morning performance.

Mulligan's brief opening pause hints at a concern that preoccupied Joyce throughout his literary career, most prominently in *Ulysses* and *Finnegans Wake*: the self-conscious subject, the subject intensely aware of the sensitive to an other's eye. When Stephen looks in the mirror later in "Telemachus," he thinks to himself, "As he and others see me. Who chose this face for me?" (6); instead of identifying with the image, he immediately envisions it as something looked at by other subjectivities. Like many other Joycean characters, Stephen is highly self-conscious, afflicted by "an obsessive sense of being watched, even when, as in 'Proteus,' there is no one present to do the watching" (Maddox 24). Bloom, too, is preoccupied with the eye of the other, wondering at lunch hour, when he sees a man wolfing down food in the Burton, "Am I like that? See ourselves as others see us" (169).

Reprinted by permission of the Modern Language Association of America from *PMLA* 104 (October 1989):882–93.

194 ◆ KIMBERLY J. DEVLIN

The Robert Burns poem that Joyce alludes to in these words suggests that, much as we may try, we never do see ourselves as others see us: "O wad some Power the giftie gie us / To see oursels as ithers see us! / It wad frae monie a blunder free us, / An' foolish notion: / What airs in dress an' gait wad lea'e us, / An' even devotion" ("To a Louse; on Seeing One on a Lady's Bonnet at Church"; qtd. in Gifford 142). The basic point that captured Joyce's attention in Burns's poems has also been explored in psychoanalytic thought. Because the conscious subject is irremediably limited, self-perception involves misperception, *méconnaissance*, the subject's field of vision inevitably containing a scotoma, a dark or blind spot. As Jacques Lacan writes in his lecture on the gaze, "No doubt, in the depths of my eye, the picture is painted. The picture, certainly, is in my eye. But I am not in the picture. . . . [I]f I am anything in the picture, it is always in the form of . . . the stain, the spot [i.e., the scotoma]" (96–97). Several points in this lecture inform my own study of Joyce's interest in attempts to transcend the limits of self-perception by seeing the self through the eye of the other.

Lacan's relevance to the Joycean corpus may not be merely coincidental, for his lecture shares a theoretical source with at least one of Joyce's fictions, his final dream book, *Finnegans Wake*. Lacan elaborates on and responds to several works, including Freud's case history of the Wolf Man ("From the History of an Infantile Neurosis"); Joyce carefully studied this Freudian text, took notes on it, and worked explicit elements of it into the *Wake* (Ferrer). Joyce and Lacan were both keenly interested in intersubjective vision, and perhaps they were drawn to the Wolf Man's case history because of what it suggests about the self in relation to the eye of the other. After briefly outlining my understanding of a few of Lacan's contentions and showing their coincidence with several features of Joycean texts, I confine my focus here to Joyce's contrasting representations of intersubjective perception in his day and night worlds and to his exploration of the negative and positive psychological functions of the other's gaze. An examination of these issues provides a clue to the logic of *Finnegans Wake*'s highly idiosyncratic structure, a problem that has long baffled critics, and also sheds some light on the sexual dynamics of intersubjectivity that Joyce represented over the course of his career.

In discussing intersubjectivity in conscious and unconscious states, Lacan suggests that dreaming involves a crucial alteration in the subject's relation to the other's eye:

we are beings who are looked at, in the spectacle of the world. That which makes us consciousness institutes us by the same token as *speculum mundi*. . . . [I]n the so-called waking state, there is an elision of the gaze, and an elision of the fact that not only does it look, *it* also *shows*. In the field of dream, on the other hand, what characterizes the images is that *it shows*. . . . So much

HCE wants to escape himself in fiction to escape society, and speaks of himself as a leader of men. "Society".

is [this insistence on showing] to the fore . . . that, in the final resort, our position in the dream is profoundly that of someone who does not see. The subject does not see where it is leading, he follows.

(75)

This insistence on "showing" gives dreams a dramatic and impersonal quality, despite their obvious subjectivity, as Freud implies in *The Interpretation of Dreams*: "a thought . . . is objectified in the dream, is represented as a scene, or so it seems to us, is experienced. . . . [T]he thought is represented as an immediate situation with the 'perhaps' omitted, and . . . transformed into visual images and speech" (572–73). In the process the self sometimes becomes its own spectacle, an object of its own theatrical viewing. The seemingly "scenic" and "objectified" status of the dream text may help to explain why Joyce chose the dramatic mode for "Circe" and why he constructs *Finnegans Wake* as a "drema" (*Finnegans* 69), as a series of densely complicated tableaux and speeches, with a central or singular narrative I/eye glaringly absent.[1] What the unconscious theatrically "shows," on one level, are images of the self and its desires that the subject does not want to recognize and that are hence elided in waking life. By day, for instance, Bloom may not fully acknowledge that he plays a role in his own cuckolding and derives pleasure from his complicity, but in the unconscious fantasies of "Circe" this guilty truth is vividly revealed to him: he envisions himself as pander to Molly and Boylan, servilely waiting on them and heeding his rival's instruction to "apply your eye to the keyhole and play with yourself while I just go through her a few times" (566). Bloom's vision also dramatizes the possibility that Molly and Boylan are very much aware of his voyeuristic presence, that they are watching him watch, that the viewing subject is also the viewed object. Joyce creates in Bloom a paradoxically blind voyeur, one whose visual acuity and curiosity are matched by psychic scotomas that blot out the images working to show the self as it would not wish to be seen.

More important, Lacan's formulation suggests that the key truth usually elided in waking life is the gaze itself, the gaze of the other that makes attitudes of "deviance" deviant to begin with, the gaze that causes various desires to be shameful and embarrassing, shame and embarrassment being strictly intersubjective responses. Dramatizations or "showings" of this normally elided gaze can be found in the case history of the Wolf Man and throughout Joyce's works. What is made both visible and literal in the Wolf Man's dream of the watching wolves in the tree is the gaze of the other, in this instance of the father himself. But of course in the primal scene that the dream supposedly screens, the father is not watching the child at all; the child only imagines the father's gaze, leveled at him, the subject, in a taboo position (the position of the voyeur)—the position that the dream's key reversal censors and yet betrays by turning the viewing subject into viewed object.[2] Although on deeper levels the son's dream may indeed express his anxieties about castration, its projection of a wholly imaginary gaze as actual more obviously dramatizes the subject's enthrallment to the other. A similar projection appears in *A Portrait of the Artist* when Stephen, affected by Father Arnall's hellfire sermon, has a paranoiac vision of his bedroom as a cave filled with judgmental inhabitants: "Faces were there: eyes: they waited and watched. . . . Murmuring faces waited and watched; murmurous voices filled the dark shell of the cave" (136). These prying eyes, like those in the Wolf Man's case history, can be read both as a momentary externalization of the self's voyeuristic transgressions: shortly after this hallucinatory vision, Stephen reminds himself, "He was in mortal sin. Even once was a mortal sin. It could happen in an instant. But how so quickly? *By seeing or by thinking of seeing*" (139; emphasis added). Lacan translates into theory what Joyce and Freud represent in fiction and case history, emphasizing both the facti- tiousness of the gaze ("The gaze I encounter is, not a seen gaze, but a gaze imagined by me in the field of the Other" [84]) and the subject's absurd enthrallment to it: "the level of reciprocity between the gaze and the gazed at is, for the subject, more open than any other to alibi" (77). The subject is always aware of the gaze, is always watching the gaze—reflexively, not intentionally or consciously—but the gaze is not necessarily watching the subject. Hence Lacan likens the gaze to ocelli, the eyelike spots on some forms of wildlife—for example, leopards, ocelots, and various butterflies— that potential predators often mistake for eyes but that of course see nothing at all. These ocelli-like eyes will reappear with a vengeance in the hallucina- tions of "Circe" and again in *Finnegans Wake*, where others are recurrently marked as "wickedgapers" (366) and "peersons" (60).

The waking subject's reflexive watching of the gaze can be seen most patently in "Lotus Eaters," where Bloom is guiltily self-conscious, marching soberly through the episode's sleepy, soporific atmosphere; he remains visu- ally alert, carefully checking to make sure that no one he knows sees him enter the post office or walk down a back lane to read Martha's most recent letter. When he retrieves the post-office-box card from his hatband but hides the gesture by pretending he has taken off his hat to wipe his brow (71), Bloom is putting on an act for an imagined other, performing for a gaze not actually there. Elsewhere in the novel, however, Bloom considers himself relatively indifferent to what others think of him, curious about the other's point of view only as a source of potential insight into himself, although he does admit, significantly, that he is sensitive to the good opinion of the opposite sex. In "Nausicaa," when an unnamed gentleman he has seen earlier passes by again on the strand, Bloom thinks to himself, "Walk after him now make him awkward like those newsboys me today. Still you learn something. See ourselves as others see us. So long as women don't mock what matter?" (375–76). As his thoughts about "parallax" suggest, Bloom in waking life sees alternative points of view as part of an intellectual pastime, as providing an interesting exercise in envisioning the way an object or person changes when looked at from a different vantage point.[3] Attuned to perceptual relativity, he is usually willing to concede the validity of others' opinions, to "look at it other way round" (380). In "Circe," however, parallactic vision is replaced by the paranoiac: the opinions and perspectives of the various phantasms are not an intellectual interest but a personal psychic threat; the gaze of the other is an agency not of insight but of exposure. In accordance with Lacan's argument, the gaze here not only looks but shows. On the level of the unconscious, Bloom is very much concerned with what the other thinks of him, with how the other sees him, as his dialectical fantasies of persecution and grandeur imply.

Over the course of "Circe," the human other gives way to the nonhuman: the nymph from the picture over Bloom's bed; the statue from the museum; the babbling waterfall, murmuring yew trees, and ruminating calf from Bloom's high school field trip to Poulaphouca; the nanny goat from his romantic outing to Howth Head (544–53)—all enter the stream of phantasms as witnesses to Bloom's polymorphous desires. These nonhuman accusers once again betray the gaze as imaginary, emphasizing the way that human self-consciousness is constituted and mediated by factitious ocelli: eyes in pictures or on statues do not really look, of course, while those of animals see without moral censure. The calf from Poulaphouca and the nanny goat from Howth are surely indifferent to the potential indiscretion of masturbating in the woods or making love in the open air—such an activity is embarrassing only to a human being envisioning a judgmental eye. Like the dream in the Wolf Man's case history, Bloom's unconscious fantasies reveal this elided gaze, his repressed and even denied enthrallment to an imaginary but ever-present other.

Finnegans Wake inherits the paranoiac ambience and perverse imagoes of "Circe," the fallen patriarchal dreamer HCE picturing himself in almost every conceivable posture of "deviance": as voyeur, exhibitionist, sadist, masochist, self-contrived cuckold, furtive adulterer, lecherous desire of the daughter, homosexual desirer of the sons. Joyce represents the dream as the site of negative epiphanies, a conception of dream he shares with (and perhaps derives from) Freud. He may have borrowed from the Wolf Man's case history in particular one possible unconscious interpretation of Christmas, the season of the epiphany, although he partially recasts its psychic significance to suit the paternal perspective of the *Wake*. Freud speculates that his patient had the wolf dream on Christmas eve (also the eve of his fourth birthday) after falling asleep "in tense expectation of the day which was to bring him a double quantity of presents" ("History" 220). The wish for material gifts from the father screens a wish for sexual gifts from the father; in the dream the boy constructs an imaginary precondition for obtaining this erotic satisfaction: recalling from the primal scene the female's position and genitalia, the patient unconsciously equates female sexual pleasure with a necessary prior castration, so that the dream memory translates "gifts" as "punishment" and turns the wish into an anxiety. Joyce's Christmas motif in the *Wake* is similar insofar as Christmas gifts consistently turn into their psychological opposite and insofar as Christmastime epiphanies seem precisely designed to shock and disturb. ALP's knapsack, which doubles as Santa Claus's sack of goodies (209), may be a Pandora's box of sorts or a dangerous document one hesitates to open ("My colonial, wardha bagful! . . . All that and more under one crinoline envelope if you dare to break the porkbarrel seal. No wonder they'd run from her pison plague" [212]). Exploring a dreaming father's fears, Joyce makes Christmas the occasion for "youlldied greedings" from oedipal offspring (308), for dramatic realizations of relentless generational succession and personal mortality: in the *Wake* the traditional season of the son's birth is frequently associated only with the father's death. Epiphany takes the form of both psychological exposure, a showing forth of repressed truths and perverse desires, and physical exposure, a showing forth of normally concealed bodily parts. When the dreamer envisions his back buttons popping off his pants (cf. Bloom's *"back trousers' button snap*[ping]" [552] in "Circe"), a voice suddenly exclaims, "How *c*ulious an *e*piphany!" (508; emphasis added).

Resembling "Circe" in structure as well as in theme, *Finnegans Wake* inverts waking subject-object relations, recurrently representing the subject as spectacle, as the object of the other's eye. In section 2.3 a vision of pub customers staring at a hunting picture on the wall (334) precedes the Butt and Taff skit, also presumably watched by HCE's clientele on the screen of a TV set; the two pieces of dream text seem homologously connected, for the televised drama turns into a hunting story, with the target being the dreamer himself. Adaline Glasheen likens the television set to the mousetrap in *Hamlet*, to the play the prince stages for Claudius and Gertrude (liv): the analogy is apt, for the set functions as an agency of exposure, as a medium that openly dramatizes embarrassing possibilities, unflattering and threatening images of the self—the father letting down his pants and defecating in public, the spying sons then shooting this vulnerable authority figure. The content and form of the dream text here are psychically related, both expressing fears of being shot—by a gun in the skit itself and by a camera in the televised structure. Later in the dream HCE's bedroom turns into a movie set (558–59), the mise-en-scène for a particularly frustrating session of intercourse. Despite all the athletic frenzy of the scene, HCE's efforts are indeed strained, and his wife is imagined laughing at his performance (583). The possibility of being poorly reflected in his wife's gaze spawns a vision of being exposed to a more general gaze, HCE fearing that his humiliating sexual showing—"the coming event" indicative of the father's decline—will be widely publicized: "The man in the street can see the coming event. Photoflashing it far too wide. It will be known through all Urania soon" (583). The dreamer is threatened by actual eyes as well as by mechanical ones ("*h*itch a *c*ock *e*ye, he was snapped on the sly" [363; emphasis added]), dreading an "exposure" of the self in every sense of the word.

Given the dreamer's fear of cameras, it is not surprising that the potentially scandalous night letter takes the shape of a photo negative (111), the written exposé becoming a visual one. HCE is figured as a cameraman whose equipment is turned on him to bring about his downfall ("you were shutter reshottus and sieger besieged" [352]) or as Charles Dodgson snapped in intimate self-portraiture with his little friend Alice ("And there many have paused before that exposure of him by old Tom Quad, a flashback in which he sits sated . . . [with] the tata of tiny victorienne, Alys, pressed by his limper looser" [57]). These visions are part of a larger dream pattern that represents HCE as representation—as a picture, a monument, a statue, or an exhibit in a wax museum. In the *Wake*an night world, the self is often imagined both as a figurative object, a person looked at by intrusive eyes in intersubjective perceptual relations, and as a literal object, a nonhuman thing examined by human others. The dreamer's subjectivity is not simply threatened and preempted by the subjectivities of others, it is inscribed imagistically as nonexistent, defunct. In the context of pervasive anxieties about human mortality, these visions of the reified self become attempts to imagine death, to think within subjectivity what it is like to be without subjectivity, to conceptualize that moment when the self is utterly and irrevocably replaced by figuration—figuration left to the hermeneutical whims of an unknown other. The gaze is inscribed as a potential perpetuity that follows the self beyond the bourn, although, as I suggest later, such an inscription records a wish as well as an anxiety.

In a similar reifying dream imago, the corporeal self is imagined as physical territory, invaded physical territory—literally invaded in the visions of homosexual rape, figuratively in the fantasies of the body as investigated terrain. Blending somatic and external worlds, the dreamer frequently perceives the self as inflated or gargantuan: visits to his property turn into tours of his body, which then becomes a landscape that others walk on and explore. This conflation of private and public premises is best seen in the sequence where the four old men investigate the father's physical plant—his house and tavern—as well as his physical form (3.4). Imagining the four watching his large shape at work on the marriage bed, the dreamer suddenly envisions himself as Phoenix Park, the "second position of discordance . . . [in which] the male entail partially eclipses the femecovert" (564), turning into an overhead view of the park's topography. His rectum becomes a gorge, cave, or well into which visitors throw an echo, while some suspicious welts and bruises on his bottom turn into belts of trees or silver mines: "The black and blue marks athwart the weald, which now barely is so stripped, indicate the presence of sylvious beltings" (564). The gargantuan imagoes of the self limn for the reader the dreamer's implicit physical condition, his sense of being heavy, sprawling, unable to move, like Gulliver among the Lilliputians; but the fantasy of being a terrain traversed by others may have a psychic rather than a somatic origin. If *Finnegans Wake* is structured largely around myths of "trespass," expressing unconscious desires to transgress lawful boundaries (Norris, *Decentered* 37–39), then the visions of intruders tromping over the body's territory, violating the self's physical boundaries, literalize the trope. If the prime transgressor is in fact HCE, who in dreaming explores his unlawful impulses, then a guilty subject-object reversal has occurred, the trespasser defensively representing himself as the trespassed against.

HCE's continual sense of the self as a viewed and explored object is connected to an elusive transgression that flickers across the surface of the dream in an endless array of forms. This mysterious fall, which HCE wants both to remember and to forget, usually involves one older man (presumably himself), two younger women, and three younger men, and in its most abbreviated form it is designated simply by the numbers one, two, three. Although the structure of the temptation is protean, representationally unstable, the two young women and three young men often haunt the dream as unwanted witnesses to transgression, taking shape as meddlers, spies, intrusive fusiliers, and forest rangers:

> it seemed he was before the eyots of martas or otherwales the third of fossilyears
>
> (40)

> The two childspies waapreesing him auza de Vologue but the renting of his rock was from the three wicked Vuncouverers Forests bent down awhits, arthou sure?
>
> (88)

> A pair of sycopanties with amygdaleine eyes, one old obster lumpky pumpkin and three meddlars on their slies.
>
> (94)

> *Fickleyes and Futilears*
>
> (176)

Joyce often represents the young men metonymically as eavesdroppers (fossily*ears*, futil*ears*) and also stresses their role as witnesses and voyeurs ("widness thane and tysk and hanry" [316]; "peep of tim boys and piping tom boys" [385]). What is psychically disturbing to the dreamer is not committing any particular sin but being seen in the act. This threat is clear even when the fall becomes literal, when it takes the form of tipsy Tim Finnegan crashing down from his ladder:

> wan warning Phill filt tippling full. His howd feeled heavy, his hoddit did shake. (There was a wall of course in erection) Dimb! He stottered from the

latter. Damb! he was dud. Dumb! Mastabatoom, mastabadtomm, when a mon merries his lute is all long. *For whole the world to see.*

(6; emphasis added)

At points, however, the *Wake*'s dreamer suspects that his watchers are unreal, that the threatening eyes are merely ocelli. He envisions himself predominantly as viewed object but also occasionally as a viewing voyeuristic subject observed only by an impervious universe, only by "the clouds aboon"—the clouds above and the clouds alone: "aither he cursed and recursed and was everseen doing what your fourfootlers saw or he was never done seeing what you coolpigeons know, weep the clouds aboon for smiledown witnesses" (29). HCE's transgression is appropriately described as "the fairest sin the sunsaw" (11)—as a sin seen by the prying oedipal offspring or maybe only by the sun, by oblivious and indifferent nature.

Instead of momentarily disappearing, the gaze more frequently multiplies, compounds itself, forming voyeuristic regresses wherein one party is watched by another party, who in turn is watched by another party, who in turn is watched by still another. The regression of gazes dramatizes the self-consciousness of the human subject of desire: the image of the self in a position of desire seems to spawn automatically a representation of the gaze, imagined as the eye of another prurient and desirous viewer, who is thus always reflexively conscious of yet another gaze. More patently, the voyeuristic regress exposes the vulnerability of the voyeur, the way in which the pruriently viewing subject, presumably safe in a position of furtive pleasure, may unknowingly also be the viewed object of yet another I/eye, or of the I/eye it is itself secretly viewing (one recalls Bloom's Circean vision of Molly and Boylan). Power is the psychic issue in images that combine seeing with being seen, for they question the self's control over its own assumed position as subject. Joyce explores the limits of this control in his early play *Exiles*—and already in the context of devious intersubjective watching. Richard tolerates Robert's dalliance with Bertha because he is able to observe its progress and thus feel some control over its course. He secretly exults in revealing his knowledge to Robert and in watching his rival's confusion, embarrassment, and disbelief ("You knew? From her? . . . You were watching us all the time?" [75]). But Joyce's notes on the play hint that Richard could have been even more ingeniously duped, that his position in the visual dialectic is not as secure as he might like to think:

In the last act (or second) Robert can also suggest that he knew from the first that Richard was aware of his conduct and that he himself was being watched and that he persisted because he had to and because he wished to see to what length Richard's silent forbearance would go.

(157)

One of the sources for the *Wake*'s complicated configurations of intersubjective watching is Joseph Bedier's *Romance of Tristan and Iseult*, a book Joyce explicitly recommended to Harriet Shaw Weaver while she was reading *Work in Progress* (*Letters* 241). Commenting on Bedier's rendering of the romance, Glasheen writes, "Ten thousand emotional miles from Wagner's, [it] is an ur and unslick bedroom farce peopled all with tricksters" (289). Much of the farcical quality derives from the elaborate spying and counterspying of the major characters. Constantly trying to catch the young lovers in a compromising position, four jealous barons goad King Mark into joining their voyeuristic pursuit of the pair, but Tristan and Iseult, having superior visual acuity, are never caught. The couple always detect their unwanted company and behave accordingly. In one scene King Mark hides in a pine tree, ready to surprise them in an illicit embrace, but they notice his reflection in the water of a well. Instead of abandoning themselves to desire, they engage in an artful conversation bemoaning King Mark's unwarranted jealousy and the barons' villainous deception of their lord (48–51). Later the pair kill one of the wily barons after Iseult perceives his shadow on the curtain of the window through which he planned to watch their tryst (100–01). Tristan and Iseult elude their pursuers because, when watched, they are always secretly watching back. What appealed to Joyce in Bedier's book, I suspect, is its representation of the human as the ontological fraud, trapped in a manipulative theater of desire; but Joyce, unlike Bedier, captures the irony of the human penchant for performance. Joycean figures, with "eyes all over them" (*Ulysses* 371), become parodic versions of the spotted beast, their ocelli warding off an other that is often merely a psychic construct.

The spying and counterspying in the *Wake* become most complicated in section 2.4—often called the Tristan and Iseult section—where all the central figures from Bedier's account appear in an intricate tableau of intersubjective gazing. The four scopophiliac ancients, analogues of King Mark's barons, are added to the familiar one-two-three configuration—the older man, the pair of young women, and the triad of young men—giving the voyeuristic regress a further dimension:

> How it did but all come eddaying back to them, if they did but get gaze, gagagniagnian, to hear him there, kiddling and cuddling her, after the gouty old galahat, with his peer of quinnyfears and troad of thirstuns, so nefarious, from his elevation of one yard one handard and thartytwo lines, before the four of us, in his Roman Catholic arms, while his deepseepeepers gazed and sazed and dazecrazemazed into her dullokbloon rodolling olosheen eyenbowls by the Cornelius Nepos, Mnepos. Anumque, umque. Napoo.
> Queh? Quos?
>
> (389)

The confusion indicated by the final puzzled interrogatives is well warranted, although in the context of the whole episode the contours of the scenario are not impenetrable. The four ancients are apparently either watching the older man watch the young lovers or else reading a version of the famous myth of triangular desire in a book by Cornelius Nepos, a Roman historian and letter writer (McHugh 389). In either event, the "gouty old galahat" spies on the couple from some point of elevation, perhaps a tree, after the fashion of King Mark, or one of the masts of the boat, the site of the initial consummation.[4] His name appropriately suggests Galehoult, the pander who in some versions of the Lancelot and Guinevere story arranges the lovers' illicit union: in the analogous myth of Tristan and Iseult, King Mark plays the pander himself, promoting his own cuckolding by appointing Tristan his proxy in love. But the verbal ambiguities and syntactical disjunctions destabilize the scenario, making it difficult to sort out who is watching whom and who (if anyone) is simply being watched. The dualistic young woman appears as a "peer of quinnyfears," but exactly who she is peering at remains characteristically uncertain. The "troad of thirstuns" gazes adoringly into her "olosheen eyen-bowls," whose sheen suggests a mirrorlike surface, a duplicitous reflector that perhaps enables the gazer to see the voyeur, like the well in Bedier's account. The afterthought "Anumque," which means "and the old woman" in Latin (McHugh 389), hints that the maternal ALP has joined the party of oglers. While the accusative case suggests that she is probably a voyeuristic object, her later appearance as a devious viewer ("his *a*mbling *l*imfy *p*eeping-partner" [580; emphasis added]) leaves her status within the visual dialectic highly ambiguous. Another possible witness of HCE's possible voyeurism, the mother compounds the paranoiac, though potentially illusory, threat of the other's gaze.

In *The Decentered Universe of* Finnegans Wake, Margot Norris explains the way the theme of the fallen father subverts the traditional attributes of patriarchal authority, dislocating the androcentric hub of religious, social, and familial orders. The fallen dreaming father

> is named rather than namer. He is uncertain of name and identity, unlocatable rather than a center that fixes, defines, and gives meaning to his cosmos. He is lawbreaker rather than lawgiver. As the head of the family, he is incestuous rather than the source of order in the relations of his lineage.
>
> (61)

The subversion, I would add, is at once visual and psychological. Instead of being an omnipotent and all-watchful patriarch, the fallen father fears he is watched by others, others who have devious designs on him ("*h*e *c*onscious of *e*nemies" [75; emphasis added]). Instead of being omniscient, he possesses limited—and hence uncertain—vision and knowledge. Far from divine, his visual capacities are frequently directed toward prurient and worldly voyeuristic ends, and they are threatened, moreover, by craftier forms of voyeurism. The very presence of his multiple voyeurs—however imaginary they may be—betrays his all too human status as thrall to others' eyes, his enslavement to intersubjective self-perception. The self-defined and self-created patriarch of Christian mythology becomes in the *Wake* the flawed father whose humanness is measured by the extent to which he derives his identity from the other.

The enthrallment to the eye of the other provides a clue to the logic behind the *Wake*'s larger narrative orientation, the odd, dispersed mode of telling that has been the source of much debate. Michael Begnal, who has identified and characterized several voices in the *Wake*, summarizes some critical perspectives on the book's structure after explaining his own view of the matter:

> The single-dreamer theory, which names Humphrey Chimpden Earwicker as the sole narrator, overlooks the use of multiple point of view . . . and creates more critical problems than it overcomes. When one realizes that several people are dreaming together, it becomes much easier to individualize them and to redefine them in greater depth.
>
> (Begnal and Eckley 20)

But if one rejects "the single-dreamer theory" on the grounds of the *Wake*'s multiple perspectives, one misses the work's central ontological paradox, the degree to which the individualized self is founded on and determined by the other. In contrast to the carefully controlled and identified subjectives in Joyce's earlier fictions, the *Wake*'s countless narrative I/eyes often remain nameless, in a dream text constructed around the hypothetical gazes of a seemingly infinite series of others. Within this decentered structure of multiple perspectives, HCE is logically identified as the dreamer, not because he is the central "speaker," but rather because he is the central "spoken of": with a compulsive predictability, the topic of discussion returns to him—or, if not to him, to a familial extension of him, to his wife, his sons, or his daughter. Frequently, though, these family members themselves compose the other, their voices constituting much of the distinguishable, personalized speech in the dream. In dreaming these various voices, HCE betrays not only his ambivalent feelings toward his nearest and dearest but also—more prominently—his fears about their potentially ambivalent feelings toward him. In her essay on ALP, Norris writes that

> we must understand the dreaming male figure in order to understand the female figure. Yet Joyce, paradoxically, sets up a hermeneutical spiral in *Finnegans Wake* through which the best insights into the condition of HCE (presumably the male dreamer) are given by Anna Livia in her final monologue.
>
> (199)

This "hermeneutical spiral," I would argue, characterizes the structure of both the final monologue and the entire dream text: although HCE does envision himself speaking at several points, most of the information (or misinformation) we are given about him is mediated, delivered through imagined others. What we confront in the *Wake* is the subject's image of himself as he imagines he appears to other I/eyes, to alien subjectivities. The human enthrallment to the gaze, in short, is a technical as well as a thematic concern in the *Wake*, a concern vividly dramatized in the book's idiosyncratic but revealing narrative form.

Because one's image in the eye of the other is elusive and unknown, the dream's fabric is contradictory and protean, resistant to any sort of fixity or consistency. The changing visions of the dreamer that are produced by even the identifiable and individualized speakers betray the uncertainty of his estimation of their estimation, of his perception of their perception; the self-image reflected through the discourse of wife, sons, or daughter is invariably incongruous, dispersed—as irrevocably fractured as Humpty Dumpty's ubiquitous shell. The wildest inconsistencies occur when one tries to reconcile not a single other's vision of HCE but the visions of the assorted others in the dream; for each gives the dreamer a different identity, as the attempt to specify his name at the end of section 1.2 suggests:

> Some vote him Vike, some mote him Mike, some dub him Llyn and Phin while others hail him Lug Bug Dan Lop, Lex, Lax, Gunne or Guinn. Some apt him Arth, some bapt him Barth, Coll, Noll, Soll, Will, Weel, Wall but I parse him Persse O'Reilly else he's called no name at all.
>
> (44)

HCE's fluctuating identity is a function of its mediated status: this is made clear in the contrasting versions of the elusive night letter, which is written to and about the dreamer but which also is the dreamer ("a *h*uge *c*hain *e*nvelope, written in seven divers stages of ink" [66; emphasis added]). We are told that "closer inspection of the *bordereau* would reveal a multiplicity of personalities inflicted upon the documents or document" (107); the singular document becomes multiple documents because its text varies according to who is imagined creating or reading it. The letter changes in form and content every time it returns in the dream because it is produced by "the continually more and less intermisunderstanding minds of the anticollaborators" (118). The night letter is another imago of the self as a textual artifact, as an artifact not simply explored and discussed by others but also written and defined by others.

Amid all the paranoid visions of being investigated, read, and spied on, there are some scenarios in the *Wake* in which being gazed on is a pleasure, a desire. At one point, for example, the dreamer imagines himself lord mayor of Dublin welcoming the king of England to Ireland and presenting him with the keys of the city (568). The ceremony is witnessed by a crowd of "peeplers entrammed and detrained on bikeygels and troykakyls and those puny farting little solitires" (567). The encrusted references to trams, trains, and cycles with varying numbers of wheels perhaps suggest the modes of transport used to arrive at the ceremony; but the metonymic one-two-three, the furtive watching implied in the word "peeplers," and the allusion to farting (flimsily disguised as the sound of air leaking from a tire) all link this grandiose event, with its pleasurable moment of self-consciousness, to the elusive sin, with its embarrassing moment of self-consciousness. The two scenes, in other words, are versions of each other and yet psychological opposites, expressing respectively the positive and negative possibilities of the gaze: the ceremony watched by a throng of impressed spectators is simply the wishful inversion, the gratifying transformation, of a culturally stigmatized act watched (or heard) by an intrusive and unwelcome audience.

Through both specific details and larger patterns, this *Wake*an fantasy of public grandeur is connected to Bloom's Circean vision of himself as lord mayor of Dublin, a vision that escalates to dreams of being coronated Leopold the First, king of the new Bloomusalem. The most salient feature of these fantasies of acclaim is the excess of cultural signifiers of significance itself: resplendent clothing, symbolic jewelry, phalanxes of titled men, a super-abundance of fanfare. Bloom's assumption of numerous titles, "emperor president and king chairman, the most serene and potent and very puissant ruler of this realm," and multiple names, "Leopold, Patrick, Andrew, David, George, be thou annointed" (*Ulysses* 482)—this excess of literal signification, frequently associated with majesty, finds its approximate counterpart in the proliferating appellations for HCE, appellations that inflate in rank and length simultaneously (as if longer names were more impressive than shorter ones): "rich Mr Pornter, a squire. . . . [H]andsome Sir Pournter. . . . Lord Pournterfamilias" (570). Attributes of excess that are potentially ambiguous—such as excessive weight—are invariably encoded favorably in these scenes. When the imagoes of the self physically inflate, Bloom and HCE turn into men (like Henry VIII or Edward VII) whose massiveness functions as a positive register of their substantiality, import, and power (and not as a negative signifier of, say, a metabolic disorder, a pathological oral fixation, or a gluttonous impulse): in "Circe" Bloom *uncloaks impressively, revealing obesity"* (487), and in section 3.4 of the *Wake* "one sees how he [HCE/Mr. Porter] is a lot stoutlier than of formerly" (570). In context these details of excess and the excess of these details ultimately betray themselves as compensatory signs, as wishful tokens of overestimation designed to mask fears of underestimation, as counters to the anxieties about disparagement and disrespect that run strongly through both "Circe" and the *Wake*an dream.

HCE's massiveness is interpreted by the other as a pregnancy, his body envisioned as the repository of several male heirs: "One would say to him to hold whole a litteringture of kidlings under his aproham. . . . [Y]es indeed, he has his mic son and his two fine mac sons and a superfine mick want they mack metween them" (570). This image can be read as the *Wake*an return of the maternal fantasy in "Circe," during which Bloom gives birth to male octuplets. As critics have noted, Joyce accentuates the children's status as socioeconomic signifiers: with their faces made of valuable metals, their auric and silvery names, their highbrow interests, and their impressive jobs (494), Bloom's eight sons are overdetermined cultural markers expressing his "petit bourgeois wish for status, power, and wealth" (Zimmerman 176–77), his "parental dream of vicarious upward mobility" (Herr 171). Gender too plays a role in the valences of this imago. In a moment of psychic powerlessness in his confrontation with the other, Bloom imagines himself as female—through a stereotypical association that will resurface when he meets Bella-Bello. But to recoup his losses, he appropriates an androcentric signifier of female desirability (i.e., pregnancy) that will also strategically play on the sentiments of the other: the Circean delivery is an attempted deliverance, a defensive maneuver to gain "clemency" and "compassion" when the crowd starts to turn on the leader it exalted moments before (494). Bloom then proceeds to produce an excess of sons (as does HCE) in part because it is the male gender that signifies within androcentric semiotics. In his manipulative efforts to ward off a potentially critical eye, Bloom reveals his thorough internalization of the engendered sign.

Amid cheering, lavish celebrating, and citywide bell ringing, Joyce's "inflated" protagonists deliver ceremonial speeches that echo one another in both structure and content:

> (*{Bloom} uncloaks impressively, revealing obesity, unrolls a paper and reads solemnly.*)
> Aleph Beth Ghimel Daleth Hagadah Tephilim Kosher Yom Kippur Hanukah Roschaschana Beni Brith Bar Mitzvah Mazzoth Askenazim Meshuggah Talith.
>
> (*Ulysses* 487)

> he [HCE] shall aidress to His Serenemost by a speechreading from his miniated vellum, alfi byrni gamman dealter etcera zezera eacla treacla youghta kaptor lomdom noo
>
> (*Finnegans* 568)

The nonsensical erudition suggested by the concatenated Hebrew and Greek words is paradoxical and finally self-subverting rhetoric. On one level each "speech" aims to make a statement: Bloom attempts to assert his place in a Judaic tradition—obviously only imperfectly remembered—and HCE attempts to stake his claim in a classical one. But at the same time, of course, their oratories are pretentious babble: the true rhetorical end of these honorific rituals is not so much to communicate as to impress (one is reminded of Gabriel's after-dinner speech in "The Dead"). Because the ultimate signifier of significance is not the position of honor and the attendant regalia but the gaze that recognizes their symbolic value, the other—more specifically, the sexual other—plays a pivotal role in these fantasies. The Circean visions of the self in positions of prestige and power occur shortly after the scene in which all eyes are turned against Bloom, after the nightmarish trial where he is accused of almost every possible transgression—mainly by indignant women. During Bloom's hallucinatory reign as lord mayor, the women have an antithetical function, his prime accusers becoming now his prime admirers: *"All the windows are thronged with sightseers, chiefly ladies"* (479). As in the *Wake*, the fantasy of acclaim, of being watched by awed onlookers, is a psychic reversal of a fantasy of humiliation, of being watched by prying and hostile eyes belonging predominantly to the opposite gender. The role of the sexual other is more veiled in the *Wake*, but the final parenthetical appositives in the description of HCE as lord mayor—"Meynhir Mayour, our boorgomaister, thon staunch Thorsman, (our Nancy's fancy, our own Nanny's Big Billy)" (568)—hint that this dream of public veneration is linked to desires for female approval. Women play paradoxical roles in these male fantasies: physically degraded or semiotically devalued, they are yet perspectivally powerful, their gaze functioning frequently as the arbiter of male value itself.

The gaze in its more gratifying form functions in Joyce's works as the final signifier of significance, as that which fulfills the self's desire to be acknowledged and recognized, to be a somebody rather than a nobody. In situations of romantic rivalry it has the power to mark the desirable, the preferred, the sexually significant. This function can best be seen in "Nausicaa," an episode structured around a gaze: the young women on the strand make almost every gesture self-consciously to catch the eye of their mysterious onlooker. The gaze plays a powerful role in the chapter, for it is with his gaze that Bloom will signify which woman he finds most attractive, most appealing, and which he will relegate to the realm of sexual negligibility; the prospect of this signifying gaze sparks the jealousy and catty competitiveness that emerge as the episode develops. It is the eventual focus of Bloom's gaze on Gerty that drives Cissy to perform so frantically and shamelessly, with the hope of capturing at least a little bit of regard for herself: she makes bold and provocative comments, runs after the twins "with long gandery strides" (359), hoping to show a little bit of skin and petticoat, and eventually even approaches Bloom directly to ask the time. This last gesture, however, may be not an attention getter at all but an act of vengeance, her way of punishing the onlooker for not choosing her as the image of desirability. The gesture interrupts—and seems aimed to interrupt—Bloom's incipient masturbation: he is forced to take his hand out of his pocket when she approaches. After Bloom thwarts Cissy's desire for sexual recognition, she vindictively tries to thwart his desire for sexual gratification. If this chapter is a modernist rerendering of the Judgment of Paris, as Norris has argued, then Cissy clearly assumes the role of the vengeful Juno, the sore loser of ancient legend. But Joyce revises the sexist myth, not only by exposing its primordially corrupt model for the judgment of beauty and desirability (see

Norris, "Modernism") but also by allowing one of the "goddesses" to return as a counter gaze in Circean hallucination, by transforming the reified female object into a critical female subject: Gerty wins the contest and the right to judge the judge as a "dirty married man" (442).

The gaze also serves as the signifier of the desirable earlier in Joyce's works, at the end of "The Dead," though it is less literal there than in "Nausicaa." At the close of the party when Gabriel watches his wife listening to Bartell d'Arcy's singing, he responds with inward joy to her flushed cheeks and shining eyes because he assumes that she is thinking of him, that her inward gaze is secretly focused on him. En route to the Gresham Hotel, he composes a fantasy script in his mind in which the object of her gaze is revealed, dramatically enacted: "When the others had gone away, when he and she were in their room in the hotel, then they would be alone together. He would call her softly: / —Gretta! / Perhaps she would not hear at once: she would be undressing. Then something in his voice would strike her. She would turn and look at him . . ." (214; Joyce's ellipsis). The revelation that this desirous gaze is wholly imaginary, that Gretta's thoughts are in fact turned backward toward her earlier lover, precipitates an ego-shattering vision of the self, a vision of the self as ludicrous, clownish, and negligible. Gabriel's self-image is predicated on Gretta's gaze, its imagined presence kindling sexual confidence, desire; its revealed absence leading to deflated self-esteem, sexual humiliation. The antithetical visions of the self produced by Gretta's gaze are reflected in the cheval glass of the hotel room: before Gabriel hears her story, he sees a paterfamilias with a "broad, well-filled shirt-front" (218); afterward the image is revised, shrinking to one of a mere "pennyboy[,] . . . the pitiable fatuous fellow he had caught a glimpse of in the mirror" (219–20).

This feeling of negligibility at the end of "The Dead" prefigures an important moment at the end of *Finnegans Wake*, the moment when HCE suffers an ontological diminution that is dramatized through images of physical diminution: the dream woman ALP is heard dolefully confessing to her spouse, "I thought you were all glittering with the noblest of carriage. You're only a bumpkin. I thought you the great in all things, in guilt and in glory. You're but a puny" (627). ALP's waning estimate of her husband is conveyed through the figures of Cinderella's carriage changing back into a pumpkin, of an impressive nobleman being exposed as a bumpkin, or of HCE—whose dominant mythic guise is the giant Finn MacCool—shrinking until he is only a puny. One can see perfectly in the final monologue the mediated nature of the dreamer's sense of self: when ALP's attitude toward HCE is positive, supportive, and loving, he is a gargantuan, albeit somewhat clumsy, man, threatening to trample on her feet; when her attitude turns more cynical and indifferent at the very end of the dream, he all of a sudden becomes small, physically and ontologically insignificant. Shortly before this image of self-diminishment, ALP concedes that her vision is fading, that she can no longer see clearly the dreamer whom she is envisioned speaking to ("Illas! I wisht I had better glances to peer to you through this baylight's growing" [626]): this disappearance of her eye foreshadows the disappearance of her voice, the voice that sustains the dreamer's very being, the voice that assures him that the other is still there. If Joyce opens his book of the emerging son, *A Portrait of the Artist*, with the voice of the other creating the self, with the discourse of the father bringing the young Stephen into being, he closes his artistic career with a reverse but complementary narrative gesture: his book of the dying father ends with the abrupt cessation of the voice of the other, a cessation logically signaling the death of the mediated self.

While the gaze of the other may be a threat, a feared intrusion, or—to borrow a Lacanian trope—an evil eye, it is also an egotistical construct, a construct of desire, whose vanishing leads to another sort of fear—a fear not of a critical other but of an indifferent other, whose stance exposes not the subject's guilts or flaws but his potential insignificance or negligibility. What is feared most in the *Wake*—even more than the gaze visualized as an agency of exposure—is the gaze visualized as an utter absence. Thus the dying dreamer's obsessive interest in his "wake" may betray a fearful and even paranoiac concern with his reputational legacy, with the opinion of the imagined perduring other; but the envisioned "wake" simultaneously expresses a wish to be remembered, to escape anonymity and oblivion, to maintain significance through posterity. Contingent on being preserved at least in the mind's eye of the other, the wake is perhaps yet another form of the gaze, a form that bespeaks most clearly the desire to negate the possibilities of insignificance and nonsignificance, of indifference and nondifference, the possibilities disturbingly figured forth in death itself.

Notes

1.   Cheryl Herr points out that the theatrical framework and references in "Circe" also emphasize that the imagoes are "cultural constructs[,] . . . not an expression of a 'natural' semiotics. . . . [T]he individual unconscious is . . . a text of culture" (147). The fabric of the *Wake* supports this characterization of the Joycean unconscious, the dream being a rich interweaving of culturally received (albeit comically transmogrified) images and phrases from a huge array of sources.

2.   It is fruitful to examine the Wolf Man's dream in the context of Freud's remarks in his later essay "The Uncanny." In discussing the psychological significance of "doubles," Freud describes the process in ego-development whereby the gaze of the other evolves in the subject's mind, the process whereby the watching wolves are created: "A special faculty is formed there, able to oppose the rest of the ego, with a function of observing and criticizing the self and exercising a censorship within the mind, and this we become aware of as our 'conscience' . . . The fact that a faculty of this kind exists, which is able to treat the rest of the ego like an object—the fact, that is, that man is capable of self-observation—renders it

possible to invest the old idea of a 'double' with a new meaning" (388). Conscience, in Freud's terms, is not only the father's law or word internalized but also the father's eye internalized.

3. Parallactic vision has been accessibly defined as "an instance of sending the observant mind in two, or more, different positions [sic] and having it compare notes" (Senn 79).

4. Joyce's use of an overhead perspective to signify voyeurism may be another borrowing from the case history of the Wolf Man. Freud writes, "[A] high tree is a symbol of observing, of scopophilia. A person sitting on a tree can see everything that is going on below him and cannot himself be seen. Compare Boccaccio's well-known story, and similar *facetiae*" ("History" 229n13).

Works Cited

Bedier, Joseph. *The Romance of Tristan and Iseult*. Trans. Hillaire Belloc and Paul Rosenfeld. New York: Vintage, 1945.

Begnal, Michael H., and Grace Eckley. *Narrator and Character in* Finnegans Wake. Lewisburg: Bucknell UP, 1975.

Ferrer, Daniel. "The Freudful Couchmare of Λd: Joyce's Notes on Freud and the Composition of Chapter XVI." *James Joyce Quarterly* 22 (1985): 367–82.

Freud, Sigmund, "From the History of an Infantile Neurosis." *Three Case Histories*. Ed. Philip Rieff. New York: Collier, 1963. 187–316.

———. *The Interpretation of Dreams*. Trans. James Strachey. New York: Avon, 1965.

———. "The Uncanny." *Collected Papers*. Trans. Joan Riviere. Vol. 4. New York: Basic, 1959. 368–407. 5 vols.

Gifford, Don, with Robert J. Seidman. *Notes for Joyce: An Annotation of James Joyce's* Ulysses. New York: Dutton, 1974.

Glasheen, Adaline. *A Third Census of* Finnegans Wake. Berkeley: U of California P, 1977.

Herr, Cheryl. *Joyce's Anatomy of Culture*. Urbana: U of Illinois P, 1986.

Joyce, James. *Dubliners*. New York: Penguin, 1976.

———. *Exiles*. New York: Penguin, 1977.

———. *Finnegans Wake*. New York: Penguin, 1976.

———. *Letters of James Joyce*. Vol. 1. Ed. Stuart Gilbert. 1957. Rev. ed. New York: Viking, 1966.

———. *A Portrait of the Artist as a Young Man*. New York: Penguin, 1976.

———. *Ulysses*. New York: Random, 1961.

Lacan, Jacques. *The Four Fundamental Concepts of Psychoanalysis*. Ed. Jacques-Alain Miller. Trans. Alan Sheridan. New York: Norton, 1978.

Maddox, James, H., Jr. *Joyce's* Ulysses *and the Assault on Character*. New Brunswick: Rutgers U P, 1978.

McHugh, Roland. *Annotations to* Finnegans Wake. Baltimore: Johns Hopkins U P, 1980.

Norris, Margot. "Anna Livia Plurabelle: The Dream Woman." *Women in Joyce*. Ed. Suzette Henke and Elaine Unkeless. Urbana: U of Illinois P, 1982. 197–213.

———. *The Decentered Universe of* Finnegans Wake. Baltimore: Johns Hopkins U P, 1974.

———. "Modernism, Myth, and Desire in Joyce's 'Nausicaa.' " *James Joyce Quarterly* 25 (1987): 11–30.

Senn, Fritz. *Joyce's Dislocutions*. Ed. John Paul Riquelme. Baltimore: Johns Hopkins U P, 1984.

Zimmerman, Michael. "Leopold Paula Bloom: The New Womanly Man." *Literature and Psychology* 29 (1979): 176–84.

The Last Chapter of *Finnegans Wake*: Stephen Finds His Mother

MARGOT NORRIS

James Joyce was a master of endings, and the metaphysical crescendo that lifts the banal life of his figures into ontological realms of loving and dying and transcendence is perhaps the most distinctive signature of his style. With the last chapter of *Finnegans Wake*, Joyce produces an ending—not just to this work but to his *oeuvre*—that not only recapitulates but surpasses the endings of all his earlier works in its metaphysical aims. Using the device of *anastomosis*, Joyce attempts, in the last chapter of his last work, to bridge all the great ontological chasms: between time and space, between life and death, between male and female. And he does so without sacrificing the narrative and psychological particularity that characterizes his earlier works. At the same time that the last chapter of *Finnegans Wake* demonstrates how dying can also be rejuvenation, how male is also female, and female, male, and how time and space are versions of one another, it also dramatizes Stephen Dedalus' *rapprochement* with his mother, resolving logically and psychologically the conflicts that torment him both in infancy and, more painfully, in adulthood at her death.

As Elliott Gose points out, Stephen, as a recent medical student, would know *anastomosis* as the physiological term for the "interbranching of fluid carrying canals in the body, as in the connection through capillaries of veins and arteries."[1] Yet in "Oxen of the Sun," a chapter whose foci include the biological relationship to the maternal body, Stephen assimilates *anastomosis* to his earlier notion of the Eden telephone, thereby giving the mythic concept of generational connection a physiological figure: "that other, our grandam, which we are linked up with by successive anastomosis of navelcords" (*U* 14.299–300). Stephen has transformed *anastomosis* from a spatial image limning the interior geography of the human body into a temporal image that historicizes the human body by imaging its continuity in time through linked umbilici. The student of *Finnegans Wake* familiar with the personifications of time and space in the figures of Shem and Shaun will recognize this reversion of *anastomosis* as alternate Shemian (temporal) and Shaunian (spatial) figures

Reprinted from the *James Joyce Quarterly* 25 (Fall 1987):11–30. Reprinted by permission of the *James Joyce Quarterly*, University of Tulsa.

of the same concept. Together they help elucidate some of the mysterious narrative configurations of the last chapter of *Finnegans Wake*, for example, the baffling relationship between the beginning of the chapter, describing the journey of St. Kevin, and its end in the dying speech of ALP.[2] The narrative link may lie in the poetic link *anastomosis* creates between son and mother. If St. Kevin's journey through the waterways of Ireland is pictured as an interior journey inside the female body—the woman's body figured as a Homeric topography in Stephen's imagination, "Tides, myriadislanded, within her, blood not mine, *oinopa ponton*, a winedark sea" (*U* 3.393–94)—then its Shemian counterpart becomes the imaginative regression in time to the origin, along the linked umbilici of the Eden telephone, perhaps the product of St. Kevin's meditation in his bathtub in the omphalos of Lake Glendalough. The chapter may begin with the son and end with the mother because its narrative moves backwards in time and takes the form of a regression rather than a progression that charts the son's return to the womb, his disappearance into the encapsulating form of the mother, and his replacement by her own regressive discourse. Joyce may have announced just such a regression when he described Shaun's *via crucis* in *Finnegans Wake* as "a postman travelling backwards in the night through the events already narrated" (*Letters I* 214).

My own procedure for reading *Finnegans Wake* employs the strategies of Freudian dream interpretation.[3] When I treat Wakean material as dream elements whose "manifest content" must be sought in the textual equivalent of a dreamer's conscious experience—Joyce's earlier fiction—I am interpreting the narrative regression Joyce promised Miss Weaver not as a backward recapitulation of Wakean events, but as a renarration of events from earlier Joycean texts. Such a procedure relies on Joyce's having embodied *anastomosis* as a narrative strategy, as an organic interbranching of Joycean stories from one text to another, so that *Dubliners, A Portrait, Ulysses*, and the *Wake* must be regarded not as fixed texts but as fluid texts that flow into one another and contain one another in various ways. One can assume the interpenetration of *Finnegans Wake* and Joyce's earlier fiction with some archival justification: the "Scribbledehobble" notebook indicates that Joyce's earliest brain-storming on his new "work in progress" used the units of the earlier fiction as organizational categories.[4] When I ask myself, therefore, where in Joyce's fiction the narrative configurations of the last *Wake* chapter have previously occurred—the bathing priest or saint related in some way to the dying mother—the answer suggests itself readily enough: "Telemachus."

That "Telemachus" might have been on Joyce's mind during his earliest thinking about the *Wake* in general, and the St. Kevin section in particular, is suggested by the inclusion of the following sentence in Buffalo Notebook VI.B.3–49 (*JJA* 29:204), the composition of which is dated summer 1923: "SD meets O. G.'s mother."[5] If this means, as one might reasonably suppose, "Stephen Dedalus meets Oliver Gogarty's mother," it suggests not only a link between St. Kevin and the figures of "Telemachus," especially Mulligan (cf. "Mulligan meets the afflicted mother"—*U* 15.4170), but also between Stephen and the mother of the "good son." Keeping in mind that Stephen identifies Mulligan with Cranly briefly in "Telemachus" ("Cranly's arm. His arm"—*U* 1.159), I see this as a completed version of the diary entry at the end of *A Portrait* where Stephen notes, "Long talk with Cranly on the subject of my revolt. . . . Attacked me on the score of love for one's mother. Tried to imagine his mother: cannot" (*P* 247–48). I will suggest that perhaps the end of *Finnegans Wake* remedies this lapsus or block of the imagination by, at last, allowing Stephen to imagine Cranly's mother, or, rather, his own mother, with himself as a "good son," as though only by rewriting himself as a "good son" can his mother's love and approval be restored to Stephen.

To imagine this intertextual completion, I find the following fiction useful: imagine Stephen going to sleep on June 17 and dreaming. What would Stephen dream after a day tormented by the agenbite of inwit of having murdered his mother with impiety? I suggest that he might dream the day over again in the image of his desire, beginning with a dawn in which he is reborn as the good son. He is now the orthodox priest his mother would have cherished more than the heretical artist—a saint even, an Irish saint like St. Kevin, clean, pure, and fair, doing his Easter duty with a vengeance. He now bathes and remains celibate and is consequently loved by Irish girls and women for his very purity, as they love their saints and priests. He defies, in a sense, his own sardonic accusation in "Proteus"— "Cousin Stephen, you will never be a saint. Isle of saints" (*U* 3.128)—by negating his own sarcasm and allowing an affirmative and ingenuous reply to emerge from his mocking rhetorical question, "You were awfully holy, weren't you?" (*U* 3.128–29). As the good son bathing in the lake, he immerses himself in the metaphor for the mother he retrieves from Mulligan's banter earlier in the day, slipping by *anastomosis*, as it were, from *mer* to *mère*. But both *mer* and *mère*, sea and mother, confront the son with the tormenting dilemma of ineluctable seductions and dangers. Its resolution is effected by acting out both choices in different spheres. In real, or waking life, Stephen chose to be hydrophobe, heretic, and the son who refused to kneel at his mother's deathbed. In imagination, or dreaming life, he enacts the other choice, allowing himself to drown in and die into mother love and mystical extinction.[6] In an alternate fiction assimilating this last chapter of the *Wake* to Stephen's maternal conflict, we can imagine Stephen grown old and dying, and in his own dying dreaming a different version of his mother's dying, one in which he had been the good son and had genuflected at her bedside not once but "whereat seven several times he, eastward genuflecting" (*FW* 605.28–29) like St. Kevin at his lakebed.

The metaphorical slippage in Book IV between *mer* and *mère* not only permits the *rapprochement* between mother and son to assume a desentimentalized, de-emotionalized poetic and figural form as submersion in sea, lake, or bath, in the *Wake*, it also initiates an exploration and reversal of the politics of metaphorization, as Mulligan practices it in "Telemachus." For in "Telemachus," SD has, in a sense, already met O. G.'s mother, if only in her metaphorical guise: "—God! he said quietly. Isn't the sea what Algy calls it: a great sweet mother? . . . *Epi oinopa ponton.* . . . *Thalatta! Thalatta!* She is our great sweet mother" (*U* 1.77–80).[7] Mulligan's appropriation of the mother for poetic ends banishes the living woman from the realm of emotion and feeling, and murders her as surely as he murders Stephen's mother when he conjures her up for Stephen as a medical school cadaver: "You saw only your mother die. I see them pop off every day in the Mater and Richmond and cut up into tripes in the dissectingroom" (*U* 1.204–06). But the *Wake* reverses Mulligan's metaphorics and transforms the sea back into the grey, great, dead, or absent mother, "our lake lemanted, that greyt lack" (*FW* 601.04–05)—our late lamented, that grey lake, that great lack, our beloved lake, our late beloved. The reversal of the metaphor in Book IV performs an ontological gesture that restores the mother, in her dying, back to life. By reversing the metaphor and using the sea as figure for the mother, the *Wake* retrieves the living woman through the waters of the last chapter and restores her subjectivity and her words, so that she does what she is barred from doing in "Telemachus": she enacts her dying from her point of view and in her own discourse.

Besides the metaphorical reversal, *Finnegans Wake* uses the conflation of adult and infantile material, organized according to a specific paradigm, to express the dilemma of the maternal conflict. The *Wake* uses adult material, usually borrowed from *Ulysses* or the later chapters of *A Portrait*, to provide the "manifest content" (that is, the pictorial elements of the representation) of the dream thoughts, while repressed infantile memories provide the clue to the "latent content" (the meaning of the inchoate, often ambivalent, feelings and desires) that impels the psychic enterprise of the dream. There is archival evidence, for example, that Joyce originally intended to conflate adult and infantile versions of St. Kevin in the July 1923 second draft. The description of St. Kevin in his concentric baptismal tubs at Glendalough is followed by an infantile history of little Kevineen on tubbing night:

As an infant Kevineen delighted himself by playing with the sponge on tubbing night. As a growing boy he grew more & more pious and abstracted like the time God knows he sat down in the plate of mutton broth. Under the influence of holy religion which had been instilled into him across his grandmother's knee He simply had no time for girls and often used to say that his dearest mother & his dear sisters were good enough for him. At the age of six he wrote a prize essay on kindness to fishes.

(*JJA* 63:38b)[8]

This little sketch introduces the *amor matris* theme that I believe links the beginning and ending of Book IV. The incestuous infantile avarice for maternal and sororal affections ("his dearest mother and his dear sisters were good enough for him") is repressed and transmuted into the animistic personifications of St. Francis of Assisi[9] in the final version: "blessed Kevin, exorcised his holy sister water, perpetually chaste, so that, well understanding, she should fill to midheight his tubbathaltar" (*FW* 605.36–606.02). This request, by St. Kevin, calling on sister water to fill his washbasin, is anticipated in less specific form by the narrator: "Now if soomone felched a twoel and soomonelses warmet watter" (*FW* 594.09–10), but in quite specific form by Stephen in *A Portrait*:

> —Fill out the place for me to wash, said Stephen.
> —Katey, fill out the place for Stephen to wash.
> —Boody, fill out the place for Stephen to wash.
> —I can't, I'm going for blue. Fill it out, you, Maggie.
>
> (*P* 174)

St. Kevin's request to sister water to fill his tub is superimposed on Stephen's adult request to his sister to do the same, as well as on a possible infantile desire to immerse his body in sister water, or just sister, perhaps the sister from the convent who is like a Sister, Isabel, the chaste and pious sibling of *Stephen Hero*. St. Kevin in his bathtub replays in poetic form the embarrassingly intimate moment in Stephen's young adulthood when he obliges sisters and mother to bathe him: "—Well, it's a poor case, she said, when a university student is so dirty that his mother has to wash him" (*P* 175).

Book IV produces a reconciliation between Stephen and his dead mother at the ontological price of loss of self, regression, and death. Stephen's dream change into the "good son" entails conditions (orthodoxy, celibacy, and obedience) that are coded in Stephen's adolescent struggles in the valences of infantilism, of regression, of the extinction of personality, of death. That his mother's love is contingent on behavior that will kill his emerging individuality, his growth into personhood and adulthood, creates the murderous dilemma that ends in Stephen's matricidal triumph.[10] *Stephen Hero* limns more clearly the lethal dangers of filial duty in the figure of his sister Isabel, the quintessential "good child," pious, chaste, and obedient, who returns from the convent to expire in saintly martyrdom in the bosom of her family. Stephen is shrewd enough to recognize that, in a sense, Isabel died twice, first as an individual and second as a mortal being:

> The wasted body that lay before him had existed by sufferance; the spirit that dwelt therein had literally never dared to live and had not learned anything by an abstention which it had not willed for itself. She had not been anything herself and for that reason had not attached anything to herself or herself to anything.
>
> (*SH* 165)

The introduction of her lifeless personality into the novel functions as a cautionary tale for Stephen and a justification for his rebellion. In *A Portrait*, the death of Isabel is replaced with the proleptic death of Stephen, already enmeshed in a poetic texture whose elements will recur in Book IV: bath (the dunking in the square ditch), baptism (Wells, who pushes Stephen, becomes a priest in *Stephen Hero*), dying (Stephen fantasizes his own funeral in the infirmary), and mother love (he implores, by letter, restoration to his mother):

> Dear Mother
> I am sick. I want to go home. Please come and take me home. I am in the infirmary.
>
> Your fond son,
> Stephen (*P* 23)

In Joycean psychology, being the good child means being the dead child. But conversely, as in *Finnegans Wake*, the dying imagination brings with it maternal reconciliation.

Whenever Stephen appears to be the good son, he feels a fraud and an impostor, or a changeling: "He felt that he was hardly of the one blood with them but stood to them rather in the mystical kinship of fosterage, fosterchild and fosterbrother" (*P* 98). This condition of imposture—which makes Stephen, as daytime ascetic and nightime libertine, an ambiguous adolescent figure—is incorporated as a salient feature of the Wakean son, as Shem the sham, or the hypocritical Shaun. In Book IV, the son as St. Kevin is therefore a changeling as well,[11] perhaps kidnapped by gypsies like Bunn's Bohemian girl, or adopted by Egyptians like Moses. Indeed, the infant Moses in his floating cradle—like Shaun in his barrel ("benedicted be the barrel"—*FW* 596.17)—appears to serve as a repressed analogue for St. Kevin. Moses scarcely appears in this chapter, except perhaps as a wandering cloud— "Insteed for asteer, adrift with adraft. Nuctumbulumbumus wanderwards the Nil. Victorias neanzas. Alberths neantas" (*FW* 598.04–06)—but the notes of *JJA* 29:18–19 contain such references as "Noah's ark," "Moses cradle," "lakeborn," "sources of Nile," "floating grass," "floating isles," "isle form-raft," that suggest that Moses in his cradle and Kevin on his raft in the water may have enjoyed contiguity in Joyce's imagination during the incubation of the chapter. Their analogy may also account for the many Egyptian and Nile references in the chapter. Joyce ends the series of Moses and Nile references in notebook VI.B.1 with the words "gypsy" and "Pharaoh." Kevin in his tub might therefore be thought of as an adopted usurper like Moses in his floating basket whom Joyce may at one time have intended for adoption by a "Mr Ptk Ramsey" or "Rameses" (two consecutive notes in *JJA* 29:57).

St. Kevin's imposture sums up in one word, "Forswundled" (*FW*

598.03), two images from Stephen's experience on Bloomsday morning in "Telemachus": first, the memory of the pantomime song his mother loved—"*I am the boy / That can enjoy / Invisibility*" (*U*1.260–62)—and second, Buck Mulligan's impersonation of priest, Christ, and anti-Christ. St. Kevin's childhood appears marked by kidnapping (like Jarl van Hoother's children by the prankquean) and disappearance: "The child, a natural child, thenown by the mnames of, (aya! aya!), wouldbewas kidnapped at an age of recent probably, possibly remoter; or he conjured himself from seight by slide at hand" (*FW* 595.34–596.01). As a child who can make himself magically disappear, St. Kevin is the boy a mother could love: an invisible boy, a boy without a self, disappeared, dead, silent. "Forswundled"—*verschwunden* and swindled—suggests that the good son is doomed to perpetual displacement. As priest, St. Kevin, "A naked yogpriest, clothed of sundust, his oakey doaked with frondest leoves" (*FW* 601.01–02), seems an impostor priest like the fair-haired Buck Mulligan, the usurper, with "light untonsured hair, grained and hued like pale oak" (*U*1.15–16). In "Telemachus" false priest and true priest are neatly juxtaposed. Diving Mulligan playing a priestly role that includes both Christ ("—*Goodbye, now, goodbye! Write down all I said / And tell Tom, Dick and Harry I rose from the dead*"—*U*1.596–97) and anti-Christ in the form of Nietzche's Zarathustra ("—He who stealeth from the poor lendeth to the Lord. Thus spake Zarathustra"—*U*1.727–28) doubles the figure of the old priest also bathing in the Forty Foot whose place he takes in the pool. I believe this old priest with his "garland of grey hair" (*U*1.689) reappears, by virtue of this "grey nimbus" (*U*1.739), a halo-like radiance or a raincloud, in the heavy concentration of cloud and raincloud images—"Cloud lay but mackrel are" (*FW* 597.31–32); "Cumulonubulocirrhonimbant heaven" (*FW* 599.25)—in Book IV of *Finnegans Wake*. Even in a dream, the figure of the Joycean priest is treated ironically.

The opening of Book IV, with its irreverent mix of sacred and profane parodies, exhibits precisely the Mulligan style of worship parody displayed in "Telemachus." As celebration of the Resurrection ("Array! Surrection!"—*FW* 593.02), this opening becomes a performance of the Easter duty ("She wishes me to make my easter duty"—*P* 239), that test of filial obedience cloaked in a specific act of orthodox piety that May Dedalus extorts from Stephen.[12] But through its retrieval of the literal semantic residues in "Easter Sunday"—of the east in Easter and the sun in Sunday—the dream technique of the *Wake* subverts the Catholic pieties with pagan resonances that constitute their veiled defiance. Mulligan's Nietzschean neo-paganism is reflected in the eruption of eastern sun worship in the Easter Sunday observance: Hellenic ("Heliotropolis"—*FW* 594.08), Zoroastrian (the Zarathustra-like invocation of the sun, "Sonne feine"[13]—*FW* 593.08), and Egyptian ("The eversower of the seeds of light . . . Pu Nuseht" ["The Sun Up" reversed]—*FW* 593.20–23). The eastern allusions have larger regressive implications as well. Unlike the thanatopsic geography of "The Dead," where dying is figured as a "journey westward" (*D* 223), dying in the last chapter of the *Wake* becomes a journey eastward precisely because it marks a regression, a movement backward in time, space, and history, like St. Kevin floating eastward from the west of Ireland, toward sunrise, the east, the origin of religion, the cradle of civilization, the origin and escape fantasy of such earlier Joycean figures as Bloom and the boy of "Araby." That this regressive journey back into primitive and eastern religious analogues is also the modernist quest is marked by the "Sandhyas! Sandhyas! Sandhyas!" (*FW* 593.01) opening of the last chapter: the transformation of the "Sanctus" of the Mass into the "Shantih shantih shantih" of the *The Waste Land*. The poetics of the *Wake*'s last chapter are produced by the *anastomosis* of literary history.

The sunrise service that opens Book IV assimilates to its sun-worship other images from morning rituals, such as the sun-soap and the image of fire-lighting. The association of soap and sun is inaugurated in Bloom's imagination in *Ulysses*, particularly in "Circe," where he imagines the soap rising like the sun in the east and invents a jingle to advertise it: "We're a capital couple are Bloom and I. / He brightens the earth. I polish the sky" (*U* 15.338–39). The aubade that opens Book IV likewise includes a soap advertising jingle in the form of a morning greeting, "Guld modning, have yous viewsed Piers' aube?" (*FW* 593.09), a version of "Good Morning, have you used Pears' soap?" (McHugh 593.09). More literally "sunlike sylp" (*FW* 594.11), a reference to "Sunlight Soap" (McHugh 594.11), repeats the motif. Bloom's imaginative experiences in "Lotus Eaters," the juxtaposition of Mass and the bath in the mosque, for example, and the thoughts of sexual regression culminating in the fetal fantasy of the bath as a return to the womb, "naked, in a womb of warmth, oiled by scented melting soap" (*U* 5.567–68), contribute many of the images of Book IV's motif of St. Kevin in his bath. The sun as fire-starter appears to be a *Brandstifter*: "Scatter brand to the renewaller of the sky, thou who agnitest!" (*FW* 594.01–02), like the rebellious figure of Zarathustra who is accused of being an arsonist by his first interlocutor, or Stephen's own imago of Lucifer, the burning light or friction match. But perhaps the best way to be both good son and rebel is to be a fine son in reverse, as it were, a "Sonne feine, somme feehn avaunt!" (*FW* 593.08–09) or a member of Sinn Fein Amhain, or a son/sun of Ireland rising on Easter 1916 to transform resurrection into insurrection, under the sunburst of the "homerule sun rising up in the northwest" (*U*4.103), as Bloom thinks of the aptly named *Freeman* in "Calypso."

The sun (or the sun god, or the father) in the chapter's opening appears to light fires, perhaps on primitive altars, or Paschal fires. "The spearspid of dawnfire totouches ain the tablestoane ath the centre of the great circle of the macroliths of Helusbelus" (*FW* 594.21–23) describes a shaft of light hitting the sacred stones of Stonehenge, like the two shafts of light that appear to ignite a fire on the flagged floor of the Martello Tower in "Telemachus": "Two shafts of soft daylight fell across the flagged floor from the high barbacans: and at the meeting of their rays a cloud of coalsmoke and fumes of fried grease floated" (*U* 1.315–17). In Stephen's imagination, the image of the fire-lighting priest (Father, father) or cleric is a privileged figure, and Father Butt in the physics theater of the university repeats the gestures of Brother Michael (perhaps the eponym, along with Michael Furey, of Shaun's guise as the Archangel Michael, or Mick) who lights the fire for him in the infirmary of Clongowes as though to prepare for a sacrificial rite whose victim little Stephen may have imagined ambiguously either as himself or Charles Stewart Parnell: "—He is dead. We saw him lying upon the catafalque" (*P* 27). But in the curious catalogue of memories of people lighting fires for him over the years that Bloom's back bent over the fire in "Ithaca" evokes in Stephen, there is a curious one of his mother: "Mary, wife of Simon Dedalus, in the kitchen of number twelve North Richmond street on the morning of the feast of Saint Francis Xavier 1898" (*U* 17.142). Surely Stephen must have seen his mother light fires thousands of times; why then does he remember her act on this specific, liturgically marked day of six years ago? I suggest it is because the feast of St. Francis Xavier in 1898 was the Saturday after the Belvedere retreat when the newly shriven Stephen, cleansed of his mortal sins and reformed and resurrected in grace, received communion and reentered a life of holiness.[14] It was a day on which he immensely pleased his mother by being the best, the purest, the holiest of sons. In deriving from Book IV, admittedly by free association, a montage of fire-lighting images, I wish to suggest that perhaps the *Wake* expresses the ambivalence of Easter as a spiritual resurrection requiring the death of the individual as surely as it required the death of Christ, but thereby producing the very sacrifice that purchases mother-love.

If *A Portrait* foregrounds his mother's bitterness and growing disappointment over her son's slippage into freethinking and heresy, Book IV of the *Wake* retrieves and relives his period of extreme, if untenable, holiness: Stephen's life of obsessional piety after the Belvedere retreat when "Every part of his day, divided by what he regarded now as the duties of his station in life, circled about its own centre of spiritual energy" (*P* 148). The concentric circles that give the St. Kevin section of Book IV its spatial imagery (and analogue to the *omphalos*-centered "Telemachus," or to the concentric geography inscribed in the flyleaf of Stephen's geography book at Clongowes) are here encoded in terms of obsessional spiritual ambition.[15] St. Kevin's journey is therefore not only concentric but spiraling (as an early note suggests Joyce intended: "∧ zigzag or spiral corsi ricorso Vico"—*JJA* 29:16), and as he circles on his way, he is endowed with increasingly elevated titles: "voluntarily poor Kevin . . . piously Kevin . . . holy Kevin . . . most holy Kevin . . . venerable Kevin . . . most blessed Kevin . . . Saint Kevin" (*FW* 605.06–606.12). It is as though the descent into the maternal maelstrom coincides with a spiritual ascent to sainthood, ending in beatific meditation: "he meditated continuously with seraphic ardour the primal

sacrament of baptism or the regeneration of all man by affusion of water"
(FW 606.10–12).

I believe one can further use its analogue with *A Portrait* to give the
encrustations of theological apparatus in the St. Kevin section of the *Wake*
(allusions to ecclesiastical hierarchies, celestial hierarchies, liturgical colors,
canonical hours, gifts of the holy spirit, sacraments, etc.) a psychological
function. With a similar supererogation of religious machinery Stephen
attempts to maintain a mechanical rigor of holiness after the emotional
energy of his retreat is spent. Mystical numerology reinforces the sense of
rationalism with which Stephen hopes to achieve some control over his
flagging spiritual enterprise: "On each of the seven days of the week he
further prayed that one of the seven gifts of the Holy Ghost might descend
upon his soul and drive out of it day by day the seven deadly sins which had
defiled it in the past" (P 148). The transposition of this passage into the
Wake preserves its fanatical irony, as mystical sevens govern St. Kevin's
hydroengineering:

> whereat seven several times he, eastward genuflecting, in entire ubidience at
> sextnoon collected gregorian water sevenfold and with ambrosian eucharistic
> joy of heart as many times receded, carrying that privileged altar *unacumque*
> bath, which severally seven times into the cavity excavated.
> (FW 605.28–33)

It is an anastomotic act St. Kevin performs here by carrying water and
creating a pool for himself, the creation of a connection between himself and
the estranged mother, the restoration of the broken umbilicus, as it were.

Although the ambitions implicit in St. Kevin's ascending spiral are
essentially spiritual, there is tenuous evidence that St. Kevin's ambitions
might reflect Stephen's dream of achieving social redemption for his family
as well, thereby becoming the good son who with Ondt-like industry and
prudence retrieves the family's failing fortunes and thus removes from himself
at last the stigma of being a "lazy bitch" (P 175). As such, Book IV would
recapitulate at least the spirit of Stephen's infantile dream at Clongowes in
which he elevates his father's status above that of all the other fathers: "His
father was a marshal now: higher than a magistrate" (P 20). That these
socially redemptive wishes would be enacted by the good son in his bath
makes sense if we think of the *Wake* scene of St. Kevin as an inversion of the
bath scene in *A Portrait*. Representing the nadir of Dedalus family life, the
family's squalor is represented in a series of circular images proleptic of those
in "Telemachus" and in Book IV of the *Wake*: the jar of drippings "scooped
out like a boghole" (that prefigures the well St. Kevin scoops out of the floor
of his hut) recalls to Stephen "the dark turfcoloured water of the bath in
Clongowes" (P 174) and reminds him to ask for a washbasin and a bath.
There are other allusions to Dedalus losses in Book IV, including a reference

to Shemian lost time in the broken clock that must be read backwards ("—How much is the clock fast now? . . .—An hour and twentyfive minutes, she said. The right time now is twenty past ten"—P 174; "Upon the thuds trokes truck, chim, it will be exactlyso fewer hours by so many minutes"—FW 598.30–31). The pawn tickets Stephen plays with in A Portrait appear to be redeemed in the Wake by the son's having become a writer ("the last half versicle repurchasing his pawned word"—FW 596.30) and the lazy bitch of a father calling the kettle black ("—Is your lazy bitch of a brother gone out yet?"—P 175) now calls the son (Kevin, Shaun, Mick) white: "and pfor to pfinish our pfun of a pfan coalding the keddle mickwhite" (FW 596.31–32). There is even a veiled reference to the possibility that little Kevin, writing "a prize essay on kindness to fishes" (JJA 63:38b), might have succeeded in reversing the family fortunes as Stephen tried but failed to do with his exhibition prizes. The essay on "kindness to fishes" might have been a version of the Grimm fairy tale, "The Fisherman's Wife," and the paradise lost reference—"You have eaden fruit. Say whuit. You have snakked mid a fish. Telle whish" (FW 597.35–36)—may refer to Grimm's Fisherman conversing with the Magic Flounder that grants an escalating series of wishes for a cottage, mansion, palace, kingship, empire, papacy, until the Edenic hubris to be God causes all to be lost. Perhaps Joyce had at one time intended little Kevin with his "prize essay on kindness to fishes" to have wished a spiral of prestigious elevations for his family, like Stephen wishing his father a magistrate or a marshal.

After several transitions, the mother returns at the end of Finnegans Wake, first in writing, then in speech; first in a letter that may well come from "the Beyond," but next in a voice that exists only in an eternal here and now. The transitions—the plebeian dialogue of Muta and Juva and the epistemological debate of Berkeley and St. Patrick—may seem to rupture, rather than maintain, the connection between son and mother unless we remember that the mother is twice the center of dialogues or debates between two intellectual men in the early works. As unlikely as it may seem, the subject of the complex, protracted conversations between Stephen and Cranly and Stephen and Mulligan is, after all, his mother. While Muta and Juva appear to recapitulate the Latinate banter of the university students of A Portrait, they discuss, almost subliminally, the state of being "full of" water, that is, being "full of" the metaphorical mother, as they talk of the kettle ("Old Head of Kettle"—FW 609.25) enclosing and evaporating her, of the hot water bottle ("May I borrow that hordwanderbaffle from you, old rubberskin?"—FW 610.30–31) that makes her warmth available, and of the water whose drinking allows the adult to ingest the metaphorical mother like the child her milk:

Muta: Suc? He quoffs. Wutt?
Juva: Sec! Wartar wartar! Wett.

Muta: Ad Piabelle et Purabelle?
Juva: At Winne, Woermann og Sengs.

(FW 610.19–22)

In the Berkeley-St. Patrick debate the mother's presence is far more oblique, indicated by metonymy rather than a metaphor. Their epistemological debate and especially their argument over the color of clothes (cf. "He kills his mother but he can't wear grey trousers"—*U* 1.122) clearly relate Berkeley and St. Patrick to "Telemachus" where the rainbow prism of colors is also reduced either to black and white (by Stephen) or to green (by Mulligan): "A new art colour for our Irish poets: snotgreen" (*U* 1.73). The mother is present, in her absence, in the metonymy of the son's clothing that announces her death in the interval between *A Portrait* and *Ulysses.* She is last seen at the end of *A Portrait* "putting my new secondhand clothes in order" (*P* 252), and our first indirect clue to her death occurs in *Ulysses* when we realize that Mulligan has taken over her function: "I must give you a shirt and a few noserags. How are the secondhand breeks?" (*U* 1.112). The snotgreen noserag reappears in the Berkeley-St. Patrick debate as "Me wipenmeselps gnosegates a handcaughtscheaf of synthetic shammyrag" (*FW* 612.24–25).

A notebook reference in *JJA* 29:241—"Mum-letterwriter" followed by "Is her libido" and "the Beyond"—suggests that Joyce was thinking of St. Kevin, St. Patrick, Tristan and Isolde, and the mother as letter-writer (with Isolde, or Isabel, her daughter, representing her libido) at the same time, as early as 1923. The note, "the Beyond," suggests that ALP's letter might be interpreted as a dream wish that her death could be reversed by substituting her letter (from "the Beyond") for the blue French telegram that was supposed to read "Mother dying come home father." The Gabler edition's restoration of the typographical error—"Nother dying come home father" (*U* 3.199)— suggests that Stephen might well have had a moment when he felt left off the hook, when the telegram might have promised "another dying," or at least a condensed "not mother dying." Perhaps in dreams Stephen gets the erroneous telegram come (literally) true in the form of a breezy letter from his mother casually announcing the death of another; "Don't forget! The grand fooneral will now shortly occur. Remember. The remains must be removed before eaght hours shorp" (*FW* 617.25–27). Addressed to "Dear . . . Reverend," the letter may be addressed to the "good son"—St. Kevin, Shaun, Father Michael, "The Reverend Stephen Dedalus, S. J." (*P* 161)— implying that had Stephen followed a vocation, become a priest, remained a good son, his mother might not have died, or that his foolish, drunken, irresponsible father, of whom he was not nearly so fond as a child, could have died in her stead. But this reading entails another possibility as well, namely that the letter to "Dear . . . Reverend" is Mrs. Dedalus' reply to little Stephen's letter from the infirmary ("I want to go home. Please come and take me home"—P 23), a letter addressed to the priest because it is too late to reach Stephen ("He might die before his mother came"—P 24) and can therefore only announce his funeral and mock his desire for fairy godmothers or forty good murderers to redress the wrong done to him by Wells ("He'll want all his fury gutmurdherers to redress him"—FW 617.18). The implications are two: that Stephen could only be the "good son" as the "dead son," the son who never reached maturity and its inevitable sinfulness, and the feeling that the mother would rather have him die at Clongowes as a good son than have him mature into lecher and heretic.

But Book IV goes beyond merely restoring the good son to the mother in the form of St. Kevin's mystical regression to her womb. It also dispels the infantile egomania that makes the son position himself at the center of her universe in such a way that the body of maternal love becomes for him an eternal prison: "Years and years I loved you, O, my son, my firstborn, when you lay in my womb" (U15.4203). The opening of the mother's letter in Book IV—"Well, we have frankly enjoyed more than anything these secret workings of natures (thanks ever for it, we humbly pray) and, well, was really so denighted of this lights time" (FW 615.13–15)—retrieves the initiatory moment of those eons of gestation and speaks its secret: that the moment of conception is a moment of sexuality, perhaps of pleasure, however benighted, plus the delights of a nice time at night with its gratitude the morning after, and that the man, the lover and father who dominates her dying thoughts, finally precedes and supersedes the son in her affections.[16] Among the layers of regression that structure Book IV we find the reversal of the Oedipus complex, as family history is rolled back in time to the effect that the son disappears (as Shaun and St. Kevin effectively do in this chapter) and the father thereby momentarily recovers his original, rightful place.

The psychology of this displacement of son by father that, at last, abolishes Stephen's agenbite of inwit, can best be illustrated with material from the Joyce biography. Although the fiction makes the son's guilt the Gothic focus of the mother's dying—"Her glazing eyes, staring out of death, to shake and bend my soul. On me alone" (U1.273–74)—the actual melodramatic apex of Mrs. Joyce's terminal illness was her husband's outrageous behavior. Stanislaus remembers how his father came drunk into the mother's room one night and blurted out:

—I'm finished. I can't do any more. If you can't get well, die. Die and be damned to you!

Forgetting everything, I shouted 'You swine!' and made a swift movement towards him. Then to my horror I saw that my mother was struggling to get out of the bed. I hurried to her at once, while Jim led my father out of the room.

—You mustn't do that, my mother panted. You must promise me never to do that, you know that when he is that way he doesn't know what he is saying.

A few days later, however, she said something to me that I am happy to remember. My mother died on August 13, 1903 at the early age of forty-four. [17]

It is interesting to note that the dying promise the mother extracts from the Joyce sons is not, as we might expect and as is the case with Eveline's mother, the care of the numerous younger children. It is, rather, the protection of her husband. And the thing she told Stanislaus a few days later that was of such a private nature that he censored it in spite of his gratification, may well have borne on the nature of her feelings toward her husband. I wish to suggest that their mother's dying disclosed to the Joyce sons something of the personal, hidden, intimate (if improbable) bond that united their parents, a bond that Joyce senior could not articulate even to repudiate his son's angry accusations after the funeral, except as a negative "—You don't understand, boy." [18] James, who hid his knowledge of his mother's feelings beneath the metaphor of the "secret" in his writings ("Her secrets," "her locked drawer," "mute secret words," "uttering a silent word," and "these secret workings of nature"), had the most direct knowledge of this hidden world of parental intimacy. After his mother's death, James spent an afternoon reading the love letters his father had sent his mother, an experience he summed up with the single word "Nothing." Both Stanislaus and Ellmann are shocked at the *sang froid* of this critique: "He had changed from son to literary critic" (*JJII* 136). But I would interrogate this moment more fully. What did Joyce read in those letters, whose contents he censored even to his brother, who subsequently burned them unread? And even if their content was banal, as Stanislaus and Ellmann infer, is it not possible that ALP's letter in Book IV is his imaginative completion of the lost half of that ancient correspondence?

The son's regression in Book IV has led to his anastomotic reabsorption into the amniotic fluid of the maternal womb, conceptually as though "Oxen of the Sun" were narrated backwards. The mother is now invisible but audible, as though the son had changed dimensions, from Shaun (space, eye) to Shem (time, ear), and can now only hear her from inside both her body and her subjectivity, as it were. For this reason, her regression, unlike his, is represented not metaphorically (as in the anastomotic sea, water, bath, and baptismal images that surrounded St. Kevin) but discursively. For ALP's soliloquy also regresses, in memory, through marriage from golden wedding to courtship, from the husband's dotage to memories of youthful vigor and beyond, to pictures, in her mind's eye, of his childhood: "I'll close me eyes. So not to see. Or see only a youth in his florizel, a boy in innocence, peeling a twig, a child beside a weenywhite steed" (*FW* 621.29–31). She sees not only son, but husband, too, as good son, "The child we all love to place our hope in for ever" (*FW* 621.31–32). In reversing her memories, she reverses, as it were, the husband's fortunes and their decline ("Rise up, man of the hooths, you have slept so long!"—*FW* 619.25), by reforming him as Mrs.

Dedalus tried to reform Stephen, getting him to visit the house of the Lord, do his Easter duty, and thereby merit, perhaps, a knighthood or a title as chief magistrate, as if to fulfill Stephen's infantile dream-wish for him: "We might call on the Old Lord, what do you say? . . . You invoiced him last Eatster so he ought to give us hockockles and everything. . . . He might knight you an Armor elsor daub you the first cheap magyerstrape" (*FW* 623.04–16). More a realist than little Stephen, however, the mother knows that she is only fantasizing: "But we vain. Plain fancies. It's in the castles air" (*FW* 623.18–19).

As the mother's voice reappropriates her life, she recasts it as an interlocution with her husband-lover-father that retrieves memory from the locked drawer to which Stephen's metaphor had consigned it and restores it rhetorically to its living function as shared experience, as gift, as living meaning. Stephen remembers his mother through a series of pallid, conventionally romantic metonymies—"old featherfans, tasselled dancecards, powdered with musk, a gaud of amber beads in her locked drawer" (*U*1.255)—that remain lifeless, fetishistic, cut off, because the fantasies of his mother's youthful beauty are too firmly sealed with death in his imagination: "I was once the beautiful May Goulding. I am dead" (*U*15.4173). Yet when ALP identifies herself as May Goulding in Book IV, she reconstitutes herself in the romantic metaphors of her lover whose flattery she now returns to him as a gift transformed by her remembrance, by having cherished it as Molly cherished Bloom's metaphor of her as his mountain flower: "I am leafy, your goolden, so you called me, may me life, yea your goolden, silve me solve, exsogerraider!" (*FW* 619.29–30). Stephen's metonymies are fleshed out by being rejoined to the lover Stephen occludes in his imaginings of his mother. Her lifeless featherfan is restored to the pulsing vigor in the whitespread wings of the archangelic Yeatsian swan beating down on the young girl, or to the massive tree fanning her with its boughs: "One time you'd stand fornenst me, fairly laughing, in your bark and tan billows of branches for to fan me coolly. And I'd lie as quiet as a moss" (*FW* 626.21–23). Even Stephen's memories of her laughter ("She heard old Royce sing in the pantomime of *Turko the Terrible* and laughed with others when he sang"— *U*1.257–59) show it folded up and forgotten like a ghostly theater program of long ago, "Phantasmal mirth, folded away" (*U*1.263). But ALP brings the pantomime back to life by reenacting the part of the Principal Girl with all the sexual thrill and rapacious danger restored to her barbarian lover, her Viking, Vulcan, Thor of a corsair Goth: "I was the pet of everyone then. A princeable girl. And you were the pantymammy's Vulking Corsergoth. The invision of Indelond. And, by Thorror, you looked it! My lips went livid for from the joy of fear. Like almost now" (*FW* 626.26–30). For Stephen the mother's life seems reclaimed by oblivion, "Folded away in the memory of nature with her toys" (*U*1.265). But in the regression of his dream, memories roll back into experience to restore the literal residue to her "toys," and with it the delight of their moment of acquisition. As ALP nears the end of her soliloquy, and the end of the book, her memories travel further and further into the past, transforming her identity regressively into girl ("I was but teen, a tiler's dot"—*FW* 626.09) and newborn ("as I was sweet when I came down out of me mother"—*FW* 627.08), until the rhetoric of memory is abandoned, and she speaks as a child, her lover having been replaced by father as interlocutor: "Yes. Carry me along, taddy, like you done through the toy fair!" (*FW* 628.08–09).

Imagine that Stephen, after Bloomsday, sleeps and dreams. Homeless, penniless, friendless, and hungry, he longs, in dream, for his mother's comfort, as he did long ago in the Clongowes infirmary.[19] He knows that to regain her love he would have to change, or rather to *have* changed, since she is dead and it is now too late. His thoughts are therefore driven to the possibilities of the past, before it was too late, and he now reenacts, in dream, his virtuous choices, becoming priest and saint, yet always with the ironic awareness that he would have been a neo-pagan impostor like Mulligan that morning, bathing, shaving, parodying Christ, impersonating Zarathustra, performing his Easter duty like a druid rite. Since he cannot imagine his reconciliation with the mother literally—such a vision is too painful and embarrassing, too fraught with sentimentality and melodrama—the mother is figured through a metaphor, the metaphor of the sea, *mer*, the homophone of *mère*. Dawn, primitive Ireland, the sea, the bath, childhood, become a series of analogous primal metaphors of the site to which he must return, and suggest to him, by logical extension, not that he must change, but that he should not have changed, should have remained a child, an infant, an embryo in her womb, where he was loved for years and years. "—Whatever else is unsure in this stinking dunghill of a world a mother's love is not," Cranly once told Stephen. "Your mother brings you into the world, carries you first in her body. What do we know about what she feels?" (*P* 241–42). In his dream bath, immersed in the metaphorical mother and reabsorbed into her body, he at last does know what she feels, for he has become her. We can also imagine Stephen grown old and dying, and in his own dying remembering his own mother's pitiless dying and imagining, as Cranly suggests, "what she feels." The imaginative physiological voyage inside the mother's body ("carries you first in her body") becomes transformed into an intersubjective voyage into her heart. As the son for the first time gains imaginative insight and empathy into what she feels, the prayer of Stephen's mother, as he himself records it, is answered: "She prays now, she says, that I may learn in my own life and away from home and friends what the heart is and what it feels. Amen" (*P* 252).

Anastomosis, the forging of life connections by the coursing of vital fluids, allows Joyce to transform the juxtaposition of death and birth—

Bloom's attendance at cemetery and maternity hospital on the same day, or the coincidence of his father's death and his grandson's birth celebrated in "Ecce Puer"—into a continuity. In *Finnegans Wake*, Joyce elaborates on ontological possibilities of the metaphor Stephen invented in "Proteus" for the hypostatic union of the generations. The linking of umbilici, "cords of all link back, strandentwining cable of all flesh" (*U*3.37), allows him to figure death as a regression, a passage not forwards into the void, but backwards as a reabsorption of child into mother, of the mother into her father, a folding back of the generations into each other through the passage-ways of childhood and parturition. The conceit of the umbilicus as a telephone cable further suggests that the passage backwards in time through the generations is not silent but audible, that one can hear them and their stories again. In dying, the Joycean dreamer's life does indeed flash before his eyes, but backwards, with all the stories in reverse, so that St. Kevin in his bath contains "Telemachus" and Mulligan in his bath, and this in turn contains Stephen scrubbed behind the ears by his mother at the wash basin at home, or shriven after the retreat, or bumped into a square ditch as a young child and wanting his mother because he feared he would die. Furthermore, the regression is pictured in different dimensions and different poetic modes, as the journey into the mother's body is pictured visually and metaphorically as befits the spatial and geographical sense of Shaun; and the journey in time, through her own history, is represented discursively, overheard through her speech, as a journey into her memory, the Shemian temporal and auditory mode.

Thus it is that Stephen, by imaginatively enacting his intellectual musings in dream, is reconciled with his mother, immersing himself and disappearing mystically into the lake that is her figure, only to become part of her own regression into childhood, through the kiss that initiated his engendering, or her engendering, reabsorbed into the oceanic semen of her father, until *anastomosis* carries him, "riverrun, past Eve and Adam's" to the beginning, the origin, of the generations and the book, that is the destination of the Eden telephone. By the end of *Finnegans Wake* it has all become reconciled; dying has become being born and gestation, male has become female, who in turn becomes male, for every son was once his mother, and every mother was once her father, and space has become time as the present retrieves all the past it embodies. The Joycean families ultimately all fold into each other, moving backwards "by a commodius vicus of recirculation," because their stories all enfold each other in a hypostatic union of the family's discourses. Perhaps ALP's words, as they are lost in her father, reemerge not at the beginning of *Finnegans Wake*, but at the beginning of *A Portrait*, which begins with the voice of the father, embedded in the voice of the child repeating "Once upon a time and a very good time it was," retelling it its own beginnings.

Notes

1. From Elliott Gose's paper at his panel, "Interbranching in the Flux of *Finnegans Wake*," presented at the Tenth International James Joyce Symposium in Copenhagen, Denmark, on June 20, 1986.

2. My thanks to Susan Swartzlander who gave me the impetus and the opportunity to investigate this puzzle by inviting me to contribute to her St. Kevin panel at the Joyce Conference in Philadelphia in June, 1985.

3. See Margot Norris, *The Decentered Universe of "Finnegans Wake"* (Baltimore: The Johns Hopkins Univ. Press, 1976).

4. See the fascinating index in *JJA* 28:1. Alas for my argument, the most explicit references to Book IV occur not in the notes under the chapters of *A Portrait* or under "Telemachus," but under the notes for "Grace": "Kevin tells story of Patrick (WBY + GM) . . . Kevin bites his nails, ring of thorns round head . . . S. Patrick infant prodigy" (*JJA* 28:77).

5. See David Hayman's introduction in *JJA* 29:xiv.

6. Sigmund Freud finds the origin of the "oceanic feeling," that is a main emotion of religious and mystical experience, in the infantile ego-phase before self and other, inner and outer are separated: "The origin of the religious attitude can be traced back in clear outlines as far as the feeling of infant helplessness," in *Civilization and its Discontents*, trans. and ed. James Strachey (New York: W. W. Norton, 1961), p. 19.

7. Roland McHugh glosses "The leader! the leader!" (*FW* 593.13) on the first page of Book IV as " 'Thalatta! Thalatta!' (cry of the 10,000 on sighting the sea)" in *Annotations to "Finnegans Wake"* (Baltimore: The Johns Hopkins Univ. Press, 1980). Further references to McHugh are cited parenthetically in the text.

8. Susan Swartzlander called this early description to my attention at the Philadelphia Symposium.

9. That Stephen might logically borrow the language of the saint we learn in *Stephen Hero*: "He had begun to be interested in Franciscan literature. He appreciated not without pitiful feelings the legend of the mild heresiarch of Assisi" (*SH* 176).

10. Mark Shechner writes, "Toward the mother who had betrayed him, Stephen appears to have harbored a murderous hostility, albeit a hostility well repressed in the service of filial piety. . . . For us, the unsentimental glare of psychoanalysis strips away the aura of principle and the sanctity of stubborn self-assertion from Stephen's refusal to pray. From this perspective, it seems quite sinister, a covertly matricidal act," *Joyce in Nighttown* (Berkeley: Univ. of California Press, 1974), p. 31.

11. In the margins of the sketch of St. Kevin's childhood (*JJA* 63:38b), Joyce scribbled, and crossed out, "The little stranger." St. Kevin is also referred to as "Coemghem, the fostard" (*FW* 603.34) in the *Wake*.

12. The use of familial affection and devotion to coerce orthodoxy occurs twice in Joyce's fiction: first in *Stephen Hero* with the dying Isabel as bait, and the second time before *Ulysses* with the dying mother as bait: "He was much annoyed that his mother should try to wheedle him into conformity by using his sister's health as an argument" (*SH* 132).

13. In Nietzsche's text, Zarathustra addresses the sun as "grosses Gestirn" rather than as "Sonne feine," although, I would argue, the import is the same. Friedrich Nietzsche, *Also sprach Zarathustra: Ein Buch für alle und keinen* (München: Wilhelm Goldmann Verlag, n.d.), p. 9.

14. Father Arnall's sermon gives us a precise calendar of the retreat which is timed to culminate in Mass and communion on Saturday, the feast of St. Francis Xavier. We know the retreat took place in 1898 because Stephen tells the priest in confession that he is sixteen.

15. An even earlier instance of Joyce's use of the concentric circle as an image of

obsessional fanaticism occurs in the descriptions of the old pervert's mind in "An Encounter" as "magnetized by some words of his own speech, his mind was slowly circling round and round in the same orbit" (*D* 26), or "His mind, as if magnetized again by his speech, seemed to circle slowly round and round its new centre" (*D* 27).

16. Kimberly Devlin explored the dark side of this parental relationship in her paper, "ALP's Final Monologue in *Finnegans Wake*: The Dialectical Logic of Joyce's Dream Text," at the Tenth International James Joyce Symposium in Copenhagen, June 1986.

17. Stanislaus Joyce, *My Brother's Keeper: James Joyce's Early Years* (New York: Viking, 1958), p. 233.

18. Stanislaus Joyce, p. 236.

19. There are many allusions to Stephen's infantile wishes from the early sections of *A Portrait* in Book IV. The dreamer of Book IV is feverish and cold and dreams of going on a journey, perhaps home, suffering, as it were, from *Reisefieber*, "resty fever, risy fever" (*FW* 597.26), agitated anticipation of a journey, much as the chilled and feverish Stephen anticipates his return home for vacation in his dream the night before he is taken to the infirmary. The dreamer imagines the journey on the "greek Sideral Reulthway" (*FW* 604.12), a kind of Milky Way express ("the vialact coloured milk train"—*FW* 604.14) that represents both fear of the celestial journey of dying as well as its transformation into a dream of returning to the infantile paradise, the land of milk and honey of the mother's breast ("She has a fine pair, God bless her. . . . I was lost, so to speak, in the milky way"—*U* 10.559,569) with its galaxies or gallons of milk, like the rattling mare-drawn milk wagon ("waggonwobblers"— *FW* 604.17) the pre-adolescent Stephen rides with his friend Aubrey Mills ("Which aubrey our first shall show"—*FW* 604.19–20).

Finnegans Wake and the Rituals of Mortality

JOHN B. VICKERY

In *Finnegans Wake* Joyce's experimental techniques of organization, selection, and perspective are, of course, brought to an apex of sophistication. It also exhibits by far the most sustained and unequivocal evidence of Joyce's familiarity with *The Golden Bough*. From "oaks of ald" to "icy and missilethroes" its pages are crowded with images, figures, and motifs drawn from Frazer.[1] Phrases like "our bright bull babe" (562:22), "the rowantree" (588:31), and "the herblord" (254:36) encapsulate some of the leading figural nodes that recur in Frazer. In so doing they confer on *Finnegans Wake* much of *The Golden Bough*'s cyclical, sacrificial, and vegetative aura. Joyce also glances with a blandly ironic eye at some of Frazer's leading ideas and the language in which they are couched. Thus, fairly early in the *Wake* he observes with something like Frazer's portentous rhetorical balance that "the use of the homeborn shillelagh . . . shows a distinct advance from savagery to barbarism" (114:12–13). In this he ironically renders one of Frazer's chief beliefs, namely, that human history is the record of a slow and painful ascent from savagery to civilization. He also with trenchant economy undercuts in a revelatory manner Frazer's penchant for solemnly uttering views of an intellectually simple order. And at the close of the third chapter when HCE's death and resurrection are being sketched, they are presented, like the illustrative instances of *The Golden Bough*, as forming "a theory none too rectiline of the evoluation of human society and a testament of the rocks from all the dead unto some the living" (73:31–33).

A similar stress on Frazer's pervasive sense of the past's intrusiveness in the present is rendered by the remark that "ancients link with presents as the human chain extends" (254:8–9). The same is true of the marginalia in the children's school lesson chapter, where one comment reads: "Primanouriture and Ultimogeniture" (300: marginalia). Frazer's emphasis on man's food supply and sexual reproduction as religion's early foci is caught in a manner that cleverly echoes his elaborate analyses of primitive means of determining familial succession by primogeniture and ultimogeniture. Such a movement "from cannibal king to property horse" (600:1) ultimately yields a full-scale

Excerpted and reprinted from *The Literary Impact of "The Golden Bough"* (Princeton: Princeton University Press, 1973), 408–23, by permission of the publisher.

parody of the scholar's effort to summarize the whole intricate course of human history:

> Signifying, if tungs may tolkan, that, primeval conditions having gradually receded but nevertheless the emplacement of solid and fluid having to a great extent persisted through intermittences of sullemn fulminance, sollemn nuptialism, sallemn sepulture and providential divining, making possible and even inevitable, after his a time has a tense haves and havenots hesitency, at the place and period under consideration a socially organic entity of a millenary military maritory monetary morphological circumformation in a more or less settled state of equonomic ecolube equalobe equilab equilibbrium
>
> (599:9–18.)

Frazer's work constitutes a central aspect of *Finnegans Wake*, which might easily merit its inclusion among the structural books of the *Wake*. Clearly, the characters HCE, ALP, Shem, Issy, and the rest continue the archetypal function of *Ulysses*. The endlessly dying and reviving god, the scapegoat of the community, and dutiful, patient, questing, Isis-like wife, to mention but the most important, enact their roles throughout recorded history as well as in the narratives of dream, legend, and myth. Instead of the classical, Judaic, and Christian cultures of *Ulysses* a pan-cultural complex is generated as Scandinavian elements jostle with Oriental, Germanic, Celtic, Romanic, and numerous others. Here the stress upon a comparative perspective found in Frazer is realized with a vengeance, as Joyce suggests when he observes: "How farflung is your fokloire" (419:12–13).

The idea of the emergence of aesthetic form from the detritus of language is, as Joyce saw, intrinsically comic. Consequently, the dying god is not allowed to retain his usual Frazerian sonorities of travail and death. The metamorphosis of his traditional ritual *sparagmos* into a comparative religion joke is caught in the declaration that "they have waved his green boughs o'er him as they have torn him limb from lamb" (58:6–7). And with his death the event acquires resurrection's divinely comic note when he likens it to "the sprangflowers of his burstday" (59:11), and also mortality's black humor when he suggests it "was a viridable godinpotty for the reinworms" (59:12). Here *The Golden Bough*'s accounts of the ritual sowing and flowering of gardens of Adonis in small pots as emblems of the god's death and resurrection are given a resolutely comic inflection.[2]

When we survey the passages from the *Wake* that reflect *The Golden Bough*, we are struck by how closely they render the major emphases of Frazer's concerns. On one level, *The Golden Bough* is an encyclopedic effort to show that man's religious expressions throughout history revolve around the ideas of sex, death, immortality, and law. Thus, his world revolves around phallic symbols, fertility rituals, solemn sacrifices, signs of resurrection, and taboos or prohibitions against crime. Substantially the same focus obtains in

Finnegans Wake. It abounds in scenes of and references to love-making, organs of generation, and other signs of sexuality as well as HCE's recurring ritual demise and revival, together with the celebrated crime in the park, which seems to symbolize the violation of man's most dread taboo. The chief difference from Frazer's treatment of these motifs of the religious impulse in man is that while *The Golden Bough* takes a cultivated and urbane but resolutely ironic attitude, *Finnegans Wake* assumes an exuberantly bawdy and vulgar, yet highly comic, stance. It is, in effect, a human comedy on man's religious consciousness, dramatizing a secularized and so comic version of the struggle between religious guilt and fear and imaginative satisfaction and sexual joy.

Informing the fear is the fact of mortality. By stressing the ritual forms of death, *Finnegans Wake* follows closely the lead of *The Golden Bough* and is particularly sedulous in using its images and figures.[3] After the wake for Finnegan the four old men declare as the third of its four constant features "(Tamuz.) An auburn mayde, o'brine a'bride, to be desarted. Adear, adear!" (13:26–27). Goldsmith's virginal girl mourns the death of Frazer's god in the fashion prescribed since the days of ancient Jerusalem.[4] Frazer's associating him with Adonis, the handsome young lover of the wanton fertility goddess Ishtar, makes his mourning by "a brazenlockt damsel" (14:7) particularly appropriate. In the same way *The Golden Bough*'s information that Tammuz means "true son of the deep water" explains why she is called a bride "o'brine."[5] When the narrator suggests we look away from the book to the natural scene, the first thing seen amid a sentimentalized pastoral setting is "lean neath stone pine the pastor lies with his crook" (14:32). Even here the aura of death and crime hangs about the serene, peaceful scene. The Christian note of gentle protection seen in the pastor and his shepherd's crook is offset by the pine, emblematic of the emasculated dying god Attis, and the ironies of criminality resident in "crook."[6] The use of the stone pine further suggests a time when the Christian pastor is recumbent beneath a different stone, equally symbolic of death.

The interrelation of Christian and Frazerian motifs is continued in the immediately following conversation between Mutt and Jute. The latter offers Mutt a bribe for betrayal and in doing so draws Parnell into the archetypal pattern of ritual murder: "One eyegonblack. Bisons is bisons. Let me fore all your hasitancy cross your qualm with trink gilt. Here have sylvan coyne, a piece of oak. Ghinees hies good for you" (16:29–32). When Mutt is paid in "sylvan coyne, a piece of oak," both Judas and the King of the Wood at Nemi become involved. To be given part of the oak forest is to be made responsible for it, to have to guard it as the priest-king of Nemi did.[7]

As if to underscore their linking Finnegan's death with the Frazerian dying and reviving god, the four old men are called upon to quiet Finnegan, aroused by the whisky spilled on him. At the outset, one with comic condescension treats him as if he were what in fact he is, the image of human death and revival: "Now be aisy, good Mr Finnimore, sir. And take your laysure like a god on pension and don't be walking abroad" (24:16). Here Joyce uses comedy where Frazer uses irony but to the same end, namely, the humanizing of deities. The Frazerian impact of the injunction is intensified also by the underlying significance of his being told to take his "laysure like a god." The ease of leisure is certainly urged on him, but so is sexual intercourse. "Sure" is both the Irish expression which here suggests the easy, assured casualness of divine copulation, as with Zeus frequently, and the more common term indicating the certainty of the act. The latter is a comic deflation of that portion of the ritual performed by the temporary king or scapegoat, the human representative of the dying god, in which he is provided with a woman for intercourse before suffering death.[8] The old man continues to urge quiet on Finnegan, and in the process reveals unmistakably that he is to be treated like a god because he is one rather than simply as a humoring gesture. Now he is not in a modern coffin but "under your sycamore by the keld water" (24:30–31). He belongs there because he is now Osiris, a point clear from *The Golden Bough*'s identification of the sycamore as sacred to the Egyptian god and associated with his effigy.[9]

The identification of the dead man with a god is matched by the ritual acts promised by the old man. Not only will his grave be cared for in the modern fashion but he will be brought offerings, as Frazer's primitive tribes did for their gods.[10] He will receive "offerings of the field" (25:3–4) including honey, "the holiest thing ever was" (25:6), and goat's milk, offerings precisely of the sort described in *The Golden Bough*.[11] In addition, his worship is spreading rapidly and even the gravestones recall him from a time when Frazerian nature-worship was rife and "every hollow holds a hallow" (25:13–14).

Even more significantly, his worshippers speak the vegetative language of *The Golden Bough*. They understand precisely why the god must die and the part that human fertility played in his perpetuation: "If you were bowed and solid and letdown itself from the oner of the load it was that paddyplanters might pack up plenty and when you were undone in every point fore the laps of goddesses you showed our labourlasses how to free was easy. The game old Gunne, they do be saying, (skull!) that was a planter for you, a spicer of them all" (25:18–23). Because he accepts his ritual death with the harvest and like Adonis sees its sexual nature, he provides for both vegetative and human fertility and is recognized as its prime occasioner. Consequently, he is elevated above all others, including Irish, Oriental, and Frazerian monarchs and chiefs: "There was never a warlord in Great Erinnes and Brettland, no, nor in all Pike County like you, they say. No, nor a king nor an ardking, bung king, sung king, or hung king" (25:27–29).

When the emphasis shifts from Finnegan to HCE, something of the same order can be found, though if anything the humor is increased. At the opening of the third chapter, various views of HCE's fate are advanced. In the course of one of these, he is described as having died painlessly on Hallowe'en night and been expelled into the great Beyond with blows "upon his oyster and atlas on behanged and behooved and behicked and behulked of his last fishandblood bedscrappers" (49:26–28). Clearly the prankish quality of Hallowe'en is appropriate to "this Eyrawyggla saga" (48:28–29). At the same time, the point of much of Joyce's humor resides in his comic appreciation of Frazer's observation about the historical diminution of the spiritually important to secular amusement. Very likely he knew that Hallowe'en and Beltane night were the two chief fire-festivals of the ancient Celts, and if he did not know it, he could easily have learned it from *The Golden Bough*.[12] Hallowe'en was the festival of the Celtic New Year as well.[13] Hosty is the figure of the dying god and the old year and expires just at the moment when the new year enters. Support for this appears earlier when the dying but reviving god Tammuz is brought into conjunction with Baal-fire's night, which according to Frazer is the popular derivation for Beltane or May Day.[14] The reviving god is linked with the day of fertility just as the scapegoat predeceases that of the new year.

This scapegoat motif is anticipated just before the "Ballad of Persse O'Reilly" in Chapter II. It is sung before a huge throng including "a deuce of dianas ridy for the hunt" (43:11), a phrase which renders one of the goddess' characteristics presented at the very beginning of *The Golden Bough*.[15] Later on the same page, however, we find the ballad of the scapegoat ritual being sung to the accompaniment of "the flute, that onecrooned king of inscrewments" (43:31–32). According to Frazer, the flute was traditionally employed in ritual music for dying gods like Tammuz and Adonis and was held to have a particularly exciting, stimulating effect in comparison to other instruments, a point perhaps hinted at in Mr. Delaney's "anticipating a perfect down-pour of plaudits among the rapsods" (43:33–34).[16]

The ballad's musical attack and ritual expulsion and death of HCE is matched on the level of reported action by Hosty's death. To emphasize the sexual aspect as a means of underscoring Parnell's involvement in the scene, he is identified as follows: "Great-wheel Dunlop was the name was on him: behung, all we are his bisaacles. As hollyday in his house so was he priest and king to that: ulvy came, envy saw, ivy conquered. Lou! Lou! They have waved his green boughs o'er him as they have torn him limb from lamb. For his muertification and uxpiration and dumnation and annuhulation" (58:3–9). Here "behung" is a description of genitality as well as mortality. In this Joyce resembles Frazer in that the dying god too has his phallic and fertile aspect in addition to his suffering and disappearing form. The suggestion that "we" are all cyclical versions of "Greatwheel Dunlop" further develops the universal, archetypal nature of HCE and the drama he enacts in the *Wake*. Thus, Parnell is not merely an Irish scapegoat victimized by society's expulsion of its own impulses to illicit passion. He is also Frazer's dying god embodied in human form from its earliest times. This is testified to by the collocation of holly, priest, king, ivy, and green boughs.[17]

At the very end of the chapter HCE's accuser demands, among other things, that he "come out, you jewbeggar, to be Executed Amen" (70:34–35). Instead of complying, HCE makes a list of the 111 names he has been called by his antagonist. The accuser describes him explicitly as a Frazerian archetype: "Earwicker, that patternmind, that paradigmatic ear, receptoretentive as his of Dionysius, longsuffering although whitening under restraint in the sititout corner of his conservatory" (70:35–71:2). His paradigmatic capacity to encompass all the names derives from his being an embodiment of the dying god whose dismemberment is the culmination of a violent assault upon him. His connection with *The Golden Bough*'s dying god is further underscored by some of the names he recites. "Wheatears" (71:11) obviously suggests the vegetative qualities of Adonis and Osiris, and "Godsoilman" (71:14) seems to carry something of their connection with the earth. "Moonface the Murderer" (71:15), on the other hand, may be a composite of myth and ritual, alluding to the moon's association with Osiris and to human sacrifices performed in honor of the moon by primitive peoples.[18] Two others stress the sexual nature of the Frazerian fertility deities and their eastern Mediterranean origin. Thus, in being called "Sower Rapes" (72:10), HCE is, among many other things, being associated with the custom described in *The Golden Bough* of orgiastic ceremonies at planting time to assure the fertility of the fields.[19] And in identifying him as an "Easyathic Phallusaphist" (72:14), Joyce elides into a single phrase Frazer's points about the dying god's Asiatic origins, role as fertility symbol, and status as a philosophical force in the primitive mind.

Not all the death images, however, focus on HCE's hanging, dismemberment, and burial. Early in the fifth chapter, the dead HCE is linked with "broody old flishguds" (73:6) and buried "three monads in his watery grave" (78:19). Like Frazer's Adonis and Osiris, he is the god whose body is committed to the waves in order to assure his return to his needy people. But in Joyce's hands this ceases to be an earnest of the harmonious relationship between the god and his worshippers. It becomes instead a comic record of the trials attendant on being the revived, life-sustaining deity who endures the ritual sacramental meal in his own person.

The comic qualities with which Joyce invests even the dying and reviving god become even more apparent in the next chapter in which Shem asks Shaun twelve questions designed to provide a series of pictures of the archetypal human family. The first question is very long and is, among other things, a sequence of descriptions of the god's or hero's powers and characteristics. It closely resembles the mythic accounts of efforts to gain power over the deity through guessing his name. Hence it has more than a slight connection with Frazer's discussion of the primitive belief that one's name was a vital part of one and its disclosure would leave one susceptible to hostile magic.[20] At another point it is remarked: "as far as wind dries and rain eats and sun turns and water bounds he is exalted and depressed, assembled and asundered" (136:5–7). Clearly one major aspect of the riddle involves Frazer's human embodiment of natural recurrence and vegetative fertility and the ritual by which his composition and dissolution is enacted. Here Joyce moves away from the note of primitive awe and civilized contemplation with which *The Golden Bough* surrounds the cyclic periodicity of nature and man. For him the unvarying round carries a note of comic absurdity in its reduction of the human figure to the dictates and movements of wind and rain, sun and water. The dying god whose dismemberment purports to be a freely elected sacrifice is in reality a puppet of the elements elevated and cast down, constituted and annihilated according to their dictates.

In another part of the same question Shem remarks: "theer's his bow and wheer's his leaker and heer lays his bequiet hearse, deep" (137:5–7). The query buried in the middle of the excerpt is a burlesque of Osiris' dismemberment and Isis' search for the parts of his body. As Frazer emphasizes, the only part not recovered were his genital organs.[21] What this does, of course, is as it were, to de-Olympianize the dying god and his consort. The exalted metaphor of the god's lost potency is shrunk to a comic image of a mislaid personal item, and mystery is replaced by mirth. The same note is continued in the question about the old maidservant Kate. Her answer contains the observation that "I thawght I knew his stain on the flower" (141:31–32). The allusion is to *The Golden Bough*'s account of Adonis and/ or Hyacinth, whose mythic deaths were memorialized by a change in the color or markings of the flower traditionally associated with them.[22]

As we have seen, Joyce refuses to allow HCE an easy escape into the role of society's victim and the noble, self-sacrificing hero. At the same time he is sensitive to the reality and value of the scapegoat and the longsuffering hero. In the fable of the Mookse and the Gripes, the explosive, dogmatic Mookse declares: "Blast yourself and your anathomy infairioriboos! No, hang you for an animal rurale! I am superbly in my supremest poncif! Abase you, baldyqueens! Gather behind me, satraps! Rots!" (154:10–13). In this Joyce draws on *The Golden Bough* for a custom easily associated with the scapegoat ritual and yet capable of revealing that contempt rather than reverence ordains the Mookse's use of it, as when he says, "No, hang you for an animal rurale!" (154:11). In that portion of *The Golden Bough* which concentrates on the various dying gods, Frazer records the custom of animals being sacrificed by being hanged.[23] The Latin form "rurale" indicates in a loosely Frazerian idiom that the sacrifice is of a wild rather than an urban, domestic creature. The image of hanging even more emphatically links with Frazer's hanged god and scapegoat, thereby making of the Gripes a sympathetic victim but one whose divine connection will assure his survival and triumph. At the same time, the language and tone used by the Mookse reveals that he is not regarding the Gripes reverently as a religious sacrifice but contemptuously as essentially a political enemy. In short, he demonstrates one of *The Golden Bough*'s most subtly emphasized points, namely, that the gradual politicizing of society's power by priest-kings results in the secularization of society and the consequent forgetting of the victim's religious significance.

Shaun's penchant for eliminating opposition by the most ruthless of means is developed more fully in the next chapter. There he recounts the nature and career of Shem, the artist as seen by his prime antagonist. He casts Shem in the Frazerian role of the ritually slain king: "perhaps, agglag-gagglomeratively asaspenking, after all and arklast fore arklyst on his last public misappearance, circling the square, for the deathfête of Saint Ignaceous Poisonivy, of the Fickle Crowd (hopon the sexth day of Hogsober, killim our king, layum low!)" (186:10–14). He feels, of course, that Shem is not actually the dying god, but he hopes that by a process of imaginative agglomeration he may be quasi-magically induced to share the god's fate. Hence he is assimilated to the "aspenking" or King of the Wood, who, as we have seen, is also represented by Parnell. What was verbal assault and symbolic sacrifice of Parnell will, Shaun hopes, become literal for Shem just as it was for the mythic figures of *The Golden Bough* like Attis, who also is invoked by the references to ivy and hogs.[24] The drift of his desire and intent is clear enough from his final speech and ritual gesture. He first declares Shem mad and then "points the deathbone and the quick are still" (193:29). In utilizing this aboriginal custom, which Frazer describes in several places in *The Golden Bough*, Joyce seeks to delineate Shaun as a comic figure of death and black magic.[25] His magic is weak and inadequate and the only stillness he can wreak on the truly living is that which the fool and dunce have always engendered in others, an inability to stay awake: "*Insomnia, somnia somniorum. Awmawm*" (193:29–30).

In the second chapter of Book II, the three Earwicker children are concerned with their school lessons. These must, according to Joyce, deal both with their immediate family's history and also with the archetypal events of the human race. Thus, they attend to what appears to be the male father-figure "dirging a past of bloody altars" (276:4). In doing so, they catch a concentrated glimpse of their natural, classical, and primitive heritage. The human sacrifices of the Irish Druids, the slaughter of Greek innocents, and the tribal appeasing of powerful gods of nature, all dealt with exhaustively by *The Golden Bough*, are implicit in this phrase, which is redolent with the regret and observances of man since the beginning of time.[26] But, as we might expect, the children must learn that there is more to the alphabet of human existence than generalized sacrifice and bloodshed. It also includes ritual destruction of persons filling a specific role in the order of society: "When men want to write a letters. Ten men, ton men, pen men, pun men, wont to rise a ladder. And den men, dun men, fen men, fun men, hen men, hun men wend to raze a leader" (278:18–21). What is humorous to Joyce, however, is unsettling to the children: "We have wounded our way on foe tris prince till that force in the gill is faint afarred and the face in the treebark feigns afear" (278:25–279:1). As Frazer indicates, Adonis was born from a myrrh tree and later suffered his fatal wound from an enemy disguised as a boar.[27] Here the children recognize that they too, as members of the human race, have attacked the god in his form of the sad young prince Tristan. At the same time, they have wound back through time from the sophisticated legend of Tristan to the primitive myth of Adonis, a journey whose result they still find somewhat puzzling: "Strangely cult for this ceasing of the yore" (279:2–3). Issy, though engrossed in the romantic sexual forms of life and myth such as the Adonis story, also senses their more somber dimensions. She remembers the dog day when she "sat astrid uppum their Drewitt's altar" (279:n.1, line 27), urges "sago sound, rite go round, kill kackle, kook kettle" (279:n.1, line 25), and muses that "it most have bean Mad Mullans planted him" (279:n.1, lines 23–24). Clearly she grasps least the dying god's ritual sacrifice and burial so copiously rendered by *The Golden Bough*.

When the action moves, in the next chapter, to HCE's pub and the plays performed there, something of what they have learned is seen. Both plays are supposedly about the overthrow of the father, which is the Freudian or domestic version of the ritual slaying of the dying god. At one point therefore Taff says: "The fourscore soculums are watchyoumaycodding to cooll the skoopgoods bloof" (346:25–26). He makes this comment "*whiles they all are bealting pots to dubrin din for old daddam dombstom to tomb and wamb humbs lumbs agamb*" (346:16–18). That is to say, everyone is engaged in the ritual noise-making that Frazer suggests may accompany both the burial of the god and the efforts to purify the area and encourage fertility.[28] Butt responds by declaring that he ranges from the extreme past to future and so has many memories of those dead who are living elsewhere and whom he identifies implicitly with the Frazerian dying god by calling them "me alma marthyrs" (348:10–11). The reference is not to the fostering mother, as the phrase "old boyars" (348:10) indicates, but to all males who like Attis are beloved by the fertility goddess and sacrifice their virility in an act of martyrdom to her honor.[29] His salutation to their memory further bears out the comedy wrought by the transmogrifying mythopoeic imagination: "I dring to them, bycorn spirits fuselaiding" (348:11). In celebrating those bygone spirits, he is honoring both the Celtic figure emblematic of liquor itself, John Barleycorn, and the Frazerian cereal deities from whom he descended.[30]

As the chapter moves on toward the children's attack on HCE and his symbolic death through drunkenness, the stress upon *The Golden Bough*'s central images of sacrifice and ritual death becomes heavier and more explicit. One tavern customer observes: "'Tis golden sickle's hour. Holy moon priestess, we'd love our grappes of mistellose!" (360:24–25). One of Frazer's chief points is that the golden bough, the mistletoe, constitutes the life or external soul of the dying god Balder and so is to be cut but once a year, on either the first or sixth day of the moon, and then only with a golden sickle as a symbolic ritual sacrifice of the vegetative form of the god.[31] Clearly what is being announced is the time for HCE's symbolic ritual demise. The customers, however, question his authenticity and accuse him of cohabiting with a known prostitute at a time "when all the perts in princer street set up their tinker's humn, (the rann, the rann, that keen of old bards)" (363:4–5). As the earlier discussion of the wren as the king of the birds made clear, Frazer identifies this folk custom as the sacramental sacrifice of the dying god in animal form.[32] The criticism of HCE, then, is not so much a moral as a ritual one. He is ignoring the message of the song, which speaks of death, not fertility or sexuality. For as Frazer points out, the mistletoe and the wren are associated by the placement of a mistletoe wreath on the pole to which the dead wren is fastened.[33] Yet to disregard the song and emblem of the dead god is also to bypass the sign of health, fertility, and protection against evil that *The Golden Bough* finds in the mistletoe.[34]

At the same time, Joyce is aware of the archetypal ritual of death as necessary for revival. He shows it by fusing the song of John Brown with *The Golden Bough*'s emphasis on the burial's occurring in the deity's sacred grove: "Shaum Baum's bode he is amustering in the groves while his shool comes merging along!" (364:8–9). Then, toward the end of the chapter, the three children incite one another to fresh indignities, urge him to participate gladly in his hanging, and then stand back to rejoice in its achievement: "Isn't it great he is swaying above us for his good and ours. Fly your balloons, dannies and dennises! He's doorknobs dead! And Annie Delap is free! Ones more. We could ate you, par Buccas, and imbabe through you, reassuranced in the wild lac of gotliness. One fledge, one brood till hulm culms evurdy-burdy" (377:36–378:5). Here too Joyce takes his cue from *The Golden Bough*. He has HCE suffer the death by hanging in order to point up his scapegoat role as the hanged god. Then, with his death announced, Joyce modulates him into a more specific form of the dying god, Bacchus or Dionysus.[35] In turn, Dionysus' association with Osiris, as pointed out by Frazer, may cast some light on the final sentence in the above passage in which Joyce suddenly associates the communion god with a flock of birds.[36] According to *The Golden Bough*, the bird was a creature known as "the soul of Osiris" and in addition was traditionally regarded as the seat of a dead person's soul as well as representing the corn spirit and serving as a scapegoat.[37] Clearly the image of the bird allows Joyce to draw into a single complex figure HCE's components as dead man, dying god, scapegoat victim, and guardian of intoxication.

As befits a book of cyclical and simultaneous structure, images of and allusions to death and the dying god continue throughout the remainder of *Finnegans Wake*. They are, however, neither so numerous nor so central to the main thrust of the narrative. They sometimes suggest the scope of time and the order of human creation, presumably through the constant of mortality, as when Shaun in the process of becoming Christ tries to love all "from the King of all Wrenns down to infuseries" (431:13). Or they invoke the ritual combat of the priest at Nemi as well as something of Frazer's antipathy to religion for the purpose of anti-clerical satire, as Shaun inadvertently does in urging the young girls to read the Archdeacon's book subtitled "*Viewed to Death by a Priest Hunter*" (440:2–3). Or they are used to suggest that the ritual death is not confined to HCE alone, as when Shem is identified as "my said brother, the skipgod" (488:22). Or they serve to reassure frightened children by being associated with the natural world of sex as when HCE tries to quiet Shem and Shaun by equating Phoenix Park and his own private parts with "the mound where anciently first murders were wanted to take root" (564:29). Or they hold out the tempting ambiguous truth about the imaginative function of death, as ALP shows when she declares: "Once you are balladproof you are unperceable to haily, icy and missilethroes" (616:31–33). To be bulletproof is to be physically immune to hail, ice, and spears of all sorts. To be immune to song and story, however, is to be unperceivable by the holy, whether Isis the savior of the dying god or Loki his slayer. And since the two alternatives are enshrined in the one sentence, one cannot choose the one without the other, Joyce avers. Thus, as *Finnegans Wake* has been insisting all along by its dramatic metamorphoses, to recognize death and mortality and to live fully with that awareness is to know the only true idea of the holy available to man in this or any other century.

Notes

1. James Joyce, *Finnegans Wake* (New York: Viking Press, 1947), pp. 4:15, 616:32. For convenience, line references are included following the colon. Subsequent references will be included in the text.

2. Sir James G. Frazer, *The Golden Bough*, 3rd ed. (London: Macmillan, 1911), V, 236 ff., 253 ff. Hereafter cited as *GB*.

3. The reliance on *The Golden Bough* for the *Wake*'s sexual pattern is equally heavy, but since the evidence does not significantly qualify the fact or nature of Frazer's impact, it is forgone in this study. For its details, see my " 'Finnegans Wake' and Sexual Metamorphosis," *Contemporary Literature*, XIII (1972), 213–242.

4. *GB*, V, 11, 17, 20; IX, 400.

5. *GB*, V, 6, 8, 246; ix, 371, 373, 399, 406.

6. *GB*, V, 264–267, 271, 277–285. The crook is also an emblem of Osiris. See *GB*, VI, 108, 153.

7. *GB*, I, 42. Additional support for this view appears in the same passage. For instance, "eyegonblack" seems to be a combination of the Greek "agon" and the German "Augenblick," which would suggest a ritual combat caught in a moment of perception. The "agon," of course was one of the crucial features of Greek tragedy and its ritual basis was outlined by Gilbert Murray, one of Frazer's most influential followers. "Bisons" obviously are "bygones," but that *The Golden Bough* indicates that they also achieve resurrection may just possibly suggest that Joyce is emphasizing that the ritual death of the dying god also issues in his revival (see *GB*, VIII, 256). Similarly, while "Ghinees" is clearly Guinness, the brewery,

it may barely conceivably also reflect Frazer's point about the existence of priest kings in Guinea (see *GB*, III, 5). The inhabitants' profound belief in dreams and their annual performance of expulsion rituals would have given Joyce additional reasons for working in such a reference (see *GB*, III, 37; IX, 131).

8. *GB*, IX, 278, 309.
9. *GB*, VI, 88, 110.
10. *GB*, VI, 194; IX, 26–30.
11. *GB*, I, 311; IV, 86; v, 85, 87; VI, 194; VIII, 288; IX, 26ff.
12. *GB*, XI, 40ff.
13. See *GB*, X, 224ff.
14. See *Finnegans Wake*, 13:26, 36 and *GB*, X, 146, 149, n.1, 150, n.1.
15. *GB*, I, 6.
16. *GB*, V, 9, 54, 225, n.3.
17. *GB*, II, 122, 251; V, 66, 72ff., 278; VI, 88, 110, 112; VII, 1ff., 30ff.
18. *GB*, V, 73; VI, 129ff.; VII, 261; IX, 282.
19. *GB*, II, 98–101, 103–104.
20. *GB*, III, 318ff., 374ff.
21. *GB*, VI, 10, 102.
22. *GB*, V, 226.
23. *GB*, V, 289–292.
24. *GB*, V, 278; VIII, 22.
25. *GB*, IV, 60; x, 14.
26. *GB*, I, 386–387; IV, 161ff.; IX, 210ff., 409 *passim*; XI, 32ff.
27. *GB*, V, 6ff., 55, 227; VI, 110.
28. *GB*, IX, 109, 111, 113, 116, 118, 120, 126, 146–147, 196, 204, 252, 256ff., 272ff.
29. *GB*, V, 263, 282–283.
30. See *GB*, V, 230, 233, 279; VI, 34, 48, 89ff., 96ff.
31. *GB*, XI, 77–78, 80, 279, 283, 315ff.
32. *GB*, VIII, 317ff.
33. *GB*, VIII, 321.
34. *GB*, XI, 77–79, 82–83, 85ff., 282–283, 294.
35. He does for several reasons. One, of course, is to link the human HCE, the drunken tavern-owner, with the mythic guardian of the vine in order to show simultaneously the perdurability and the metamorphosis of the archetype. Another reason is that in assuming the form of Bacchus, HCE also blends, as Frazer points out, with Dionysus (see *GB*, VII, 2). Bacchus' legendary association with an Athenian festival of swinging may also contribute to Joyce's linking of him with a hanged god "swaying above us" (see *GB*, IV, 281–283). This association also renders accessible the comic vision of the traditional communion meal, a vision which like that of *The Golden Bough* emphasizes the continuity existing between primitive pagan and Christian versions of the observance. Dionysus, of all Frazer's dying gods, was the one whose ritual preeminently involved not only dismemberment but devouring of the god or his representative (see *GB*, VI, 98; VII, 13–14, 17–18, 25; VIII, 16). That these sacrifices sometimes included children would help to explain also why in anticipating the ceremonial drinking of the god's blood, the celebrants should speak of it as an "imbabe through you" (see *GB*, IV, 166 n.1).
36. *GB*, VI, 113, 127; VII; 3.
37. *GB*, VI, 110; VII, 295ff., VIII, 296; IX, 35ff, 51ff.

The Politics of *Finnegans Wake*

DAVID PIERCE

There is no more daunting task for criticism than an enquiry into the politics of *Finnegans Wake*, a text whose epigraph is perhaps best captured in the schoolboy Latin of the interrogators in chapter 15:

Magis megis enerretur mynus hoc intelligow.

(478.17–18)

Indeed, the more *Finnegans Wake* is explained, the less at times it is understood—which is a not uncommon pattern of response. Fog, together with cloud and rain, constitutes the natural ambience of this text, and becomes in turn emblematic of the relationship between it and the reader. At the opening of chapter 3 the reader is invited to "Chest Cee!" But the fog is "Sdense" that the reader becomes the object of scorn, out of place, a "spoof of visibility in a freakfog" (48.1–2). Nothing is clear—not even the reader's desire for clarity, which is being in some way spoofed—though there may be temporary, if misplaced, relief in that it is only a "freakfog." For much of the text, the reader is like "Head-in-Clouds" (18.23), anxiously awaiting the proverbial breaks in the clouds for a view of the earth below. But the fog continues. The first and last chapters of Book 3 begin with a reference to it—"White fogbow spans" (403.6); "What was thaas? Fog was whaas?" (555.1)—and it is not until the final chapter that we are confidently, though perhaps ironically, informed by someone that the "smog is lofting" (593.6–7). Not for nothing did Joyce refer to *Finnegans Wake* as his "experiment in interpreting 'the dark night of the soul.' "[1] We can go further and, in the light of Roland Barthes's attack on the distinction between the "before" and "after" of writing,[2] add that this experiment is intensified for the reader by Joyce's familiar coupling of experience and writing, by which means he underscores the fact that writing too is "experience."

Fog, dreams, the night—these are useful metaphors for the unknown territory here being charted. Joyce didn't need Ezra Pound to tell him how difficult (that is, how painful) it was for the reader. He knew exactly what was involved: hence the constant promptings and encouragement to the

Reprinted from *Textual Practice* 2 (Winter 1988): 367–80, by permission of Routledge, Chapman and Hall, Ltd.

reader not to give up. "Phew!" (10.24) as we exit from the Willingdone Museyroom. "What a warm time we were in there." Indeed. Elsewhere we are told: "Cry not yet!" (20.19), or, more simply, "Smile!" (55.2). Later, words are put into our mouths: "This is nat language at any sinse of the world" (83.12). We are even told who constitutes the ideal reader—someone "suffering from an ideal insomnia" (120.13–14). Suffering, yes, but then even this purchase on the text is undermined by the humorous collocation of insomnia with ideal. It is a "book of Doublends Jined" (20.15–16), "Work in Progress," a "most moraculous jeeremyhead sindbook for all the peoples" (229.31–2), "all about crime and libel" (419.34). But "the unfacts, did we possess them, are too imprecisely few to warrant our certitude" (57.16–17). Indeed, we might not unreasonably conclude that *Finnegans Wake* is the "last word in stolentelling!" (424.35). Lies, distortion, voices from afar (3.9, 407.14), impenetrable riddles and stories, history as "fabled by the daughters of memory" (*Ulysses*, p. 20), together underline the difficulty (some might say the folly) of ever being able to determine the politics of *Finnegans Wake*. Then, too, we are unsure—yet it belongs to an early stage of any such investigation—if we are dealing primarily with parody, pastiche, or burlesque. Is the "collideorscape" (143.28) showing us a universe where, following Nicholas of Cusa, there is a coincidence of opposites, or a world where things are linked arbitrarily? What is being mocked in bringing together disparate material in this way—one or more of the items referred to, or the human desire to make sense of such disparate material? Such questions serve to remind us of a wider modern fascination, which stretches across the sciences and the humanities, with Heisenberg's "indeterminacy principle," and perhaps it is for this reason that we need to address issues of clarification rather than increase the epistemological doubt never far from the surface of Joyce studies.

To prevent adding to the confusion, it may be helpful if we isolate three areas for consideration in an approach to the politics of *Finnegans Wake*: the political context of *Finnegans Wake*, its political message, and political readings. The first belongs to a form of historical investigation and placing, to what Robert Weimann calls "past significance";[3] the second to the author's implicit or explicit political message as contained in the text; the third to our own contemporary political interpretation of *Finnegans Wake*, or to what Weimann terms "present meaning." Of course, these three areas significantly overlap, and Weimann would be the first to insist on the unity of the first and the third, the historical with the evaluative. But in *Wake* studies we are still some way off integrating the historical with the evaluative, and we need therefore to put down some markers. Too often in critical discussions of the politics of *Finnegans Wake* the tendency has been to focus on one area with little or no thought given to the other two areas. The best discussions—and I include here the work of John Garvin, Hugh Kenner, W. J. McCormack, and Seamus Deane—have come from investigations into historical context;

less satisfactory—and I here instance the work of Phillip Herring, Diarmuid Maguire, and, though excellent in other ways, Dominic Manganiello—have been those which centre on the second area; the third area remains the least explored but, given the advances of recent feminist theory, the most promising.[4] Here I concentrate on presenting an overall picture of what I take to be involved in discussing the politics of *Finnegans Wake*. In the first section I point up certain lines in recent developments, in the second section my intention is to clarify difficulties, while in the third I touch on alternative approaches to this particular topic.

POLITICAL CONTEXT

The political context of *Finnegans Wake* embraces a wide field of enquiry, which, for illustrative purposes, can be grouped under a series of headings labelled Irish, Anglo-Irish, European, myth, and history, and with further subheadings referring to pre-modern history, the nineteenth century, the Fall of Parnell, the Easter Rising, the Irish Civil War, and the inter-war years. In this regard we might note the significance of the date when *Finnegans Wake* was begun, for 1923 marked the end of the Civil War and of the revolutionary period ushered in by Easter 1916. Just as *Ulysses* belongs to a period of expectancy that found its now perennially hopeful expression in the one day in June in 1904, in a parallel way *Finnegans Wake* gives voice to the disorder and disillusionment that befell Irish politics in the immediate aftermath of the Anglo-Irish War, when civil war and internecine feuding broke out between the warring brothers Shem and Shaun.

Shaun, as John Garvin makes clear, is not unlike the figure of Eamon de Valera, the "dogmestic Shaun" (411.23), who rose from being a "math-master" (4.4) to becoming "through deafths of durkness greengrown deeper . . . [the] vote of the Irish, voise from afar" (407.12–14). This connection between Shaun and de Valera receives further support from Sean O'Faolain's equally critical biography of the Irish leader published in the same year as *Finnegans Wake*. One passage might well be about "frank" Shaun:

Fundamentally his political integrity was unimpeachable. . . . If only . . . De Valera would once or twice say, "I am not infallible. I am no hero. I am no saint. I had to contradict myself. It was for Ireland"—the heart would open more readily to him, and one could without detriment either to the symbol or the man create the hero in full admiration.[5]

De Valera refused to acknowledge Lloyd George's Anglo-Irish Treaty, which had been negotiated under duress in December 1921 by Arthur Griffith, Michael Collins, and the other Irish leaders. Instead, he proposed an amendment known as Document Number Two, which sought a looser association between Ireland and Great Britain. It was a narrow point of principle: effectively, the Irish delegates had been outmanœuvred by the British, who had used the familiar tactic of divide and rule. As someone once quipped, the only difference between the two documents was that one was signed and the other one wasn't. Throughout *Finnegans Wake* there are references to Documents Numbers One and Two (see 358.30, 369.24, 386.20, 528.32, 619.19), and in chapter 15 "Keven" (a Shaun figure) finds "dogumen number one . . . an illegible downfumbed by an unelgible" (482.20–1). What distressed Joyce about de Valera was his moral uprightness, his dogmatic insistence on a formula of words, his narrow view of Ireland, and his willingness to plunge his country into civil war and thereby subject Nora and the children in April 1922 to "the premier terror of Errorland" (62.25) (a phrase that yokes together de Valera as President of Dail Eireann, his parsimonious role in the treaty negotiations, and the ensuing terror which accompanied the breakdown of order). "The devil era" (473.8), which is interpreted, significantly, in the context of the treaty negotiations as "a slip of time between a date and a ghostmark" (473.8–9), had begun.

In many ways the primary political context for *Finnegans Wake* is the Civil War, so much so that Hugh Kenner has suggested that the figure being waked is perhaps a participant in that conflict.[6] Certainly, apart from de Valera there are enough references to other figures and events, as well as to fratricide, violence to the person, and decidedly sinister encounters, to support the notion that *Finnegans Wake* is a Civil War text. The presence of Erskine Childers, whose father Hugh Culling Eardley Childers (1827–96) was nicknamed "Here Comes Everybody," is relevant here. Author of the thriller *The Riddle of the Sands* (1903), Childers took part in the Howth gunrunning in July 1914; he later joined de Valera's Republican side in the Civil War, and, having been caught with a pistol in his possession (given him by Michael Collins when the two were on the same side), was executed in November 1922 by a Free State firing squad. He is mentioned at 473.9, "chilldays embers," and at 596.5, "hailed chimers' ersekind," where there is a play on his (and HCE's) Englishness; he is possibly being referred to in the first question in the picture gallery chapter in the phrase "made a summer assault on our shores and begiddy got his sands full" (132.20–1), and perhaps he is there, when the Document is being scrutinized in chapter 5, as "the eternal chimerahunter . . . the sensory crowd in his belly coupled with an eye for the goods trooth bewilderblissed by their night effluvia with guns like drums" (107.14–17).

Drawing attention to this particular context to *Finnegans Wake* returns us as a matter of course to the less ambiguous period preceding the Troubles and to the "Surrection!" (593.2) of Easter Week 1916, "our hour or risings" (598.13), and to the Proclamation of the Republic: "Eireweeker to the wohld bludyn world" (593.3). The beginning of the last chapter of *Finnegans Wake* is a celebration of a new dawn, part of which takes its cue from 1916.

"Surrection!" is both resurrection and insurrection; "Eireweeker" is both Eire, Easter Week, HCE, ear, and weaker; "the whole bludyn wohld" is reminiscent of the papal address "Urbi et Orbi" given at Easter and therefore linked with the 1916 Proclamation of the Republic from the General Post Office; it also picks up the phrase in chapter I used after the "erection" of the wall—"For whole the world to see" (6.11–12). Throughout the final chapter there are references to the wider nationalist struggle for Irish independence: Sinn Fein, whose slogan we might notice did service for Joyce's own ideological perspective, reinterpreted now as "oursouls alone," is mentioned at 614.14 and 623.28–9; Patrick Pearse appears at 620.24; at 614.17 Parnell's insistence that "newmanmaun set a marge to the merge of unnotions" is dusted down again (compare its earlier formulation at 292.26–7); the unofficial nineteenth-century Irish national anthem and rallying call written by Thomas Davis appears as "Innition wons agame" at 614.17–18; while Michael Dwyer, the 1798 rebel, has a walk-on part at 600.18. The celebration of Easter 1916, however, is short-lived, and with the ricorso we are back to the opening chapter again with "snake wurrums everyside" (19.12), "sneaks" (19.13), "racketeers and bottloggers" (19.19), the ante- and post-bellum period, as it were, of "bloody wars" (14.9) and "Killallwho" (15.11). However, we can perhaps hear in the very last words of the chapter the Sinn Fein slogan, not now "ourselves alone" but simply "a lone" (628.15). For, if *Finnegans Wake*—caught as it is between 1916 and 1923—is concerned in no small measure with the theme of loss, then part of that loss turns on the historical failure of the Irish revolution to bring forth a new Ireland.

In identifying the period 1916–23 as one of the strands that constitute the political context for *Finnegans Wake*, it is as well not to claim too much. For of course there are other strands, some of which are Irish, others of which are not. Some critics, for example, might wish to argue for priority to be assigned to the Roderick O'Conor sketch, which was the earliest passage of *Finnegans Wake* to be written. At the Treaty of Windsor in 1175 Rory O'Connor, the last High King of Ireland, pledged his allegiance—"suck up" (381.30) is how this is described in the text—to Henry II, and thus was initiated the modern phase of Irish history, caught between subservience to and rejection of the Crown. Others, aware that Joyce's focus is on his native country but now broadened to include all kinds of material much of which is non-Irish, might wish to claim that the primary political context for *Finnegans Wake* is that of the exile in Europe, keenly alive to politics but guarded about taking sides, especially in a period that tended to see the destiny of man exclusively, as Thomas Mann observed, in political terms.

Equally, we need to bear in mind that the relationship between text and context in the case of *Finnegans Wake* is perhaps qualitatively different from that which obtains with other works. The defeat of the left at the Battle of the Ebro in 1938 is a moment that haunts Malcolm Lowry's "thirties" novel *Under the Volcano* (1947). It is not only significant for the British consul's brother Hugh, who was a correspondent for *The Globe* in Madrid, but it is also associated with the growth of fascism in Mexico—the British consulate in Cuernavaca is on the point of being closed, the Nazi German presence is increasing, and at the end of the novel the consul is murdered by fascist police. The political context for the novel, it can be legitimately argued, is the Spanish Civil War, its repercussions and meanings, which can now be felt worldwide. Among the political themes dealt with in the novel are: the defeat of the left, the image of life as an "arena" where diametrically opposed viewpoints or political systems are in conflict (Mexico is described as being at the center of the earth, Cuernavaca as the place where the American-style highway peters out, while a bullfight occupies a central episode of the novel), the shadow of world war, the problem of commitment especially for the writer, and the possibility or otherwise of private life in an age of politics. The political context for *Under the Volcano*, a novel that is often seen in non-political terms, is in fact especially sharp and revolves around quintessentially thirties concerns.

Finnegans Wake (which is also in part a thirties text) cannot be tied back so neatly to any one political context. This, though, has nothing to do with its being more "universal" or tackling "universal" themes. Rather, it centres on Joyce's rewriting of the relationship between text and context and the consequent disarray for the critic in determining what constitutes his or her role in such matters: there is no political unconscious in *Finnegans Wake* awaiting the supplementary attention of the critic. Hence the political context for *Finnegans Wake* needs augmenting by two other sorts of investigation, one concerned with Joyce's intentions and message, the other with a second-order enquiry where the concept of a political context or ideas about the relationship between text and context are themselves subjected to scrutiny under what can be termed political readings.

POLITICAL MESSAGE

In looking for a clue to Joyce's politics in *Finnegans Wake* we might well recall Shaun's cautionary note in his portrait of Shem in chapter 7: "not even then could such an antinomian be true to type" (172.17–18). Possibly in reaction to his Jesuit education and Catholic upbringing, Joyce hated to be pinned down. As an undergraduate, Stephen Dedalus refuses to sign Tsar Nicholas II's petition for peace; as an established Irish writer, Joyce refused to join the newly formed Irish Academy of Letters. He even turned down an invitation to a St Patrick's Day party at which the Irish ambassador was to attend, for fear that his presence might be misconstrued as a tacit endorsement of the Free State.[7] In the biography, Richard Ellmann tells us that Joyce "refused to commit himself publicly in any way."[8] But in a sense of course he already had, for from the moment of his exile from his native country in 1904, which was a deliberate disengagement from Ireland, there developed a parallel and increasingly public commitment to writing. Unlike many British writers of the thirties, such as Edward Upward, W. H. Auden, Christopher Isherwood, or George Orwell, Joyce remained unimpressed by the distinction between writing and action. Hence the absence in his work of the exploration of the border, whether as symbol or reality. For him, writing was experience, and it remained the most effective instrument for reshaping and changing the world. Hence the significance (in part at least) of the image of the telescope in *Finnegans Wake*. At the same time, his commitment to writing went hand in hand with a Flaubertian desire as an author to refine himself out of existence and to make the paraphrase of his work formidable and, perhaps with his final work, impossible. These factors need to be kept in mind as we try to discover what it is Joyce intended by *Finnegans Wake*.

In the late eighteenth century Edmund Burke voiced his opposition to Grattan's Protestant Parliament on the grounds that, if the connection with Westminister were broken, the rights of Irish Catholics—which, he knew, were precariously few under English law—would be further eroded. Joyce's view—and it is one that he never seems to have radically altered—was that genuine freedom for the Irish people was not to be equated simply with breaking the cross-channel link. Like Stephen, he understood how he was a servant of two masters—England and Rome. Historically, with the establishment of the Free State in 1922, the links with the Crown were broken, but the other tyranny continued and indeed—at least in the field of censorship and social legislation—flourished. "Healiopolis" in the figure of Tim Healy—and we might recall Joyce's childhood poem "Et Tu, Healy," which contains (presumably) a scathing attack on Healy for his part in the fall of Parnell—was now in charge at the Viceregal Lodge in Phoenix Park. If Joyce was a Republican, then it was of the Parnellite Home Rule variety; that is, he desired to break the connection with England—but not entirely (after all, he was in receipt of a Civil List pension and continued to travel under a British passport). I think it is against this background that we should interpret his remarks in *Finnegans Wake* about "freestouters and publicranks" (329.31): he is not saying a plague on all your houses, whether Free Stater or Republican, but rather he is showing impatience with the narrowing of the political options available for his country.

He was equally irritated with the Border and with the Border issue. In the encounter between the attacker and the adversary, "the boarder incident prerepeated itself" (81.32–3), while in the portrait of Shem in chapter 7 Shaun declares: "He even ran away with hunself and became a farsoonerite, saying he would far sooner muddle through the hash of lentils in Europe than meddle with Irrland's split little pea" (171.4–6). To muddle through rather than meddle with—here is the characteristic Joycean emphasis, now augmented with the familiar opposition between Europe as opportunity and Ireland as backward and provincial. It isn't the whole story, of course, for what is *Finnegans Wake* doing if it isn't meddling with "Irrland's split little pea"? Indeed, throughout his writings Joyce strikes at the narrow definitions of Irish identity increasingly apparent from the 1880s onwards. Think of the censure of the Celtic Revival in "A Mother," of the celebration of the outsider in Irish culture in *Ulysses* and its twin attack on Mr Deasy's Orangeism and the Citizen's one-eyed nationalism, or of the deliberate choice in *Finnegans Wake* of a hero who uses a "British to my backbone tongue" (36.31–2) and whose surname is derived from a West Sussex directory. Who now, Joyce seems to be saying, can tell the difference between Mutt and Jute, the indigenous Irish from the foreign invader? "Become a bitskin more wiseable, as if I were you" (16.24–5). Conversely, who now can claim proprietorial or exclusive rights to English, given the writing of *Finnegans Wake* and given the way in which Joyce—like the Gaelic-speaking King—"murdered all the English he knew" (93.2)?

It is appropriate to concentrate in the first instance on the Irish and on the Anglo-Irish context of Joyce's message, but it is not enough. The audience for *Finnegans Wake* is an international one which, as Louis MacNeice put it, may or may not care "Who is the king of your castle."[9] Joyce's message, in other words, exhibits more than an Irish inflection and contains a much wider appeal for a modern audience. Here we might single out two aspects: the theme of peace and the right to individual liberty.

As chapter 1 demonstrates, human history in general and European and British history in particular has been a history of warfare, of "wills gen wonts" (4.1). Hear its sounds of guns and wailing: "Brekkek Kekkek Kekkek Kekkek! Koax Koax Koax! Ualu Ualu Ualu! Quaouauh!" (4.2–3). What better place to capture the essence of human history than a museum dedicated to war. In the opening chapter Joyce gives us the Willingdone, that monument to war and to the arrogant use of male sexual power which stands guard not only over the sexual misdeeds of HCE but also as it were over the whole text. In Joyce's *Notebook*, VI.B.22 (p. 150), he lists a series of foreign words for peace, for *paix*—"Hoping," "Takiya," "Hoa bink," "Thai bink," "Soc," "Kuam samakkhi," "berdamai," "ju jen pen suk," "shanti," "sainte," "si-anta," "al-solhe," "soulhe," "soulke," "Khagagouthioun," "dama." As the first three words of the last chapter remind us, *Finnegans Wake* is a call for peace: "Sandhyas! Sandhyas! Sandhyas!" (593.1). *Samdhi*, like *shantih*, is Sanskrit for peace, and so it is appropriate that, just as the first chapter begins with the fall of human history, the last chapter begins with an expression of hope, a turning of the page of human history, a coda to what has gone before. The Sanctus triplet is here perhaps the least ambiguous of all its appearances in the text—earlier we have had "Xanthos! Xanthos! Xanthos!" (235.9), "Shaunti and shaunti and shaunti again!" (408.33), and "Shunt us! Shunt us! Shunt us!" (454.33). It also contrasts with the "Shantih" of the last line of T. S. Eliot's *The Waste Land* (1922), which is in Eliot's gloss "The Peace which passeth understanding."[10] Peace in Joyce is never associated with some higher realm of consciousness, but is invariably located in time and place, and we shouldn't be surprised if the opening to the last chapter also mimes the Easter Rising, or indeed if hope for the future is shadowed by the hopes for the future in the past.

The second aspect concerns Joyce's constant references to individual liberty. In chapter 3, HCE is called a list of what he assumes are abusive names—"Firstnighter, Informer, Old Fruit," and so on. Though hurt, he does not rise to the bait; he is going through a period of religious reform, we are humorously informed, helped by "the dominican mission for the sowsealist potty" and "the rowmish devowtion known as the howly rowsary" (72.23–5). Instead, his response, captured in the lowly comma, in the change of typeface, and in the use of free indirect speech, is muted, defensive, and verbose: "but anarchistically respectsful of the liberties of the noninvasive individual, did not respond a solitary wedgeword beyond such sedentary" (72.16–18). Again, we cannot expect the antinomian to be true to type (in both meanings of that phrase), but I think we can detect in *Finnegans Wake* a plea for the rights of the individual to be respected. In this regard we might notice how such rights are seen not so much in terms of democratic or consumer rights but rather as the more basic right to be an agnostic, or not to have a gun pointed in one's face, or perhaps—bearing in mind the special difficulties of the owner of a public house—not to have people invade one's private space.

Finnegans Wake does not contain the kind of political message that is to be found in, say, Sean O'Casey's *The Star Turns Red* (1940) or in the great plays of Bertolt Brecht's period of exile. Joyce shied away from the role of teacher, and the only lesson the Shem figure teaches is a subversive one, namely the geometry of ALP's vagina (which is also presumably a sideswipe at the "mathmaster's" sterile approach to reality). It must be confessed that the political message outlined here amounts to very little. After all, there are few who don't want peace or the right not to be unduly disturbed—especially at night. Compare the insightfulness about war everywhere apparent in Brecht's *Mother Courage and Her Children* (1939), as in the Sergeant's opening remark about "Peace—that's just a mess; takes a war to restore order . . . no order, no war," or in the Chaplain's opinion that "war satisfies all requirements, peaceable ones included," or in Brecht's own view of the play—that war is "a continuation of business by other means," that "no sacrifice is too great for the struggle against war."[11] By comparison, the discourse on peace in *Finnegans Wake*, especially when we recall its date of publication, is too generalized and bland, too lacking in the necessary edge and focus, to ultimately challenge us. This remains one of the central difficulties in centring a discussion of the politics of *Finnegans Wake* on the text's political message, for even after the political platform has been identified, which is no easy task given the Flaubertian inheritance, there still remains the problem of the insightfulness or otherwise of what is being said.

POLITICAL READINGS

In outlining the political context and message of *Finnegans Wake*, a number of political readings have already been touched on. In this section the focus is on Weimann's "present meaning." A common objection to *Finnegans Wake* from the left and others is that reality is complex enough and that in writing *Finnegans Wake* Joyce has merely compounded it. Given that such a charge can be answered, another one often follows, for as Marx said in his "Theses on Feuerbach": "The philosophers have only interpreted the world, in various ways; the point, however, is to change it."[12] Put differently, could the time needed to understand *Finnegans Wake* be better spent changing the world? Is there not a tyranny on Joyce's part in requiring so much time and attention from the reader? Have all the words written by the professors in interpreting the text contributed to anything significant beyond the Joyce confederacy? Has *Finnegans Wake*, in Brecht's words, shortened "the age of exploitation"?[13] These questions are difficult to answer but are worth raising because they challenge us to develop a more finely tuned political reading of the work—even if in the end we remain consumed by self-doubt, conscious perhaps, like Shem, of not "having struck one blow" (176.29) (for Ireland or freedom).

Among the many political readings of *Finnegans Wake*, two strands in particular can be mentioned here. The first concerns the way in which Joyce has widened a discussion of politics to include material often designated as outside its scope. In this regard his assault on the phallocentricity of language is telling. Nothing in *Finnegans Wake* has a single meaning; nothing can be tied back to a single source of meaning. This links, of course, on the one hand, with the "metaphors" of fog, the night, and dreams and, on the other, with the confusion and doubt that surround the letter, the names of "characters," or the significance of the title. But there is more to it than this. Phallocentric discourse is marked by the display and exercise of power: it assumes that the human subject controls, precedes, or exists outside language, that the position of the subject in language is unproblematic, and that its task as discourse is mastery over the world through science, rationality, and logic. *Finnegans Wake* radically questions such assumptions and makes us aware of the decentred subject, the problematic relationship of the human subject to language, and the central importance of excess and of what Hélène Cixous calls "*écriture féminine*" or "feminine writing." In this regard, HCE's stutter, linked with his sexual guilt and with the cluster of meanings that surrounds the word "hesitency," reminds us of a phallocentric discourse under pressure, and contrasts with the flow of language, with "gramma's grammar" (268.17), as articulated by ALP and the female voices, and with the accompanying attack on the patriarchal order.

According to Derrida, meaning is never truly present in discourse but is ceaselessly deferred (or, we might add in the light of *Finnegans Wake*, recalled). Against the metaphysics of presence, Derrida posits the free play of the signifier. So it is with *Finnegans Wake*, a text which is fundamentally caught between the eye and the ear, between writing and speech. Two systems constantly hit off against each other, and at any one time both are co-present, but in such a way as to prevent the possibility of full presence. The form this lack of full presence takes is, like everything else in *Finnegans Wake*, varied. When some words are read out loud, their meaning becomes restricted, as, for example, with the word "boarder" in the phrase "the boarder incident" (81.32–3); in writing we see both meanings, but when it is spoken hear only one. Sometimes it turns on a syllable, as in the word "husbandry" (38.11), which can be pronounced either as "husband dry" or "husbandry." The eye can take in both meanings, but in reading the word aloud we are of necessity forced to jettison one of the meanings. Sometimes behind the written word we can hear other words, as, for example, with "dumbestic" (dumb, domestic, beast) in the phrase "dumbestic husbandry" (38.11). At other times—and this needs a more extended gloss—we repeatedly notice "that patternmind, that paradigmatic ear" (70.35–6), as Earwicker is called.

Language, according to Saussure, is made up of paradigmatic and syntagmatic (or vertical and horizontal) relationships. In *Finnegans Wake*, many of the syllables, words, phrases, and sentences anticipate or echo each other and come to form a paradigm, a set of vertical relationships that lift them out of the syntagmatic relationships of the particular sentence in which they are embedded. Sometimes when this happens the reader is unable to integrate the two sets of relationship, seeing one, then the other, but never the two together as a unity. Thus "deltic dwilights" (492.9) recalls Yeats's Celtic Twilight, but it also revives "cultic twalette" (344.12), and so the reader is momentarily caught between an extratextual reference and an intratextual paradigm. At the level of individual words, "deltic" exists within a series of lexical sets which are perhaps related to each other only because of a common word: "deltic origin" (Delphic oracle) (140.9), "deltas twoport" (318.13) (death do us part), "triagonal delta" (297.24) (ALP's triangular delta). Similarly with "dwilights," "cultic," and "twalette." On the other hand there are paradigms, such as St Augustine's *felix culpa*, or refrains such as "The wren, the wren, the king of all birds," or prayers such as the Hail Mary, that include many variations, so many in fact that the paradigm draws the reader away from the surrounding syntagmatic relationships, and it is at this point that we perhaps recognize the force of Derrida's concept of the free play of the signifier.

Finnegans Wake—and this in part accounts for the problematic status of its political message—refuses the distinction between denotation and connotation, being, as Samuel Beckett once proclaimed, "not about something; it is that something itself."[14] Furthermore, it mocks our legitimate readerly desires for a paraphrasable content. The aesthetics of high modernism here meets the more recent discussion that takes its bearings from psychoanalysis, semiotics, and linguistics, and is in turn given a radical and social nuance. Thus an aesthetics which had its origins in defeat and alienation—the fate of art after 1848—takes on a political meaning in the work of critical modernists such as Brecht and Joyce. In Brecht it is closely allied with the struggle against fascism and for socialism; in Joyce it takes its most prominent form in the struggle against the identity of word and world. In the long run both struggles were—and are—necessary, and we should take care not to counterpose the two and assume we are obliged to choose one and dismiss the other. *Finnegans Wake*—and we need perhaps to invoke a distinction here between a political message and a political meaning—is a subversive text, which not only contributes to a strengthening of a potentially radical theory about language, gender, and the human subject but also continues to extend and test such a theory.

For the second approach to a political reading of *Finnegans Wake* I turn to Mikhail Bakhtin's discussion of Rabelais and to his concept of *chronotope* (chronos + topos):

> Rabelais' task is to gather together on a new material base a world that, due to the dissolution of the medieval world view, is disintegrating. The medieval wholeness and roundedness of the world . . . had been destroyed. There was destroyed as well the medieval conception of history—the Creation of the World, the Fall from Grace, the First Expulsion, Redemption, the Second Exile, the Final Judgment—concepts in which real time is devalued and dissolved in extratemporal categories. In this world view, time is a force that only destroys and annihilates; it creates nothing. . . . A new *chronotope* was needed that would permit one to link real life (history) to the real earth. It was necessary to oppose to eschatology a creative and generative time.[15]

There is much here that is relevant to an understanding of Joyce's project. Think, for example, of the usefulness of the phrase "gather together" in connection with *Finnegans Wake*, a text that is the supreme example in literature of the concept of bricolage, where disparate, heterogeneous material is brought together not for any reason inherent in the material but because it can be assigned meaning and used to form part of a new view of the world. Joyce doesn't reflect the world; he gathers it together. Or think of his "generative" view of time. He deliberately eschews the apocalyptic sensibility and primitivism of many of his modernist contemporaries. Taking a longer view of history—which had been assigned to the Irish by the triumphs of the British—he saw the workings of much larger cycles than were available to those immediately involved in the establishment or protection of empire. This is summed up in an enigmatic phrase that recurs in *Finnegans Wake*: history is "the seim anew" (215.23), "the same renew" (226.17), "Sein annews" (277.18). It is Joyce's answer to the pre-Socratic dilemma of permanence and change, of whether or not it is possible to step into the same river twice. Here lies one of the key tensions in his last work, between the known pattern of human history, with all its "Killykillkilly" and "wills gen wonts," and the future destiny of the race and its ability or otherwise to live in peace. The Liffey has much to tell us, not only about the guilty secrets it has seen—"O tell me all about Anna Livia! I want to hear all about Anna Livia" (196.1–3)—but also about bringing human history into a closer alignment with the natural world, about listening to rhythms and sounds which predate the rise of civilization and within which our modern world should be enfolded.

The comparison between Rabelais and Joyce is more complex than this, not least because Joyce recognized that the Irish "are still fundamentally a medieval people" and that "*Ulysses* also is medieval."[16] In *Finnegans Wake* we are told that Shem is "weird . . . and middayevil down to his vegetable soul" (423.27–8). Aquinas and scholasticism were among Joyce's fathers and stood him "in good stead" when he embarked on his voyage away from medieval Ireland and medieval Dublin towards the modern world of Europe and Paris. The historical irony is that Joyce, whose head was saturated with medieval ideas, whose natural bias was "the backward look," and whose perspective was invariably long-term, came to be regarded in the inter-war years as the leading exponent of the avant-garde. But then Joyce had the advantage over his contemporaries of being more directly exposed to contradictory ways of perceiving the world and therefore of sensing more sharply the plight of being in some way disinherited. In giving up his religion and in exiling himself from Ireland, family, and friends, Joyce lost much of the ideology which bound him to the social structure and which lent him a sense of coherence and purpose. However, from his Catholic upbringing and Jesuit education he retained structures and forms and an interest in taxonomy which not only served him well in the period of *The Waste Land* and in the aftermath of the Irish Civil War, but which also stood him in good stead when he began to pick up the pieces of a disintegrated world and rediscover anew the "strandentwining cable of all flesh" (*Ulysses*, p. 32).

Notes

Quotations from Joyce are taken from the Faber edition of *Finnegans Wake*, (1939), and from the new Penguin edition of *Ulysses* (1986).

1. *Selected Letters of James Joyce*, ed. Richard Ellmann (New York: Viking Press, 1976), p. 327, to Harriet Weaver, 14 August 1927.

2. Roland Barthes, *Image—Music—Text*, selected and trans. Stephen Heath (London: Fontana, 1979), pp. 142–8.

3. See the chapter entitled "Past significance and present meaning in literary history" in Robert Weimann, *Structure and Society in Literary History: Studies in the History and Theory of Historical Criticism* (London: Lawrence & Wishart, 1977), pp. 18–56.

4. For recent contextual studies, see, *inter alia*, John Garvin, *James Joyce's Disunited Kingdom and the Irish Dimension* (Dublin and London: Gill & Macmillan; New York: Barnes & Noble, 1977); William J. McCormack, *Ascendancy and Tradition in Anglo-Irish Literary History from 1789 to 1939* (Oxford: Clarendon Press, 1985); Seamus Deane, "Joyce and Nationalism," in Colin MacCabe (ed.), *James Joyce: New Perspectives* (Brighton: Harvester; Bloomington: Indiana University Press, 1982), pp. 168–83; Hugh Kenner, *A Colder Eye: The Modern Irish Writers* (Harmondsworth: Penguin, 1983). For Joyce's political message, see Phillip Herring, "Joyce's Politics," in Fritz Senn (ed.), *New Light on Joyce from the Dublin Symposium* (Bloomington: Indiana University Press, 1972), pp. 3–14; Dominic Manganiello, *Joyce's Politics* (London: Routledge & Kegan Paul, 1980); Diarmuid Maguire, "The Politics of *Finnegans Wake*," in Giorgio Melchiori (ed.), *Joyce in Rome: The Genesis of Ulysses* (Rome: Bulzoni, 1984), pp. 120–8. For the third approach, see, *inter alia*, Margot Norris, *The Decentered Universe of Finnegans Wake* (Baltimore: Johns Hopkins University Press, 1976); Colin MacCabe, *James Joyce and the Revolution of the Word* (London: Macmillan, 1978); Suzette Henke and Elaine Unkeless (eds), *Women in Joyce* (Urbana, Ill.: University of Illinois Press, 1982); Bonnie Kime Scott, *James Joyce* (Brighton: Harvester, 1987).

5. Sean O'Faolain, *De Valera* (Harmondsworth: Penguin, 1939), p. 173. On pp. 174 and 175 the word "frank" appears twice. In September 1932 at the League of Nations, de Valera, his biographer tells us, "spoke with so much frank forcefulness about the League"; in the same speech de Valera declared, "Let us be frank with ourselves."

6. Hugh Kenner, *A Colder Eye: The Modern Irish Writers* (Harmondsworth: Penguin, 1983), p. 290. Characteristically, Kenner is being provocative.

7. See Richard Ellmann, *James Joyce: New and Revised Edition* (New York: Oxford University Press, 1982), p. 643 n.

8. Ibid., p. 708.

9. Louis MacNeice, *Collected Poems*, ed. E. R. Dodds (London: Faber, 1979), p. 134. The phrase is from section XVI of "Autumn Journal."

10. T. S. Eliot, *Collected Poems 1909–1962* (London: Faber, 1963), p. 86. Actually, modern students of comparative religion are reluctant to see equivalences between religions in the way Eliot does. It can also be noted in passing that *samdhi* and *shantih* are to be distinguished and cannot adequately be translated by the one word "peace." Perhaps the use of the two words in *Finnegans Wake* is another example of Joyce intent on showing his superior knowledge over his rival Eliot.

11. Bertolt Brecht, *Mother Courage and Her Children*, trans. John Willett (London: Methuen Student Editions, 1983), pp. 3–4, 53–4, and xvii.

12. From Marx's "Theses on Feuerbach," in Karl Marx and Frederick Engels, *Selected Works* (London: Lawrence & Wishart, 1970), p. 30.

13. From his poem "A Bed for the Night," in Bertolt Brecht, *Poems 1913–1956*, eds. John Willett and Ralph Mannheim (London: Eyre Methuen, 1976), p. 181.

14. From Beckett's essay "Dante . . . Bruno. Vico . . . Joyce," in Samuel Beckett *et al., Our Exagmination Round His Factification for Incamination of Work in Progress* (London: Faber, 1961), p. 14.

15. Mikhail Bakhtin, *The Dialogic Imagination: Four Essays*, ed. Michael Holquist, trans. C. Emerson and M. Holquist (Austin and London: University of Texas Press, 1983), p. 205. The connection between Bakhtin and Joyce, especially in the context of dialogism,

carnivalesque, and the grotesque, has been the subject of recent critical attention; see, for example, the first chapter of Patrick Parrinder, *James Joyce* (Cambridge: Cambridge University Press, 1984), pp. 1–16. Bakhtin's insights into the workings of literary history could well be applied further in Joyce studies.

16.   Arthur Power, *Conversations with James Joyce* (London: Millington, 1974), pp. 92–4.

The General and the Sepoy: Imperialism and Power in the Museyroom

VINCENT J. CHENG

Colin MacCabe has suggested that *"Finnegans Wake*, with its sustained dismemberment of the English linguistic and literary heritage, is perhaps best understood in relation to the struggle against imperialism."[1] This statement seems to me all the more accurate since the struggle against imperialism and the structures of colonial authority is itself already such a major and overt topic in the *Wake*. I wish here to re-present the *Wake*'s Willingdone Museyroom as a site, and a case study, of colonial power dynamics. The Museyroom passage on pages 8 through 10 is a deservedly celebrated passage, wonderful and rich and full of resonant meanings to pursue. Henriette Power has previously investigated, in her essay on "Shahrazahde" in *Finnegans Wake*, the intricacies of the Museyroom's "hinndoo seeboy" as a "hidden," "seeing" boy within the contexts of voyeurism and concealment.[2] I would like to focus on his identification as a "Hindu sepoy" reacting to the great British general, the Iron Duke of Wellington.

Dominating the wax museum that is the "Willingdone Museyroom" (8.10)[3] is Arthur, Duke of Wellington on his big white horse, Copenhagen. Around him are the Lipoleum(s), the three young insurgents who sometimes seem one and are collectively represented by their "triplewon [three-in-one] hat," the "Lipoleumhat" (8.15–16); they are aided by the female "jinnies" (Jenny was a blackmailer of Wellington). Thus, the Duke of Wellington is presented as an archetypal patriarch and wielder of Authority and power, sitting on his high horse over the children who try—in the universal power struggle—to unhorse the Father and the Law of the Father, and make Humpty have a great fall. Appropriately, the passage is peppered with hundreds of references to famous battles and martial conflicts, especially those from Wellington's own life, which Joyce obviously knew in intimate detail. For example, in these three pages we find not only many references to Wellington's celebrated horse Copenhagen (the "Cokenhape," and so on) but to Wellington's many battles: "inimyskilling" (Inniskilling dragoons at Waterloo), "Belchum" (Waterloo, Belgium), "Dispatch . . . Dispitch" (*The*

This essay was prepared for this volume and is published here for the first time by permission of the author.

Dispatches of the Duke of Wellington during his Various Campaigns, 1834–9), "thin red lines" (Wellington's famed Thin Red Line), "Salamangra" (Salamanca 1812), "hundred days'," "Tarra's widdars" (Torres Vedras 1810), "blooches" (General Blucher), "solphereens" (Solferino 1859), "Almeidagad!" (Almeida 1811), "Arthiz too loose!" (Orthez 1814, Toulouse 1814), "Cumbrum!" (General Cambronne at Waterloo), "ousterlists" (Austerlitz 1805), "Dalaveras fimmieras" (Talavera 1809, Vimeiro 1808), "hiena" (Jena 1806), "lipsyg" (Leipzig 1815), "insoult" (French Marshall Soult, Waterloo's nemesis all through the Peninsular War), "Hney, hney, hney!" (French Marshall Ney), "upjump and pumpim" (Wellington's famed "Up, guards, and at them!"), "cursigan" (Corsican Napoleon), "Basucker" (Bussaco 1810), and so on.[4] I would like, however, to concentrate on the lesser-known Wellington references—the numerous allusions here to his military campaigns in India (prior to battling Napoleon in the Peninsular War), in which he was instrumental in expanding England's Oriental empire.

"This is the Willingdone on his same white harse, the Cokenhape . . . his big wide harse" (8.17, 21). The Iron Duke of Wellington seated on his big white horse is, like all such equestrian statues, a stylized symbol of the power of Authority over those it rules. Wellington himself is an ideal embodiment of such imperial power—having been first a general who fought brilliantly in India during the Mahratta War and expanded England's colonial power in the Orient; who then defeated Napoleon in the Peninsular War and again at Waterloo; and who later became England's prime minister. As such, he is a symbol of domination by patriarchal power and violence; it is appropriate that in Dublin he is represented by the phallic Wellington Monument in Phoenix Park, embodied in the Museyroom by Willingdone's erection ("Willingdone git the band up" in 8.34 and 9.09) and by his phallic "mormorial tallowscoop Wounderworker" of "Sexcaliber hrosspower" (8.35–36), combining phallic telescope, candle (tallow), obelisk memorial (marble "mormorial"), sex, power, and violence (six-caliber and Excalibur). (In fact, I suspect that Joyce's "tallowscoop" comes from a story associated with a painting of Wellington [see illustration 1] in which he was originally depicted with a watch in his hand, but—in truly militaristic fashion [notice the phallic sword hanging from his legs]—expostulated: "That will never do. I was *not* 'waiting' for the Prussians at Waterloo. Put a telescope in my hand, if you please."[5])

Wellington on his white horse is only the most prominent and frequent of many references in *Finnegans Wake* to rulers on white horses (including Napoleon on his white charger Marengo), all figures denoting imperial and colonial rule. Such an emblem of empire is especially appropriate if we remember that the "white horse" was the specific emblem of the House of Hanover, the English ruling dynasty (later the Windsors), a fact Joyce makes reference to in "his whuite hourse of Hunover" within a passage clearly about empire and colonialism (388.13–18; cf. McHugh, 388). Even more notably,

Reproduction courtesy of Wellington College, Crowthorne, Berkshire, England.
1. Wellington 1824. Portrait painted for Peel by Sir Thomas Lawrence. The artist began by putting a watch in the Duke's hand, as if waiting for his Prussian allies, but the Duke expostulated, "That will never do. I was *not* 'waiting' for the Prussians at Waterloo. Put a telescope in my hand, if you please."

the white horse was a personal symbol for William III, King Billy, the Protestant and Dutch Prince of Orange and Nassau, victor of the Battle of the Boyne, which sealed English domination over Ireland, and the scourge of Irish Catholics. As Adaline Glasheen, citing J. T. Gilbert's *History of the City of Dublin* (Dublin: McGlashan and Gill, 1854; reprinted, Shannon: Irish University Press, 1972, III, 40–56), points out, "In Dublin (before the Free State), the Ulsterman's brazen calf was a lead equestrian statue of King Billy on College Green which, on Williamite holy days, was painted white (a white horse in a fanlight is still a sign of Protestant sympathies) and decorated with orange lilies . . . and green and white ribbons 'symbolically placed beneath its uplifted foot.' Catholics retorted by vandalizing the statue, tarring, etc., and in 1836 succeeded in blowing the figure of the king off the horse."[6]

The particular symbolism of the uplifted foot of King Billy's white horse, ready to crush rebellious Irish Catholics, appears in *Ulysses*'s "Wandering Rocks" episode, when the Viceregal parade rounds College Green: "Where the foreleg of King Billy's horse pawed the air Mrs Breen plucked her hastening husband back from under the hoofs of the outriders."[7] The effectively ambiguous grammar here suggests an equal danger to Dubliners of being crushed by King Billy's horse and by the Viceregal hooves—for they are both metonymies for the same thing, imperial (and Protestant) England.

Similarly, in *Finnegans Wake* HCE-Porter ("missed a porter") is again described as a king, imposing the law of the father: "Dutchlord, Dutchlord, overawes us . . . like the prince of Orange and Nassau" with his "great wide cloak . . . and his little white horse" (135.08–22). The "Dutchlord" is both Protestant King William III, the Dutch prince of Orange and Nassau who overawed Catholic Ireland at the Boyne and who rules on the white horse, which is the hated sign of Protestant sympathies—and another empire-mongering King William, Kaiser Wilhelm (*Deutschland, Deutschland über alles*). (As Glasheen [302] points out, Wellington is not to be distinguished from all conquering Williams.) In another passage about battles and empire building (including references to Hittites, Bulgars, and many battles), we learn that "Hittit was of another time, a white horsday . . . along about the first equinarx" (346.36–347.02). McHugh (347) glosses this equine "White Horse Day" as "12 July in Ulster: King Billy on a White Horse," celebrated by Ulster Protestants as the victory at the Boyne over the papists. That equestrian statue of King Billy's white horse, which Catholics repeatedly tried to deface, returns in the description of HCE as "*he*, conscious of enemies, a kingbilly whitehorsed in a Finglas mill" (75.15, my emphases; McHugh notes that William III stayed at Finglas after the Battle of the Boyne).[8]

In the Museyroom, the description of Wellington on Copenhagen is indistinguishable from King Billy, for he is "the big Sraughter Willingdone [combining William and Wellington], grand and magentic [like His Majesty] in his goldtin spurs and his ironed dux [Iron Duke] and his quarter brass woodyshoes and his magnate's gharters" (8.17–19). McHugh (8) notes that "brass money and wooden shoes" was an "Orange Toast to William III." And, sure enough, two lines later we find the lipoleums described as "the three lipoleum boyne grouching down in the living detch" (8.21–22): three rebellious Irish boys crouching down on the ground in a living ditch (i.e., Ireland, the peat bog and old sod; as opposed to the Orange King on his high horse) waiting for King Billy at the Boyne. Thus, Wellington on his white horse (as conqueror of India and defender of the empire against challengers like Napoleon) and King Billy (as conqueror/oppressor of Catholic Ireland) unite in a collective figure (in which Ireland and India are correspondingly united as a collective victim of English imperialism), a symbol of colonial domination and power politics. The centerpiece of the Museyroom is but a wax version of at least three famous equestrian statues that symbolize the imperial, Protestant, English rule: the statue of King Billy on College Green, Dublin; the giant Wyatt equestrian memorial to Wellington in London (see illustration 2); and an equestrian statue of Wellington in the center of Madras.[9]

After all, as we learn, the lipoleum "boyne" in the ditch, living like dogs, are not merely Irish colonials, but include those of the Empire's darker Oriental races. The Museyroom tour guide goes on to point out the three: "This is the bog lipoleum mordering the lipoleum beg. A Gallawghurs argaumunt. This is the petty lipoleum boy that was nayther bag nor bug. Assaye, assaye!" (8.24–26) While the first two boys are similar (like bog and beg, with perhaps an echo of "murdering Irish"), it is the third boy who is neither "bag nor bug" and is perhaps the most rebellious ("*nay*ther"). While the first two are Irish rivals "mordering" each other or holding an argument among Irishmen (Gallaghers' argument), the identity of the third boy, who is neither "bag nor bug," is hinted at quite obliquely and Orientally: for "Galwilgarh" and "Argaum" were both battles in the Mahratta War (1803) Wellington conducted in India; they followed upon the heels of the most decisive and bloodiest battle of that war, Wellington's great victory at Assaye. These three battles broke the powers of the Mahrattas, and treaties were agreed to forthwith.[10] (The museum visitor's startled reaction to the discovery of this hidden identity is "I say! I say!") Confirmation of the Indian identity of the third lipoleum occurs three lines later: "This is Mont Tivel, this is Mont Tipsey, this is the Grand Mons Injun" (8.28–29)—in which the third lipoleum is pegged as an "Injun."[11]

These identifications all occur on page 8, the first of the three Museyroom pages. After much description of Willingdone's skirmishes with the jinnies on page 9, the Museyroom episode concludes on page 10 with the lipoleums' attack on Willingdone. Again, these "nice young bachelors" (like Willingdone with his "tallowscoop," they are quite nicely "hung" themselves) are identified by the tour guide: "Lipoleums is nice hung bush-

Reproduction courtesy of the Victoria and Albert Museum, London.
2. Wellington funeral procession, passing by the Decimus Burton Arch with Matthew Cotes Wyatt's Statue of Wellington.

ellors. This is hiena hinnessy laughing alout at the Willingdone. This is lipsyg dooley krieging the funk from the hinnessy. This is the hinndoo Shimar Shin between the dooley boy and the hinnessy" (10.03–7). The first two appear to be Irish—Hennessey and Dooley—or perhaps Irish and American, since Irish-American comic P. F. Dunne wrote a book called *The Dooley Philosophy*, featuring two Irish-Americans named Dooley and Hennessey (Glasheen, 76, 127). The third is a Hindu named Shimar Shin. Standing "between the dooley boy and the hinnessy," "hinndoo" as the third is a combination of the other two ("Hinnessy" plus Dooley)—one ("hinn") plus two ("doo") equals "hinndoo." Whether Irish, American, or Hindu, all are English colonials. Their three-in-one solidarity is again symbolized by "the threefoiled hat of lipoleums" (10.08)—not only Napoleon's tricornered hat but a "trefoil," suggesting the Irish shamrock, St. Patrick's emblem of Ireland's trinitarian Catholic faith. In Joyce's pencil sketch[12] of Waterloo, the signs "∧ ∕⊏ ⊏" show Shaun (∧), Shem (⊏), and standing between them ∕⊏ as their composite substance (see McHugh, ix, and Glasheen, 127)—suggesting a religious mystery in this holy trinity of the collective "hinndoo." Furthermore, as Brendan O Hehir (also McHugh, 10) points out, *siomar sin* is Irish for "that fair-dark trefoil (or shamrock)" (Glasheen, 127). Thus, the "hinndoo Shimar Shin" is a combination of the fair Irish and the dark Hindu in a tripartite unity, joined in a religion of rebellion from subservience (motto: *non serviam*) whose religious symbolism is a shamrock-like trefoil, the "threefoiled hat." Just as the figure of Willingdone on a white horse unites William III (who conquered and tyrannized the Irish and whose symbol was a white horse) and Wellington (who conquered the Hindus in the Mahratta War, and was himself notorious for opposing Irish Catholic emancipation) on Copenhagen, so also the three lipoleums unite into a collective archetype (Irish, American, Hindu) and united cause of colonial insurrection against the imperial power.

As so frequently happens in colonial uprisings, the immediate cause of conflict is the colonizer's religious arrogance or intolerance. Just as the Orange faction's repression of Catholic Ireland led to terrorist acts (such as blowing up King Billy's horse), so also the incident in the Museyroom is precipitated by Willingdone's arrogance toward the lipoleums' religious icon: "This the wixy old Willingdone picket up the half of the threefoiled hat of lipoleums fromoud of the bluddle filth. . . . This is the Willingdone hanking the half of the hat of lipoleums up the tail on the buckside of his big white harse" (10.07–11). Not only does Willingdone yank the mystically joined, sacred trefoil-icon in half, but he then uses it to wipe his horse's ass. "That was the last joke of Willingdone. [by the First Duke of Wellington, and it was a direct] Hit, hit, hit! This is the same white harse of the Willingdone, Culpenhelp, waggling his tailoscrupp with the half of a hat of lipoleums to insult on the hinndoo seeboy. Hney, hney, hney! (Bullsrag! Foul!)" (10.11–15). Stung by the direct hit of Willingdone's cruel "insoult" to their religion, the colonial "hinndoo" (Irish and Indian) can only cry "Foul!"—but even that cry is a marginalized discourse silenced and bracketed by an authoritative grammar of parentheses: "(Bullrag! Foul!)"—in contrast to the loud and uncontained laughter (ha, ha, ha) of Willingdone ("Hit, hit, hit!") and his horse ("Hney, hney, hney!"—the neigh and "insoult" also mock Napoleon's marshals, Ney and Soult).

Can the subaltern speak?[13] Silenced into the bracketed margins of official discourse, but angered by the insult to his religion and thus moved by a cultural desire to represent himself, the Irish-Hindu colonial "hinndoo" responds in the only effective discourse available to him, violence—the bomb: "This is the hinndoo waxing ranjymad for a bombshoob" (10.09; "Ranji," aka "Jam Sahib" [Glasheen, 243], was a popular Rajput cricketer who played for England and made over 3,000 runs, thus a Hindu who can make "hits" of his own). Mad as a hatter in his anger, the "hinndoo" responds to Wellington's famed rallying cry ("Up, guards, and at 'em") with a Hindu war cry of his own: "This is the seeboy, madrashattaras, upjump and pumpim, cry to the Willingdone: Ap Pukkaru! Pukka yurap!" (10.15–17). "Madrashattaras" combines Madras (a Mahratta city, dominated by an equestrian statue of Wellington) and the Mahratta War won by Wellington; the "hinndoo" war cry suggests that things are no longer *pukka* (genuine, first rate) for Willingdone and sounds suspiciously like either "Bugger Europe!" or "Bugger your arse!" (the "harse" is, after all, the seat of Willingdone's power). "This is the Willingdone, bornstable ghentleman, tinders his maxbotch to the cursigan Shimar Shin. Basucker youstead!" (10.17–19). Wellington's verbal response to the cursing Hindu (also Corsican/Napoleonic) upstart is one offering ("tinder"-ing) battle (Wellington's victory over Napoleon at Bussaco, Portugal), massacre ("Basucker youstead" sounds like "Massacre *usted*" [Spanish for "you"]), and firepower ("tinders" and "matchbox" ["maxbotch"]).

It is significant that our "hinndoo" lipoleum, both Irish and Indian, becomes newly identified three times at this point as a "seeboy"—a term that has very interesting connotations in this context. A "sepoy" (who is literally and militaristically a colonial "subaltern") is "a native of India employed as a soldier by a European power, esp. Great Britain" (*Webster's*) and is a term derived from the Hindi and Persian words for "cavalryman." In other words, a sepoy is a native imitation of a British dragoon—playing at being British (for the British) in the European war games that involve cavalry charges and so on—a native attempt to mimic the "horsepower" of Wellington mounted on Copenhagen. Indian sepoy brigades were famous for their ferocious effectiveness and loyalty in fighting for the Crown, just as Ranji became a star for the British at their own game of cricket. But, as Homi Bhabha has so incisively noted in "Of Mimicry and Man: The Ambivalence of Colonial Discourse," one of the distinguishing qualities of a colonial relationship is what he calls the "colonial mimicry" induced in (and expected of) the subject race taught to imitate (resemble, and *almost* become) the dominant race, in a form of cultural desire, but—in the dilemma of being "almost the same" but "not quite/not white"—never being actually granted the privileges and freedoms that come with sovereignty, dominion, and citizenship. The object of such colonial mimicry, from the colonizer's viewpoint, is, as Bhabha puts it, to "ensure its [own] strategic failure, so that mimicry is at once resemblance and menace"[14]—menace, that is, if the mimicry is too successful (as in the case of Paul Scott's Hari Kumar in *The Raj Quartet*[15]). The sepoys can be proud, like British Tommies, of serving the Crown; but since they must not claim the other rights and privileges accorded to the Crown's own citizens and soldiers, rebellion—once the sepoys have been insulted to the point of being "ranjymad" and "madrashattaras"—is inevitable, as eventually happened in the bloody Sepoy Mutiny of 1857–58.

"Sepoy" is a particularly interesting term in relation to the Duke of Wellington. When he first took on Napoleon in the Peninsular War, he was known only for his very successful Indian campaigns, and Napoleon foolhardily wrote him off as merely a "Sepoy General" (*Britannica* vol. 29, 735); Wellington was subsequently and frequently referred to as "The Sepoy General" or even just "The Sepoy." The label of "sepoy" is doubly ironic because, in a sense, he *was*: born in Dublin and raised Irish, Wellington was one of the dark horses that, in this ambivalent discourse of colonial desire, trains to become a white horse in a white horse world, as does a Hindu sepoy or a Rajput cricketer—going to Eton and then fighting for England, becoming its leading military figure and eventually prime minister (in the process opposing Irish Catholic emancipation as long as he could). In Wellington, the mimicry was so authentic that it became authoritative (even in his own mind), and he grew to symbolize (to both himself and the world) the dominant, not the subject, race. This is an irony Joyce shows us he is quite aware of in describing Willingdone as "bornstable ghentleman" (also referring to Wellington's role in the Treaty of Ghent), for, when asked if he were Irish, Wellington's famous reply, disowning his own native heritage as one of the colonized (in the stables, in the living ditch) in favor of the colonizer (in the ducal manor/manner), was: "If a gentleman happens to be born in a stable, it does not follow that he should be called a horse" (McHugh, 10).

Furthermore, in calling our insurgent "hinndoo" a Hindu and a sepoy, Joyce is invoking the notorious Sepoy Mutiny of 1857, thus forecasting the eventual results of Wellington's aggressive campaigns in India. As with Irish Catholic uprisings against Orange forces and as with the lipoleum's bomb response to the attack on their trefoiled icon, the Sepoy Mutiny had its origin in the empire's religious insensitivity and was sparked by a religious "insult": To load the new Enfield rifles, "lubricated cartridges had to have their ends bitten off by the sepoys" but "the grease used for this purpose was a mixture of pigs' and cows' lard, an insult to both Muslims and Hindus."

(This is perhaps why the pained cry of the Hindu "seeboy" at Willingdone's insult is "[*Bull*srag! Foul!]"). The sepoys at Meerut refused the Enfield cartridges; "as punishment, they were given long prison terms, fettered, and put in jail." Incensed at this injustice, numerous sepoy companies mutinied and marched on Delhi—and thus began the Sepoy Rebellion. Unfortunately, the English response, like Willingdone's, was massacre, "tinders," and "maxbotch": "In the end the reprisals far outweighed the original excesses. Hundreds of sepoys were shot from cannons in a frenzy of British vengeance."[16]

In *Finnegans Wake*, the Museyroom episode climaxes with the lipoleum's response to the religious "insult" by Willingdone and his horse. Driven "ranjymad" and "madrashattaras," the "dooforhim seeboy" (two-for-one, Irish and Indian, "Hinnessy" and Dooley; Dufferin was the "first marquess" and ruler of annexed Burma, according to Glasheen, 79) picks up his "bombshoob" and uses it to close the episode: "This is the dooforhim seeboy blow the whole of the half of the hat of lipoleums off the top of the tail on the back of his big wide harse. Tip (Bullseye! Game!) How Copenhagen ended" (10.19–22). Like the Sepoy Mutineers, the incensed "seeboy" ("madrashattaras") rebels and blows the big white horse, emblem of imperial authority, to bits. The cry of "Bullsrag! Foul!" is now replaced by the children's glee at their own bull's eye, which ends the game and literally unhorses HCE (and the Law of the Father) by destroying his horse ("*How Copenhagen ended*").

Thus, in the *Wake* Indian colonial domination by, and resistance to, English imperial rule is re-presented (or co-presented) by Joyce as parallel to and synonymous with Catholic Ireland's subservient relationship to Protestant England—for the "hinndoo" sepoy blowing up Willingdone's big white horse is but another version of Irish Catholic Hennesseys and Dooleys tarring, defacing, and then (in 1836) blowing up King Billy's white horse on Dublin's College Green. (I understand that the Wellington equestrian statue in Madras has had a similarly perilous history.) The Museyroom thus becomes a collective case study of colonial politics and the dynamics of power. In suggesting that *Finnegans Wake* is "best understood in relation to the struggle against imperialism," MacCabe ruefully concludes that "*Finnegans Wake* is a primer for a failed revolution, one that would have allied Ireland to Europe rather than simply separating twenty-six counties from Britain" (MacCabe, 5). Perhaps the *Wake*'s pluralistic vision of a polylogic, universal discourse, displacing the monologic discourses of nationalism, is as yet "failed," even utopian. But I would add that, even in 1939 (long before the independence of India and Pakistan), Joyce would have at least known that—whether in the 26 counties of Ireland or in the many provinces and princedoms of England's Oriental colonies—failed revolutions are a tragic and bomb-laden reality that only temporarily derail, but do not finally deny, the inevitability of sovereignty and home rule.

Notes

1.   Colin MacCabe, *"Finnegans Wake* at Fifty," *Critical Quarterly* 31.4:4; hereafter cited in text as MacCabe.

2.   Henriette Lazaridis Power, "Shahrazade, Turko the Terrible, and Shem: The Reader as Voyeur in *Finnegans Wake,"* in *Coping with Joyce: Essays from the Copenhagen Symposium,* ed. Morris Beja and Shari Benstock (Columbus: Ohio State University Press, 1989), 248–61.

3.   All citations to *Finnegans Wake* are taken from the New York: Viking Compass, 1959 edition.

4.   Among the references to battles *not* connected to Wellington are "Saloos" (Salo, Loos), "magentic" (Magenta), "goldtin spurs" (Golden Spurs), "pulluponeasyan wartrews" (Peloponnesian War), "boyne," "Mons," "crimealine," "phillippy," "hastings," "fontannoy," "agincourting," "stampforth" (Stamford), "camelry" (Camel), "floodens" (Floddens Field), "action" (Actium), "their mobbily" (Thermopylae), "panickburns" (Bannockburns), "bunkersheels," "marathon," "spy on" (Spion Kop). Some of these are listed in Roland McHugh, *Annotations to "Finnegans Wake"* (Baltimore: Johns Hopkins University Press, 1980), 8–10; hereafter cited in text as McHugh.

5.   Elizabeth Longford, *Wellington: Pillar of State* (New York: Harper & Row, 1972), illus. 14.

6.   Adaline Glasheen, *Third Census of "Finnegans Wake"* (Berkeley: University of California Press, 1977), 309; hereafter cited in text as Glasheen.

7.   *Ulysses* (New York: Vintage, 1986), 208.

8.   The preceding three paragraphs are indebted to a much longer essay of mine on Joyce's equine symbolism, "White Horse, Dark Horse: Joyce's Allhorse of Another Color," in *Joyce Studies Annual 1991*, ed. Thomas F. Staley (Austin: University of Texas Press, 1991), 101–28 (see especially pages 104–5 and 114). In fact, this present essay unfolds a detailed analysis of the Museyroom passage first conceived (but not developed or elaborated) on pages 115–16 of the "White Horse" article.

9.   I am indebted to Hemalatha Chari for telling me about the Wellington statue in Madras.

10.   *The Encyclopaedia Britannica*, 11th ed. (Cambridge: Cambridge University Press, 1911), vol. 28, 507.

11.   "Mons Injun" is also Mont St. Jean, where Napoleon's troops were centered at Waterloo.

12.   *A First Draft Version of "Finnegans Wake,"* ed. David Hayman (Austin: University of Texas Press, 1963), 50.

13.   I am of course borrowing the title of Gayatri Spivak's complex and cogent treatment of the intricacies in positing subaltern discourses, "Can the Subaltern Speak?" in *Marxism and the Interpretation of Culture*, ed. Cary Nelson and Lawrence Grossberg (Champaign: University of Illinois Press, 1988), 271–313.

14.   Homi Bhabha, "Of Mimicry and Man: The Ambivalence of Colonial Discourse," *October* 28 (Spring 1984): 126–27, 132.

15.   Paul Scott, *The Raj Quartet* (New York: Avon, 1979).

16.   *The New Encyclopaedia Britannica* (micropaedia), 15th ed. (Chicago: Encyclopaedia Britannica, 1975), vol. 6, 289.

Index

♦

Campbell, Joseph, and Henry Morton
    Robinson, 2–3, 10–11n6, 36,
    72n12, 89–90, 182
Carens, James F., 3, 8
Carlyle, Thomas: *Sartor Resartus*, 145
Carroll, Lewis, 186, 199; *Alice's Adventures
    in Wonderland*, 35; *Through the
    Looking-Glass*, 75, 170
Cary, Joyce: *The Horse's Mouth*, 27
"Casey Jones," 43
Cervantes, Miguel de: *Don Quixote*, 34, 38
Chari, Hemalatha, 268n9
Chase, Robert Howland, 178
Chaucer, Geoffrey, 59; *The Canterbury
    Tales*, 34
Cheng, Vincent John, 8, 9, 99, 103n5,
    268n8
Childers, Erskine, 246; *The Riddle of the
    Sands*, 246
Childers, Hugh Culling Eardley, 246
Christiani, Dounia Bunis, 11n9
"Cinderella," 175n3, 209
Cixous, Hélène, 252
Collins, Michael, 245, 246
Connelly, Michael, 70
Connolly, Thomas, 4, 142n3
Cooper, J. C., 103n6
Cory, Charles E., 181
Costello, Daniel, S. J., 72n5
Cromwell, Oliver, 37
Curran, Pearl Lenore, 181–82
Czarnowski, Stefan, 93

Daedalus, 63
Dailey, Abram H., 184n5
Dalton, Jack, 5, 27, 28, 33n24
D'Annunzio, Gabriele, 179, 185n10
Dante Alighieri, 186; *The Divine Comedy*,
    31, 34
Davis, Thomas, 247
Deane, Seamus, 244
Deane, Vincent, 5
Deming, Robert H., 9, 10n1
Dermot and Grania, 139
Derrida, Jacques, 8, 75, 81–82, 84n5,
    84n12, 253
de Valera, Eamon, 102, 245–46, 256n5
Devlin, Kimberly J., 9, 230n16
DiBernard, Barbara, 7
Dickens, Charles: *The Pickwick Papers*, 24;
    A Christmas Carol, 104
Dillon, John M., 6, 11n9
Dionysus, 236, 240, 242n35

Dodgson, Charles. *See* Lewis Carroll
Dohmen, William F., 94n3
Dostoevsky, Fydor: *The Brothers Karamazov*,
    38; *Crime and Punishment*, 120
Dreiser, Theodore, 121
Dunleavy, Janet Egleson, 11n6
Dunne, P. F.: *The Dooley Philosophy*, 264,
    267
Dwyer, Michael, 247

Eckley, Grace, 6, 8
"Eileen Aroon," 79
Einstein, Albert, 44
Eliot, T.S.: *The Waste Land*, 219, 250–51,
    255, 256n10
Ellmann, Richard, 1, 10n2, 32n3, 33n24,
    60, 65, 68, 117n1, 143, 225, 248
Epstein, Edmund L., 165n20
Eve. *See* Adam and Eve
Everyman, 21
Eve White and Eve Black. *See* Chris
    Sizemore; Corbett H. Thigpen and
    Hervey M. Cleckley: *The Three Faces of
    Eve*

Fabre, Henri, 38
Fagerberg, Sven, 16–17
Falconer, John, 60, 65
Ferrer, Daniel, 8
Findlater, Adam, 101
Finn. *See* Finn MacCool
"Finnegans Wake" Circular, A, 5
Fischer, Doris, 182–83, 184n2
Flaubert, Gustave, 249, 252
Foucault, Michel, 160
Francis of Assisi, St., 54, 216, 229n9
Francis Xavier, St., 54–57, 220, 229n14
Franz, Shepherd Ivory, 179–80
Frazer, Sir James George: *The Golden
    Bough*, 231–42
French, Percy, 43
Freud, Sigmund, 7, 9, 18, 40, 59, 80,
    84n11, 90, 145, 150, 160, 163n5,
    163n6, 184n4, 194–95, 197–98,
    210–11n2, 211n4, 213, 229n6, 239
Frost, Robert, 121

Gabler, Hans Walter, 97, 223
Garvin, John, 6, 244, 245
Gaskell, Philip, 33n27
Genette, Gerard, 129
George, Lloyd, 245
Gifford, Don, 88, 194